## The Official Guide

# SOFTIMAGE | XSI® 5

CD Included

Anthony Rossano

The Thomson Course Technology PTR logo and related trade dress are trademarks of Thomson Course Technology and may not be used without written permission.

**Publisher and General Manager, Thomson Course Technology PTR:** Stacy L. Hiquet

**Associate Director of Marketing:** Sarah O'Donnell

**Manager of Editorial Services:** Heather Talbot

**Marketing Manager:** Heather Hurley

**Executive Editor:** Kevin Harreld

**Marketing Coordinator:** Jordan Casey

**Project and Copy Editor:** Brian Proffitt

**Technical Reviewer:** John Freitas

**PTR Editorial Services Coordinator:** Elizabeth Furbish

**Interior Layout Tech:** Sue Honeywell

**Cover Designer:** Mike Tanamachi

**CD-ROM Producer:** Brandon Penticuff

**Indexer:** Kelly Henthorne

**Proofreader:** Karen Gill

The Softimage Press and/or Official Guide are used by permission of Avid Technology, Inc. All rights reserved.

Avid, Softimage, SOFTIMAGE|XSI, and Pro Tools are registered trademarks of Avid Technology, Inc. in the United States. Maya is a registered trademark of Alias Systems Corp. All other trademarks are the property of their respective owners.

*Important:* Thomson Course Technology PTR cannot provide software support. Please contact the appropriate software manufacturer's technical support line or Web site for assistance.

Thomson Course Technology PTR and the author have attempted throughout this book to distinguish proprietary trademarks from descriptive terms by following the capitalization style used by the manufacturer.

Information contained in this book has been obtained by Thomson Course Technology PTR from sources believed to be reliable. However, because of the possibility of human or mechanical error by our sources, Thomson Course Technology PTR, or others, the Publisher does not guarantee the accuracy, adequacy, or completeness of any information and is not responsible for any errors or omissions or the results obtained from use of such information. Readers should be particularly aware of the fact that the Internet is an ever-changing entity. Some facts may have changed since this book went to press.

Educational facilities, companies, and organizations interested in multiple copies or licensing of this book should contact the publisher for quantity discount information. Training manuals, CD-ROMs, and portions of this book are also available individually or can be tailored for specific needs.

ISBN: 1-59200-581-0

Library of Congress Catalog Card Number: 2004114490

Printed in the United States of America

06 07 08 09 10 PH 10 9 8 7 6 5 4 3 2 1

**THOMSON**

✦

™

**COURSE TECHNOLOGY**

Professional ■ Technical ■ Reference

Course PTR, a division of Course Technology
25 Thomson Place
Boston, MA 02210

http://www.courseptr.com

*I dedicate this book to my wife Andrea,*
*for her understanding and support during*
*and after the many long nights I spent hunched*
*over a monitor, researching and writing this book.*
*My life is complete!*

# Acknowledgments

A book is a collaborative work, and the author is just the guy tapping the keys the most. Many other people have worked to make this book happen, and to help me while I worked on this book. First and foremost, my thanks go to the men and women at Softimage who have toiled to bring this amazing piece of software to all of us users, answered my annoying questions and requests, and humored me in general.

I thank my Executive Editor, Kevin Harreld at Thomson Course Technology, for making the book happen, and Project Editor, Brian Proffitt, for making me look good by painstakingly correcting my grammatical and syntactic errors. The difference between an amateur and a professional is a good editor.

Many thanks to my boss at Omation, Jason Barlow, and all the other creative and technical people at "the Barnyard." You folks inspire me!

I send tremendous thanks to those who contributed images and tutorials to the book, Malachi Bazan (spin.killer@gmail.com) for his wonderful angel model, Charlie Winter (moneyhouse@gmail.com) for the interior images of the Nautilus, and Nick Lozides (nick@nickloz.com) for images of the Maserati Birdcage, building exterior and the droneship model and images. I would also like to thank Randal Dai for his wonderful tutorial on Rigid Body Dynamics that appears in Appendix A.

A special thanks goes out to Shinsaku Arima, who was a contributor on the first versions of this book back in 2000. Little bits of his ideas and style are still strewn throughout my work here.

Finally I'd like to thank the hottest bartenders in the OC, at Ole's Tavern in San Clemente for their hard work and inestimable contribution to my Thursday nights. I'll miss you, Ole's!

# About the Author

An author, teacher, lecturer, and producer, **Anthony Rossano** has been developing the art of multimedia and animation for over fifteen years.

Anthony has taught professionals and students in the U.S., Canada, Europe, the Middle East, and India. The author of four technical books and contributor to two more, Anthony's writings have been translated and published in Spanish, Japanese, Mandarin, Cantonese, Italian, and Polish.

Since founding Mesmer fx in the early days of the multimedia revolution, Anthony Rossano has been writing and producing DB, CD-ROM, DVD and Internet applications using languages like Lingo, 4D, PHP, Perl, and C. His clients have included Microsoft, REI, Delta Airlines, The Seattle Art Museum, Edmark, Cendant, and many other businesses and government agencies.

Anthony has contributed to the films *Star Wars Episode Three—Revenge of the Sith*, Dreamworks' *Sharkslayer* and Paramount's *The Barnyard*, and trained countless teams from Microsoft Games, EA, Valve, Maxis, Psygnosis, the FBI, CIA, DoD, NTSB, and other top-notch studios around the world.

Anthony is currently the Lead Technical Director at Omation studios in Southern California, working on the CG animated feature *The Barnyard*.

Anthony is a member of the Acacia Advisory Board, and sits on the board of directors of IOActive Inc., a fast-growing Internet security firm.

He lives with his wife Andrea, their cat Musetta, and rabbit Lola in Seattle, Washington, where he occupies his free time in fixing and racing vintage Italian cars, gardening, and photography.

Anthony can be reached in cyberspace at anthor@mesmer.com and www.mesmer.com.

# Contents

## Chapter 10
## Deformations and the Generic Attribute Painter.............197

# Introduction

Dear Readers,

This is the fourth edition of my beginner's guide to SOFTIMAGE|XSI. From the humble origins of version 1, XSI has grown up and matured into a remarkably powerful and fully featured creative environment for the development of visual content. This book has grown with XSI, and is now 13 chapters and 480 images long, covering everything from modeling through animating to rendering, compositing, and even grooming hair.

But with power comes complexity, to paraphrase Spider-Man. This book is designed to reduce XSI's inherent complexity by explaining how the architects of XSI put the tool together, how they intended for the user to get information and feedback from the interface, and by giving some few examples of the results possible from XSI and methods of achieving them.

I have attempted to structure the material in such a way that topics build upon each other as the book progresses. The initial chapters are very simple, and spend a great deal of time discussing concepts and fundamental ideas that lay underneath all 3D applications. In the middle of the book the pace accelerates and new topics are introduced rapidly. The end of the book covering image compositing and hair is advanced material. If you read the book from the beginning and work through until the end you'll find that your understanding of the software grows naturally as you progress.

This book was designed with teachers and students in mind. Teachers will find *SOFTIMAGE|XSI 5: The Official Guide* easy to plan lessons around, with digestible chapters and clear tutorials. The tutorials frequently start with sample scenes from the CD-ROM that comes with the book, and completed versions of the tutorial scenes are available for comparison and reverse engineering. Students will find the language precise but approachable. I have tried to make the explanations of topics, ideas, tools, and workflows as concise and accurate as possible, both comprehensive and comprehensible.

This book cannot possibly cover all the features and capabilities of XSI version 5.0. Other fine books cover character building in XSI, including my own *XSI Illuminated: Character* which is available on the Web as a free PDF file. The documentation which comes with XSI in searchable HTML format is also a wonderful source of precise reference information.

Please also take time in working through the book. After each topical section you should practice, explore, and sleep on what you have learned. People new to 3D animation programs frequently report to me that they dream vividly, and experience the world differently while learning XSI, sometimes seeing things in wireframe or becoming aware of colors, textures, and lighting that they previously passed by without noticing. This is normal. Enjoy the ride.

Anthony Rossano

November 1$^{st}$, 2005

# Chapter 1
# The XSI Interface and Concepts

In this chapter you will:

◆ Launch the software
◆ Navigate the interface layout
◆ Set application user preferences
◆ Explore the five modules—Model, Animate, Render, Simulate, and Hair
◆ View display styles
◆ Open and save scenes and manage your project folder
◆ Use the camera and view navigation hotkeys
◆ Understand objects and properties
◆ Use stickiness lock, and recycle in PPGs
◆ Find objects using the Explorer and the Schematic View
◆ Try the XSI explorer and memo cams

## Introduction

SOFTIMAGE|XSI 5.0 is, as of this writing, the latest version of Avid Computer Graphics flagship integrated animation, rendering, special effects, and compositing software. XSI is the most modern of high-end Computer Graphics Imagery (CGI) applications, and as such it is certainly the most comprehensive, the most powerful, the easiest to use, and the most capable of creating professional quality, breathtakingly beautiful results in games, film, and television.

XSI has powerful modeling tools for creating, editing, and manipulating NURBS, polygon models, and subdivision surfaces, which make organic character modeling much easier and more fun (see Figure 1.1). XSI uses as an internal renderer: the mental ray. It's the most powerful distributed shader-based ray tracer in the industry today, though you can also plug in additional renderers.

XSI has an animation core built around the concept of non-linear animation, with an Animation Curve Editor, a Dopesheet Editor, and an Animation Mixer. XSI has a complete rigid body dynamics, soft body dynamics, fluids, hair, cloth and particle simulation module for creating physical effects.

XSI is completely scriptable and programmable, so you can build your own tools to speed workflow, or to add new capabilities to the software. XSI 5.0 brings new tools for the game development and content creation industry, including prelighting, normal mapping, and real-time shading features. Finally, XSI integrates both a powerful image compositor and a 2D paint system, so that animators have a complete multi-pass rendering, compositing, and effects all rolled up into one package on their desktop.

SOFTIMAGE|XSI 5.0 runs on computers that use the Microsoft Windows XP and Linux operating systems. Linux variants from Red Hat and SUSE are officially supported, but with some reconfiguration, XSI can be made to run on many different flavors of Linux.

If you are considering a hardware purchase, you should first visit http://www.softimage.com/ to find

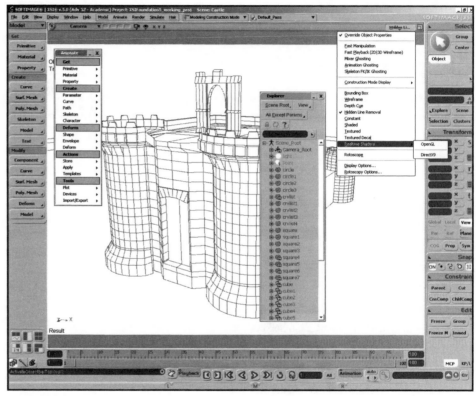

**Figure 1.1**
Tools you'll use.

out more about hardware requirements. Anyone can download the free version of XSI, called the XSI Foundation 5 Trial, from http://www.softimage.com, and students and faculty can purchase an unrestricted version of XSI very inexpensively from one of several educational resellers, also listed at the SOFTIMAGE Web site.

This book is designed to introduce you to the most basic features and capabilities of XSI version 5.0; to familiarize you with the interface and XSI operating conventions; to teach you how to build models; to show you how to use material shaders, textures, and lights to get the look you want; to demonstrate the basic keyframing and animation editing tools; and finally to teach you how to use the renderer to generate image files, and play them back.

This book is divided up into simple, easy-to-understand chapters that tackle discrete concepts and teach specific skills.

You will find the scenes referenced in this book on the CD-ROM that accompanies it.

## Which XSI Is Right for You?

XSI is available in several different versions: the free Trial version, the low-cost Academic version, and three commercial grades, Foundation, Essentials, and Advanced.

While the Trial version is a boon to the home user looking to evaluate different software packages, it is not appropriate for any sort of production use, as it saves files in a non-interchangeable '.exp' file format, limits the size of image you may render, and watermarks all images (including render regions in the view ports).

The Academic version is not hampered with these limitations. It is fully functional and feature equivalent to the Advanced commercial version. You should not use the Academic version to do work for hire. On the commercial side, the Essentials version is much less expensive, but it lacks a few features such as Cloth and has fewer rendering licenses.

Although XSI is identical in functionality on Linux and Windows platforms, launching the application is slightly different within each operating system.

## Starting SOFTIMAGE|XSI on Windows and Linux

On Windows systems, go to the Start menu on the main taskbar and then click on Programs > SOFTIMAGE Products >SOFTIMAGE XSI 5.0. Then click either XSI Advanced or XSI Essentials, depending on which version you are using.

On Linux systems, log in to the user account that has been configured for XSI, and get a shell window. In that shell, type xsi and press Enter to launch the program. If the installation created a shortcut on your desktop, you may double-click on it to launch XSI.

> On Windows, the OS creates an artificial delay when showing menu items. This slows down your work. You can change the delay to something more reasonable, like zero, with the Registry.
>
> Open the Registry with Start > Run > Regedit and then navigate to My Computer > HKEY_CURRENT_USER > Control Panel > Desktop and look in the right pane for the Menu Show Delay property. Double-click it to set the value, and choose 0. Close the Regedit window. Log out and log back in to see the changes.

# The XSI User Interface

XSI uses a very standard windowing interface that is the same on all platforms (see Figure 1.2). The User Interface (UI) has standard menus along the top window title bar, custom drop menus collected in buttons throughout the interface, Windows Explorer-like lists of objects and properties, context-sensitive menus that pop up at your mouse location, and graphical buttons to click on or toggle.

The interface is completely customizable, and comes with several different layouts, organizing the graphical tools in different ways for different uses.

Those fortunate to use several monitors will find layouts pre-made to spread across two desktops, including a clever option called the Autohide layout that slides the MCP and menu stacks out of the way when they are not being used. (Try out the View > Layouts > Autohide menu command.)

## Top Menus

The standard menus along the top of the window replicate all the functions found in the Graphical User Interface (GUI) in case you need something in one layout that is only found in another. Because all the options in the application are available in the top menu system (shown in Figure 1.3), you can flexibly re-configure and customize the GUI to suit your needs, while still being sure that you can get to any command you might want. For purposes of consistency, this book will use only the standard layout to show examples.

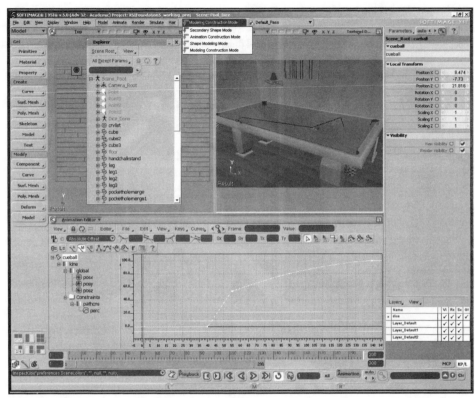

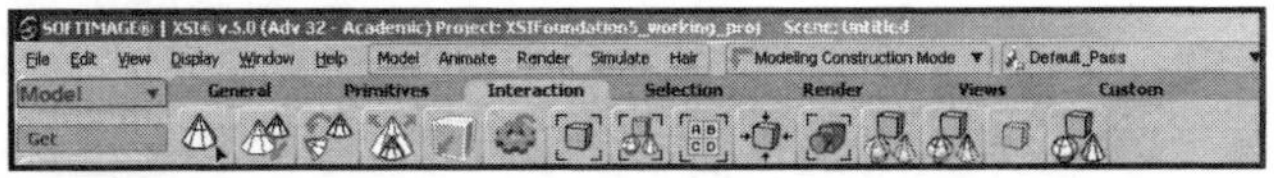

**Figure 1.2**
The entire XSI interface.

**Figure 1.3**
The top menu bar has all the menu options and features in XSI.

Most of the menus can be "torn off" by opening the menu and clicking on the dashed line with the scissors icon at the top of the menu. This makes the menu free floating, so it remains until you close it with the Close box in the upper-right corner. This saves a lot of clicks in cases where you plan to use several menu items from a menu repeatedly (see Figure 1.4).

The menus that are not duplicated elsewhere in the interface are the File, View, Display, Window, and Help menus.

The File menu, shown in Figure 1.5, contains all the commands necessary to open, Save, Import, Export, and merge scenes and models. It also contains the User Preferences and Keyboard hotkey mappings. The File menu also contains the Project Manager. The Project Manager helps you organize all your scenes into different projects and also assists in sharing scenes among multiple people working on the same team. You also use the File menu to import models from other programs; export your models, scenes, and other data to other applications including game engines; and to load custom plug-ins, called Add-Ons in XSI-speak.

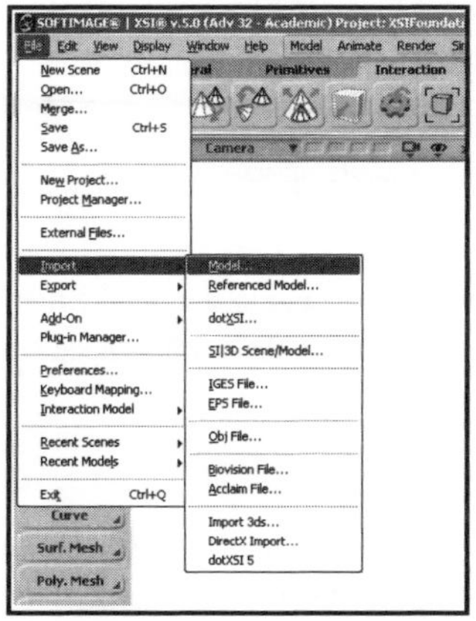

The View menu is new to XSI 5 (see Figure 1.6). It collects all the commands and user interface tools for switching between layouts, popping up floating view windows, creating and using custom commands and toolbars, and managing which panels (timeline, playback, etc.) are visible on screen.

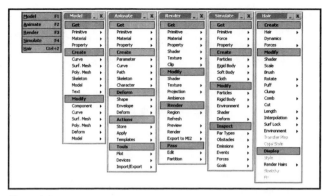

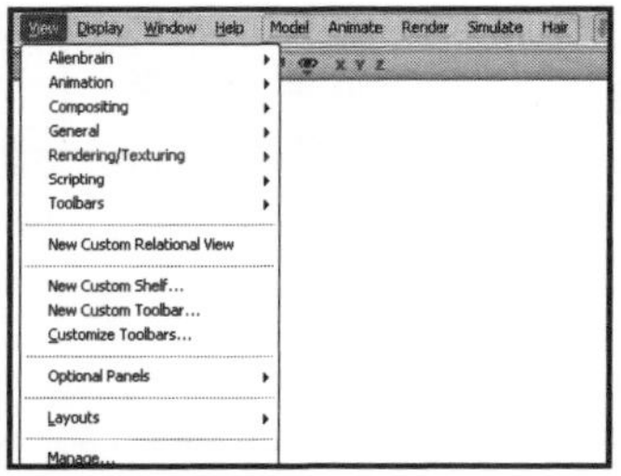

**Figure 1.4**
The hotkeys to switch between the modes are 1, 2, 3, 4, and Ctrl-2 for Hair.

**Figure 1.5**
The File menu.

**Figure 1.6**
The View menu.

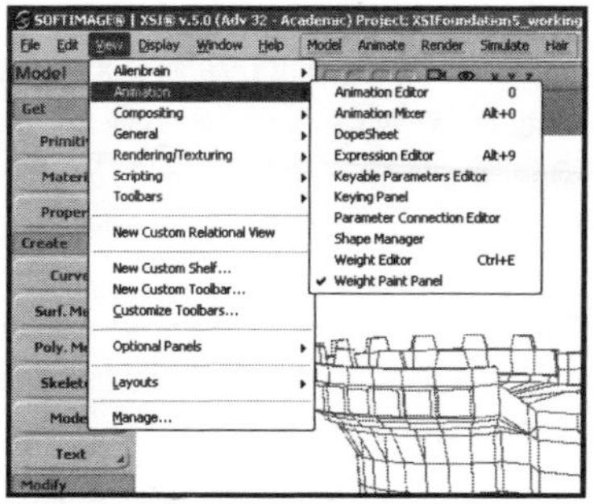

**Figure 1.7**
The View > Animation submenu.

The View > Animation submenu displayed in Figure 1.7 has the commands to open the Animation Editor, the Animation Mixer, the Dopesheet, and other animation tools as floating windows that you can move around the screen—even outside of the main XSI window. These windows then float above the rest of the interface, even on a second monitor. They can be temporarily collapsed by double-clicking on their title bars. This helps save screen space and decrease clutter. There are keyboard shortcuts for these floating windows. Try tapping the 8 key to bring up a floating Explorer (or the F8 key if you use the XSI command map). Experiment with the other number keys to see which views pop up. You may also hide a floating window with the Minimize button in the upper-right corner of the window, then recover that window with the Window menu, which is always at the top of the screen.

The View > Layouts submenu is responsible for all the tasks related to creating and editing custom user interfaces.

The Display menu at the top left of the screen contains some options that seem redundant, but in fact operate in slightly different ways from the other areas of the interface where the commands are found (see Figure 1.9). When you make changes to the selections in the Display menu, your choices apply to all the 3D views. If you use the Eyeball menu in a specific 3D view, your choices apply only to that single 3D view.

For instance, toggling Display > Attributes > Points on will show points in all the View windows, whereas toggling Show > Points from one window title bar (in the eyeball icon menu) will display points in only that view.

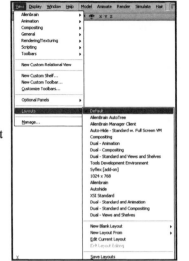

**Figure 1.8**
The View, Layouts submenu.

**Figure 1.9**
The Display menu.

The Help menu has access to the excellent searchable documentation, called the XSI Portal and located in the Help > XSI Guides menu command, to the software development kit portal in the SDK Guides option, to the SOFTIMAGE Web site, and to the XSI download site. You can use the download site to retrieve new versions of XSI, or patches that improve performance and stability.

## The Five Workflow Modules and Menus

Proper workflow organizes to the process of animation. It creates a process with an achievable result. Workflow defines the most efficient manner of producing the result required. If you create a single object, animate it, apply color, model it some more, add more color, create another object, and then follow the same meandering path again, it will be very difficult for you to complete your work. Segmenting the various duties of animation into workflow steps allows you to move through the process more efficiently, in an assembly-line fashion.

In the default layout that we will use for all examples in this book, the major tools and functions are divided into five modules: Model, Animate, Simulate, Render, and Hair. Each module is designed to present you with a set of tools that are all related to one part of the creative process. When you select a module by mouse or by keyboard, only the tools relevant to your current task show up in the left-hand stack of menu cells.

You can enter the Model, Animate, Render, Simulate, and Hair modules (see Figure 1.10) either by clicking on the module name that is currently active (in the top-left corner of the interface) and selecting a new module from the drop-down list or by pressing the hotkeys on your keyboard that represent them: 1 for Model, 2 for Animate, 3 for Render, 4 for Simulate, and Ctrl-2 for Hair (don't use the numeric keypad for this).

As of version 5.0, you can access any menu commands from any module by choosing them from the module menus at the top of the screen.

**Figure 1.10**
Modules are always available at the top of the user interface.

In XSI 5.0, each module (Model, Animate, Render, Simulate, and Hair) is available as a regular menu with submenu options or as tear-off menus (see Figures 1.10 and 1.11) from the module menus at the top of the screen. These are color coded to match the coloration of the modules in the left-hand menu stack. These are very useful in cases where you find yourself in the wrong module but need a specific tool, or where you want to tear off a menu to use within a different module.

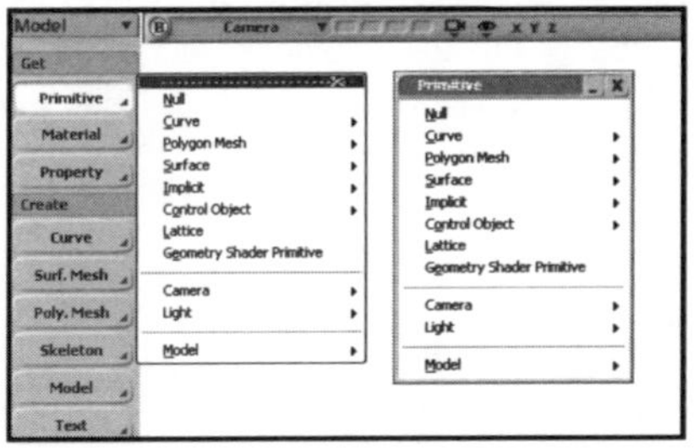

**Figure 1.11**
Most menus can be torn off.

## Model

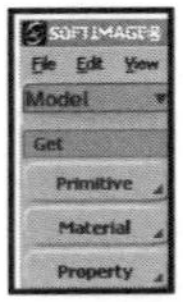

You start your workflow in the Model module, where you construct all your scene elements. Model's tools enable you to create objects from primitive shapes, draw curves, develop surfaces from those curves, and do all manner of editing of the models you make. Here you may also create cameras, lights, and new object properties. The Model module contains all the tools for editing polygonal objects, for Booleans, for blending and merging, and for working with subdivision surfaces. The Model module is where you can create 3D text and where you manage referenced models (models stored externally to your scenes or shared among different scenes).

## Animate

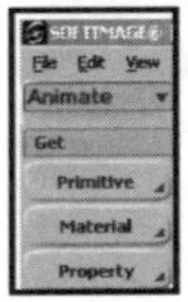

While regular animation keyframing and playback controls are always available from the Animation menu button at the bottom of the screen, the Animate module contains all the commands for adding different animation effects to your scene.

Here are the special menu commands for attaching objects to a path, for adding animatable deformations, and for creating custom property pages.

The Animate module also contains the special tools for setting up virtual actors, assigning inverse kinematic skeletons, assigning skin, adjusting skeletal deformations, and weighting the skin to the Inverse Kinematics (IK) skeletons.

Finally, the Animate module contains the Actions menu cells, which Store, Load, and Save animation actions for use in the Non-Linear Animation Mixer, and the Shape menu, which controls shape animation, sometimes called morphing in other programs.

## Render

In the Render module, you can assign color and texture to the objects in your scene, create lights and cameras, work with the Render Tree to build complex shader networks, and set up render passes and partitions.

Also in the Render module are the controls for the Render Region, the full frame preview, and the final render. The Preview button is located in the Render module, and is one way to take a look at how your scene will appear when it is completely rendered. XSI also has a Render Region, which will render a portion of your scene into any view, and keep it updated as you make changes.

## Simulate

The Simulate module organizes all the dynamic simulations tools together into one workflow area. In the Simulate module, you can invoke physical forces like gravity, wind, turbulence, and vortices. You can then make objects in your scene react to those forces, with the Cloth, Hair, Softbody, and Rigid Body properties. You can create fluid simulations to imitate water flowing or splashing. You can add particle systems to simulate the look of rain or fire. You can create cloth simulations to drape material over a model. You can set up soft body collisions on objects so that collisions and gravity affect your characters.

## Hair

The Hair module is where you can add a new hair emitter object to part of a model or the whole thing. Then you can groom that hair or fur into the form you require, add dynamic properties like inertia, collision, gravity, and turbulence to the hair, and edit the shaders that give the hair its rendered look.

The Hair module also has tools for displaying the hair on screen in real time. Chapter 13, "Hair and Fur," covers the Hair module in detail.

## Organization Within Modules

Inside each module, the menu commands on the left side are further organized to help you figure out where the tools you need are located. Within the Model module, the stack is subdivided into three areas: Get, Create, and Modify. The tools in the Get area help you bring new pre-made objects (like cameras, lights, or primitives), while those in the Create section help you make things from scratch. Finally, the Modify section contains tools you need to clean up models, modify the surface, move points, etc.

The Animate module is divided into sections labeled Get, Create, Deform, Actions, and Tools.

The Render module contains sections for Get, Modify, Render, and Pass.

The Simulate module contains sections for Get, Create, Modify, and Inspect.

The Hair module uses the verbs Create, Modify, and Display to organize the contents.

When you read or speak the name of a command, it helps to say the section of the module it is in, like "Create a Curve with Sketch" which would correspond to the Create > Curve > Sketch menu command in the Model module. Often in this book, the name of the module is left out. You will quickly learn which module to be in for each kind of task.

## Construction Mode Menu

Construction modes in XSI allow you to step back in time through the creation and animation of an object. Even after an object has been animated, you can turn back the clock to the modeling phase and make further modeling changes by choosing the Modeling Construction Mode from this menu (see Figure 1.12). Within any viewport, you can view your scene at the state resulting from any one of the four Construction modes (Modeling, Shape Modeling, Animation, and Secondary Shape) with the View Style > Construction Mode Display menu item.

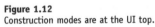

**Figure 1.12**
Construction modes are at the UI top.

Using construction modes is an advanced XSI feature.

## The View Switchers

As the XSI application has grown, new User Interfaces (UIs) enabling new features have come into existence. Sometimes these new features have been added into the existing UI by replacing the screen real estate occupied by the workflow modules. The three small buttons at the bottom of the menu stack are examples of this concept.

Called view switchers they swap out the left-side menus entirely, making way for the weight painting tools and the color palette controls. The first view switcher, which looks like four panes stacked on top of one another, restores the original workflow modules.

## 3D Viewports

In the middle of your monitor are the views, which can show you the 3D space in your scene, the view from a camera or a spotlight, or any number of other perspectives on your world.

You can quickly switch between two and four views, or a combination of 3D and other views The six small view switcher buttons are at the bottom left of the interface.

You can also dock the Animation Editor, the Dopesheet, the Explorer, a file browser, a Property Editor, the Render Tree, compositor output, the texture layer editor, or even a Web browser into these view windows.

Alt-right clicking in view windows will often bring up a context-sensitive menu. This menu will show you options for use in that window, or if you are in the middle of modeling, it will show you various modeling operations you could perform at that point.

Context-sensitive menus are called context sensitive because what you are doing at the time, the window your mouse is in, and what is selected all influence the menu that pops up when you Alt-right click (or just right click, depending on your interaction preferences).

## The Main Command Panel

The right-side menu and button stack is called the Main Command Panel (MCP, shown in Figure 1.13), and it contains all the functions that you are likely to use most often as you work in XSI. Using the MCP, you can move, scale, and rotate objects, select objects and components of objects like points and knots, look at the animatable properties of objects, duplicate and delete objects, and organize your scene into hierarchies, groups, and layers. The MCP also has controls for enabling the snapping options, which make precision modeling a lot easier; for using proportional modeling, which turns your models into rubbery skins that are easy to stretch and mold; and for drawing symmetrical curves. You can swap out the MCP with the Keyable Parameters layout when animating.

## Timeline

The timeline at the bottom of the scene shows you the duration of your scene, generally in frames (see Figure 1.14). It has both a scrubber for you to manually set the current frame, and complete playback controls to play the animation in your scene forwards or backwards, rewind, or advance one frame at a time or one key at a time. When you have set keys on an object, little red tick marks show up in the timeline when that object is selected for additional feedback.

**Figure 1.13**
The Main Command Panel.

> You can adjust which properties get tick marks by right-clicking on the timeline and choosing from the Show Keys menu option.

**Figure 1.14**
The timeline controls.

The area below the timeline contains the basic keyframing tools, named the AutoKey, the Keyframe button, and the Animation Marking List. This area also contains the Playback menu, which is where the menu command to call up the FlipBook is located. The FlipBook is how you will review your previously rendered frames to evaluate your work.

## Feedback Line

At the very bottom of the screen is the feedback (or status) line. This critical area can be a huge help to you as you learn and use XSI. Each time you activate a command, the feedback line will show the name of the command on the left side and a diagram of how each of the three mouse buttons will work with that command. For instance, if you decide to draw a curve with the Create > Curve > Draw Cubic by CVs menu command, the status line will tell you that the left mouse button will add a point to the end of the curve, the middle mouse button will add a point in the middle of the curve wherever you point the mouse, and the right mouse button will open a context-sensitive curve menu.

Many commands require you to execute the command and then pick one or more objects to complete the command. For instance, if you are lofting to create a skin over a series of ribs, you would execute the Create > Surf. Mesh > Loft command. Then you would look into the feedback line to see that you must now pick with the left mouse button on each rib in turn. Finally, you would complete the command by clicking the right mouse button, which is labeled End Picking in the feedback line at the bottom of the screen.

It is almost always a good idea to turn off or complete a command when you are done with it, to avoid accidentally using it again in a way you do not intend. Often you can exit from a command by clicking the right mouse button, but you can always exit a command by tapping the Esc key on your keyboard. Pressing Esc before a command is completed will cancel that command, while pressing Esc after a command is completed will return you to the Nil tool (if you have the Preference for Interaction > Tools > Default 3D Tool set to 'Nil Tool'), which means that you won't accidentally do anything you don't want to do.

Whenever you have a question about how to proceed, check the feedback line.

# XSI UI Conventions

The designers of the XSI interface built in subtle cues to tell you where to find more information, and consistent ways for the user to get information to XSI and feedback out of XSI. Some of these UI conventions are detailed here.

## Triangles Mean Drop Menus

Whenever you see a small triangle anywhere in the interface, it indicates either that it is a drop menu, or that you can use it to expand or collapse a group of options. For instance, most of the menu cells in the left-hand stack have a diagonal triangle in the bottom-right corner, indicating that if you click on them, a list of options will pop out. In the same way, the Camera View has a triangle that, if clicked, can change the camera view into some other view. The Snap buttons in the MCP have little triangles pointing up and left, which means that if you click the right mouse button on them, you will be rewarded with a context-sensitive menu offering up further options.

Property pages have a different kind of triangle. It either points down, indicating that the list of properties under that section is fully expanded, or it points right, indicating that the section is collapsed and no properties in that section are showing. You can click on the triangle to toggle it back and forth.

Triangles also show up in the Render Tree to signify that nodes are collapsed, and that clicking on the triangle will expand the node to show more information.

## Undo and Redo

XSI has a potentially unlimited undo stack, although by default it is limited to 50 undoes. Every single thing you do during a session can be undone, in the order that you performed the operations. This is called the "undo stack" because new operations are added to the top of the stack, removed from the top when you undo, and placed back on the stack when you redo.

The XSI undo uses the standard Apple/Windows control keys: Ctrl-Z to undo, and Ctrl-Y to redo.

You can view the most recent command on the top of the stack in the feedback line at the bottom left of the screen, and the most recent 25 commands by clicking on the triangle next to it.

You can change the default number of default operations that are undoable by going to the File > Preferences menu from the top of the screen, which will pop up a Preferences dialog box. If you click on the icon (really a property page) labeled General, you can set the number of undo levels.

## Select, Shift, and Ctrl

To select objects in XSI, you hold the spacebar to enter the standard selection mode. While the spacebar is held down, you can draw a rectangle that touches some part of the object you want selected. When you release the mouse, that object will become selected, and show highlighted in white in your 3D views.

> Please make certain that your selection options are set correctly: In the Select menu of the MCP on the right side, verify that all three menu items at the bottom are checked on: Select Single Object in Region, SOFTIMAGE 3D Selection Model, and Extended Component Selection. For consistency in this book, all three options are toggled on at all times.

When you want to select objects, parameters, or properties in XSI more than one at a time, you will use the standard Shift and Ctrl keys to extend, shrink, or toggle the selection. For instance, if you had three spheres and one was selected, you could hold Shift and then select the others to add them.

Since holding the spacebar, Shift, and Ctrl while accurately clicking requires the manual dexterity of a concert pianist, you can also use just the spacebar and the Ctrl key while clicking on objects to toggle them between selected and unselected states. In other words, if you had three spheres, and two were already selected but one was not, holding the spacebar and Ctrl and then clicking on a sphere would select it if it was not selected, but would deselect it if it was already selected.

There are many other methods and tools useful for selecting things in XSI. The Select menu at the top-right corner of the MCP holds all of these options. Feel free to explore. The default (and most useful) tool mode is Select by Rectangle, which is toggled on and off at Select > Tools > Rectangle. You will find yourself becoming a faster and more precise XSI animator if you remember to use the spacebar whenever you need to select an object.

## Context-Sensitive Menus

In some places other than the regular geometry view menus, clicking with your right mouse button (RMB) will pop up a context-sensitive menu with special commands that are active only there and on the object you were over had selected.

For example, in the Explorer and Schematic views, you can inspect, change names, and much more by right-clicking on the name of an object. In the Mixer, the right mouse button pops up clip and track options. In the Animation Editor, the right mouse button has curve options. In the Camera View (the 3D perspective view) right-clicking in an empty grey area pops up a menu with options to Select the Camera or Interest of the Camera, Frame the Selected Object or All Objects in the Scene, Orbit, Dolly, or Roll the Camera, and a number of other useful options.

When in doubt, try right-clicking. When a tool has the RMB already mapped to something else, you will need to exit the tool to get at the context-sensitive menu, by tapping the Esc button on your keyboard, thereby activating the Nil tool. In the Nil tool, the RMB always pops up the context-sensitive menu. If you want to pop up the context menu without leaving the tool you are in, you may hold the Alt button while clicking the RMB.

## Interaction Models

Different folks like different setups for how the software will react to them, so XSI has very detailed user preferences that each user can set to his liking. Very broadly, these are called interaction models. There are four default, built-in interaction models available to start with in the File > Interaction Model menu command.

### Stickiness

One method used by SOFTIMAGE|XSI to enhance your workflow is the concept of stickiness. When you choose a menu command that might be executed many times in a row, SOFTIMAGE executes the command on the first object you specified and stays in that command mode until you click the right mouse button (sometimes), press the Esc key, or choose another menu command. This makes it easy for you to group your tasks into processes and apply a command to many objects in a sequence.

If you have completed modeling a large number of objects individually and now need to group them into hierarchies, for example, you would click on the Parent button. XSI then remains in the Parent mode as long as you need it, allowing you to construct many elaborate hierarchies without choosing the Parent command over and over again. When you are done with a command, make a habit of pressing the Esc key to put the command away, which avoids unintentional use of that tool the next time you click an object. Not all tools in SOFTIMAGE work like this—just the ones that can be executed without calling up a dialog box.

### The SOFTIMAGE|3D interaction Model

Hotkeys can also be "sticky" (if you have turned this option on in the File > Preferences > Interaction > Tools property page). When you tap the space bar lightly, for example, XSI stays in selection mode. When you tap the O key, XSI stays in Orbit mode.

> Turning on the Sticky key option in the User Preferences is a bad idea. If you become very fast and proficient with XSI, the time delay that defines "tapping" a key will begin to become ambiguous, and hotkeys will start acting sticky when you don't want them to. It's a good idea to leave Enable Sticky Keys off. This option is located in File > Preferences > Interaction > Tools, along with the Default 3D tool, which should be set to Nil.

**13**

The stickiness and Shift-Ctrl selection methods just described can become slow and confusing when you are working fast with multiple objects. The old method used in SOFTIMAGE 3D|Extreme has been preserved, and it accelerates working with selections, node/branch/tree selection, selecting tags, and working with selection and other tools at the same time. To use the SI3D model (recommended strongly), go to the File > Preferences > Interaction dialog box. In the Tools tab, turn off 'Enable Sticky Keys' and set the Default 3D Tool to 'Nil Tool.' Close the dialog box and then in the Select Menu in the top right of the MCP, make sure that all three bottom options are on: Select Single Object in Region, SI3D Selection model, and Extended Component Selection (see Figure 1.15). To select objects, you hold the spacebar down and pick at or draw a rectangle over objects, branches, and trees. The tag selection tool (hotkey T) works to add, subtract, and toggle tagged selections. You can still use Shift to make multiple selections.

There are other setting in the File > Preferences that make using XSI easier and more fun. In the Display property page you may wish to toggle on the Update All Views During Interaction option to avoid having different windows refreshing at different times and rates.

As you become proficient, you will want to toggle off the Interaction > Pop Up Property Editors on Node Creation option, so that you may deliberately decide what properties to view and when to view them. If this option is on, Property Pages will be popping up on their own as you work, which means that you will waste time closing them when you do not want to see them.

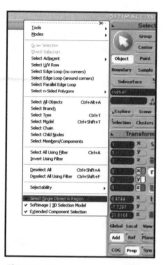

**Figure 1.15**
The Select menu showing the correct settings for the SI3D selection model.

If you toggle off the option Select Contents of Text Boxes on First Click, you can more easily edit values. If you do want to select the entire field, just click in it with your middle mouse button, and the whole string will be selected so that you can cut it or overwrite it.

If you are a user coming to XSI from Alias Maya, you can switch many user preferences and hotkeys over to be more like Maya by choosing the File > Interaction Model > QWERTY Tools and Alt Camera Navigation menu command.

# View Windows

The majority of the screen is given over to the View windows. The View windows provide a glimpse into your scene in a number of different ways: in a 2D orthographic view, as a 3D perspective corrected view, as a linear list of components, as a schematic diagram of interconnected models, and many other ways. You can also use these View windows to browse what's on your hard drive, surf the Internet (I love Google images), and to work in other interfaces within XSI, like the Animation Editor and the Animation Mixer. You can arrange your interface to have as many as four or as few as one View windows, but the default configuration is to show four of these views into your scene.

At the top of each view window is the title bar. At the left of the title bar is a letter identifying that view, and then a drop menu showing what type of view it is. You can click directly on that title, which has a small triangle next to it (indicating that it is a drop menu), to select a different kind of view. The Cameras option lists all the cameras in your scene, and will change the view to look through whichever you choose. You can look through a spotlight using the Spot Lights option. The User option is a perspective view that does not correspond to any defined camera. It's useful when you want to work in your scene without disturbing the placement and settings of the cameras. The Top, Front, and Right views are orthographic views, meaning that they look into the scene as if it were in two dimensions, without perspective (see Figure 1.16).

> If you want a 3D orthographic view, you can create a new ortho-graphic camera with Get > Primitive, Camera > Orthographic. Then you can look through it by selecting the new camera (named Camera1 by default) in the Cameras drop list of the View menu (the colored menu in each view window).

## Cartesian Space, Views, and Cameras

SOFTIMAGE|XSI sets up a virtual 3D world for you that is almost infinitely big but completely empty. This 3D space is organized according to the Cartesian coordinate system. This means that any point in the SOFTIMAGE virtual world can be located precisely with three values: the point's location along the X-axis, the point's location along the Y-axis, and the point's location along the Z-axis.

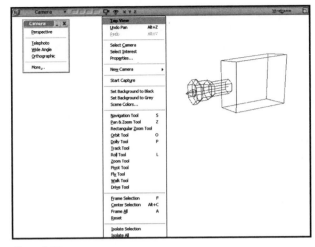

**Figure 1.16**
The Camera view window.

Each of these three axes—X, Y, and Z—is an invisible straight line (a vector) stretching infinitely far in both directions. Each axis runs at a right angle (90 degrees) to each of the other axes. In other words, each axis is perpendicular to the other two axes (see Figure 1.17).

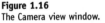

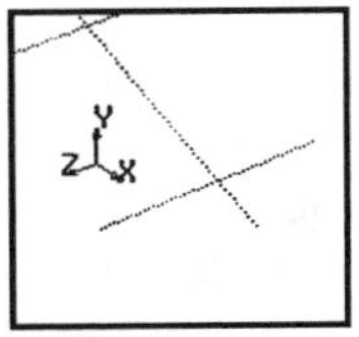

**Figure 1.17**
The X, Y, and Z axes.

If you are sitting in front of your computer looking in SOFTIM-AGE|XSI's Front View window, the X-axis is usually visualized as running from left to right, directly in front of you, like a horizon line. The Y-axis is the "up" axis and is usually visualized as running from the bottom to the top of your screen. The Z-axis is invisible to you because you are looking at the exact end of the line, running in and through your screen.

Each of these axes runs through a point in the exact center of the virtual 3D world called the global origin. All the axes meet as they pass through it. As they proceed through the global origin, they extend in both the positive or negative directions (see Figure 1.18).

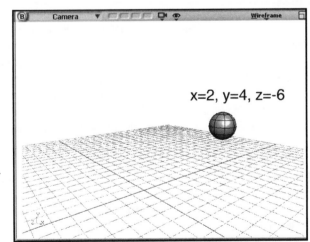

$x=2, y=4, z=-6$

**Figure 1.18**
The global origin at the axes' intersection and a point defined by the values on each axis.

**15**

Every point along an axis has a value, expressed in SOFTIMAGE Units. But how big is a SOFTIMAGE Unit? What does a SOFTIMAGE Unit correspond to in the real world? The answer is simple: A SOFTIMAGE Unit is whatever you want it to be. Just wave your magic wand and chant, "let the units be centimeters" or "let the units be parsecs," and it is so. SOFTIMAGE Units are generic decimal units. They can be anything, but where they need to map to the real world they are considered to be 100 cm each.

Because every position on the individual axes can be measured, you can define a point in space by choosing one point on each axis. Any point in space can then be located in a Cartesian coordinate system by specifying the values of the three axes, as in X=7, Y=41, Z=30, or, in shorthand, XYZ = 7,41,30.

SOFTIMAGE|XSI has the job of converting the 3D virtual space I just described into a 2D virtual space that it can draw on a flat computer monitor for you to see and work with. The program does this by projecting each point in the virtual 3D space onto a 2D plane (called the projection plane) and drawing it to a View window.

Each of SOFTIMAGE|XSI's View windows can display the projection plane from a different perspective, called the view plane. By default, the windows use the Top, Front, Right, and Camera view planes. Each view plane comes with a small icon showing you the orientation of the three axes in that view, so you can orient yourself in 3D space. Because each plane is really only a two-dimensional construct, it can show you only two out of the total three axes in the 3D space. The Top view shows the X- and Z-axes, which make up the XZ plane, the Front view shows the XY plane, and the Right view shows the ZY plane. Each of these views is orthographic, which means that all parallel lines are projected to the screen as parallel. In this way, you see a view that acts as a flat view port into the 3D world.

The last window is the Perspective View window. In SOFTIMAGE|XSI, the Perspective View window is by default the first camera window. This is the view that your camera sees when you render your animation, although you may add in other cameras later to view the scene from other angles. This window doesn't have to stay parallel to two of the major axes, although it's still a 2D view plane. In other words, you can move the camera freely throughout the 3D virtual space and look at the scene from any angle, not just the top, front, and right sides. This View window is not orthographic, but perspective, which means that SOFTIMAGE performs perspective-correction projection when it draws the 2D view plane. In this way, SOFTIMAGE can show you a 2D simulation of 3D space that provides you with a simulation of depth. Parallel lines converge into the distance, and objects seem to grow smaller as they move farther away. The severity of these effects changes depending on the width of the camera view angle used, so that you can easily simulate a fish-eye lens or a telephoto lens.

## Moving Around with the Hotkeys

Hotkeys are keyboard shortcuts essential to working with SOFTIMAGE|XSI. Hotkeys work differently in XSI than in most other applications. You hold them down for as long as you want them, and when you let go, the hotkey goes away and you are returned to whatever function you were in before you used the hotkey. This means you can chain together two commands and flip back and forth rapidly. This sort of use is the opposite of 'Sticky' hotkeys, where once you tap the key, the function is on until you choose something else.

To move around in the Top, Front, and Right View windows, position your mouse anywhere inside of one View window, hold down the Z key on your keyboard and the left mouse button, and drag your mouse around. The Z key is the Pan & Zoom hotkey.

Now try using the Z hotkey with the middle mouse button. This zooms into the View window. Try the right mouse button to zoom out of the View window. Now hold down the Z hotkey and look at the status bar at the bottom of the screen. The status bar shows you the result of the hotkey for each of the three mouse buttons.

If you use the Z hotkey to zoom in and out of the Camera window, you aren't just scaling the view, you're increasing or decreasing the field of view of the camera lens, which affects how distorted your Camera view gets. It is a good idea to use the P hotkey instead of the Z hotkey in the Camera window whenever possible. The P hotkey is the Dolly hotkey, which actually moves the camera back and forth to see more or less instead of changing the view angle of the camera. Try it out in the Camera window.

The P hotkey has another feature that is common to many functions in SOFTIMAGE|XSI. When you hold down P, each of the mouse buttons does the same thing but in varying amounts. For instance, the left mouse button dollies at a normal rate, the middle button dollies more slowly, and the right mouse button dollies rapidly. This way you can get the exact amount of control you need for big moves or for small precise ones.

Another crucial hotkey that works in the Perspective window is the Orbit (O) hotkey. The Orbit hotkey allows you to change the view plane of the camera, by orbiting it around the camera interest (the point in space where the camera is aimed). Try it out in the Camera window (it doesn't work in the Top, Front, or Right views). The Orbit key allows you to see your work from any angle. As you orbit, watch how SOFTIMAGE|XSI uses perspective correction to make the part of the grid that's farther away seem smaller. This effect is the basis of simulating a 3D space with a 2D image plane.

The last hotkey does the job of all the previous keys. It's Zoom, Dolly, and Orbit all rolled into one key, named the S hotkey. Hold down the S key and drag with the left, middle, and right mouse buttons to control the view plane.

Some other hotkeys are useful to know, too. The F hotkey frames the selected element, showing you the entire element in the active View window. This is often faster than zooming around until you can see the whole object. The A hotkey frames all the objects in the scene. You may also zoom into a rectangular selection onscreen by simultaneously holding down the Shift key and the Z hotkey and dragging a rectangle onscreen with your left mouse button. Doing the same with your right mouse button zooms out of a rectangular area of the screen. Take a few moments to try these hotkeys.

## Rearranging the View Windows

You can customize the view that you see while working with SOFTIMAGE|XSI. You will generally work with four or fewer View windows onscreen at any one time, but you can arrange the windows to your liking by changing their orientation, the plane they show, and their relative sizes.

First, note that all the views are designated with a letter: A, B, C, or D. Each view can show you an orthographic view, like the Front view or the Top view. It can show you the view from a camera you have placed into the scene, or even the view from a spotlight in the scene.

## Resizing the Views

On the top corner opposite from the letter is a small Resize box. Clicking a View window Resize box with the left mouse button expands the window to fill the entire screen, removing the other windows from view. Clicking the Resize box with the middle mouse button causes that window to grow horizontally, replacing the window to the right or left of it, but leaving the other windows to the top or bottom alone. Clicking again with the middle mouse button causes it to regain its former size. Clicking the Resize box with the right mouse button gives you a drop menu with other options.

You can also click and drag the dividing line between windows to resize them to any size. Try it out!

To restore the windows to occupy even quadrants of the screen, click exactly on the middle where the dividing lines between the panes come together with the middle mouse button.

## The Camera Drop Menu

Next to the View window drop menu lies the Camera drop menu (identified with a small camera-shaped icon). The Camera menu, shown in Figure 1.19, primarily contains the menu equivalents for the navigation hotkeys like Pan, Zoom, Orbit, Frame, and Reset. However, it contains two other useful features: the ability to immediately select the camera or interest for that view, and the capture options. Capture starts a playback but records the contents of the chosen view as a series of frames to disk. Then it pops up the Flipbook window, which contains the controls for playing back the frames to review your work. Reviewing your timing and poses is an essential part of the animation workflow, so having easy access to see the results of your work here is very useful.

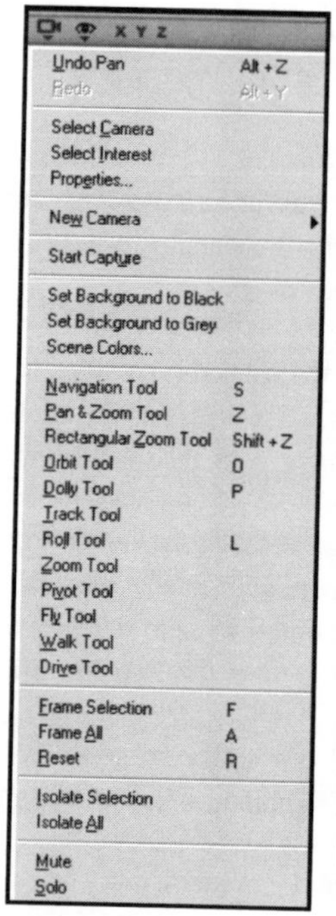

## The Show Menu

The Show menu (eyeball icon) immediately to the right of the Camera menu in the View title bar toggles the visibility of different kinds of information that you could view in the window (see Figure 1.20). Since XSI can show you so much information about each object in the scene, it is necessary to filter that information, showing only what is most useful for the stage of the project that you are currently in.

You can turn on and off cameras, 3D geometry, curves, lights, nulls, chains, and texture controls for each view independently. You can also show components like points, knots, centers, and normals differently in each view.

**Figure 1.19**
The Camera drop menu.

**Figure 1.20**
The Show drop menu.

The toggles in the Show menu (eyeball icon) are generally the same as the toggles in the View menu at the top of the screen, but they apply only to that window.

At the bottom of the list of showable items is the Visibility Options command. This pops up another property page with even more options for how you may look at your scene, and new kinds of information to display. In the last tab, named "Stats" try toggling on Show Frame Rate, Show Selection Info, and Show Scene Info. These options will layer more information over the View window to show you the size of the selected model in triangles and other information.

## Display Method

When you are viewing the scene through either an orthographic or perspective view, you have some options for how the view is displayed.

In the top-right corner of each View menu bar is the menu for the view Display Style. It will have the name of the currently active method, which will be one of the following: Bounding Box, Wireframe, Depth Cue, Hidden Line Removal, Constant, Shaded, Textured, Textured Decal, Realtime Shaders, or Rotoscope (see Figure 1.21).

Load a scene from the project data for this book using File > Open so that you will have something to look at.

Load the stonehenge_done scene.

If you do not have the digital content for this book installed, you may install it from the CD-ROM that accompanies this text.

## Wireframe and Hidden Line

The first option, Wireframe, is the view that you have used up to this point. Wireframe view mode doesn't actually show the surfaces of objects, just the curves that make up the surfaces. Each object is transparent, so you can also see the curves on the back of each object and those objects that are behind it. This can become confusing. The Hidden Line Removal view style located below the wireframe draws only those curves on the surface that face towards the camera, hiding the back-facing portions of each surface. Hidden Line Removal also sorts the objects by order of distance from the camera, so that closer objects obscure farther ones. This view method is quite fast and provides a better sense of depth in the scene (see Figure 1.22).

## Constant

The Constant view option covers your models in a constant color, unaffected by lights, depth, or other shading. At first this seems useless, but actually it's a great help when viewing weight maps and painting over them on models.

## Shaded , Textured, and Realtime

Shaded view, shown in Figure 1.23, uses the OpenGL graphics hardware in your workstation to display the surface of each model in your scene, using a simple shading method. It can show light and color, but not transparency, bump, or most special effects. (SOFTIMAGE|XSI creates a default infinite light for you automatically, in case you don't have your own yet.)

**Figure 1.21**
The different display modes.

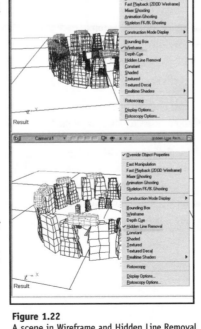

**Figure 1.22**
A scene in Wireframe and Hidden Line Removal view styles.

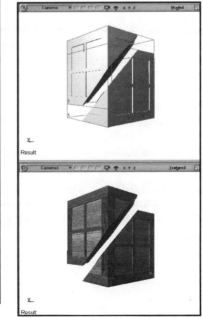

**Figure 1.23**
A scene in shaded and textured modes.

**19**

The Shaded view can give you a better visual representation of where things are in your scene and what they will look like in the final render, but it can be quite slow if the complexity of the scene exceeds the capabilities of your OpenGL hardware. You can customize your shaded view to suit your needs by adjusting options in the Shaded > Display Options menu. The changes you make will apply to all objects in that view as long as the toggle Override Object Properties is off in the Display Style menu. Each view camera can have different view mode settings.

The XSI display system is much more flexible than that, however. You can specify different display methods for objects based on whether they are selected or unselected, being modified or holding static, or playing back in an animation or not (see Figure 1.24). In the same property page (Shaded > Display Options) in the Display Mode tab, change some settings so that the selected object will be shaded, but the other objects will be displayed in hidden line removal, by setting the Static and Interaction modes in the Unselected Objects column to Hidden Line Removal. Now as you select objects in your scene, they will change from Hidden Line Removal to Shaded.

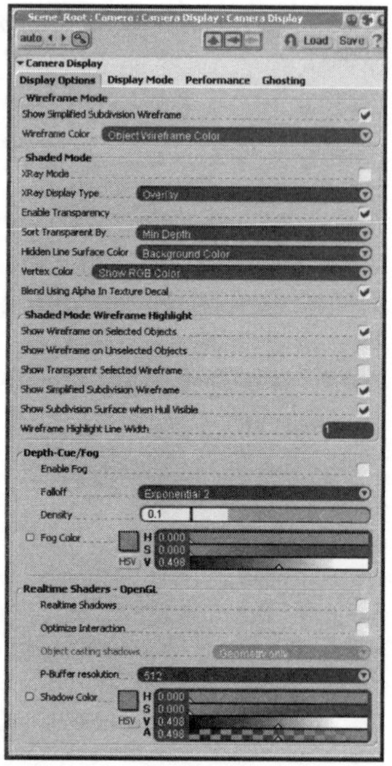

> Advanced users will find the Display property on each object. In fact, the Display mode can be set differently on each object in the scene, if need be.

The Textured view mode adds any surface 2D image textures on top of each shaded object so that you can see texture placement. The Textured view relies on the OpenGL graphics hardware of your computer to draw the textures. If your card has insufficient texture memory, this can be very slow. In addition, XSI only shows the last applied texture, so multiple layered textures will not be shown very accurately. Procedural textures and shaders won't show at all.

The Textured Decal option shows the last selected texture (or the texture in use in another view) with full lighting, so you can easily see the results of your work without worrying about what the lights in the scene are doing.

**Figure 1.24**
You can have different display types for selected, unselected, near, and far objects.

The Realtime Shaders view bypasses the traditional display model and lets you attach shaders to objects that are interpreted and drawn directly to the screen by your 3D Display Acceleration hardware—in other words, by your graphics card. There are several competing standards for languages that describe the display of 3D graphics to screen. SOFTIMAGE|XSI supports the OpenGL standard, which is available on all current (circa 2005) graphics hardware, the DirectX9 Microsoft spec (less common), and the up-and-coming NVIDIA Cg shader language, supported now on only new NVIDIA-based graphics cards. These options will be of use to game content developers, but we'll stick to the regular Wireframe, Hidden Line Removal, Shaded, and Textured Decal views in this book.

## Rotoscope

The Rotoscope view mode is a tool that allows you to bring in a sequence of frames as a background image and then see the images behind your work in SOFT-IMAGE (see Figure 1.25). This roto-scoping technique is often used in film work where real-life film contents ("practicals") are integrated with Computer Graphic Imagery (CGI).

For example, if you are adding an animated character to a scene in which a group of computer-generated characters sit down for dinner in a real-life restaurant, you

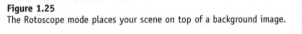

**Figure 1.25**
The Rotoscope mode places your scene on top of a background image.

could shoot film of the table in the restaurant, with waiters wandering by and real people dining in the background. The film would be developed, scanned into a computer, and provided to you as digital frames. You could then bring these background plates into SOFTIMAGE so that you can verify the correct placement of the computer-graphic characters you are animating.

When you toggle on Rotoscope, the Camera Rotoscopy property page is opened and you can choose an image or sequence of images to view behind your work. Try loading an image from your own collection by clicking on the New button, choosing the New From File option, and navigating to your My Pictures directory (in Windows).

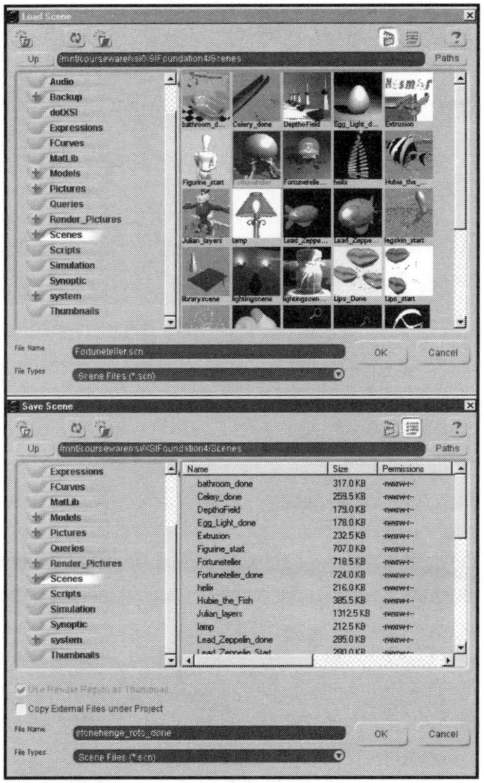

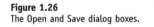

**Figure 1.26**
The Open and Save dialog boxes.

# Opening, Saving, and Projects

XSI uses totally custom Open and Save dialog boxes that are not based on any particular OS. As a result, they look a little different and have some new features.

Use File > Open from the menus at the top of the screen to see the Load Scene dialog box (see Figure 1.26).

On the left side of the dialog box is the list of folders under the current place in the file system (hard drive or servers). Only folders are shown here, not files. Where you see a plus sign next to a folder, that folder has something in it. You can click on the plus to reveal the contents. When you have clicked on a plus, the list cascades out, and the plus turns into a minus. You can click on the minus to collapse the folder.

If you click directly on the name of a folder, the contents of that folder (both folders and files) will be shown in the larger right panel of the Open or Save dialog box.

## *Browsing the Path*

The 'path' is your current location in the file system. The path starts with a / on Irix and Linux, which means the root, and c:\ on Windows, which means the top of drive C. After that is a list of each folder you traversed down into to get to this point on the disk. For instance, /disk2/people/bobby translates into English as in the bobby folder, which is in the people folder, which is on disk 2, which is at the root of the file system.

You can type directly into the path line and then press Enter to go there, or you can browse by clicking the up button to go up the path, getting closer to the root, or by double-clicking on folders on the right side to descend down into them (see Figure 1.27).

All the contents of the folder at the end of the path are shown in the larger right side area.

The contents of the right side can be shown as either text listings or as thumbnails by clicking on the Clapper and List icons in the upper right corner.

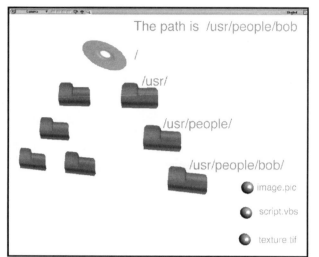

**Figure 1.27**
A path is the way you find your work in the computer and on the network file system.

A very useful icon is the Paths button on the right side, under the Help question mark.
The Paths button will show you all the projects that you have listed in the Project Manager, in addition to the default location of the software installation, and the Sample scenes that install with the software. This is almost always the fastest way to get to a specific scene.

There are more icons on the left side of the browser to aid in navigation. The first icon is the Favorites button, where you can set up your own favorite locations, first navigating to the location you want to mark, and then choosing the Add to Favorites option. If you need to access files located on another server or computer on your local network, use the second icon, the Network Neighborhood icon, to browse your network. If you don't see a file in the browser that should be there, use the third icon from the left to refresh the file list in the browser.

On Linux and Windows, you can only save into folders that your user has permissions for (a smart security precaution). Unfortunately, XSI defaults to the installation path, which should never be the path to your user account. You will want to use Project Manager immediately to set the default path to your own user account so thatyou can save and open files without browsing through the file system so much.

The bottom of the window shows the OK and Cancel buttons. If you are in the Save Scene dialog box, you can pick an existing scene and then click OK to save over it, replacing it, or you can enter a new file name in the File Name line and then click OK to create a new scene file.

## Project Management

XSI has a sophisticated project management system that is designed to make it easy for you to manage multiple jobs at once, and keep revisions within each job organized. This is accomplished with the Project Manager dialog box, located in the File menu (File > Project Manager; see Figure 1.28).

The major container for all your work in XSI is called a project. You may have as many projects as you wish on your machine, and you can also share projects that are located on a central server. You might wish to create a new project for each new client you take on or each new project that you undertake.

Each project is really just a folder system, containing sub-folders that organize the different parts of the work that you create.

Those folders are: Actions, Audio, Backup, dotXSI, Expressions, Fcurves, Models, Pictures, Queries, Render_Pictures, Scenes, Scripts, Shaders, Simulation, and Synoptic.

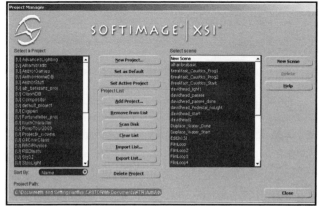

**Figure 1.28**
Use the Project Manager dialog box to organize your scenes.

Your scenes are mainly saved into the Scenes folder, but you can also choose to save models externally into the Models folder. Your rendered frames will end up in the Render_Pictures folder, and the Pictures folder is a good place to put texture maps. Audio clips used for sync should be placed in the Audio folder.

Within each project, you may have as many different scenes as you wish. A scene file binds up all the models, lights, cameras, textures, shaders, and everything else into one file. To completely save all your work during a session, you use the command File > Save or File > Save As, which writes a new scene into your current project.

It's a good idea to give your scenes a descriptive name and a version number so that you can always get back to your previous work if you decide to go back a few steps. For example, if you were working on a character animation for the PuffyStuff company, you might name the scene puffystuffCharacter1. XSI will append the file extension .scn to your name for you automatically.

You can also save an image thumbnail of the scene along with the file, to help you see which one was which at a later date. To do this, draw a render region on screen somewhere in the Camera view. Then when you choose File > Save, check the button marked Use Render Region As Thumbnail.

### Examining and Switching Projects

You can see what project you are currently working in, switch to a different one, or even create a new project with the Project Manager. To see the Project Manager, click on File > Project Manager.

The list of projects is found on the left-hand side of the Project Manager dialog box. The scenes contained within that project are listed on the right-hand side. You can pick items from either side. You can also use this dialog box to delete entire projects or scenes. Be very careful of these options. Only use them if you really want to throw away all your hard work.

You can create new projects here in the Project Manager, or you can use the File > New Project menu item. Remember that you can save new Project folders only to areas of the file system that you have privileges to. If you try to save a project to an area you do not have permissions to change, you will see an alert saying "The disk is write protected." Save somewhere else, contact your SysAdmin, or change the permissions yourself.

### Moving Scenes from One Project to Another

You can move scenes from one project into a new one by simply opening the scene, then switching projects in the Project Manager, and doing a Save. Or you can use Save As, navigate to the location of the new Project in the path, and save the scene into the Scenes folder. When you do that, be sure to also check on the box in the Save dialog box that is marked Copy External Files Under Project. This will automatically look into your scene and copy any textures, shaders, or other files used in your scene from the old project to the new one.

## Objects, Parameters, and Property Pages

XSI is deeply object-oriented. Each object in it exists in a structure of objects, each with its own attributes, called properties or parameters. Since everything in XSI is an object with distinct properties, all objects can be treated in similar ways. Each can be selected, moved around in space, or in the list of all objects called the XSI Explorer, be copied, pasted, and so forth. Each can also be inspected in a standard interface box called a property page, or Property Editor (see Figure 1.29).

The Property Editor is the single most ubiquitous interface element in XSI. Each object has myriad different property pages telling you about values of the object, like location in space, visibility options, material attributes, and much, much more. To explore properties, get a primitive NURBS Sphere with Get > Primitive > Surface > Sphere. Then change your lower-right view to be a Schematic view by clicking on the name of that view (it probably says Right) and pulling down the drop list to Schematic.

Also open an Explorer in the Top view (click on Top > Explorer) to see a linear list of the elements in your scene, including the sphere you just made.

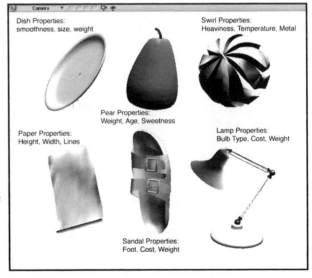

**Figure 1.29**
Real-world objects and their properties.

There are several different ways to inspect the properties (or parameters) of an object.
One method is to locate the object of interest in either the Schematic view or the Explorer view, and click just once with the left mouse button on the colored icon to the left of the object name (zoom in closer if you do not see the icon. Also check that the View > Show Icons toggle is on in the Schematic menu bar.) Another method is to right-click (or Alt-right-click if you have another tool already active) and choose Properties > General from the context-sensitive

menu that pops up. This causes the general property page for that object to pop up. If the object you clicked over was a sphere, you will be able to edit the radius of the sphere, its name, and the number of U and V isolines in the sphere. If the object was a light, you will be able to change those properties that are specific to the light, such as the color, the falloff, the spread, and whether or not it casts shadows. Each object has different properties, and you can even add properties to them as you work within SOFTIMAGE|XSI.

## Property Groups

Properties in similar areas are grouped into tabs within the General property page. These tabs have a title (like Geometry, or Sphere) to identify them within a horizontal gray bar in the interface, along with a small triangle. The triangle can collapse or expand that tab to limit which properties you see in the General property page.

The tabs along the top of the PPG (shorthand for PropertyPaGe), shown in Figure 1.30, and the horizontal collapsing section breaks are the same thing. Showing them both is redundant. The File > Preferences > Interaction > Tab Style Property Editors toggle changes this behavior to be more reasonable.

There is a shortcut to the General property page for any object. You can simply select the object and press the Enter key. Using the combination Alt-Enter will inspect all the object's properties in one long property page. You can also use the Edit menu in the MCP (right side, Edit > Properties) to look at the General properties, the Modeling properties, the Animation properties, the Rendering properties, the Viewing properties, or any Custom properties that you have added, as illustrated in Figure 1.31.

Properties can be organized into sets that you look at together:

◆ General properties include the name of the object.

◆ Modeling properties include how the object was made, its surface UV detail, and any geometry or deformation operators that have been applied.

◆ Animation properties include the object's current scale, rotation, and translation, in addition to velocity, acceleration, and any positional or rotational limits that have been applied.

◆ Rendering properties include the object material and shaders, the geometry approximation for the object, the object visibility to the camera and in reflections and refractions, and links to the ambient light in the scene.

◆ Viewing properties control specifically whether or not, with what level of detail and in what draw style, the object is rendered to the screen,.

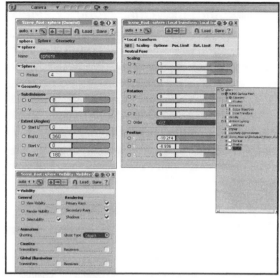
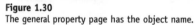

**Figure 1.30**
The general property page has the object name.

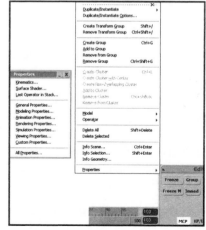

**Figure 1.31**
You can get the property page you want from the Edit menu.

## *Locking and Recycling Property Pages*

Many views, like the Property Editor or the Animation Mixer, will show you whatever object is currently selected. Sometimes you will want to keep a specific object open for editing while going on to select other objects. Generally you do this by locking the window or property page. To lock a window view, click on the Lock button in the title bar of the window. To lock a property page, click on the small lock icon in the top-right corner of the page. This will keep the property page open for that object and that property. If you inspect a different property, it will pop up in a new property page. When you are done with that locked property, you can either close the property page with the small X in the top-left corner, or turn the page back to recycle by clicking on the three-sided swirling recycle icon in the top-left corner of the property page (see Figure 1.32).

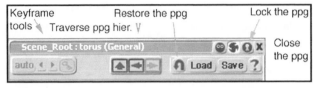

**Figure 1.32**
Each property page has the same buttons in the header.

In some views (like the Render Tree), the lock icon is a small padlock, and the recycle icon has two arrows swirling together instead of three swirling lobes. In either case, the meaning is the same. Recycle means reuse this display for whatever is selected while lock means don't change - I need this information!

Each property page also has buttons to load and to save the object or property. These are the small Load and Save buttons in the top of the page directly below the Lock and Recycle buttons. If you have a render region defined, it will be added to the saved property page as a thumbnail. These saved property pages are called presets. The preset mechanism means that you can save anything at all from XSI from any object, at any time, and reload it later from disc. This applies to simple things like material colors, and complex things like shape animation morph targets. Store this information away in your brain for later, more advanced use.

## *Docking the Property Page*

Because you will use properties so frequently, they can often clutter the screen and obscure the interface or parts of the scene that you would rather see (see Figure 1.33).

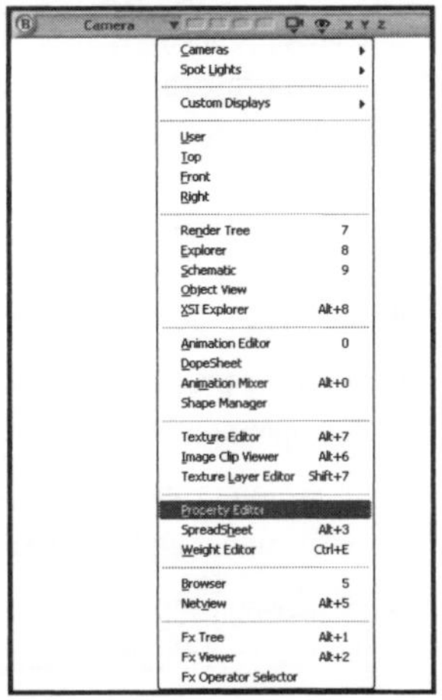

One idea to reduce the clutter is to allocate one of your View windows to show all the property pages that pop up. You can do this by clicking on the View title (Top, Right, Camera, etc.) and selecting the Property Editor option near the bottom of the list. Now all new properties will be drawn into that window, and if they are too long, they will scroll. This is called docking the PPG. However, the downside here is that one view is taken up with the PPGs. A better solution is to use floating PPGs, and then either collapse the title bar, minimize PPGs, or just close them when you don't need them. Let's explore (pun intended) how to show floating properties most easily.

# The Selection Explorer

Since each object might have many properties, there is a way to pop up a property page that doesn't show everything, but just has the information you want to work with. That's the Selection button, and it's located on the right side of the screen in the Main Command Panel (MCP), directly below the text entry boxes. When you click on the Selection button,

**Figure 1.33**
You can show property pages in a window.

a drop box appears showing all the properties of the currently selected object as a series of cascading icons and names (see Figure 1.34). Simply click on the icon of the property you want to edit, and a property page showing just that info will pop up. If you click on the name of the property, something different will happen: You will have now selected the property itself, and the object that owns it will not be selected. This is not usually what you want, so be careful to click just on the icon next to the property name to display the property page.

Seeing only the properties you are interested in will help your understanding and workflow a lot. Get used to using the Selection button whenever you want to work with the properties of the selected item. Remember that clicking on the *icon* of the property, not the name, is what you want to do. It saves clicks, and prevents frustration and error later.

## *Organizing Objects and Properties with the Explorer*

Because there are so many new objects and properties, organizing them to find what you need is an important consideration. The Explorer view is another way to organize all the objects in your scene.

To enter the Explorer view, click on the colored View drop menu in an existing view window and select the Explorer option, or tap 8 to call up the floating Explorer window. You can select objects in the Explorer by clicking on their names.

In the Explorer view, all objects in the scene can be listed, or the list can be filtered to show only objects in the current layer, partition, render pass, group, or selection. This complete view of everything in your scene can be useful, but more often the quantity of information available there makes it hard to find what you want (see Figure 1.35).

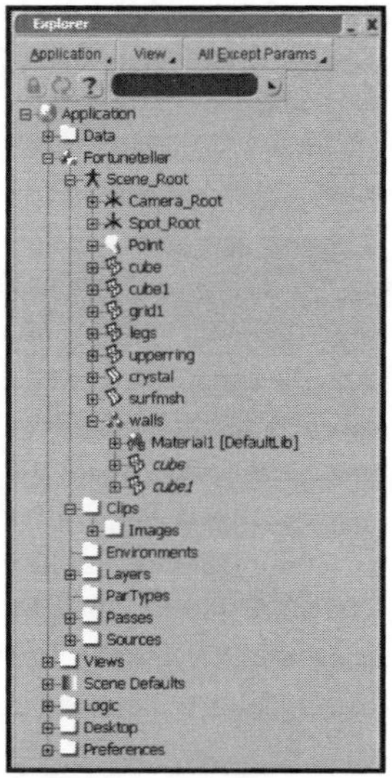

By default, the Explorer shows all the objects in your scene. This is called Scene Scope. You can change the scope of the Explorer with the leftmost drop menu in the Explorer window. Setting it to Application scope will show you more objects and properties, and setting it to Selection will show you fewer. The hotkey to zoom in on one object in the Explorer and set the scope to Selection is E.

If you find yourself overwhelmed by the Explorer, stick with using the Selection button in the right side Main Command Panel (MCP) to find properties.

The Explorer window is dynamic, which means that it will update with whatever you have selected. If you have a sphere selected and show the Explorer with Selection scope (so it shows only that one sphere), you'll see the sphere's properties. But then when you select a cube, the Explorer window will automatically update to show you the properties on the cube. This concept is called focus because the Explorer focuses on whatever you have selected (in Selection Scope). To prevent this from happening, and make sure that the sphere stays loaded in the Explorer, you can use the Lock button. In the Explorer, like many other views and the property pages, locking means that it will not update automatically based on what you have selected.

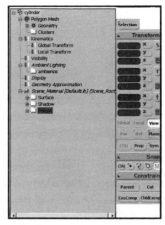

**Figure 1.34**
The Transient selection explorer shows you just the properties on the currently selected item.

**Figure 1.35**
The Explorer can show a lot of information.

The XSI Explorer view is a variation on the Explorer theme. The XSI Explorer (maybe we should call it the new explorer) shows two panes: a list on the left and a blank view on the right. If you open the new XSI Explorer (Alt-8 is the hotkey), and then change the scope to Selection (hotkey E, with an object in the scene already selected), you can then use the Viewer button in the menu area at the top of the XSI Explorer to set the second blank pane to a new view, such as the Object view or the Texture Editor. This makes for a very convenient interface to work on a single object at a time without being confused (or slowed down) by all the other stuff in your scene.

## The Schematic View

The Schematic view can be used to arrange your scene, select models, view the relationships between objects in a hierarchy, see constraints between objects, and work with materials and textures. The hotkey to pop up a floating Schematic view is 9 (see Figure 1.36).

The Schematic view window is a pretty important window in XSI, and it can quickly get cluttered. Feel free to move the items in the Schematic window around as much as you like, by holding the M key (move tool), clicking with the left mouse button, and dragging. You can also hold down the Shift key, and drag a selection rectangle to select multiple objects at once.

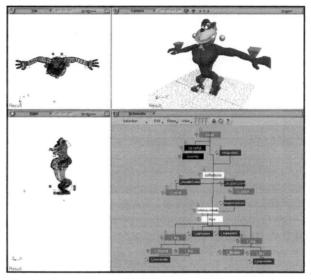

**Figure 1.36**
The Schematic view is useful for visualizing what's in your scene.

It's a good idea to lay out the items in some sort of order that makes sense to you in relation to the model you are building. For example, if you are building a human figure, you would place the body in the middle of the schematic, with the head on top, the hands out to the sides, and the feet below. That way you can easily choose whichever body part you want to work on, without struggling to find it in the scene.

You can also turn on or off different types of information in the Schematic view. If you are working on adding materials, you might want to use the Show menu to display materials in addition to models. You can also choose to see constraints, expressions, operators, and simulation links as colored lines connecting models in the schematic. If the number of links showing in the schematic gets overwhelming, look in the Show menu from the Schematic title bar and toggle on the option to Show Links on Selected Nodes Only.

The Schematic menu has a very useful context-sensitive menu that you can show at any time by right-clicking in the Schematic window. If you click over empty space, you will get a menu offering to frame, rearrange, select, pan, or zoom. If you click over an object, you can inspect properties, rename the object, delete it, duplicate it, create instances of it, and much more.

You can show and hide objects in the Schematic view by selecting the object and tapping the H hotkey (for Hide) on your keyboard. Hidden objects still appear in the schematic, but have an outline form to differentiate them. To unhide the object again, press the H hotkey. You can reorder and sort the contents of the Schematic view with the options in the View menu.

You can collapse hierarchies to save space in the Schematic view by clicking on the parent object (the top of the hierarchy) with the right mouse button and choosing Collapse Node.

The Schematic view has memo cams just like the regular view menus. These are the four empty divots in the top portion of the Schematic view menu bar. They let you save a view you like in the schematic for later recovery. For instance, imagine you have a hand hierarchy in the schematic, and you will be using it a lot. You could zoom in to frame the hand objects in the Schematic view and then middle-click in an empty memo cam slot to store that view. Zoom and drag to a different part of the Schematic and save another memo cam. Now you can switch back and forth between the saved views by left-clicking on the memo cam buttons. You can erase memo cams by right-clicking over the memo cam slot.

## Searching For Objects

XSI also supports the use of searching, complete with expressions and wildcard characters for finding and selecting scene objects.

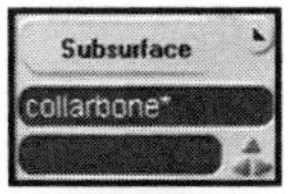

You can search for and select objects by entering a string to match in the text entry box near the top of the Main Command Panel (see Figure 1.37).

**Figure 1.37**
You can read the name of the selected element, and enter a name to search for.

For instance, if you have a cylinder named mycylinder and a sphere named mysphere you could select either one by entering its name into the top text box in the MCP and pressing Enter to search for it.

You can also use wildcards to select more than one object. You could, for instance, type my* in the text selection box, and XSI would select both mysphere and, mycylinder. Entering *cyl* would select the cylinder, or all the things named cylinders if more existed in the scene.

You can also use this feature to select a branch (an object and all its children), by adding a B: (for branch) before the name of the object. If you have a hand named my.right.hand that is the parent of five fingers, you could enter B:my.right.hand to select the whole hand branch.

## Conclusion

Whew! That was a long chapter about a great deal of important, but sometimes dry, information. It's important because you will use the tools for finding, organizing, and selecting objects constantly as you work within XSI. You should consider reflecting back on this chapter a few months later, after you have had a chance to work in the software. You will likely find quite a few useful tidbits that escaped your notice the first time through.

# Chapter 2
# Basic Terminology & Modeling

In this chapter, you will:

◆ Start a fresh scene

◆ Learn basic names for objects and components

◆ Create models from primitive shapes

◆ Learn all about polygons

◆ Learn all about NURBS (Non-Uniform Rational B-Splines)

◆ Move, scale, and rotate objects

◆ Efficiently select objects, hierarchies, and components

◆ Model organically by pushing and pulling points

# Introduction

In this chapter, you will learn a lot more about the terminology used in XSI (and most other 3D applications) to describe the objects you will work with in the software. You will learn about objects and centers, control points and vertices, and knots and boundaries (see Figure 2.1).

You will soon have a chance to put together a simple scene and view your work.

## Starting from Scratch

When you want to get rid of everything on the screen without saving changes, or if you simply want to load a fresh scene to work on, use the File > New Scene menu command (Ctrl+N) to clear the scene (see Figure 2.2). This command removes all objects from use, clears the undo stack, and cleans up memory. Now with a new scene, you have the computer equivalent of a blank sheet of paper to start work on.

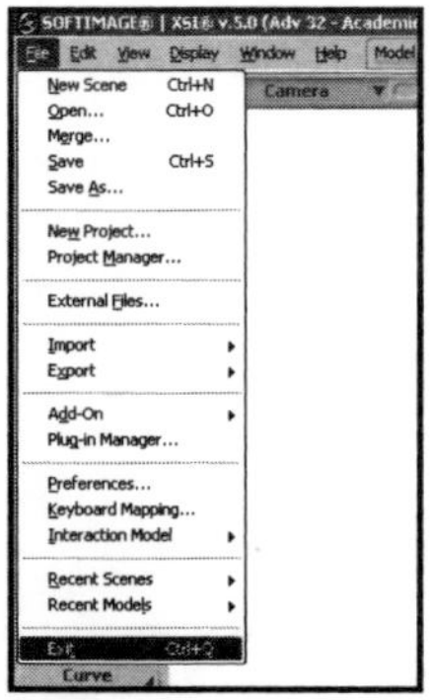

## Basic Nomenclature: Points, Curves, Polygons, Surfaces

Before you can get started using the tools in SOFTIMAGE|XSI to make models and scenes, you'll need to learn the body of terminology used throughout this book and the SOFTIMAGE|XSI product. Most of these terms are used in ways that are standard to the 3D animation world, but some are not. If you take the time to understand the terminology now, even when it becomes technical, you will have an easier time using SOFTIMAGE|XSI to create good work.

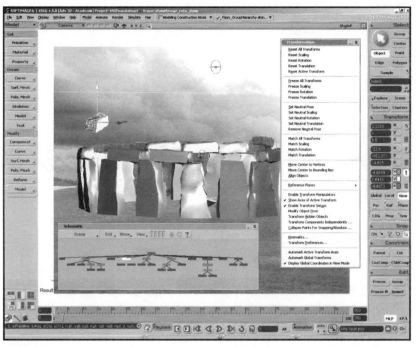

**Figure 2.1**
Tools you'll use.

**Figure 2.2**
The File menu.

Almost everything in SOFTIMAGE|XSI is constructed by placing points in 3D space. A point is simply a zero-dimensional location in 3D space, usually given by the X, Y, and Z coordinate system. Two connected points can define a straight line. If something is linear, it is composed of straight line segments, each with a point at either end. Each linear segment is a one-dimensional object, because two end points define a one-dimensional vector. In fact, a straight line is the definition of one-dimensional. If two segments are joined together, they become a two-dimensional object, because they now have three points, which defines a plane. A two-dimensional plane is easiest thought of as a triangle floating in space. If three segments are joined together so that each segment is perpendicular to the other two, they become a three-dimensional object, like the sides of a cube, or the 3D axis on each view port in XSI (see Figure 2.3).

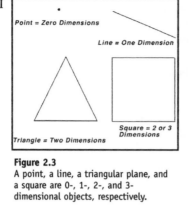

**Figure 2.3**
A point, a line, a triangular plane, and a square are 0-, 1-, 2-, and 3-dimensional objects, respectively.

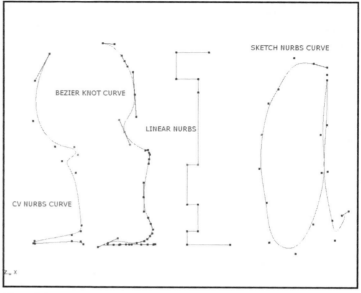

**Figure 2.4**
These are all different kinds of spline curves. All are also called NURBS.

## Splines, Curves, NURBS

A spline is a line shape that is defined by two or more points plotted in space. A synonym for spline is curve. SOFTIMAGE|XSI uses both terms interchangeably. There can be linear curves, even though the names seem to be exclusive of one another. SOFTIMAGE|XSI uses both Bezier curves and NURBS (Non-Uniform Rational B-Spline) curves (see Figure 2.4).

Bezier curves are the type found in common Mac and PC drawing applications, where each point on the curve also has two handles—one before, and one after—that determine how the curve transitions into the points before and after. These handles are called tangent handles. You can draw Bezier curves in XSI with the Create] > Curve > Draw Cubic by Bezier-Knot points tool.

NURBS curves are more complex. They're the most useful type of curves found in any 3D program.

All NURBS are actually composed of a number of segments, although you as the user perceive an unbroken curve. The segments are joined together at invisible intersections called knots (see Figure 2.5). The knots usually do not lie at the same place as the control points that you see when you create a curve, because the NURBS curve finds a best fit through the control points that you lay down when you plot out the curve. For a basic Cubic NURB, four control points are required to create the smallest segment.

Being composed of a series of knots makes a curve "piecewise," which emphasizes that the curve is actually a compound made up of lots of smaller pieces that are joined together at the ends. NURBS curve segments can be of various orders and of different parameterization, which is to say that the knots connecting the segments can be spaced in different ways.

If you draw a curve, with Create > Curve > Draw Cubic by CVs in the Model module, and then turn on Show Points and Show Knots (remember, Show is the eyeball menu above each view), you can see the difference between the points (called control vertices, or CVs) and the knots.

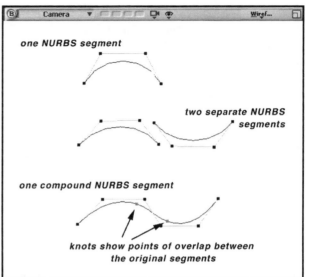

## Curve Order

The mathematical formula that describes each line segment between knots can be of varying complexity. A first-order curve has a linear equation, a quadratic equation is used

**Figure 2.5**
Each NURBS curve is created from smaller pieces, connected together at knots.

for second-order curves, and a cubic equation is used for third-order curves. Third and higher-order curves maintain positional and tangential continuity as one segment joins another. This creates very smooth curves that seem to be one unbroken filament.

The order of the curve segment defines how smoothly it transitions into a neighboring segment. In a linear curve, the segments share a knot and a point, but they are not tangent to each other at that knot, so you see a sharp edge there. Two segments that are not tangent to each other seem to break into a sharp angle at the point at which they intersect. Second-order curves are perfectly tangent to each other where they join, transitioning smoothly from one to the next, so that without the control points showing, you wouldn't know where one segment ends and the next begins.

The NURBS curve has several benefits. The points can be unequally weighted, so that one point attracts the curve more closely than the others. This is what makes the curve rational. It enables the creation of corners in an otherwise smooth curve. It may also be trimmed to any length, because the knots defining the ends of segments can be placed at any point along the curve.

If a spline is closed, the end of the last segment of the curve is co-located with the start of the first segment, creating an unbroken path. By themselves, splines are invisible to the rendering engine, because they have no real surface.

## Centers

Each object is located in Cartesian space. The coordinates of the object are given by the position of the object center relative to the global center (also called the origin). This means that every object in SOFTIMAGE|XSI has an object center, called a local center.

The local center is the point from which the object scales, so if the local center of a ruler is in the geometric center of the ruler, it grows equally outwards from the middle when you scale it. If you move the center to the bottom of the ruler and scale it, the ruler grows up from the bottom edge.

Similarly, the object rotates around the local center (see Figure 2.6). Put another way, the local center is the axis of rotation for that object. To make a door object swing open appropriately, you would need to move the local center to the hinge edge of the door. Then the door rotates around the edge of the door instead of the middle.

This local center is fundamental to the behavior of every object in the XSI 3D environment.

**Figure 2.6**
Each object has a local center.

When you have an object selected, and are transforming it with the Main Command Panel (MCP), you can see several buttons beneath the Translate cells. One of these buttons is Local. When Local is active, you are translating the object relative to its local center. Another button is Global. When Global is selected, you are moving the object relative to the global center. COG is an option that creates a new, temporary center to transform the object, at the geometric middle of the object bounding box. If you need to transform the object around some other arbitrary point, you can create your own pivot while transforming by holding down the Alt key on the keyboard. The Alt key creates a temporary pivot that you can relocate to somewhere more convenient for you.

## Polygons

The polygon is another basic building block in the SOFTIMAGE|XSI object system. A polygon is a shape defined by three or more points, called vertices (plural), arranged in space. Each vertex (singular) is connected to at least two neighboring vertices with straight-line segments called edges. This method of linking points in space by edges creates the geometric shapes called polygons.

There are several kinds of polygons. The most basic polygon has only three sides and is called a triangle. The next size up from a triangle is a rectangle, also called a quad, which has four vertices and four sides. From there on up, polygons are called n-sided (see Figure 2.7).

You can see and select polygons with different numbers of sides by selecting a polygon object (try a sphere) and using the Select > Select n-Sided Polygons options in the MCP.

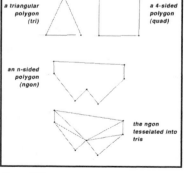

**Figure 2.7**
The parts of a polygon: vertices, edges, normals, and polygons of different types.

## Polygon Meshes

An object can be composed of a single polygon or a group of polygons. An object composed of many polygons is called a polygon mesh. A polygon mesh object is composed of one or more polygons that share vertices and edges (see Figure 2.8).

If two polygons share two or more vertices, they also share an edge between those vertices. Polygons like this remain connected at the edge like conjoined twins connected at the hip: Move one polygon, and the other has to stretch to stay joined at the edge. Polygons that share edges can be broken up so that they no longer share edges. Edges that are not shared are called boundaries. You can show them with Show > PolyMesh Boundaries and Hard Edges.

Because each vertex contains a value for the X position, the Y position, and the Z position, polygon datasets can be quite large.

XSI takes polygons in a whole new direction with subdivision surfaces. In XSI, all polygon objects are also subdivision surface cages. A subdivision surface is a very smooth organic surface implied by the shape of the polygonal object (then called a polygonal cage). Subdivision surfaces (also known as SubDees) can be thought of as smoothed polygon objects, though there is more to them than that. In XSI, SubDees are completely integrated, and anything that you can do with a polygonal object can also be done with a subdivision surface.

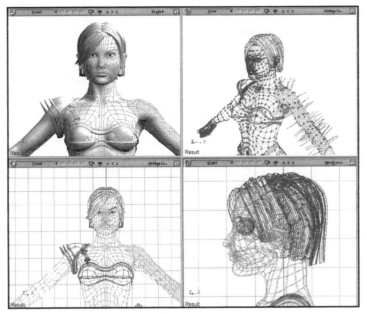

**Figure 2.8**
A simple character made of a polygon mesh.

## Normals

Both polygons and NURBS have another important component called the normal. The normal is a vector line segment emanating from the each polygon or NURBS patch that indicates which way the object is facing—that is to say, which side of the polygon is the front side and which is the back. Imagine putting on your socks this morning. The first thing you checked before you put them on was whether they were inside out or right side out. Surfaces in XSI can be just like socks—either side could be showing. Swapping sides (turning an object inside out) is called inverting the surface. For polygonal meshes, it becomes very important that all parts of the mesh have coherent normals that all point out in the same direction. Imagine if part of your sock was inside out but another part was not (see Figure 2.9).

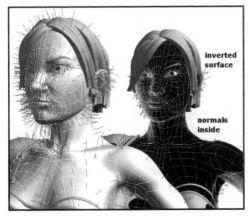

**Figure 2.9**
Normals help in shading, and also show which way the surface is facing.

SOFTIMAGE|XSI uses this information in several important ways. First, it determines at render time which surface is facing the camera and renders only that part, to save render time. Second, XSI uses the normals during the render to smooth the shading on edges between polygons, helping to reduce the typical jagged, faceted look of polygonal models.

The normals can be shown or hidden differently in each view window of SOFTIMAGE|XSI with Show > Normals. When shown, they look like thin, blue hairs sprouting from the surface of your models.

## NURBS Patches, Boundaries, U and V

So far we've talked about NURBS curves, but we can also make NURBS surfaces, as shown in Figure 2.10. NURBS surfaces are a patchwork of smaller rectangular patches. The patch can be thought of as a network of spline curves, with the intersections between the curves connected by a web of geometry, creating a surface.

The edges of a patch are often called the boundary curves because they define the boundaries of the patch. One boundary runs in the U direction and one boundary runs in the V direction, as shown in Figure 2.11. U and V are just like latitude and longitude on the Earth—they always run perpendicular to one another.

When the patch is more or less rectangular, the boundary curves look like they are the edges, but when the patch looks more like a sphere, the boundary curves look more like the poles of a planet.

To see this in XSI, get a primitive surface sphere and a primitive surface grid, and then show the boundaries in the Camera view by toggling on the NURBS Boundaries option in the Show menu. (Show looks like an icon of an eye, located in the menu bar of the Camera view.) The U boundary shows in red, and the V boundary shows in green.

Each location in UV space exactly describes a location on the patch surface, just as every longitude and latitude combination describes a unique location on the Earth. This precise capability to locate positions in the UV parameter space is one of the main advantages that NURBS patches have over polygon objects.

Patches, like splines, can be closed or open. In an open patch, the two U edges, or the two V edges, are connected. A patch with one edge (or parameter) closed looks like an unbroken ribbon. A patch with both parameters closed looks like a solid object where the U and V parameters stretch completely around in an unbroken surface, like a sphere or a torus. It's very useful to remember that, no matter what the shape, NURBS patches are always made up of small rectangles.

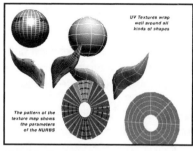

**Figure 2.10**
Each NURBS object has a UV parameter space that follows the contours of the object.

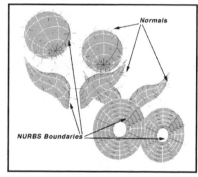

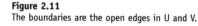

**Figure 2.11**
The boundaries are the open edges in U and V.

## Approximation and Tessellation

Because XSI renders only triangles, a patch is really only an approximation of a surface made of lots of very small triangles. How closely the polygonal surface approximates the mathematical precision of the patch determines how smooth and accurate the final surface is. The process of approximating the surface by breaking it down into a number of triangles is called tessellation (see Figure 2.12).

As a general rule, the more triangles that are used to approximate the patch, the better it looks (see Figure 2.13). The degree of approximation used to tessellate the patch into triangles at render time can be controlled precisely for each object in SOFTIMAGE|XSI. You can set the Step parameter (in the Geometry Approximation property page in the Surface tab, with the Parametric U and V step), or you can allow the mental ray to choose the proper level for you by enabling the Length/Distance/Angle option in the same property page. The Step is the number of times each UV patch section is divided into smaller sections before it is finally divided into two triangles. This capability to easily trade off between surface smoothness and the number of triangles is another key advantage of using patches over polygons in your modeling tasks.

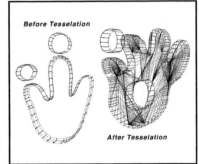

**Figure 2.12**
Tessellation is when the NURBS surface is reduced to many small triangles for rendering or display.

## Special Features of NURBS Patches

Because the knot of a NURBS curve can be located at any point along its length, a NURBS curve can be trimmed to any length. Similarly, a NURBS patch can be trimmed to any shape by projecting another NURBS curve onto the first surface, in the same way that you trim a cookie out of a sheet of dough with a cookie cutter (see Figure 2.14). The trim curve can be projected onto the surface for later use, it can define a hole in the surface, or it can become the outer boundary of the surface, causing everything outside the curve to go away.

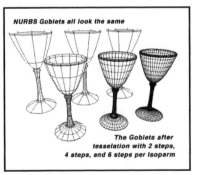

**Figure 2.13**
This object has been tessellated with different U and V steps to make different levels of detail.

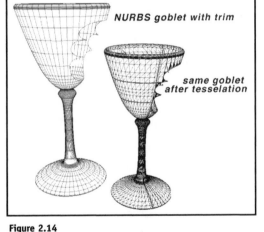

**Figure 2.14**
Trimming can make a hole in a NURBS.

Because of the more flexible parameterization of NURBS patches, it is possible to connect two separate NURBS patches into one contiguous surface by merging the two original surfaces. Another method of achieving a similar result is to create a third surface that blends evenly between two original surfaces to create a joint between them, much like using putty to fill in the crack between sections of drywall when building a house. This is called a NURBS surface mesh, or a NURBS assembly.

XSI has all the tools you will require to build NURBS surfaces, trim them, build multi-patch objects from them, and even extract new NURBS curves and surfaces from parts of an original NURBS surface.

# Selecting Objects

When you want to do something with an object, first you need to select it.

The simplest way to do this is to use the special selection hotkey: the spacebar on your keyboard. Whenever you have the spacebar held down, you are telling XSI that you will now point at an object and select it. You can click directly on an object, or you can drag a box around an object, touching at least one part of it to select the object.

To select more than one object, you must hold down the Shift key along with the space bar and click or drag with a mouse button.

Which mouse button you use also is important. If you want to select a single object (a "node"), you click with the left mouse button. To select a branch, meaning any object and all the objects below it in its hierarchy, use the middle mouse button. To select an entire tree (everything in the hierarchy), use the right mouse button (see Figure 2.15). In XSI, the right mouse button is also used to select the entire model, which is a tree hierarchy that has been defined as a special kind of tree. Models can have their own name space, and can be saved separately from the scene file to facilitate importing and exporting, sharing, and collaborative workflow. We'll discuss the hierarchy in a later chapter. For now just use the spacebar with the left mouse button.

XSI introduces another selection method called the Lasso tool, which is like a lasso selection tool on a Macintosh. Using this, you can draw an irregular shape and select objects that are either inside the lasso or are touched by the line you draw. The hotkey for the Lasso tool is F8, but you can also activate the Lasso tool from the Select Tools menu at the top of the MCP.

The last new selection method in XSI is called freeform. When freeform is on (hotkey F9), you draw a scribble line on-screen, and any objects touched by the line will be selected.

## *The Select Menu*

The Select menu in the MCP has each of these selection methods, and you can turn them on and off here when you forget the hotkeys (see Figure 2.16).

The Select menu also has the useful options Select All Objects, which means select all objects, and Select All Using Filter, which selects components using the filter currently chosen in the Filter menu. (It'd easy to miss; it's the little triangle directly above the Object Name box in the MCP.)

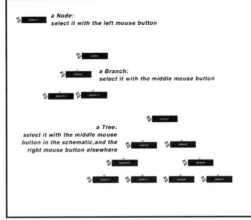

**Figure 2.15**
Use a different mouse button depending on how much, or how little, of a hierarchy you want to select.

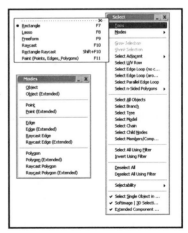

**Figure 2.16**
The Select menu can remind you about selection options.

Perhaps the most useful option is the Invert Using Filter option, which works like the Invert Selection command in Adobe PhotoShop. Sometimes it's easier to select the stuff you don't want, and then toggle everything, than to select all the stuff you do want. Later, when you begin doing serious poly modeling, you will use the options for selecting edge loops, growing polygon selections, and changing between different types of component selections.

## Get Primitives

SOFTIMAGE|XSI includes a variety of pre-made primitive shapes that are useful in basic modeling. These primitives include both splines and surface shapes, and can generally be made as either polygonal meshes or NURBS surfaces. These are often a good starting place in your modeling tasks (see Figure 2.17). There are nine types of primitives in XSI, in addition to cameras and lights, which are also found in the Primitives menu.. Each has a property page where you can interactively customize the primitive to fit your needs.

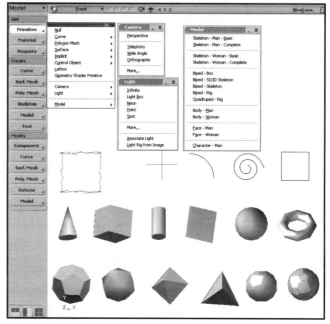

**Figure 2.17**
The Primitives menu is where you can choose a building block to start with.

- ◆ Null: A null object, used for organizing hierarchies.
- ◆ Curve: Default arcs, circles, spirals, and squares.
- ◆ Polygon meshes: Cones, cubes, cylinders, discs, grids, spheres, and toruses.
- ◆ Surface: NURBS discs, grids, spheres, and toruses.
- ◆ Implicit: Implicit objects are the base primitives used to make the polygon and NURBS models.
- ◆ Control objects: Physical forces used in simulations: waves, attractors, gravity, vortices, wind.
- ◆ Lattice: A deformation cage that you can control manually.
- ◆ Geometry ShaderPrimitive: This is a placeholder for an object that will be created at render time by a procedural shader. Writing Geometry shaders is an advanced topic.
- ◆ Model: Pre-built models that you can use. There are complete human forms, IK skeletons, IK control rigs, and customizable facemakers located here.

To try using a primitive, choose the Get > Primitive > Surface > Torus menu command.

You can show the property page for the primitive object by tapping the Enter key on your keyboard (with the object selected).

The property page that pops up when you create a primitive (the General property page) is there for you to customize the primitive to your needs. Start by changing the name from Torus to MyTorus. Then click on the Torus tab of the property page to see the variables that are specific to the torus: radius and cross section. Change these to your liking. Finally, click on the Geometry tab of the property page. Increasing the subdivisions will give the object more detail that you can use while modeling.

Starting with a primitive shape and then cutting, transforming, or deforming that shape into something else is the most basic form of modeling, and it's a quick way to get things done. Experiment with the primitives in the Get > Primitive menu to see what's there.

The Polygon Mesh geometrics (Dodecahedron, Icosahedron, Octahedron, Tetrahedron, and Rhombicosidodecahedron) are fun to start with, as is the very cool Soccer Ball primitive shape.

You can also bring a new camera or light in to the scene with the Get > Primitive menu (shown in Figure 2.18).

**Figure 2.18**
The Get > Primitive menu also has lights and cameras.

### Null Objects and a Few of Their Uses

In the Get > Primitive menu, you will find a command that seems a little obscure at first, called Get > Primitive > Null, which brings a special kind of object into being. A null is an object that has no geometry—no lines, no points, no polygons, no surface at all. It is really just an object that consists of a local center. The tremendous utility of the null comes from the fact that when objects are linked in a hierarchy, each parent node adds transformations to all the child nodes. This means that a null object can be used as a parent in a hierarchy when you just want all the children objects to be linked together at the same level. The whole null grouping can then be scaled, translated, or rotated together, by selecting the top of the hierarchy as a branch. That null can also be animated, and the animation on the null will cascade down into the child nodes connected to it.

Nulls are also a critical part of inverse kinematic (IK) skeletons in XSI, and they can help out tremendously in constraint-based animations.

## Transformations: Scale, Rotation, Translation

The three basic operations for all objects are the transformations: Scale, Rotate, and Translate. You will use these commands to move objects around your scene, make them bigger or smaller, and spin them into the desired position. When you begin animating, you will most likely spend the majority of your time setting keyframes on scale, translation, and rotation, and mixing up animations based on these changes. Together, scale, rotate, and translate are called by the shorter term "transformation."

The interface buttons for Scale, Rotate, and Translate are located on the right edge of the interface in the Main Command Panel, under the menu heading Transform"(see Figure 2.19). To transform an object, first select it with the space bar, and then click on one of the transformation buttons with the letter corresponding to the type of transformation you want: S for scale, R for rotation, and T for translate. Finally, click and drag the mouse in your scene with the left mouse button to make the change interactively.

**Figure 2.19**
The transformation cells in the Main Command Panel (MCP).

There are hotkey keyboard shortcuts for the transformations. Tapping (or holding) the X key will activate the Scale menu cells, pressing the C hotkey fires up the Rotate cells, and pressing the V key will activate the Translate cells. A mnemonic device to remember which goes with which is "XCV = SRT," where the order of the letters matches up.

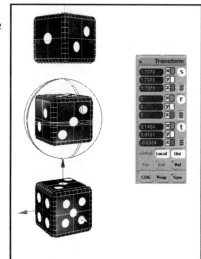

With Transform Manipulators toggled off in the MCP Transform menu, each of your three mouse buttons acts on a different axis. When you have one transformation active (say, scale), the left mouse button scales in X, the middle in Y, and the right in Z. The status line will remind you which is which, but again the keys go in order of the mnemonic "XYZ = LMR" so that XYZ matches which button you use—left, middle, right—when you click the mouse. The use of the Transform Manipulator option is covered later in this chapter.

Each of these functions can be performed relative to one axis, two axes, or three axes at a time. For instance, you can rotate an object around the X-, Y-, or Z-axis. Rotating all three at the same time will cause an object to tumble.

## *Manipulators*

To help you remember which axis is which, and to make it easier to use the local axes when the object is all out of whack with the global axes, XSI has a type of user feedback called a Manipulator. The Manipulator is slightly miss-named, since you don't actually grab it with your hand (or your mouse), but it does show you which axis is which and provides you with clues about what the Transforms will do (see Figure 2.20).

**Figure 2.20**
Manipulators also show you directional cues.

When you activate the Translation menu cells, a manipulator shaped like three arrows, color coded Red, Green and Blue to match the colors of the local axes, pops up at the center of the object. These arrows point in the direction that the object will move when you drag the mouse with either the left, middle, or right mouse button.

When you activate the rotate menu cells, a manipulator pops up showing three gimbals, again color coded red, green, and blue and indicating which way the object will rotate with different mouse buttons. When you drag with a mouse button, the manipulator shows how far you have rotated the object.

When you activate the scale menu cells, the Manipulator is a set of color-coded axes with small cubes at the ends to show you how you might scale the object.

> Users of "the other program" may turn on the option called 'Transform Manipulators' in the Transform menu of the MCP (right side of the screen) to make the manipulators behave more like those in Maya, or choose the File > Interaction Model > QWERTY Tools and Alt Navigation option to set the selection, transformation, and navigation tools to be very Maya-like.

When you scale an object in all axes at the same time, the object grows or shrinks while retaining its proportions. But if you scale in only one axis, it will grow or shrink along that axis (see Figure 2.21).

To transform an object in just one axis, you can also choose to click only on that part of the transformation in the Main Command Panel. In other words, you can click only on the X button in the S area of the transformation cells. To get back to activating all the axes, click on the icon with the three black bars below the S, R, or T I buttons.

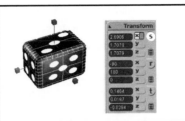

**Figure 2.21**
You can scale in just one axis.

For instance, if you wanted to scale a cube into a rectangular tabletop, you could click in the Y button in the Scale part of the MCP panel then drag the left mouse button down to make the cube shorter. To scale the tabletop uniformly again, click back on the uniform icon (three black bars) below the S icon.

When you have one axis of a transformation active (say, scale just in Y), each of the three mouse buttons does the same thing, but in different amounts: The left mouse button goes slowly, the middle mouse button goes more rapidly, and the right mouse button performs the action at the fastest rate. By using each mouse button, you can get exactly the level of control that you need: left to right, slowest to fastest. Look to the status area at the bottom of the screen to see a description of each mouse button's function within the menu cell. If you click directly into the area of a transformation button where the decimal number reads out, you can enter a value directly into that box. Pressing the Enter key, or selecting another cell, causes the change to take place.

> You can also enter simple formulas into the transformation cells. If you type "5+" into the Translate Y cell, your object will go 5 units higher. If you type "R(1,9)" your object will pick a random height between 1 and 9. This also works on multiple selections: try making 10 spheres, and with them all selected, entering L(1,20) in the Translate X cell to make a linear adjustment to their translation in Y from 1 to 20 over the range of spheres.

When you need to scale, rotate, or translate an object uniformly, hold down the Shift key while you drag. This causes the object to scale uniformly along all axes, to rotate in discreet 15-degree increments, and to translate in perfect one-unit increments along whatever axis you are using.

## Transform Manipulators

In the previous section on Manipulators, I mentioned that they are really more of an indicator than a manipulator. This may seem odd to people who have used other 3D applications where the user may click directly on the manipulator indicator to transform the object selected. Many people find these types of Transform Manipulators easier to use, particularly when working in a perspective view, because they don't have to remember which finger maps to which mouse button and which mouse button maps to which local axis (see Figure 2.22).

**Figure 2.22**
Turn on Transform Manipulators.

XSI has a setting to Enable Transform Manipulators, located in the Transform menu in the MCP directly above the SRT menu cells. If you toggle the option on, you can select an object, activate a transform by clicking on the S, the R, or the T, and then click directly on the colored portion of the Transform Manipulator to move, scale, or rotate the object. As you hover your mouse over the Manipulator, XSI looks to see which axis or plane between axes you are closest to, and gives feedback by changing the mouse pointer.

If you right-click while in a Transform Manipulator tool, you can see a pop-up context-sensitive menu allowing you to change the transform mode, for instance from local to global. This repeats the functionality of the mode buttons (Global, Local, View, COG, etc.) in the MCP under the Transforms.

## Transform Modes

When you move something through space, the big question you should be asking is "What am I moving the object relative to?" All transforms are relative to something. An object gets bigger than it was, rotates more than it was rotated before, or translates through space relative to other objects. Sometimes changing the transform of an object is easier when relative to one thing than another (see Figure 2.23). For instance, sometimes it is easier to translate an object

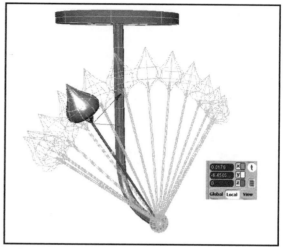

**Figure 2.23**
Transform relative to what?

relative to the 2D view your mouse is in than it is to translate it relative to the 3D global axes. Sometimes it makes more sense to rotate an object relative to its own parent than to its local axis. Sometimes you want to choose a completely different pivot point to rotate relative to, or scale from. You can make these choices with the Mode buttons underneath the transforms. These buttons change depending on which transform (scale, rotate, or translate) is active.

When scaling an object, you might wish to scale it relative to its own center (Local mode), scale it uniformly in all axes, (Uni mode), or scale it so that its volume remains constant for squash and stretch (Vol mode).

When rotating an object, you might wish to rotate it relative to its own axes (Local mode) or relative to the static Global axes shared by everything (Global mode). Or perhaps you want to spin it only around one axis, like a wheel or a propeller (Add mode).

Translating an object is the only time the View mode will be useful, and then generally only in a top, front, or right view. Avoid the use of the View mode when translating objects in the camera perspective view. You might, however, wish to move an object relative to its parent (Par mode), its own Local center (Local mode), or even the axes of some other unrelated object or component of an object (Ref mode).

# Stonehenge: At a Glance
## Topics Covered

In this tutorial, you will get a chance to practice moving blocks of stone around in 3D space.

You'll learn how to:

◆ Create primitive objects

◆ Move objects in space

◆ Scale, rotate, and shape objects

◆ Pan, zoom, and orbit to look around in your scene

### Materials Required

The tutorial uses the stonehenge_start.scn'scene from the courseware on the CDROM that accompanies this book.

You may use WinZip to unzip the PC version, and use the command gunzip to extract the linux version.

Finally, use the File > Project Manager to add a project, browse to the place on your computer where you un-zipped the XSIFoundation5 project, and use the Select button to add it to your list of active projects.

**Figure 2.24**
The completed Stonehenge scene.

## Tutorial: Stonehenge

Let's try all this out by creating a simple scene constructed only of primitive cube objects of varying sizes and proportions, and placed in space to simulate the collection of obelisks found at Stonehenge, in Wiltshire, England (see Figure 2.25).

Of course, it was the Druids' idea first, and creativity counts for a lot in this world whether you're a druid or an animator. What do you suppose was on the other side of those portals?

### Step 1: Open the Stonehenge_start Scene

The Stonehenge_start scene has all the component posts, lintels, altars, and other small stones you will need to build Stonehenge. Load the scene with the File > Open menu command, use the Paths button in the top-right corner of the Open dialog box to navigate to the XSIFoundation5 project, select the Stonehenge_start scene from the list, and load it with the OK button. Now all you will need to do is arrange the stones into the right shape. Before we start moving posts and lintels, let's mark out the plan for the area so we know where things go.

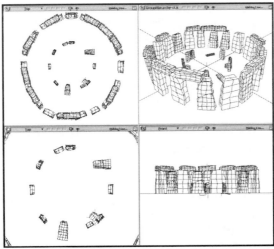

**Figure 2.25**
A layout diagram of Stonehenge.

Look at the overhead view, the top view (the XZ plane), and click the A hotkey with your mouse somewhere in that view to frame all objects.

## Step 2: Make Some Guides and a Ground Plane

Now create a primitive circle with the Get > Primitive > Curve > Circle menu command.

We'll use this circle as a guide when we place the stones, but since it was created in the XY plane, and we want it in the XZ plane, we'll have to rotate it first. With the circle selected, click directly into the numeric area of the Rotate X menu cell with your middle mouse button and enter the value 90, which means 90 degrees. Press the Enter key to execute the command. In the top view, you should now see the circle.

> To open a PPG, make sure the circle is selected and then click on the Selection button mid-way up the MCP. Click directly on the icon (not the name) at the top of the list and click through the tabs of the PPG that pops up to find the Radius property.

In the Circle property page, check the radius. It should be 4 units. This will be the inner circle of smaller stones.

Make another circle out of the first by duplicating it with the Ctrl-D hotkey combination.

Change the new circle's radius to about 11 units. This will be the guide for the larger ring of bigger stones.

Name the smaller circle innercircle and the bigger one outercircle using the general property pages.

Start by building a ground plane with a simple grid object. Use the Get > Primitive > Surface > Grid menu command to bring a grid into existence. If you have the preference for Auto-Popup of Property Editors on, the general Property Editor for the grid will pop up instantly. If it doesn't, click on the Selection button in the MCP to browse the properties of the grid, locate the Geometry property, and click directly on the small icon to the left of the word Geometry to view the grid's properties.

Now that you are looking at the Grid property page, leave the U and V length alone, but increase the subdivision in both U and V to 15.

A grid is created, but it isn't large enough to cover the area in front of us in the scene, so we'll need to enlarge it. Use the Scale area of the MCP to make the grid bigger in X and Z, to form a base for our monuments. Now the grid stretches to the horizon, but it's awfully flat looking.

Let's bump the grid up in a random rolling fashion by using a randomize command on the grid. In the Model module, choose Deform > Randomize (with the grid still selected), open the Randomize Operator property page from the transient selection explorer (the Selection button in the MCP), and change the displacement Y multiplier to .8. Experiment with the other sliders to get the look you want. The Randomize effect will randomly move the location of each control point in the grid a little bit, creating a rolling hillside. Look at it in shaded view (see Figure 2.26).

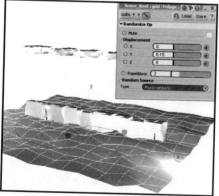

**Figure 2.26**
The ground under Stonehenge.

## Step 3: Arrange the Stones

Open a schematic view and zoom out in it to see all the objects there. The stones are organized into groups according to type. Start placing the smaller stones onto the inner circle by translating them in both top and front views.

Refer to the images here of the Stonehenge layout for assistance. Place the post on the circle and flush with the ground plane, with the translation menu cells. Then in the View translation mode, click with your mouse in the top view to drag the post to the circle. Use the front view to adjust the position in Y.

> The stones are easy to move into position in the top view, using the View mode under the Transforms.

> The stones might not be at the right ground height. Move one to the right elevation and look at the Translate Y edit box in the MCP to see how high it is. Select all the other stones and type that number into the same edit box to make them all the same height.

Remember also to rotate the stones around Y so that they all face the middle. Some stones may be laid down on the ground, as if they toppled during the intervening 20 centuries.

Next, place the larger upright stones around the outer circle.

## Step 4: Move a Lintel

The lintel is the flat, broad piece of stone that caps the two posts. Use the Translate and Rotate menu cells to place each lintel roughly on top of and resting on the two posts (see Figure 2.27).

## Step 5: Make the Other Doorways

Copy the stones you've built and place them in groups to match the layout of Stonehenge in the figures here, or if you wish, construct your own mystical portals and lay them out as your spirit dictates. Because we haven't yet learned how to group objects, you will have to scale and rotate the giant stone blocks one at a time.

## Step 6: Examine Your Work

Place your camera wherever you wish in the scene by using the O, P, and Z supra keys within the perspective window.

View your work in shaded mode by selecting Shaded from the View Style drop menu at the top of the Camera view.

When you are done, save your work with File > Save As and examine the finished scene by loading Stonehenge_done for comparison.

The Stonehenge exercise helped you pull together a scene into a cohesive, visible work of art.

Seeing the collection of shapes come together into a scene is the most rewarding part of the animation process (outside of seeing your name in the credits at the end of the show).

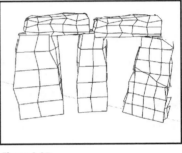

**Figure 2.27**
Two posts and a lintel.

## Multiple Selections

You may have noticed that if you selected multiple objects (with the Shift key held down during selection) and then scaled them, or rotated them, each object was transformed relative to its own local center. For instance, if you selected two posts and a lintel and tried to rotate them in Y so that you could align them with the circle, each part would spin on its own, losing contact with the other pieces. Similarly, if you wanted to scale a portal smaller, using the Shift-Select method makes all the parts smaller, and then you have to reassemble the pieces. That's not too hard when the model is made of three cubes, but for more complex models, it would be unforgivable. There is a better way—build a hierarchy.

## Hierarchy

When objects are in a hierarchy, they can be transformed relative to their parent's local center, instead of their own. And, if the hierarchy has several levels to it, each level can be a different local center for the transformations. That means that if the portal was in a hierarchy (for example with the lintel the parent of both posts,) selecting the whole hierarchy with the right mouse button and the spacebar would allow you to move, scale, and rotate the portal as you wish, and its parts would always remain in the correct proportions and orientation. In

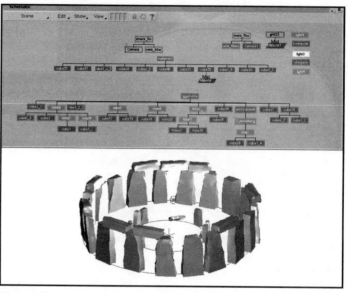

**Figure 2.28**
Hierarchies make transforming easier.

addition, most animation can be performed on hierarchies, at the node, branch, and tree levels. This is a concept of great importance in SOFTIMAGE, because without it you can never build and animate anything with more than one piece. Hierarchies are covered in the next chapter.

I'll award extra credit for those who know about hierarchies already.

One way to organize your work is to create a parent-child hierarchy. Try this out by creating a null object (Get > Primitive > Null) and making it the parent of all the smaller posts around the inner circle.

Use the Escape key when you are done to avoid accidental parenting (if only it was this easy in real life . . . ouch).

Now make each lintel the parent of the stones below it. Finally, make the ground plane the parent of all the lintel hierarchies, and examine your hierarchy in the Schematic view.

# Selecting and Transforming Centers, Points, and Clusters

All objects are made up of smaller things called components. Examples of components are points, lines, polygons, isolines, boundaries, and knots.

Sometimes you will want to select and move just a component of an object, not the whole object. For example, the local center of the object is a component and you will often wish to change the position of the local center when modeling and animating. Each point is a component, and can be moved separately. A saved group of points is called a cluster. Clusters can be transformed, too. On surfaces, each isoline can be selected and translated, and the boundary edges can be selected and transformed. There are many more components that respond to the transform menu cells. You can see a complete list by clicking on the Component Filter button, in the Selection panel of the MCP, which is the top part, directly under the big arrow symbols, in the tiny triangle drop menu (see Figure 2.29).

This component filter works in two ways. First, your selection tools will only work to select whatever kind of item is active in that list. The active item is the item that is printed on the menu button when you let go of the menu.

Second, when you have a component selected in the filter, the transformation cells will only operate on components of that type.

Some components are so commonly transformed that they have their own buttons and hotkeys.

Holding down T selects vertices (called 'tagging', not to be confused with vandalizing trains), the E hotkey selects edges, and the Y hotkey selects polygons.

## *Object Mode*

Object mode means that whole objects and hierarchies can be translated, rotated, and scaled. Object is the most common mode; you used it to move, scale, and rotate objects for the Stonehenge scene. When in Object mode, the transformation keys work on all the vertices of the current object equally. There is an Object button in the Selection panel of the MCP, and you can use this to switch back to Object mode after using one of the other component filters. The spacebar hotkey switches to Object mode (see Figure 2.30).

**Figure 2.29**
The Component menu allows you to pick just what you want.

**Figure 2.30**
Spacebar is the hotkey for Object mode.

## Center Mode

When Center mode is selected, then the transformation keys operate only on the local center of an object. The object vertices remain located in global space where they were. Moving the center of an object allows you to change the axis of rotation, determine where the object scales from, and from where the object's position in space will be measured (see Figure 2.31). This change is permanent, and is reflected in the operator stack (look at the Selection button in the MCP) with a Center operator.

If you want the center somewhere else for only a short time, or you want to keep the center where it is for one transform (say, rotation) while using a different center for another transform (say, scale), there is a temporary center called a pivot. You can see the pivot and move it with the Alt key, while an object is selected and a transform tool is active.

## Point Mode

When you enter Point mode, by tapping or holding the M hotkey, you can point at and transform individual points, one at a time. You can also define groups of vertices (verts) or points, which is called tagging (see Figure 2.32).

Tagging is so commonly used in XSI that there is a hotkey for it: T. Whenever you hold down the T hotkey, you can select and deselect points to add to the current tagged group for that object. Then, when points are tagged, you are automatically placed in Point Filter mode, and the transformation menu cells to work only on that tagged group. Try it out by tagging points on a sphere with the T hotkey and then translating them to make a pear. Check the status bar when you have the T hotkey held down to see how the three mouse buttons will operate differently. If you are not using Extended Component Selection, you have to use Shift and Ctrl in addition to the left mouse button to add and remove tagged points to and from the selection. If do you use Extended Component Selection and the SI3D selection model (much better for this), then the left mouse button adds to the group, the middle buttons removes from the group, and the right button toggles tagged points back and forth. You can check your selection model by looking at the bottom of the Select menu in the MCP.

## Clusters Mode

Normally, when you are done manipulating tagged points, you move on and tag a new group of points, and the tagged group that you had originally selected is lost. You can save that group if you want, by turning it into a cluster, with the Cluster button in the lower portion of the MCP under the Edit menu.

**Figure 2.31**
Center mode transforms the local center.

**Figure 2.32**
Point mode is used for tagging verts.

Now that cluster can always be selected again, by selecting the object in Object mode and then clicking on the Clusters button in the MCP at the bottom of the Selection area to display a list of clusters on that object, as shown in Figure 2.33.

# Selecting Polygon Components with the Filter

Polygonal meshes are made up of polygons, and polygons are made up of vertices and edges.

Each component of a polymesh (polygon, edge, and vertex) can be selected so that you can work with it. You can select just one at a time or groups of components. You cannot, however, select edges *and* vertices at the same time; it has to be one component type at a

**Figure 2.33**
A cluster is a saved group of components.

**Figure 2.34**
You can select points, edges, and polygons.

time. This one-at-a-time selection method is called a filter. With the Polygon Selection filter active, you can only select polygons; with the Edge filter on, you just select Edges; and so on.

The Selection filter is located in the MCP near the top. Since Point, Edge, and Polygon filters are so common, buttons for just those filters appear automatically in the MCP whenever you have a polygon object selected. They do not show when you have a NURBS object selected (see Figure 2.34).

When you click on the Point button, you can select points using the standard selection tools, by holding the space bar and clicking on vertices or dragging a rectangle around them. Similarly, if you click the Edge button at the top left of the MCP, you can select groups of edges. The Polygon button filters the selection tool so that it only works on polygons.

## *Setting Selection Preferences*

There are two selection methods in XSI—the standard Windows method, which uses Shift and Ctrl to extend selections, and the Extended Component Selection SOFTIMAGE 3D Selection model. We'll refer only to the SOFTIMAGE 3D Selection model in this book, because it makes it much easier to make complex selections. To make sure that your XSI preferences are set the same as this book, open the Select menu from the top of the MCP and make sure that the three bottom items are all toggled on: Select Single Object in Region, SOFTIMAGE 3D Selection Model, and Extended Component Selection (see Figure 2.35).

**Figure 2.35**
Make sure you understand the Selection options.

> You need a good three-button mouse for polygon modeling, because you need to use one finger per button to use all three axes—X, Y, and Z. The kind of mouse with a wheel in the middle just won't do, because your middle finger doesn't stay there easily.

## *Component Selection Hotkeys*

While there are buttons in the MCP that activate the component filters, using them would be very slow. You would have to take your eyes off the object you are working on, move the mouse cursor up to the MCP, make a change, go back to the object, hold the space bar, and make the selection. Since you'll be doing this thousands of times each day as you sculpt, that method just won't do. The faster way is to use the hotkeys for component selection.

### Selecting Vertices

If you hold down the T key with your left hand, you can select, deselect and toggle vertices with the three mouse buttons. With the T hotkey down, drag a rectangle selection around some of the vertices on your sphere. Note that the vertices become tagged in red (hotkey T for tagged). Note that the Point filter is automatically enabled.

If you want to add to the group of selected points, just hold T again and drag a rectangle around those points. They will be added to the others already tagged in red. If some points became selected that you didn't want, drag a rectangle around those with your middle mouse button and note that they are removed from the tagged group. Try dragging a rectangle around the whole sphere with the right mouse button, and see that the tagged group is inverted: those that were not tagged now are, and those that were are no longer. This convention, where the left mouse button adds to the group, the middle removes, and the right toggles is called the Extended Component Selection model. It works for all components.

You may use the T hotkey on polygonal mesh objects and NURBS objects.

### Selecting Edges

If you hold down the E key with your left hand (hotkey E for edge), you can select, deselect, and toggle edges with the three mouse buttons by dragging a rectangular selection marquee. The left mouse button adds edges to the selection, the middle button deselects edges, and the right button toggles edges. Selected edges show in red and deselected edges show in amber. Drawing a selection rectangle will select all edges that are within the rectangle or touch the rectangle, on both sides of the object.

Sometimes this method makes it hard to precisely select just one edge, since you are likely to cross one or more other edges by accident. There is another edge selection hotkey—the I hotkey. I selects edges by raycast, which means that if you hold down I to invoke the command and then drag across a polygonal object with the left mouse button, only those edges directly below your mouse cursor will be selected. In Wireframe Display mode (or X-Ray Shading mode), raycast shoots straight through the object, and selects edges on both the front and back side. In Hidden Link Display mode, I will only select front-facing edges that you can see—leaving those on the hidden backside of the object alone.

You may use the E and I hotkeys on polygonal mesh objects only, not NURBS. That's because NURBS don't have edges—they have isolines and boundaries instead.

### Selecting Polygons

Polygons are special because they have two different component selection hotkeys. The Y hotkey selects polygons in the same way that you select edges and vertices, by dragging a rectangle that selects all the polygons that are entirely within the selection rectangle.

The selected polygons will show in translucent red. The problem is that while you are working in shaded view, you might be selecting polygons on the back of the object without knowing it, and messing up your model. To solve this problem, the U hotkey was pressed into service. When you hold the U key, you can click over the middle of a polygon, and only the polygon facing out of the model towards you will be selected. This is called ray-casting, and it is very useful. You can also hold U while dragging a stroke across the model to paint in a selection. As usual, the extended component selection model means that the left mouse button adds to the selection, the middle mouse button removes polygons from the selection, and the right mouse button toggles polygons.

You may use the U and Y hotkeys on polygonal mesh objects only, not NURBS. That's because U and Y select only polygons (see Figure 2.36).

Remember that the hotkeys are crucial to fast, efficient workflow. Practice with them until they are second nature. Hotkey E works on edges, T selects vertices, Y selects polygons by rectangle, and U selects polygons by raycasting.

For the truly adventurous, each of these can also be modified with the other selection tools, freeform and lasso, although this requires the manual gymnastics waggishly called finger olympics.

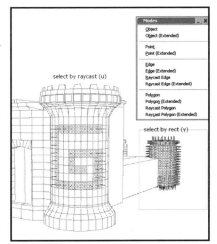

**Figure 2.36**
The U and Y hotkeys select polygons.

## Selecting Ranges and Edge Loops

You can also tag rows or columns of points on either poly or NURBS objects.

On a NURBS surface, the rows are called the U parameters and the columns are called the V parameters. With a NURBS object selected, hold T and also Alt. Now when you choose two points with the left mouse button, all the points in a row or column between the two are also selected. If you hold T and Ctrl and then click on two points, an entire row or column is selected on the object.

You can do the same thing on polygons to select ranges of points and edge loops. Get a polygon mesh, and then use the T and Alt hotkeys at the same time to select ranges of points, and the T and Ctrl hotkeys at the same time to select edge loops (see Figure 2.37).

If you find it hard to make the hand stretched required for this to work, you can use the Select Edge Loop options in the Select menu at the top of the MCP.

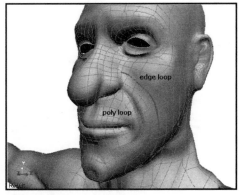

**Figure 2.37**
Look for polygon loops and edge loops.

You can also select edge loops of polygons and edges. This is often an easier way to make a selection. Try getting a polygonal object and holding I (which is Select Edge by Raycast) and Alt at the same time. Then you can choose two edges that connect with a few empty edges in between. This selects the range between the edges you select.

**53**

I and Ctrl selects loops of edges.

The U hotkey (select polygon by raycast) and Alt makes selecting ranges of polygons easy, while U and Ctrl makes selecting polygon rows and columns a breeze.

### Growing Component Selections

Sometimes when you need to make a selection of polygons or points or edges in an irregular, hard-to-see model, it is easy to select just some components and then grow the selection until you have what you need.

You can grow any selection of components with the Selection > Grow Selection command, which has the convenient hotkey Shift +. (That's the Shift button and the plus button on the regular part of the keyboard. The plus button on the numeric keypad is reserved for something else: increasing subdivision refinement.)

If Grow gets you close, you can finish off the selection by adding or removing the remaining polygons, points, or edges more easily.

### Switching from One Component Selection to Another

Each component type has a memory on each object. If you select a group of polygons, select a group of edges, and then return to polygon mode again with the U hotkey, the original polygon selection is still there.

But you can also convert one type of component selection into another. If you have some points tagged, for instance, and you want polygons, use Select > Select Adjacent > Polygons. You can experiment with the different Select Adjacent options to see what they do.

A related tool is the Select > Select Members/Components. If you have a cluster (discussed in detail later) and want to get a selection of the components within the cluster, try that command. It also selects the individual object members of a group.

## Selecting and Transforming Texture Supports

When your object has one or more texture maps on it, you will often need to move those maps around, rotating and scaling them to the exact placement you want. This is done by selecting the texture projection in the 3D view window, or in the Explorer and using the transformation cells in the MCP just as you would on any other object. If you have created a texture projection, it will show up in the 3D view as a green Wireframe object (see Figure 2.38).

You can also see Texture Projections (if you have created them) in the Explorer view, by opening up an object to see if it has any children. If you select a Texture Support, you can modify how it covers the object manually and interactively with the Modify > Projection command in the Render module. The hotkey for modifying a texture projection is J, but it only works if you have a texture projection

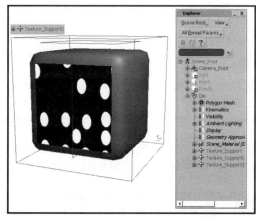

**Figure 2.38**
Texture Supports project textures onto objects.

selected. Texture projections are always children of an object. You will learn to create texture projections later in this book.

## Selecting and Transforming NURBS Components

If you have a NURBS object selected, you can choose NURBS-specific options from the Selection filter list.

Isopoint selects a location anywhere on the surface of the model, and reads back to you the location in U and V of that point.

U and V knot curves select an entire knot line in the surface.

U and V isolines selects an isoline on the surface and reads back its position.

Boundary selects only U and V edges in the surface.

Unfortunately, while you can select these components, you cannot directly manipulate them the same way you can points (actually Control Vertices, or CVs). These component selections must be used with other tools that are specific to their use (see Figure 2.39).

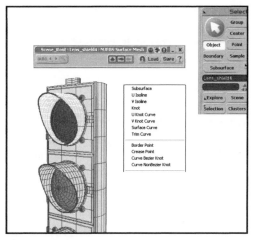

**Figure 2.39**
NURB surfaces have different components.

## Transformation Options

When you have one or more of the transformation menu cells activated, some new buttons will become active below the SRT area, just above the Constraint menu. These buttons control what the transformation is performed relative to. For instance, you might wish to translate the object relative to the global center (Global mode), or you might prefer to translate it relative to the object's own local center (Local mode) (see Figure 2.40).

If you want the object to move relative to the axes of its parent (the object above it in the hierarchy), you may use Parent mode (Par on the button).

When you are in View mode, the object moves relative to the view mode that your mouse is over when you drag.

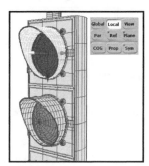

**Figure 2.40**
Objects transform relative to these modes.

### Uniform Transformations

When you are transforming objects after modeling them, and you want them to scale up evenly in each axis, one way to do it is to hold down each of the three mouse buttons at the same time while you drag. The problem with this method is that you may not get each mouse button depressed at exactly the same instant, which would cause the model to become distorted slightly as it scales up. If you hold down the Shift modifier while dragging with the Scale cells active, you will be assured that the model will scale uniformly. As an added bonus, the left mouse button will grow the object slowly, the middle mouse button will grow the object at a medium rate, and the right mouse button will make the object grow most rapidly. If you toggle on the Uniform scaling mode with the Uni button in the MCP, all axes will grow or shrink at the same rate (see Figure 2.41).

Often you will want to scale an object while keeping the volume of the object constant. This happens a lot in cartoon animation when you create squash and stretch. The Vol button in the MCP becomes available only when you have the scale cells active, and will try to keep the volume constant. To see the effect, get a primitive soccer ball, enter Center mode (top of the MCP), and move the center of the ball with the Y translation cell to the bottom most point on the ball, where it would contact the ground. Then switch back to Object mode (top of the MCP), activate all three scale cells, toggle on Volume scaling mode, and try scaling the ball shorter only in Y to see it get fatter at the same time in Z and X.

This conservation of volume is an important part of cartooniness.

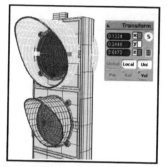

**Figure 2.41**
Uniform Scale means all axes grow equally.

## Freezing, Resetting Transforms, and Aligning objects

There are quite a few other miscellaneous options to save you time when transforming objects. These functions are located in the MCP, under the Transform menu, as shown in Figure 2.42. The basics are Reset Transforms, Match Transforms, and Freeze Transforms.

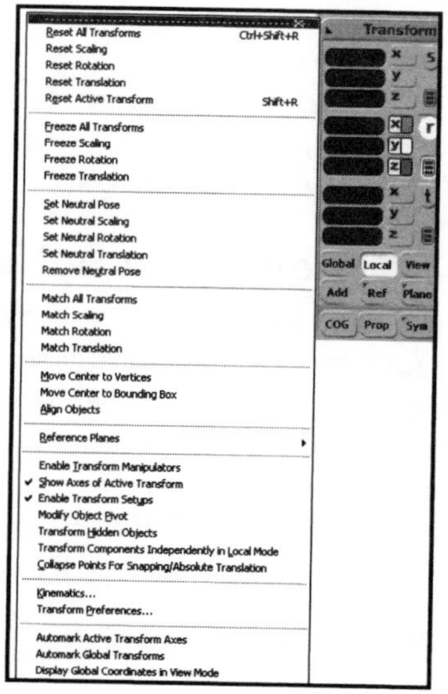

Once you have an object transformed, you may wish to un-transform it. You can easily return it to the position where it was created (or the position in which it was frozen) by choosing the Reset All Transforms option from the Transform menu. This returns scale to 1,1,1, rotation to 0,0,0, and places the object back at the global center. The hotkey combo is Ctrl-Shift-R. Resetting transforms actually changes the shape of the object, removing the effects of the scale, rotation, and translation on the vertices.

Sometimes you will want to set all the transformations back to the starting point without changing the shape of the object. This is called freezing the object. Each vertex is held precisely where it is, but the center of the object is returned to 0,0,0 and scaled to 1,1,1 without rotations.

You can reset or freeze any single transform (scale, rotation, or translation), the currently active transform, or all the transforms at once with the Transform menu in the MCP.

**Figure 2.42**
The Transform menu.

You can also use the Transform menu in the MCP to match the scale, rotation, or translation of one (or many) objects to another object. To quickly match one object using another, select the first, untransformed object, and choose one of the Match commands from the Transform menu. Then pick on the target object, that already has the rotation, translation, or scale that you want to match to complete the command.

XSI includes a very handy Align feature, also in the Transform menu. Any number of selected objects can be aligned in space (translated) to either the middle point of the group, or the highest point or lowest point in the group, or with the first object that was selected.

XSI can also return a center to the geometric middle of an object (or to any other place you require) with the Transform > Move Center to Vertices tool. To use it, tag some points (or all points) on the object, and execute that menu command. The center will move to the middle of those tagged points. If you do not tag points, the center will go to the middle of the object bounding box.

Set Neutral Pose is an option added to mimic the behavior of another 3D animation program, Maya. It adds an offset to the Local Transforms PPG of an object that takes off the visible transform, while leaving the object the same as it was. In other words, it hides the transform from the user. If you rotate and scale a cube and then use Set Neutral Pose on it, the cube will remain rotated and scaled, but the transform cells in the MCP will read out a scale of 1,1,1 and a rotation of 0,0,0. This is used in character rigging to set a neutral pose to animate from. To the animator, it means that each bone starts out with no rotation at all, making it easier to think about.

> Set Neutral Pose is hiding the true rotation of the bone (or other element) from you. As a character rigger, I can tell you that this is a bad idea. Just because that's the way it's done in Maya doesn't make it smart.

## Organizing the Schematic View

The Schematic view window is a pretty important window in SOFTIMAGE, and it can quickly get cluttered. Feel free to move around the items in the Schematic window as much as you like, just as you would move objects around the scene: with the translate menu cells (see Figure 2.43).

There are also automatic commands to clean up and organize the Schematic view, located in the menu bar at the top of the Schematic view window. The View > Rearrange All tool will spread out all the items in the Schematic view, while keeping the shape of each tree just the same as before, so your hard work in arranging the schematic to your liking is not lost.

## Organic Modeling: At a Glance

In this tutorial, you will practice what you have learned by creating some primitive objects and making a bowl of fruit out of them. You will create them by changing their geometry properties in a property page, and by pushing and pulling points and groups of tagged points on the surface.

You'll learn how to:

◆ Create primitive objects
◆ Modify object properties
◆ Sculpt shapes by moving points

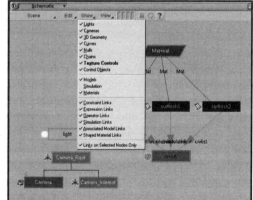

**Figure 2.43**
The drop menu in the schematic has tools to reorganize things for you.

◆ Sculpt objects by tagging and translating groups of points

◆ Make selections with the Edge Loop tools

◆ Duplicate and transform objects

# Tutorial: Making a Bowl of Fruit

Very often, pushing and pulling points is a good way to quickly create simple shapes. Smooth, organic shapes are the easiest to create in this manner. In this tutorial, you will quickly create a bowl of simple fruit shapes by moving points and by tagging and transforming the tagged group of points (see Figure 2.44).

## Step 1: Make a Bowl

Get a primitive surface disc. In the General property page, drag the Disc > Inner Radius slider as low as it will go, so that there is no longer a visible hole in the middle of the disc.

Tag the outermost three points that sit close to the last row (V) around the outside of the disc. Use the T hotkey and the three mouse buttons to add and subtract points from the tagged group until you have the ones you want selected. You are automatically in Point filter mode because you used the T hotkey.

Translate those points up in Global Y to form the lip of the fruit plate, as shown in Figure 2.45.

This would be a good time to try out the hidden edge loop selection tools. Try using T and the Ctrl keys at the same time and then clicking on a two adjacent points to select the entire row of points at the rim of the disc.

**Figure 2.44**
Rendered bowl of fruit.

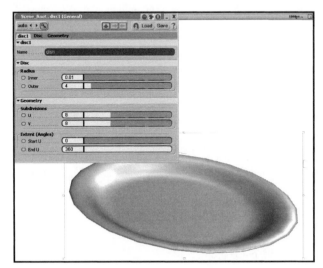

**Figure 2.45**
The bowl is just a disc with a lip.

## Step 2: Make a Pear

Get a primitive polygon mesh sphere, and in the Geometry tab of the General property page, add more rows in V (V subdivision) so you have some more points to tag when making the shape of the pear. Eleven or twelve rows in V should be fine. In the Sphere tab of the property page, change the name of the object to pear (see Figure 2.46).

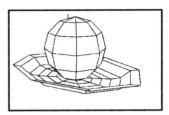

**Figure 2.46**
The pear begins life as a sphere.

In the front view, frame the pear and tag the rows of points at the top pole and the next row down. Translate them up in positive Y to make a neck for the pear.

Untag those points and tag the next two rows down. We want to make these thinner, scaling them down in X and Z. To do this, activate all the scale cells and hold down both your left and right mouse buttons. Then drag to make the neck of the pear smaller, as shown in Figure 2.47.

Make the rows at the base flatter and fuller. Sculpt the base of the pear to your liking using the same method: selecting rows of points, and scaling and translating them. You can also select rows of polygons with U, or even the U Ctrl hotkeys for polygon loops, and then scale the loops to squeeze the pear into new shapes.

Remember, you can always undo with Ctrl-Z if you do something you don't like.

Keep your pear framed in the perspective view so you can see how it looks as you work.

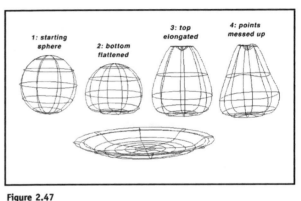

**Figure 2.47**
With some points tagged on the sphere, you can shape the pear.

Rough up the pear with the M hotkey. In the perspective view, show the points on the surface by pulling down the Show menu (eyeball icon) and toggling on the Points option. Now you can see each point even when it is not tagged. Hold down the M hotkey and click and hold the left mouse button over a point. Then drag the mouse to move just that point in space a bit. Do this repeatedly on different points to make the pear less uniform. Orbit the pear with the O hotkey as needed while moving points.

Each move you make results in a move operator, which you can see by clicking on the Selection button in the MCP. These illustrate that you can undo any one of these moves at any time. When you are done, it's a good idea to flatten all these move operators. Click the Freeze M button (which stands for Freeze modeling) at the bottom of the MCP to flatten the operator stack and cook all the moves down into a final shape for the pear. If you cannot see the very bottom of the MCP because the Windows Taskbar is on top of your interface, you should use the Start bar properties in Microsoft Windows to make the Start bar auto-hide.

Place the pear in the dish. Scale and translate the pear as needed to fit it onto the dish you made. Rotate it a bit so it doesn't look so stiff. Duplicate the pear and transform the second pear so it is a different size, in a different place on the dish, leaning against the first pear.

### Step 3: Make More Fruit

Make some other fruit as desired, using the same methodology of tagging and moving points. Try an apple, a plum, or an orange. You get extra credit for modeling a banana.

> Back in the early 1990s, building a banana was considered such a challenge in a 3D program that a 3D modeling tool for the Macintosh had the code name 'Banana' before it was launched. That tool (MacroModel) was proud of its lofting features.

# Conclusion

Now you have had some good basic experience creating objects, moving them around, selecting components, and doing basic organic modeling. In addition, you should have a firm grasp of NURBS and polygon terminology and differences.

You should understand the rather fully featured selection tools in XSI, and be able to limit your selection to the objects or components that you want to work with. You should understand loops and ranges of components, and recognize where it would be easier and faster to use them.

You should be able to use to the Show menu in each View window to limit what you see in each view to just the stuff that is important to you.

# Chapter 3
# Organization, Hierarchy, and Groups

In this chapter, you will:

- ◆ Learn the terminology for hierarchies, parents, children, trees, models, and groups
- ◆ Discover why hierarchies are so useful in animation
- ◆ Use and organize the Schematic view
- ◆ Select by node, branch, and tree
- ◆ Learn how to use and organize the Explorer

## Introduction

In this chapter, we will discuss how to create a relationship between objects called a hierarchy. We will explore XSI terminology and metaphors behind the concepts. We also will learn how to use the Schematic view and Explorer to build a hierarchy by parenting and cutting objects (see Figure 3.1). At the end of the lesson, we will create a robot arm out of multiple objects, all connected by a hierarchical relationship.

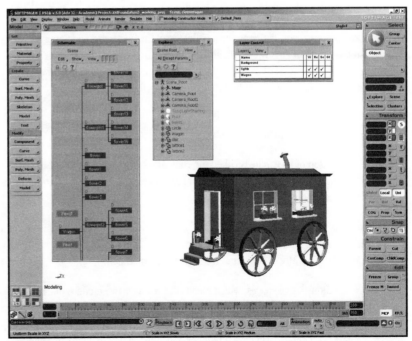

**Figure 3.1**
Tools you'll use.

# Hierarchy

As your scene grows with more objects, lights, and other elements, you have to find a way to organize your scene in some way. Without clear organization, simply selecting an element can become a very tedious job. A hierarchy is one way to organize scene elements to create an understandable structure. The hierarchy also assists you in moving, rotating, and scaling scene elements, and the hierarchy makes animating complex scenes much easier and more understandable.

Imagine that you have modeled and arranged a robotic arm, with an upper arm section, a lower arm section, a wrist, a palm, and some fingers. That robotic arm must be arranged into a hierarchy before it can be animated.

You can imagine an uprooted and upside-down tree as a hierarchy with its roots up in the air and branches and leaves pointing down.

In the robot arm metaphor, the upper arm is the top of the hierarchy. The upper arm is also the parent of the lower arm, and the lower arm is the parent of the wrist. The wrist is the parent of the palm. In turn, the palm is also the parent of fingers, since the palm is higher up in the hierarchy than the fingers (see Figure 3.2).

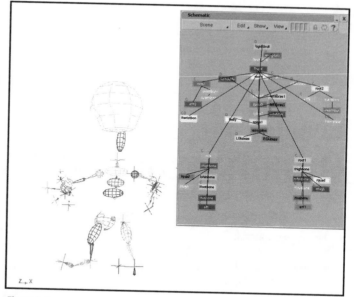

**Figure 3.2**
Basic arm hierarchy structure.

This whole hierarchical structure (the entire arm) is called the tree.

Consequently, the top of hierarchy is called the root. Any sub-hierarchies under the root are called branches. So the upper arm is the root of this particular hierarchy, and the connections between the palm and fingers are branches. If nothing is attached to or is below the element, you can simply call it a node. The term node can refer to any single object.

A Model node is a special kind of object in XSI used to organize lots of hierarchies together in a scene. The Scene Root object in the explorer is actually a Model node. It has an icon of a man doing jumping jacks. You can turn any hierarchy into a model by selecting the root of the hierarchy and choosing the Create > Model > New Model command from the Model module.

Models create unique name spaces, which means that if I have two models, one named Bob and the other named Fred, I can have objects with the same names in both Bob and Fred. For instance, both Bob and Fred could have a control object named right_hand_control, which is not possible without using a model as the root of a hierarchy. Within a single model, each element name must be unique. If you try to name something with the same name as another object, the name you choose will have a number appended to it, like hand1 or leftfoot3.

Groups are another organizational tool in XSI. You can think of a group as a bag of objects, where there is no particular structure within the bag. The elements are simply loose in the group.

When a property is applied to the group, that property overrides similar properties on the objects within the group. This makes groups ideal for adding materials to many objects at once, or changing the render properties of a bunch of similar objects.

We will explore how to apply groups later, in the tutorial at the end of this chapter.

## Inherited Transformations

Organizing your work space into hierarchies of objects has an additional benefit: The child nodes will inherit the transformations of the parent node. Each parent node in turn inherits the transformations of its parent, all the way up to the root. If the root moves, scales bigger or smaller, or rotates, all the child nodes under it will scale, rotate, and translate, too.

To visualize this, imagine a truck wheel composed of an axle, a hub, a rim, a bunch of lug bolts and lug nuts, and a tire. In real life, when the axle turns, all the other parts of the wheel assembly rotate properly, and when the axle moves through space (let's say, jumping "Dukes of Hazzard" style), all the lug bolts and nuts move along with it automatically (see Figure 3.3).

**Figure 3.3**
A hierarchy makes all the parts of the wheel easy to animate.

If you modeled this arrangement of parts and you wanted to animate your car, you could select each part individually and move it, setting keyframes as you go. But that would be tedious, and the parts would probably come apart from one another.

A better idea would be to put the parts into a hierarchy.

While there are several ways you could do this, the arrangement that makes the most sense would be this. Make the axle the parent of the hub, the hub the parent of the rim, the rim the parent of all the lug bolts. Also make the rim the parent of the tire. Finally, make each lug bolt the parent of its lug nut.

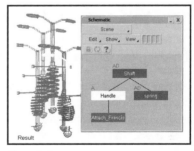

**Figure 3.4**
Different parenting methods create different results.

In this way, you can choose to spin the whole assembly by rotating the axle, or just spin each lug nut around its bolt (see Figure 3.4).

Hierarchy can be done incorrectly, too, and can have a negative impact on animation. If you accidentally made a lug nut the parent of the rim, for instance, instead of the other way around, then when you moved and the rim, the lug nut would not follow. When you rotated the lug nut, the wheel would spin around that bolt. That would be bad, because it would make the wheel very hard to animate. When that happens, you should look in the Schematic view to find a graphical representation of the hierarchy and then select and move parts of the wheel until you understand where you made a mistake. You can then select the child node that is incorrectly hooked to a parent and cut it loose. Finally, hook it up again in a better order.

You can Shift-select all the parts of a hierarchy and then use the Cut button to cut them *all* loose, all at the same time. You could also select the whole hierarchy by selecting it with the spacebar-right-click key combo, and then use the 'Select Members/Components' command from the Select menu at the top of the right-hand MCP (Main Command Panel) to select each node individually. Then use Cut to chop up the whole hierarchy.

## Inherited Operators and Properties

In just the same way that child nodes inherit the transformations of the parent, child nodes can also inherit new properties and operators. This makes it easy to apply changes to many objects at once. The tactic of propagating operators and properties down the tree from a branch to all of that branch's children is called branch applying. For instance, in the case of the wheel and lug nuts, you would want one material to be applied to all the nuts and bolts. Because they are all in a hierarchy, under the rim, you could branch-select the rim and then apply a material, which would filter down from the rim and be applied to all the lug nuts, as long as they did not have their own material already.

You can use this technique to apply operators, like deformations, and properties, like Motion Blur, to lots of objects in a scene at once.

## How to Create a Hierarchy

You can quickly create a hierarchy by using the Parent button, which is located on the right of the Main Command Panel, just below the Constrain menu.

Select an object and then click the Parent button, that puts you in Parent mode. While in Parent mode, left-clicking an object will make it the child of the object you have selected, middle-clicking an object will make it the parent of the object (or objects) you have selected, and right-clicking (or tapping the Esc button) will end Parent mode (see Figure 3.5).

If you have the Schematic view open, you can now see lines connecting the objects.

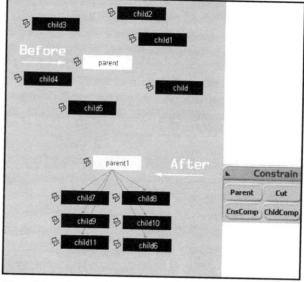

**Figure 3.5**
A simple hierarchy.

XSI has a convention called SOFTIMAGE|3D Selection Model that you can check on and off in the Select menu at the top right of the user interface. When SOFTIMAGE|3D Selection Model is on, you can use the left, middle, and right mouse button s in conjunction with the space bar to select nodes, branches, and trees, respectively.

### Single Node Selection

Left-clicking will choose any node as a single object. The selected objects will be highlighted in white.

### Branch Node Selection

Middle-clicking on a parent will branch-select, which means that the node you clicked on becomes selected and shows in white wireframe, and all the child nodes of that parent also highlight in gray, to indicate that whatever you do now will affect them, tool.

For example, if you middle-click on Camera_Root, you will select the entire camera branch, including the actual Camera and the Camera_Interest.

In the Schematic view, you can move the entire hierarchy by holding M and then clicking and dragging a node with the middle mouse button.

### Tree Node Selection

Right-clicking on a node will select that node, all the nodes beneath it, and all the nodes above it. In other words, it selects the entire tree that the clicked node belongs to. The root of the hierarchy will show onscreen in white wireframe; all the other nodes will show gray.

## Cutting Hierarchy

When you make a mistake or you want to rearrange a hierarchy, you need to cut the connection between the parent and child with the Cut button, which is located by the Parent button, at the bottom-right corner of the MCP.

Simply select the object you want to detach from the hierarchy, and click the Cut button. Now the connection line between the objects is gone. If you have many objects that are in a hierarchy, you can Shift-select them all rapidly by drawing a marquee around them and then use the Cut button from the MCP. Each will be cut from its parent, and there will be no hierarchy among those selected nodes.

## Using the Schematic View

The Schematic view is used to analytically view hierarchical and other relationships in between. You can change a view port to Schematic view by left-clicking on the View menu to get a pull-down and then selecting the Schematic view. If you just started a new scene, you will see default Scene_Material, a light, and a camera, with two constraints and two nulls (see Figure 3.6).

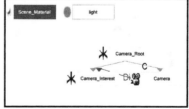

**Figure 3.6**
The default schematic in an "empty" scene.

The boxes represent elements. Connections, such as hierarchy and constraints, are shown as a line between boxes. You can choose what kinds of relationships to show in the Schematic diagram by checking on and off items in the Show menu. By default, the Schematic always shows parent-child hierarchy relationships between nodes.

You can use the normal hotkeys to move around in Schematic view. For example, you can pan and zoom with the Z key, and frame selected objects with the F key. Selecting works the same in the Schematic as it does elsewhere. The spacebar and left mouse button (LMB) selects individual nodes, spacebar and middle mouse button (MMB) selects branches, and spacebar and right mouse button (RMB) selects whole trees.

You can automatically rearrange the nodes in the Schematic view with the View > Rearrange All and View > Rearrange Selection menu commands. The first will automatically rearrange the entire scene, while the second will change just the organization within the selected node.

You can manually rearrange nodes in the Schematic view to help you visualize the relationships between and among objects, by holding the M hotkey and then left-clicking and dragging to move the nodes around.

You can collapse whole hierarchies down to a single box in the Schematic view by Alt-right-clicking on a branch or a root node to see the context-sensitive menu, and choosing Collapse Node. The Collapsed node shows up as a series of outlines around a regular node box. You can expand it back to show all the nodes in the hierarchy by popping open the context-sensitive menu and choosing Expand Node, with your mouse hovered over the same node.

There are context-sensitive menus in the schematic view, but since the right mouse button is in use for Tree selection, you must use Alt-RMB to access them. When you Alt-RMB in the empty space of the Schematic or on a node, a window will pop up, giving you a range of options. You can, for instance, rearrange a hierarchy to vertical or horizontal, delete a node or a branch, duplicate, and show properties of selected elements.

You may collapse and expand the hierarchy. This is very useful if you have many hierarchies in your scene. When a branch is collapsed, the parent will show three lines under it, as if it is stacked on top of some other nodes, so you can tell it can be expanded.

To collapse or expand a hierarchy, Alt-right-click over it and choose either Collapse Node or Expand Node from the context-sensitive drop menu, or just double click on the node in the schematic with the left mouse button to collapse or the middle mouse button to expand.

Hierarchy creation and editing can be done using other views, too, but the Schematic view is simple and provides good visual feedback for artists.

## Using the Explorer to Edit Hierarchy

You can also use the Explorer to view and edit hierarchy. The Explorer can be opened by changing an existing view from whatever it is to the Explorer view, or XSI Explorer (see Figure 3.7). You can also open a floating Explorer window by choosing View > General > Explorer from the top menu bar, or better yet, by tapping the 8 hotkey from the numbers above your keyboard (not the number 8 on your numeric keypad).

The Explorer will display hierarchical structure a little differently than the Schematic view. The Explorer shows hierarchy branching out from left to right; the farther right you, the lower you are on the hierarchy. Connections are displayed with vertical lines. If a node has a + or – sign, the element contains a hierarchy tree underneath. Clicking + expands the tree, and clicking – collapses the tree. You can hide any unnecessary hierarchy this way, to create a clutter-free display. You can also navigate through elements by using the arrow keys, as long as your mouse cursor is within the Explorer window. The up- and down- arrow will move up and down the node in the hierarchy. The right-arrow will expand hierarchies, and the left- arrow will collapse them. You can also move branches from one

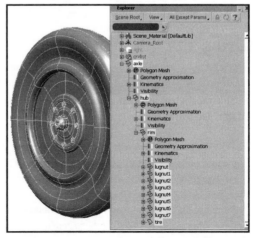

**Figure 3.7**
The Explorer view.

parent to another easily in the Explorer. Simply hold the left mouse button on the node name, and drag it on top of the parent-to-be.

> This is called Drag n' Drop parenting.

If you want to cut the relationship, just drag the node to the Scene_Root node, which makes it a child of the top of the scene. In XSI, all nodes must be children of something, so by default all new objects come in as children of the Scene_Root model node.

Renaming nodes is also very easy. Just right-click on the node and select Rename from the list that pops up. "So why do we even bother with Schematic view?", you might ask. The great advantage of the Schematic view is that it is much more graphical, and you can arrange your hierarchies in any shape you like. For example, if you create a very complex human skin and skeleton setup, you can arrange the hierarchy to resemble a human, to speed up your selection process.

## How to Group Objects Together

If you want to apply the same operators, materials, and textures to many objects at the same time, you can use Group instead of hierarchy. A group is a container that holds references to any number of scene objects within it. The objects are not actually "in" the group—just a pointer to the object is in the group. References (also called links or pointers) show in italic type in XSI.

You can create groups by selecting any number of objects and clicking the Group button, located in the Edit panel. If you want to add more objects to the group, first select the group you want to add objects to, Shift-select the objects you want to add, and choose Edit > Add to Group from the Edit panel. Edit > Remove from Group will take selected objects out of a group.

The easiest and fastest way to add items to a group is to use the Explorer window. Groups show up at the bottom, below objects, when you are in the Scene Root scope of the Explorer. You can then click and drag objects from the Explorer over a group, let go to drop them into the group.

> This is called Drag n' Drop grouping.

If you expand a group by clicking the plus sign next to the group name, it will expand to show you the members of the group. If you right-click over a group member, you'll get a context-sensitive menu that includes a command Remove From Group.

When the group is selected, you can add properties to it that are propagated or shared with all the members of the group (see Figure 3.8).

Let's practice what we have learned so far with the following tutorial.

**Figure 3.8**
Group overrides hierarchy.

## Robotic Drone: At a Glance
### Topics Covered

Previously, the structure of a wheel was used to explain the concept of hierarchy. In this tutorial, we'll continue to explore the hierarchy by constructing a robotic drone out of prebuilt components and assembling those components into a functional hierarchy (see Figure 3.9).

You'll learn how to:

◆ Create a hierarchy by using the Parent button

◆ Use the Schematic view to edit the hierarchy

◆ Use the hierarchy to take advantage of inherited transformations

◆ Propagate a branch material to parts of the drone arm

◆ Use a group to override material properties for other parts of the robotic drone

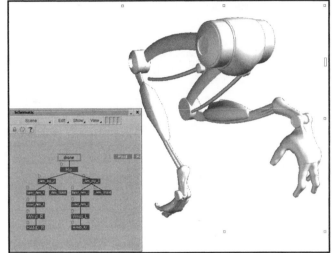

**Figure 3.9**
Let's make a drone!

## Tutorial: Robotic Drone
### Step 1: Check Out the Drone

Open the drone_start scene from the material that accompanies this book, and take a look at the objects in the scene. The drone has a center part named the Hip, which will be the top of the hierarchy. When you select the hip as a branch and translate it, you will want all the other parts of the drone to move along exactly with the Hip. The Hip will be connected to the Upper_Arm_Hip_Joint, which will be connected to the Upper_Arm and Upper_Arm_Stablizer. The Upper_Arm will be connected to the Lower_Arm, which will be connected to the Wrist, and then to the Hand.

Each part will need to be a child of the part above it, and the child will need to have the local center in a certain place so that the child rotates properly. For instance, the hand needs to have the center at the top round pivot object. That way, when the hand rotates, it will look correct. Examine the location of the local center by selecting some of the drone objects and activating the Rotation transform cells in the MCP, and experiment with rotating the parts to see how they move independently of one another.

## Step 2: Make the Hip the Parent of the Right Upper Arm Hip Joint

When building a hierarchy, you can either start with the child and work up the hierarchy, or start with the parent and move down. Let's start with the top-down approach for the right arm, and then we'll try the bottom-up method for the left arm. Select the hip and activate the Parent button in the lower-right corner of the MCP.

Your cursor changes to the pick cursor, which means you are ready to left-click on the object that you want to be the child of the hip, which is the Upper_Arm_Hip_Joint_R.

Right-click or tap the Esc key to end the parenting pick session.

Open your Schematic view (hotkey is 9) and see that the Upper_Arm_Hip_Joint_R is connected to the Hip, just like Figure 3.10.

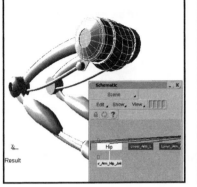

**Figure 3.10**
The Upper_Arm_Hip_Joint is now a child of the Hip.

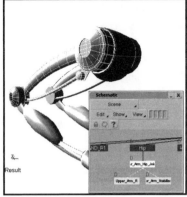

**Figure 3.11**
The Upper_Arm_Hip_Joint has two children.

## Step 3: Add in the Upper Arm

Now, if you started another parenting session with both the Hip and the Upper_Arm_joint selected, and then you picked an object, that object would become a child of whatever was at the top of the hierarchy, which is not what we want. We want each part of the arm to be a direct child of the part above it.

To make sure this happens, select just the Upper_Arm_Hip_Joint now, and then click on the Parent button to enter parenting mode. After that, pick on the Upper_Arm_R to make it a child of the Joint. We also want the Upper_Arm_Stabilizer_R to be a child of the same Arm_Hip_Joint, so with the Arm_Hip_Joint still selected, also pick on the stabilizer. Check Figure 3.11 to make sure you have the right idea.

## Step 4: Add the Lower_Arm_R and Parts Below

You don't actually have to leave the parenting mode in between moves. If you hold the spacebar, you temporarily turn off parenting and turn on selecting. Hold the spacebar and select the Upper_Arm_R. Then release the spacebar, and you are back in Parent mode, ready to pick the Lower_Arm_R.

Repeat this process, making the Lower_Arm_R the parent of the Wrist_R, and the Wrist_R the parent of the HAND_R (see Figure 3.12).

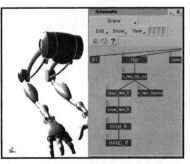

**Figure 3.12**
The completed arm hierarchy.

**69**

## Step 5: Do the Other Arm

Previously, we have selected the intended parent, clicked the Parent button, and then picked the child. Let's use a slightly different method for the second arm, the left arm of the drone. With the HAND_R1 selected, click the Parent button. Look at the Status line at the bottom of the screen; it says middle-click to select a parent. So, middle-click on Wrist_L to make it the parent of the hand. The advantage of parenting from the bottom up is that you don't have to stop to change the selection all the time. To add the Lower_Arm_L, just middle-click on it.

Use these same techniques to add all the rest of the left arm, finally connecting it to the Hip. Both the Stabilizer (Upper_Arm_Stabilizer_L) and the upper arm should be children of the Upper_Arm_Hip_Joint, which means you'll have to add one or the other to the hierarchy after you have parented all the way up to the Hip_Joint.

## Step 6: Move the Arm: Inherited Transformation

You are all done! Please make sure that the Transform Manipulator option in the Transform menu is toogled off for testing, so you can easily rotate the arm relative to each part's local axis. To move this arm, you can simply branch-select from the Upper_Arm or Lower_Arm or even wrist joint and rotate Local X. Try this: Middle-click on the Upper_Arm_Hip_Joint_L in the Schematic view, the Explorer, or 3D view. Make sure the Upper_Arm_Hip_Joint_L is highlighted in white and everything else below it in the arm is highlighted with gray, indicating that the Upper_Arm_Hip_Joint_L is branch-selected, and the children will inherit the transformations.

Activate Local transform, and rotate in X to flex some muscle. The Lower_Arm, wrist, and hand should follow the Upper_Arm_Hip_Joint_L rotation since they are children of that node. We call this concept inherited transformation, and it's a huge help, because you can arrange the moving parts of a model in a hierarchy that makes animating them simpler.

The Schematic view is also very helpful when selecting objects and hierarchies, since you can see the entire structure and you don't need to be in a selection mode to select objects. 3D animation can be very time-consuming, so the speed and efficiency these tools give you is very important.

## Step 7: Materials on Hierarchies

You can also add materials to hierarchies. Select the entire hierarchy as a tree (hold the spacebar and RMB-click on any part of the hierarchy) and choose Get > Material > Phong from the left-side menu stack. Now switch to the Render module with the button at the top of the menu stack or with the hotkey 3 on your keyboard, and click the Modify > Shader button to open the Material PPG if it is not open already. Modify the color by dragging the color sliders around to your liking. You can see the color in the shaded view, but not in wireframe or hidden line.

The color propagates to all the parts of the arm, because you applied it to the whole hierarchy in branch mode. This is called a bnranch material (see Figure 3.13).

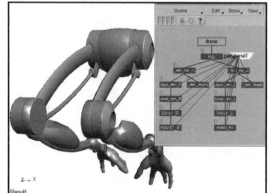

**Figure 3.13**
A branch material colors everything below the node it is applied to.

### Step 8: Now Let's Try Making a Group

Select just the Hand and wrists of both arms, using Shift to extend the selection. Make a group with the Group button, and open the Explorer (hotkey 8) to see it. Make sure the group is selected, and change its name (use the context-sensitive menu) to HandGroup.

With the group selected, add a material shader and modify it as shown in Figure 3.14.

You will see the material color from the group override the material from the hierarchy. Properties on groups take precedence over properties on hierarchies.

If you added a material directly to an object, say a finger bone, that property would pre-empt the property of the hierarchy, but not the property of the group. We call this concept of some properties overriding others precedence.

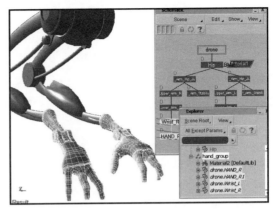

**Figure 3.14**
Objects not in the same hierarchy can be colored with a group material.

## Conclusion

You learned all about the advantages of using hierarchies to organize your scenes, to build simple animation rigs that transfer animation from parents to children, and how hierarchies can be used to propagate operators, properties, and materials down from a parent node to many children all at once.

You learned how to create hierarchies using the Parent button and how to destroy hierarchy relationships with the Cut button.

You learned how to work in the Schematic view, and you learned how to drag and drop in the Explorer view.

Finally, you learned how to use groups to apply materials to lots of objects at once, even if they are not together in a branch or a tree.

# Chapter 4
# Simple Polygon Modeling

In this chapter, you will learn:

◆ How to choose whether to work on polygons or NURBS

◆ All about polygon terminology

◆ How to use the polygon-building tools

◆ How to create objects starting with a polygon primitive

◆ The process of sculpting and gradual refinement

◆ What Subdivision Surfaces are, and how they work in XSI

◆ The SubDee modeling technique

## Introduction

XSI uses two main surface types for building objects: NURBS and Polygons. Each has distinct advantages and disadvantages, and so each one is better for some tasks than for others. NURBS are mathematically defined curving surfaces that are infinitely smooth, while polygonal surfaces are made up of many straight-line segments. This means that it is easier to make (and edit) a really smooth NURBS surface than a really smooth polygonal surface.

However, NURBS are always rectangular patches, and they are very hard to connect into more complex shapes. Using polygon modeling tools and techniques, an artist can easily make shapes of whatever topology he wishes (not just rectangular), and separate polygon objects are easy to merge into one object and won't show seams. Since polygon objects are also Subdivision Surfaces in XSI, and since Subdivision Surfaces can be made very smooth, polygons are now the most useful surface type in XSI (see Figure 4.1).

**Figure 4.1**
Tools you'll use.

Copyright 2005 Charlie Winter.

# Polygon Modeling Tools

First, let's go over a little conceptual background. In a surface modeler like XSI, objects have no density, no material inside their shapes. Objects are just infinitely thin shells surrounding nothingness. Those shells tend to be built of many small line segments, connecting the dots to form a surface mesh. In surface meshes, the simplest way to connect the dots is with straight lines. An object created from a series of dots connected by straight lines is called a polygon mesh.

## Polygons as Guides for NURBS Modeling

Even when your character will really need to be created with multiple NURBS patches and stitched together, it is often easiest to build a low-resolution polygonal model of the character first to use for prototyping. You can make quick and easy adjustments to shape and proportion, and then trace that polygon mesh with NURBS curves to build the final NURBS surface patches. XSI has great tools for you to draw perfect curves right on polygonal characters, making it much easier to build the patches you need (see Figure 4.2).

The snapping tools in XSI make this possible. Try this simple series of steps to practice the technique.

1. In the MCP, click on the Snap to Point button (it looks like a dot under the Snap menu) and toggle off the Snap to Grid option.

2. Next, click the On button to activate snapping.

3. Get a polygon mesh object to experiment with, and set the Display mode to Hidden Line Removal.

4. Now use the Create > Curves > Draw Cubic by CVs tool, and point your mouse over the polygon mesh.

   Hold down the left mouse button, and move your mouse to see that the first point of the curve will snap to the vertex of the polygon nearest to the mouse cursor, within the snapping reticule. Click to drop a point on the NURBS curve when you have the vertex you want. That point on curve the you have added is called Control Vertex, or CV for short.

5. Repeat the process, clicking and holding down the left mouse button, and then sliding the mouse around the polygon surface to choose where to drop it. The snapping tool will try to drop the CV on one of the polygon vertices, so it will be right on the surface of the polygon mesh. Drop additional points until you have the curve you want.

6. Select the original polygon mesh you were using as a form, and hide it with the H hotkey. Observe that you have drawn a NURBS curve directly on the polygon surface (see Figure 4.3).

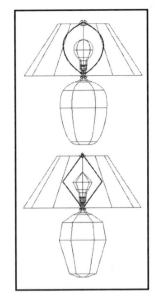

**Figure 4.2**
NURBs can be converted into polygons.

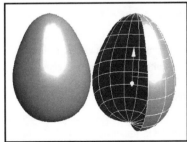

**Figure 4.3**
Surfaces in XSI are hollow.

# Polygon Terminology

Polygons are simple, but there is some terminology to learn before we begin exploring the polygon tools in XSI. First, let's change the feedback that XSI gives us so that we can see the parts of the polygon that we are talking about. In the Camera view, go to the Show menu, which is located under the eye-shaped icon at the center of the View title bar. Make sure that Points, Normals, and PolyMesh Boundaries and Hard Edges are checked on, so they will show up in the Camera view (see Figure 4.4).

Now get a Primitive > Polygon Mesh > Sphere and examine it in the Camera view. Each polygonal mesh is made up of many smaller individual polygons. A polygon is a geometric shape with at least three sides. Three-sided polygons are called triangles, four-sided polygons are called quads, and polygons with more than four sides are called n-sided polygons. A polygon can have as many as 255 sides, but it's a much better idea to keep them simple (see Figure 4.5). A complex polygon with many sides can always be broken up into more polygons, each with fewer sides.

## Edges

The side of a polygon is called an edge. When an edge of one polygon abuts the neighboring polygon, we say that the edge is shared, or closed. When the edge is on the outside of the shape, or abutting a hole, we say that the edge is open. Open edges are called boundaries in XSI. They can be shown (if the model has some) with the Show > PolyMesh Boundaries and Hard Edges toggle.

## Vertex, Vertices

The points in space that connect the edges are called vertices. A single point is called a vertex. Vertices are located in Cartesian space with values for the X-, Y-, and Z- axes, so we might say that a vertex is at -3, 5, 8, which would mean that it is 3 units in the negative direction of X, 5 units up of Y, and 8 units forward of Z, relative to the global center.

## Normals

Each polygonal mesh, being an infinitely thin shell of a surface, has an inside and an outside. Since the render can render just the inside, just the outside, or both, it's important to know which way the surface is facing.

If you built an object that was inside out (and this happens a lot), then it might not shade or render correctly. The best way to check the direction of the surface is to examine the normals. Use the Show > Normals toggle in each viewport to turn on the display of normals in that view, or use the Display > Normals menu from the top of the screen to show the normals in all the viewports.

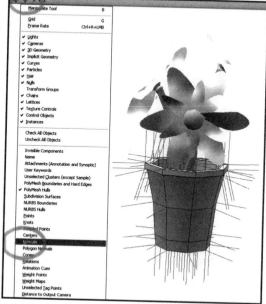

**Figure 4.4**
The Show menu is where you can toggle on different feedback options.

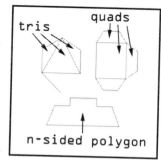

**Figure 4.5**
Polygons can have any number of sides from 3 to 255.

Normals are the thin blue lines radiating from each vertex like spiky blue hair. Normals extend in the outside direction of the surface. Technically, they are perpendicular to the surface, but sometimes we just call that "normal to the surface." If the normals are pointing inside your object, the object is inside out and needs to be inverted. Try using the Modify > Surf. Mesh > Invert Normals command on your sphere to see what that would look like.

It is very important that all the polygons in a mesh have normals facing the same direction. Imagine that if some of the polygons faced out in your sphere and some faced in, it would be really hard to figure out how to render it correctly. If you were developing the model for use in a real-time renderer, it would show strange holes and artifacts in the object that would look bad. As a result, you should pay attention to the normal direction as you build polygon objects. Generally, XSI tries not to let you create such mixed polygon surfaces, but should you accidentally create one, you can select just one polygon (covered next) and invert that selected polygon with Modify > Poly. Mesh > Invert Polygons. So, to repeat our terminology, polygonal meshes are made up of polygons, and polygons are made up of vertices and edges. Polygons, vertices, and edges are called components. You will work with each type of component using that component mode from the filter selection at the top-right of the Main Command Panel (MCP) (see Figure 4.6).

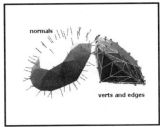

**Figure 4.6**
The components: vdges, vertices, and normals.

## The Polygon Components Filter

Each component type (polygon, edge, and vertex) can be selected so that you can work with it. You can select just one at a time or groups of components. You cannot, however, select edges and vertices at the same time; it's one component type at a time. This one-at-a-time selection method is called a filter. With the polygon Selection filter active, you can only select polygons; with the edge filter on, you just select Edges, and so on.

The Selection filter is located in the MCP near the top. Since Point, Edge, and Polygon are so common, buttons for just those filters appear automatically in the MCP whenever you have a polygon object selected. They do not show when you have a NURBS object selected.

**Figure 4.7**
Use the hotkeys U, E, and T instead of these buttons.

### Selecting Components

While there are buttons in the MCP that activate the component filters, using them would be very slow. You would have to take your eyes off the object you were working on, move the mouse cursor to the MCP, make a change, go back to the object, hold the spacebar, and make the selection. Since you'll be doing this thousands of times each day as you sculpt, that method just won't do. The faster way is to use the hotkeys for component selection (see Figure 4.7).

### Selecting Vertices

If you hold down the T key with your left hand, you can select, deselect, and toggle vertices with the three mouse buttons, respectively. With the T hotkey down, drag a rectangle selection around some of the vertices on your sphere. Note that the vertices become tagged in red (hotkey T for tagged). Also note that the Point filter is automatically enabled. If you want to add to the group of selected points, just hold T again and drag a rectangle around those points using the left mouse button, and they will be added to the others already tagged in red. If some points became selected that you didn't want, drag a rectangle around those with your middle mouse button and note that they are removed from the tagged group (see Figure 4.8). Try dragging a rectangle around the whole sphere with the right mouse button, and see that the tagged group is inverted: those that were not tagged now are, and those that were are no longer. This convention, where the left mouse button adds to the group, the middle removes, and the right toggles, is called the Extended Component Selection model. It works for all components.

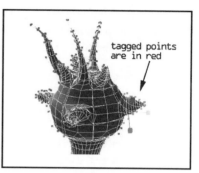

**Figure 4.8**
Tag, untag, and toggle vertices with T and the left, middle, and right mouse buttons.

### Selecting Edges

If you hold down the E key with your left hand (hotkey E for edge) you can select, deselect, and toggle edges with the three mouse buttons. The left mouse button adds edges to the selection, the middle button deselects edges, and the right button toggles edges (see Figure 4.9). Selected edges show in red, and deselected edges show in amber. Drawing a selection rectangle will select all edges that are within the rectangle or touch the rectangle, on both sides of the object.

### Selecting Polygons

Polygons are special. They have two different component selection hotkeys. The Y hotkey selects polygons in the same way that you select edges and vertices, by dragging a rectangle that selects all the polygons that are entirely within the selection rectangle. The selected polygons will show in translucent red. The problem is that while you are working in shaded view, you might be selecting polygons on the back of the object without knowing it, and messing up your model. To solve this problem, the U hotkey was pressed into service (see Figure 4.10). When you hold the U key, you can click over the middle of a polygon, and only the polygon facing out of the model towards you will be selected. This is called raycasting, and it is very useful. You can also hold U while dragging a stroke across the model to paint in a selection. As usual, the extended component selection model means that the left mouse button adds to the selection, the middle button removes polygons from the selection, and the right mouse button toggles polygons.

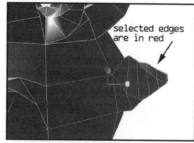

**Figure 4.9**
Tag, untag, and toggle edges with E and the left, middle, and right mouse buttons.

## *Transforming Edges, Vertices, and Polygons*

Once you have a component or a group of components selected, you can sculpt the shape of the polygon object by transforming them. Polygons, vertices, and edges can be scaled, rotated, and translated to change the shape of the object.

The Tweak tool (hotkey M) is a spiffy way to move any type of component (see Figure 4.11). When you hold M and move your mouse over the surface of a selected object, the edge, vertex, or polygon under your mouse will light up. When you left-click and hold the mouse button down and then drag, you can drag the component freely. When the Move tool active, you'll see three small icons in the

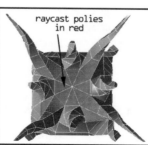

**Figure 4.10**
Tag, untag, and toggle polygons with E and the left, middle, and right mouse buttons.

**Figure 4.11**
The new Tweak tool has an onscreen UI.

lower middle of the viewport you are working in. These icons let you change how the move tool works. The first icon shows three axes, and it allows you to freely drag the edge, vert, or polygon freely in the view. The second icon looks like a horseshoe. It's a magnet icon, and when you click on it and then drag a component, that component will try to stay in the plane defined by the neighboring components. The third toggle is, weld, and it looks like a cross over a vertex. With this toggle on when you drag a vert, it will snap to neighboring verts and weld itself to them, collapsing the edge in between and reducing the point count of the model by one.

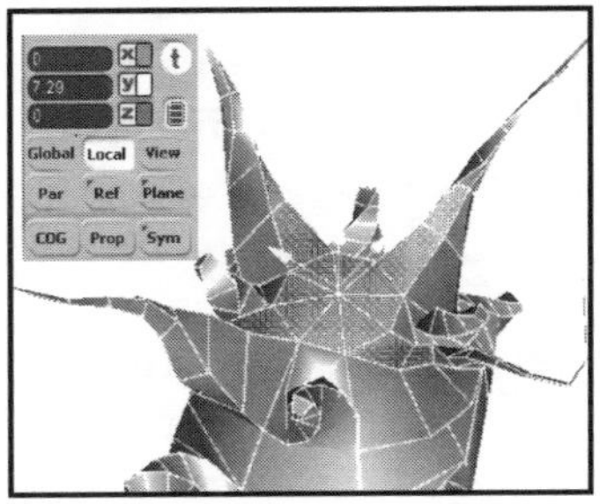

When you have a component or group of components selected and you plan to transform them, the big question is always, "Transform them relative to what?"

You can change the way that the components are transformed by clicking on the mode buttons in the MCP, right below the Transform cells Global, Local, and View (see Figure 4.12).

**Figure 4.12**
Local, View, and Global are all useful in different circumstances.

The selected components will automatically have a local center, called a local reference frame, which is the geographic center of the group. Sometimes you want to transform the selected components using a different local reference frame. You can use any point, polygon, or edge on any object as the new reference frame. Choose a new reference frame by right-clicking on the Ref button in the MCP, select the type of reference you wish to use, and then click once on the reference object and again on the reference component (edge or polygon) in the 3D view.

Generally, the most useful method when working with components is the Local mode. When you translate a single component in the Local mode, that component moves relative to its local axis. When translating a polygon, for instance, local Y is always normal to the surface (out from the surface) no matter how the polygon is facing in global space.

When you have more than one component selected in a contiguous block (the components are touching), then there is only one local axis for all the touching components together. That axis is the average of all the individual axes. Keep in mind that when the components are not touching, each has its own axis.

Now try out transforming the components:

1. Try selecting every other polygon in a ring around the equator of your sphere (use U to raycast polygons), and in Local mode, carefully translate them in each axis to see the effect.
2. Try selecting all the edges around the middle of the sphere with the E hotkey, and scale them uniformly. See the effect that shortening them will have on the circumference of the sphere.

You can also select a loop of polygons around a sphere with the U hotkey and the Ctrl modifier, which allows you to use two polygon selections to define a polygon loop (see Figure 4.13).

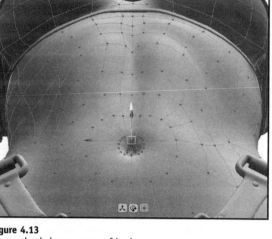

3. Try selecting a group of vertices near the top of the sphere with T, and then extend that selection to include the similar points around the bottom with T and the right mouse button. Translate, scale, and rotate these vertices to see the effect.

4. To see how choosing a reference frame might work, create a cap of polygons around the top of the sphere by selecting the third or fourth row of polieys around the sphere and deleting them with the Backspace key on your keyboard. Now select just the cap, the polygons around the top of the sphere. Activate the Rotation menu cells. Imagine that we want all these to hinge at one side and rotate up.

With the cap selected, right-click on the Ref button in the MCP, choose Pick Edge Reference, and then pick on one edge at the perimeter of the cap. Now you can rotate the selected polygons around the edge you chose as a reference frame.

**Figure 4.13**
Edge and poly loops are your friends.

## *Drawing Polygons from Scratch and Aligning Edges*

You may also draw polygons one at a time by plotting points in space for the vertices, either starting from scratch or by sharing an edge with an existing polygon (see Figure 4.14).

The important thing to understand when manually drawing polygons is that the polygons you draw must be kept facing the same direction as those around them. In other words, you want the normals of the new polygons you are drawing to match the direction of the normals all around them. If you drew one polygon with normals facing the wrong way, that might show up as a hole, or create problems later in modeling.

The direction that you draw the vertices of the polygon (either clockwise or counter-clockwise) determines which direction the normals will face (see Figure 4.15). XSI will also warn you when you create a bad polygon by highlighting the edge between the good and bad polygons in green, as long as you have turned on Show Boundaries and Hard Edges on the Show menu (eyeball icon) at the top of the View window you are using.

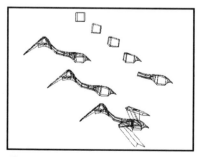

**Figure 4.14**
The evolution from a cube to a Quezlecoatlas quetzal.

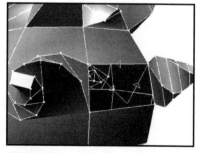

**Figure 4.15**
The arrows show which direction to click in while adding polygons.

To draw a polygon from scratch, choose the Add/Edit Polygon tool from the Modify > Poly Mesh menu in the Model module (hotkey N), and click with the left mouse button to drop the first vertex in space wherever your mouse cursor is pointing.

Move your cursor and click again to drop the next vertex. A line will connect the two, showing where the edge will be, with an arrow showing the correct direction of the polygon. Click a third time to drop the next vertex, and complete the most basic polygon, a triangle. You may continue to click if you wish to create a polygon with more edges. If you click with the middle mouse button, you will start a new polygon and choose a new edge to draw from. Whenever possible, the Add Polygon tool will connect the new polygon you are drawing to the existing polygons that you have drawn already. If you roll your mouse over an edge of the selected polygon while in the Add Polygon tool, that edge will be used and shared with the polygon you draw, and any edges that can be automatically assumed will also be added and shared. This intelligence ensures that your polygon geometry is as accurate as possible, that it shares vertices and edges whenever possible, and that all the normals point in a consistent direction.

If you click on a vertex while in the Add/Edit Polygon tool, you can move that point to adjust where it ended up.

When you are done with that tool, tap the Esc key on your keyboard to escape the tool and stop dropping vertices. Try to use the hotkey for Add Polygon, which is N, instead of the menu command.

# Serious Poly Modeling

Often the most productive manner of polygon modeling is to start with a primitive object, and then refine that shape gradually to get the shape that you want. When you use this method, there is no right or wrong command to use at any given time, no set sequence of steps that must be followed, and no clear point at which you are done. You just look at what you have, imagine how you could make it better, and gradually refine the model. By turning it in the Camera view, you examine the form of the model, and make decisions about how you could move polygons around, where you could add more edges to increase detail, and where you could translate vertices to make a more perfect shape. You may choose a primitive object that is similar in some way to the shape of the object you are modeling. Most people start with a cube (easiest), a cylinder, or a sphere. As you create more detail on the object by adding edges and duplicating polygons, the model takes on the shape you want. Since this is a process of refinement, it makes sense to approach the task with more of an artistic, sculptural approach than the technical engineering approach required of NURBS modeling.

## *The Operator Stack, Immediate Mode, and Freeze*

When you execute a command on the polygon primitive object, it becomes an operator in the operator stack. Every move—each added vertex, each added edge, and each transformation of a component—is logged. In many ways, the model is actually still a primitive, and XSI rebuilds it constantly, repeating each command you have ever made. Since you'll make hundreds or thousands of changes to the model while sculpting it into a new shape, this method is overkill and will slow down your productivity. There are two options to resolve this problem.

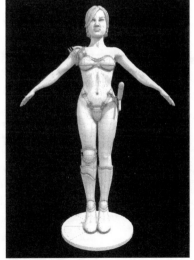

Angel by Malachi Bazan
(spin.killer@gmail.com
www.vfs.com/~malachib/).

## Freeze

When you use the Operator > Freeze Modeling command from the Edit menu in the MCP, or click the Freeze M button near the bottom of the MCP, which does the same thing, all the changes that have been preserved in order in the operator stack will be combined and cooked down into the final shape of the mesh. Then they'll be discarded. If you cannot see the Freeze M button, your Edit panel may be collapsed. Try right-clicking to expand it. You may also collapse other menu sections in the MCP with a right-click to get more room on screen.

After a Freeze M operator stack command, you will be left with a simple polygon mesh in the same shape it was before, but with no modeling operators (see Figure 4.16). While you cannot edit those operators, you can always undo (Ctrl-Z) to restore the operator stack. Freezing the modeling operators removes move point operators and the like, but it does not remove deformation operators, shape animation operators, envelope operators, or other operators that you might want to keep around for animation purposes.

## Immediate Mode

It seems like a hassle to create a big operator stack and then freeze it to remove the stack, so the Immediate mode was invented. When the Immediate mode is toggled on with the Immed button at the bottom of the MCP, operations are frozen as soon as they are completed, so that no giant operator stack is created.

This does not mean that undo won't work—it still remembers the last 20 things you've done so you can recover from mistakes. If the operator is something that never requires you to see a Property Editor, like moving a point with the M hotkey, the operation will just be done and frozen without further intervention on your part. If the operator requires a Property Editor to take input, like the Extrude Along Axis command, the Property Editor will open as a modal dialog box with OK and Cancel buttons. You can make changes, and when you click OK ,the command will execute and the operation will be frozen. Immediate mode is frequently the most convenient way to work when polygon modeling.

## Add Edge

A good way to add more detail is to split one polygon into two. XSI has a fantastic tool for dividing polygons exactly how you want them, called Add Edge. Using Add Edge, you can create a new edge stretching from two existing vertices on the same polygon, add a new vertex along the edge of a polygon and connect it to an existing vertex, or create another new vertex to join it to with a new edge (see Figure 4.17). The tool provides excellent feedback as you work and will not let you create bad edges.

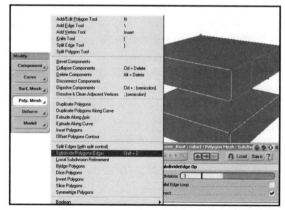

**Figure 4.16**
Freezing compacts the operator stack.

**Figure 4.17**
Adding an edge subdivides a single polygon into two polygons.

To use Add Edge, select the polygon object, click on the Polygon Mesh > Add Edge Tool menu command, and move your mouse over the mesh.

Note that as you move over vertices and edges, they are highlighted in red to indicate which you are about to split. Click to approve a starting vertex or edge, and then move your mouse to the opposite vertex of the same polygon, and click to select it. A new edge will be created connecting the two vertices. The tool cannot connect vertices that are not part of the same polygon. Tap the Esc key on your keyboard to complete the tool so you can start over fresh.

Try it again. This time start with an edge, and rather than clicking, click and hold your left mouse button to keep the command active, and slide the point back and forth along the edge by dragging the mouse left and right. When you have the spot you want, let off the mouse button. Wave your mouse over another edge of the same polygon (Add Edge cannot work across multiple polygons in one shot), and click again to split the polygon in two. Note that this time new vertices were created, in addition to the edge.

You can use the Add Edge tool to chain together edges, each one starting where the last left off. On your sphere, start in the middle of an edge, and click in the middle of the next edge over. Then immediately click with the left mouse button again on the next edge along the sphere to continue the edge, and keep going around the sphere. When done, you can click the right mouse button to stay in the tool but choose a new starting position for a new edge. You can stay in the tool as long as you have edges to create. Then tap the Esc key on your keyboard to quit the tool.

Finally, it is possible to add edges that terminate in the *middle* of a polygon. Imagine that you have a single polygon, and you want to make a vertex in the middle and radiate new edges off to the vertices from there. You can use the Add Edge tool to start from an outer vertex, click in the middle of the polygon to drop a new vert in the interior of the polygon you are splitting, and connect it with an edge to your starting point. You can continue to add edges from this newly created vertex. You must continue the edge to the other side of the polygon, because it is a bad idea to let edges terminate in the middle of a polygon. If you don't keep going with the new edge, the dangling part will be removed when you exit the tool.

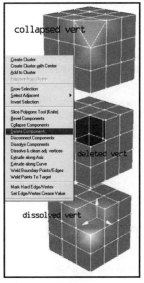

If you hold the Alt key while adding edges with \, XSI will automatically add extra edges for you when your mouse is inside a polygon.

You can also split polygons with the Shift-D hotkey.

## Deleting Polygons, Vertices, and Edges

Just as you can add more polygons, vertices, and edges, you can also delete them. When you select a polygon or group of polygons with the hotkey U, you can delete the polygons with the Delete key on your keyboard, or the Edit > Delete menu command from the MCP, leaving holes in the model (see Figure 4.18). This tool is great for creating windows, doors, and other openings in polygonal models.

However, if you select either a vertex or an edge and use the Delete button or the Edit > Delete command, that component is removed and XSI tries to patch the space by creating a bigger polygon surrounding it. This method of removing polygons is called dissolving.

**Figure 4.18**
Delete, Dissolve, and Collapse all remove verts with different results.

**83**

### Collapsing Polygons, Edges, and Vertices

When you collapse a component, something entirely different happens. Collapsing a polygon or an edge generally means shrinking that component to a single point in space and then replacing it with a vertex. This keeps your surface whole and unbroken, which is generally a good thing.

However, when you select a vertex and use the Poly Mesh > Collapse Components tool, it removes that vertex and all the edges that were connecting it. Then it creates a new polygon to patch the hole.

### Dissolving Edges, Vertices, and Polygons

Dissolving a component is like deleting a component, but the resulting hole is filled in with a new polygon so that the surface is still complete and unbroken.

## From NURBS to Polygons

Both polygonal surfaces and NURBS have unique advantages and downsides. When you are using the curve-based modeling tools (extrude, revolve, loft, etc.), you can choose whether the resulting object should be a NURBS surface or a polygon mesh surface by choosing the right command (see Figure 4.19). If you want to end up with NURBS surfaces, use the modeling commands from the Create > Surf. Mesh menu. If you crave polygon mesh objects, use the commands in the Create > Poly Mesh menu. The key is to use the right tool for the right job, and sometimes that means swapping from NURBS to polygons and vice versa. XSI has some wonderful tools to do just that.

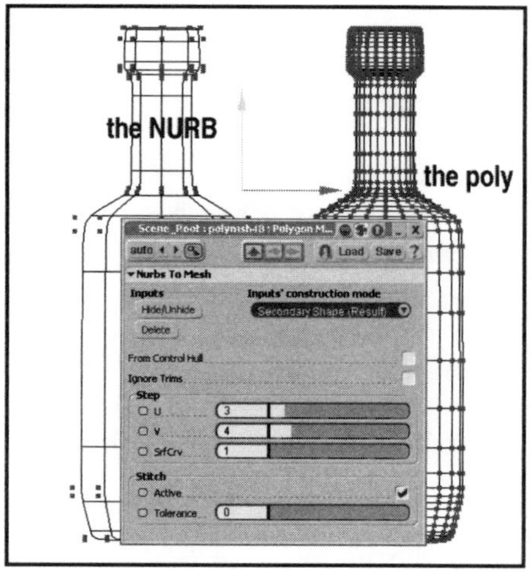

Getting from NURBS to polygons is easy, since all NURBS are eventually broken down (tessellated) into a polygon mesh anyway. XSI has a neat operator called NURBS to Mesh that will tessellate for you, while giving you control over the level of detail in the resulting polygon mesh. This level of detail is even animatable (until you freeze the operator stack). Simply select a NURBS model and choose the NURBS to Mesh command in the Create > Poly Mesh menu command. A new object is created, with an operator in its operator stack. If you open that operator into a Property Editor, you can adjust the Step in U and Step in V sliders to gain more or less detail in the resulting mesh. NURBS curves can also be converted into polygonal faces, and polygonal meshes can be reduced to fewer polygons, called filtering in XSI. Both topics are covered later in this book, after you have more experience building polygon meshes.

**Figure 4.19**
NURBS models can be converted down to polygons.

## Poly Tools for Games

One of the big advantages of polygons is that they are simple to display on-screen. All a computer has to do is transpose the straight lines onto a view plane, fill in the shape with a solid color, a shade, or a texture map, and move on to the next polygon.

As a result, where computers need to draw to the screen rapidly, polygons often have been used. Almost all the terrains, sets, props, characters, and special effects in modern computer games are created with a polygon toolset. In order for you to wander the 3D environment of your favorite game, the game engine has to draw the entire world from your point of view many times per second. The faster it can draw the world to the screen, the smoother the motion seems and the better your gaming experience. How many times each second the game can draw the screen is largely dependent on how many polygons are in the scene. More polygons are going to take more time to draw. As a result, early game systems had very limited polygon 'budgets', and were able to display only 2,000 to 5,000 polygons per frame while drawing 30 frames per second. More modern machines like the Xbox, GameCube, and PlayStation2 have increased in power to the extent that they can easily draw more polygons per frame than there are pixels onscreen, resulting in near-perfect resolution, crisp images, and few visible polygon artifacts. Certainly the next step will be to use the ever-increasing computational power to draw more complex curved surfaces, but for now games still rely heavily on polygonal modeling (see Figure 4.20).

Since XSI is such a great tool to use for creating game content, there are a number of helpful tools (Like the Half-Life 2 Mod Maker and the Epic Unreal Actor X) to aid you in moving your work from XSI to the game engine. However, the portion of the process where the models are created, UV information is laid out, and texture maps are applied requires nothing more than XSI. For the most part, creating good clean game content out of polygons is all about keeping the geometry simple, using edges only where you need to make a visible change of contour, and staying within the specifications of the game engine. Of course, there is much more to creating game art, but let's focus on the basics of using polygons efficiently.

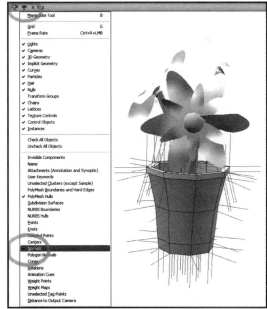

**Figure 4.20**
The Show menu is where you can toggle on different feedback options.

## Proper Number of Sides

By definition, a polygon has many sides. In fact, a polygon must have at least three sides, and in XSI it can have as many sides as you want. Using text curves to generate a polygon mesh, for instance, will create polygons with many, many edges to represent the outline of the letter properly. Game engines, however, have special needs. In order to make drawing polygons, texturing polygons, and lighting polygons fast, most game engines require that all the polygons have a consistent number of sides—usually three sides (called a triangle) or four sides (called a quad). If you plan to make game art, you need to keep this in mind, and where you build models containing polygons with five or more sides, you should tessellate those polygons into three and four sides. The first step is knowing which polygons have more than three or four sides.

Since looking by eye would be challenging and error-prone, there is a tool to show you all the polygons that meet certain criteria in the Select menu of the MCP. If you select a model and choose Select > Select N-Sided Polygons > Five Sides or More, XSI will highlight (select) all the polygons in your mesh that need attention (see Figure 4.21). Now you know which polygons you need to change, and you can use the Add Edge command to break them up into smaller polygons. XSI also has automated tools for converting (or tessellating) n-sided polygons. If you want to end up with triangles, select the object or just the polygons you wish to work on, and use the Modify > Poly Mesh > Triangulate command.

If you want quads, use the Modify > Poly Mesh > Quadrangulate command (see Figure 4.22). In many cases, the Quadrangulate automatic tool will not tessellate all the polygons you select, even after you adjust the rather cryptic controls in the PPG, and in some other cases it works but doesn't choose the best way to split the polygons for your particular model. There is no substitution for manually adding the edges you want .

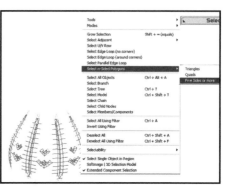

**Figure 4.21**
Use the Select tools to find bad polys.

## *Cleaning Up Imported Polymeshes*

Inevitably when doing work, you will need to use someone else's models. Either you will be importing models created in a different program or created by a different modeler, or you will be purchasing models for use from the Internet. Equally inevitably, those models will have problems when you look at them in XSI. XSI has a more rigorous definition of what constitutes proper geometry, so many models created in sloppy programs exhibit defects in XSI. Common problems are edges that are not shared between adjacent polygons, two (or more) identical polygons laying exactly on top of one another, infinitely skinny polygons where there should only be an edge, vertices that lay on one another and so are redundant, and adjacent polygons with normals flipped relative to one another.

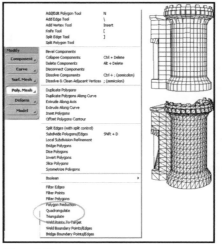

**Figure 4.22**
Use Triangulate and Quadrangulate to clean up your models.

**Figure 4.23**
The filter tools.

XSI has tools to correct these and other problems. These sorts of tools are called filters (see Figure 4.23). When you have a model imported, the first thing to do is check it out for problems and run a few filters on it. First, give yourself some feedback about the number of triangles and components in the selected model. Use the eyeball menu to open Show > Visibility options (Shift-S), and from the last tab, toggle on Stats > Show Selection Info. Now you have a nice heads-up display showing info on the selected object. Take note of the number of triangles. Also from the Show menu, toggle on Show > Polymesh Boundaries and Hard Edges. Orbit the model and look for telltale blue lines indicating unshared edges. These are bad. Let's filter them.

## Filter Points

Start by filtering the points. With the entire model selected, choose the Modify > Poly. Mesh > Filter Points command. Now use the Selection Explorer to open the FilterPointsByDistance PPG so we can make some changes. We want the operator to look at each point and its neighbors, and if they are too close together, maybe they are irrelevant to the model shape, or worse, they are laying on top of one another. The size of the model in SOFTIMAGE units will determine the proper distance setting. You can adjust the slider until you see the model change shape and the number of triangles in the Selection Info change, and then back up a bit. Note the change in the number of triangles from before and after applying the operator. If the number of triangles decreased, but no visible change to the model took place, there were bad polygons and vertices that were removed, because the Cleanup options in the FilterPointsByDistance PPG were toggled on.

## Filter Edges and Polygons

Next, use the Filter Edges command, also from the Modify > Poly. Mesh menu, and inspect its PPG. This tool collapses edges that are very short. Again, the scale of your model and the level of detail will determine the right setting for the Edge Length slider in the PPG. Adjust it while watching the triangles count and the model shape. Finally, filter the polygons with the Modify > Poly. Mesh > Filter Polygons command. Inspect the PPG. You can choose from two methods: Filter by Incidence Angle or Polygon Area.

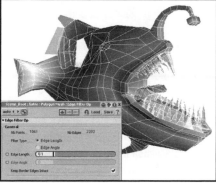

If you use the Polygon Area method, the operator looks for very small polygons and removes them. For instance, if you used Ctrl-D to duplicate a polygon and then moved the resulting poly only very slightly, you created border polygons with very small areas. This tool would remove them and connect the adjacent edges again. The polygon area method will also remove fine detail, so it is a way to reduce the polygon count of a model, too. The Incidence area method examines the angle at each edge between the polygon on one side of the edge and the polygon on the other. If the angle is very slight, the tool assumes that the feature defined by that edge is not very important, and the two polygons are combined into one. This will turn triangulated models into quadrangulated models where the pairs of triangles are close to co-planar. Be careful with this tool, as it can create n-sided polygons very easily. In fact, if you used the filter Points and Filter Edges tool, the Filter Polygons tool is not needed to clean up models. Finally, freeze your modeling operator stack to get rid of the filter operators. Now you have a clean model (see Figure 4.24).

**Figure 4.24**
Filtering can remove small polygons.

# Modeling with Subdivision Surfaces

Subdivision surfaces are a wonderful way to create organic models with sculptural detail and character. The best part is that you already know how to build SubDee models in XSI, because that's what you were doing in this chapter without even knowing it.

All polygon models are also subdee models in XSI, and the tools for working with them are the same. To see the subdee representation of the surface under a polygon model, just tap the + key on your numeric keypad (not the plus key next to the Backspace). XSI will show you the first-level subdivision model. Tap + again to see the second level of subdivision. Tap the - key (minus on the numeric keypad) to reduce the level of subdivision and head back toward a simple polygon object (see Figure 4.25). The plus and minus keys are really just changing the subdivision levels in the Geometry Approximation PPG, under the Polygon Mesh tab. If you inspect that PPG with the Selection Explorer, you can change the sliders yourself. It is also possible (and useful) to set one level of subdivision for modeling onscreen and another higher subdivision level for the renderer, so your objects automatically come out smooth and beautiful. You can continue to model on your objects while they are represented as subdees. Have fun!

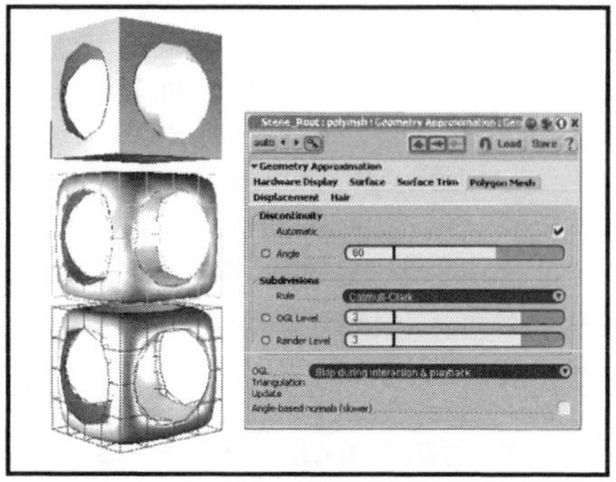

## Poly Tools for Games

Frequently when building game art, you will need to reduce the number of polygons that are used to represent the shape of a model. Even though modern game systems can push a lot of polies, there is no sense in leaving more polygons in an object than are really needed to represent the shape.

The XSI Polygon Reduction tool can help you here (see Figure 4.26).

You can apply the Polygon Reduction operator, interactively enter exactly the number of vertices and polygons you want to have in the finished model, and immediately see the results.

The Polygon Reduction tool will even make levels of detail! To use the Polygon Reduction tool, simply select the mesh you want to reduce and then apply the Poly Mesh Reduction operator by choosing the command Polygon Reduction from the Modify > Poly Mesh menu in the Model module. Locate the operator now on the poly mesh portion of your object's operator stack, and open that PPG to adjust the controls.

## Jellyfish: At a Glance

In this tutorial, you will learn:

◆ All about basic polygon modeling

◆ How to select polygons, edges, and vertices

◆ How to grow selections

◆ How to select loops of polygons

◆ How to sculpt shapes by transforming components

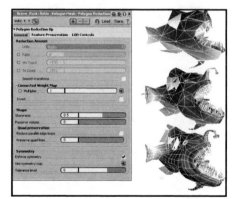

**Figure 4.25**
A polymesh hull and several levels of subdivision.

**Figure 4.26**
The Polygon Reduction tool is a gamer's friend.

◆ How to duplicate and extrude polygons and vertices

◆ How to extrude polygons along a curve

◆ How to smooth polygonal objects

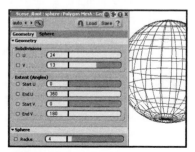

## Tutorial: Jellyfish

Our goal in this tutorial is to use the most basic polygon modeling tools in XSI to create a beautiful, elegant, and simple model, starting from a basic polygonal primitive (see Figure 4.27).

We'll duplicate polygons, edges, and vertices, we'll move polygons and components around singly and in groups, we'll add edges and vertices, and we'll extrude polygons along a curve. Starting from a polygon mesh sphere, we'll quickly create a very cool jellyfish that we can animate in an interesting way later on.

**Figure 4.27**
Simple polygon modeling applied.

We'll focus on sculpting the general shape of the jellyfish, creating tentacles and contours, without worrying too much about the finished surface. When we are done, we can adjust the smoothness of the polygon mesh to put the finishing touches on the jellyfish.

Remember, polygon modeling is a creative endeavor. There is no one correct way to do it. If you have ideas of your own that you want to try, please do experiment and improvise.

If you want to be able to get back to where you were before an experiment, duplicate your object and then hide it periodically as you go so you can always return to a previous version.

### Step 1: Start with a Simple Object and Then Refine It

Get a polygonal mesh sphere and open the Geometry property page. (Immediate mode must be off at this point.) We need to have enough detail around the equator of our jellyfish to pull out little bumps and nodules, but the sphere currently has only eight polygons around the middle, which is not enough.

We want a pattern of bumps around our jellyfish like this: little bump, twisted tendril, little bump.

This pattern will repeat eight times around the jellyfish, and there are three bumps and tendrils per pattern, so we'll need 8×3 or 24 subdivisions around the middle of the sphere. Set U to 24 in the Geometry Property Editor (PE).

Set the V subdivisions to 13 so we have enough detail in the sphere, from top to bottom, to work with (see Figure 4.28). The odd number (13) of subdivisions ensures that one row of polygons will go perfectly around the equator.

**Figure 4.28**
Add enough rows in U and V to make sculpting easy.

## Step 2: Freeze the Operator Stack Before Continuing

Now with the basic aphere ready to go, we no longer need to have an operator stack recording each move we make. So, freeze the sphere with the Freeze button and then turn on the Immediate mode toggle button near the bottom of the MCP. If you cannot see the Freeze and Immed buttons, expand the Edit stack in the MCP.

When Immediate mode is on, each move and tool will be frozen after it is completed, which will make our job faster and simpler. We can always turn Immediate mode back off at any time.

## Step 3: Make the Bell Shape of the Jellyfish.

Select three rows of polygons at the equator of the sphere using the polygon Select by Rectangle hotkey, which is Y. Now scale the three rows in Global Y to make them half as tall as they were. These will become the lip of the jellyfish. We want more fine detail here, so we made the rows smaller.

Deselect the rows using the Y hotkey and the middle mouse button so that you don't accidentally transform these polygons by mistake later on.

Now, tag all the points in the lower half of the jellyfish (not including the points around the very middle) and scale them in Object mode Y to completely invert the lower half inside the upper half.

Object mode means that the points will scale relative to the center of the sphere object.

One way to select these points is to tag the bottommost row and then grow the selection with Shift-+ (shift and the plus key).

Gently scale these same points in X and Z (hold down the left and right mouse buttons at the same time) to make the inside membrane slightly smaller inside the outer shell. Stop when the top row of tagged points is even with the bottom of the equator and untag just that top row, and then keep going. Untag all the points (T and the middle mouse button) when you are done turning the sphere inside out to form the jellyfish.

Now we want the bottom lip of the jellyfish to be fatter. We'll do this by selecting a loop of polygons at the bottom of the creature with the special Select-Loop-by-Raycast hotkey, and scaling up the loop. Orbit under the jellyfish and identify the rim of the shape, the bottommost row or loop of polygons. Hold U (Select Polygon by Raycast) and the Ctrl key, and then select two adjacent polygons in that loop. Magically, XSI will select the rest of the polygons in the loop. Now gently scale the loop so that the lip is fatter.

## Step 4: Add Some Detail to the Top of the Jellyfish

The top of a jellyfish has areas that are thicker, arranged in a star shape radiating from the center. On our jellyfish, we can do the same thing by selecting some polygons in a pattern and duplicating them, and then raising them up and out just a little bit. Using the polygon Select by Raycast hotkey U, select a stripe of four polygons, starting with the second from the top and extending down almost to the equator.

Our jellyfish will have six of these bumps, so repeat this pattern every fourth column. Refer to Figure 4.29 to get some ideas about neat patterns for this, and experiment with your own.

With these patterned polygons around the top half of the jellyfish bell selected, extrude them with the Extrude Polygon on Axis hotkey, which is Ctrl-D. This creates new polygons, which lay exactly on top of the other ones.

We need to move these new polygons a little bit. Activate the transform area of the MCP, and make sure that you are in Local transformation mode. When in Local mode, each group of polygons will move according to its own axes, which is often useful.

**Figure 4.29**
Select your own pattern if you wish.

Now, translate the selected polygons only in Y, which will move the polygons up and out from the center just a little ways. You may also scale these polygons down in X and Z slightly, also in Local mode.

We've just created contours like a topographical map. Don't worry about how blocky it looks now. It will become smooth later. Deselect all the polygons since we are done with them now (see Figure 4.30).

## Step 5: Pull Out the Underside of the Jellyfish

Using your best artistic judgment, select some polygons in the middle of the underside of the jellyfish and translate them in global Y to add more mass to the middle of the jellyfish.

Deselect those polygons, and then tag the point in the absolute middle of the bottom of the jellyfish. Translate the tagged point down in global Y just a bit. We want the middle of the bottom of the jellyfish to drop down a ways more, but we need more detail. When you extrude a tagged point, new edges and polygons are created that would give us more detail (see Figure 4.31).

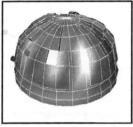

**Figure 4.30**
Extrude the pattern of selected faces to create contours.

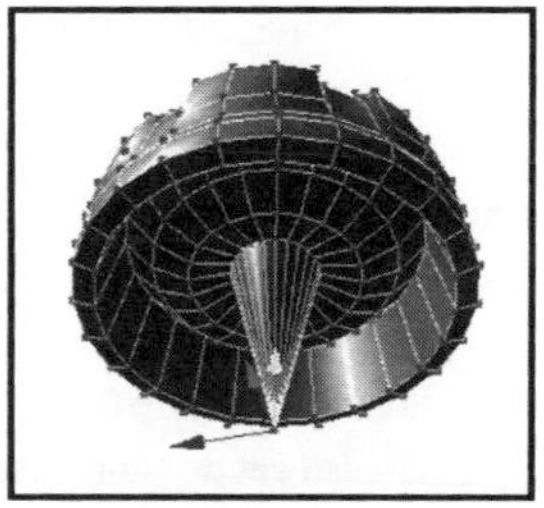

**Figure 4.31**
Extrude the selected polygons to create contours.

Extrude the tagged point with the Ctrl-D hotkey. Now move the selected center point down a little more, repeat the Ctrl-D action again, and move it down some more. Untag that point when you're done.

## Step 6: Add Some More Shape to the Bottom

We could add more detail to the polygons surrounding the bottom point we just pulled out to create some ridges that would look interesting. Look at the edges connected to the center point that we pulled in Step 5, and select every fourth one with the Select Edge by Raycast tool (hotkey I).

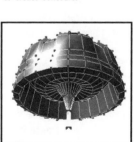

**Figure 4.32**
Extruding the center vertex adds more polygons.

When all six edges are selected extrude them just like we extruded the points and the polygons, with Ctrl-D. New edges, new points, and new polygons will be created. Translate these new edges in local Y to make them move out from the center just a little ways (see Figure 4.32).

## Step 7: Add Some Small Bumps and Tendrils

On the underside of the rim of the jellyfish, there are 24 polygons. We can use these to create small bumps and tendrils in the pattern bump-bump-tendril repeating around the rim (see Figure 4.33).

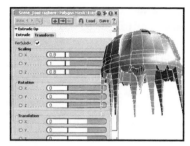

**Figure 4.33**
The longer fringe parts.

Select every third polygon and extrude it with Ctrl-D. Then translate it in local Y a little ways from the lip and scale it down a bit in local X and Z. This will make a small bump when it's finally smoothed.

Deselect these polygons, and select every third polygon next over along the rim. Repeat the extruding and scaling process, but make these bumps a different length and size.

Deselect those polygons, and select the remaining eight polygons of the lip. These we will extrude in a different way to make more interesting tendrils.

We want to adjust the properties of the tendrils after we execute the command, which would not be possible in Immediate mode, so turn off Immediate mode (see Figure 4.34). This means that when we do our extrusion, we'll get a property page for it where we can make changes (or even animate them).

**Figure 4.34**
Immediate mode keeps your operators manageable.

With Immediate mode off, execute the PolyMesh > Extrude Along Axis command in the Modify > Poly Mesh menu. You can also get this command by holding down the Alt key on your keyboard and left-clicking over one of the selected polygons.

The polygons will be extruded slightly, but we want to do much more. Search in the Selection button of the MCP to find the Extrude Op. Open it by clicking on the icon. In the Extrusion Op PPG, make sure that the Frame...Component radio button is on. That will transform each polygon relative to its own local axis and make it easier to control and more interesting.

Next, adjust the extrusion Length slider to about 4, and increase the number of subdivisions to 7 to make the tendril more detailed. In the Transform tab of the PPG, you can adjust how each subdivision of the extrusion is scaled, translated, or rotated. Adjust the rotate in Y to about 15 degrees, and make the scale in X and Z about .80, which means that each new segment in the extrusion will be 80% as big as the prior one. As you make these changes, you will be able to see the tendril grow and change.

Make sure you close the PE (Property Editor) and deselect the polygons at the ends of the tendrils before you move on (see Figure 4.35). Now we have nice bumps and tendrils around the rim of the jellyfish.

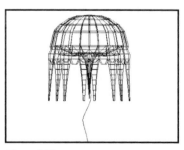

**Figure 4.35**
Extruding the tendrils without Immediate mode.

## Step 8: Make Four Larger Tentacles

Our jellyfish needs four larger, longer tentacles that will trail behind, contracting and expanding as the creature swims. These need to be animated eventually. The clever way to do this is to extrude some polygons from the base of the creature along a curve. Then the extrusion itself can be animated and the curve shape can be animated.

Examine the underside of your jellyfish (is it a boy or a girl?), and select four polygons (every sixth in a circle) somewhere near the middle of the underside.

We want these polygons to be quite flat in the XZ plane, so they extrude straight down. Make them flat by scaling them in Object Y. Then scale them slightly larger using Local X and Z, and translate them down a ways so they become good foundations for the tentacles (see Figure 4.36).

Using the Create > Curve > Draw Cubic by CVs NURBS curve tool, draw a serpentine curve in the Front view, starting at the global center with about six control points. This will become the shape of the tentacles, as shown in Figure 4.37.

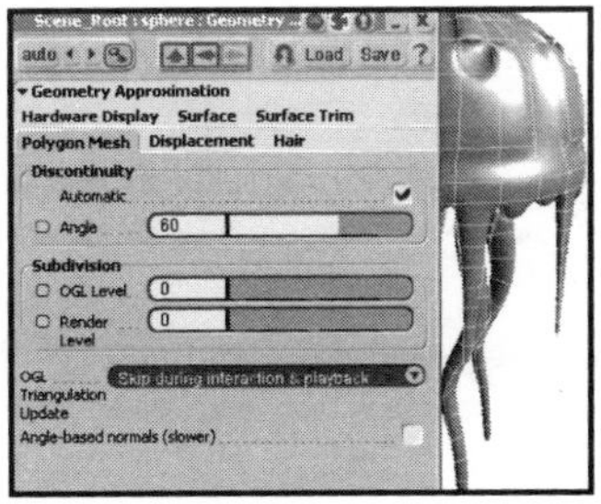

Select the jellyfish again and activate the polygon selection by tapping the U hotkey or by clicking on the Polygon filter button in the MCP.

Choose the Poly Mesh > Extrude Along Curve tool, and then pick on the curve to finish the command (see Figure 4.38), again, select the jellyfish as an object or enter Object mode, open the Extrude PE (there will be two now —we want the top one) and check that auto rotate is off and perpendicular is on.

Increase the number of subdivisions to 12 to make for a smoother tentacle, and again adjust the scale of each subdivision in the Transform tab to perhaps 0.9 in Scale X and Scale Z, with a small rotation in Y for additional interest.

Try out the End slider in the Extrude tab of the PPG to see that this makes the tentacles extend and contract. You could animate this later as the creature swims.

OK—we are done with the polygon modeling!

## Step 9: Smoothing the Surface

Select the jellyfish as an object, and in the Selection button, find the Geometry Approximation PE and open it. By default, the Geo Approximation property is shared with all objects. We want one specifically for the jellyfish, so in the dialog box, choose to create a local copy.

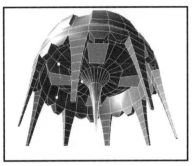

**Figure 4.36**
Here come the tendrils.

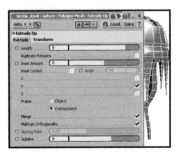

**Figure 4.37**
The NURBS curve will shape the tentacles.

**Figure 4.38**
The tentacles extruded on a curve.

**93**

In the Polygon Mesh tab, increase the Subdivision OpenGL Level to 1 and the Subdivision Render Level to 2. Then examine your jellyfish in the shaded view and the render region. The Geo Approx PPG can set different levels of smoothing for view onscreen and at render to make your interaction with the model faster, and the final render smoother.

It looks good (see Figure 4.39)! Apply a cool translucent material, and then save the jellyfish so you can animate it later.

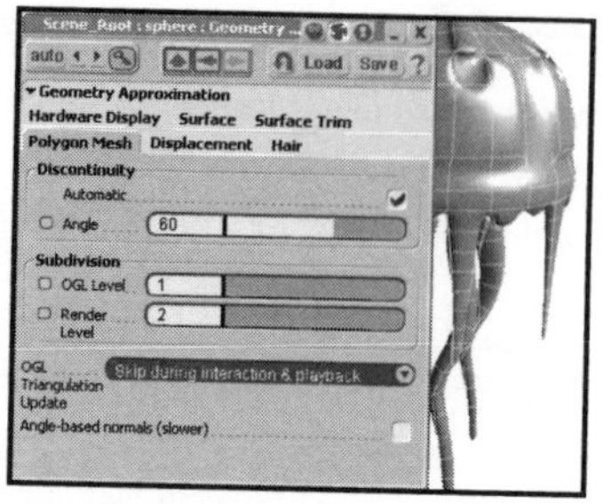

## Conclusion

The polygon toolset in XSI is fantastic. it brings a new level of sophistication and a standardized ease of use to both beginning and sophisticated polygon modelers. XSI's ability to work with vertices, edges, and polygons all in the same way certainly makes life much easier and more productive. On top of that, having Subdivision Surfaces so fully integrated—and in fact interchangeable with polygon objects—really makes the modelers work easier to work with, more productive, and more fun.

**Figure 4.39**
The smoothed jellyfish.

# Chapter 5
# Basic Animation and Keyframing

In this chapter, you will learn:

◆ Fundamental animation concepts and terminology

◆ How to start making animation by keyframing

◆ How to use the animation panel, the timeline, and the playback control

◆ How to use the Property editor to add and erase keyframes

◆ How to use the marking widget to selectively keyframe properties

◆ Techniques to enhance your animation

## Introduction

Animation can be a very complex endeavor, but by learning XSI's sophisticated animation tools, we can achieve any desired motion. In this chapter, we will learn basic keyframe animation concepts that are derived from traditional 2D animation. We will also cover how to apply these keyframing techniques to 3D animation, by utilizing XSI's many animation tools to create and preview animation (see Figure 5.1). SOFTIMAGE|XSI allows you to animate almost all parameters in the property page, which puts you in the director's chair giving you total control to move, pulsate, and morph anything you want.

**Figure 5.1**
Tools you'll use.

95

# What Is Animation?

Technically speaking, animation is the result of showing sequential images, one after another, at a sufficient rate that our eyes interpret the changes between the images as life and motion. This phenomenon is sometimes called persistence of vision, but it also includes elements of suspension of disbelief. Because we see the same objects in each frame, we intuit that those items actually exist in some reality between the frames. Good animation seems to live on well after the images stop flashing in front of our eyes.

The sequences of images in computer animation are called frames. A frame is the shortest unit of time in animation. The actual length of a frame is dependant on which media you are creating animation for. To create animation for the North American NTSC video format, you need 29.97 of these frames to represent one second's worth of animation. In other words, one frame is about one-thirtieth of second. European PAL format, on the other hand, displays 25 frames per second. Film requires 24 frames for a second.

Even though NTSC television can display about 30 frames per second, it is not completely necessary to have 30 different frames each second. Some frames can be held for much longer, to reduce production costs. That's why kids' animation on Saturday morning television seems so choppy.

Our second definition of animation comes from the fact that the word animate means "to give life to" and "make alive." Using this definition, animation is a technique for giving the illusion of life through the generation of a sequence of computer-generated images. Animation can invent new characters and imbue them with life, interest and vitality; it can stir emotion; and, of course, it can entertain. Bringing life through animation is easier said than done, but we will discuss some of the basic animation techniques later in this chapter.

# Basic Terminology

There are lots of ways to make animation, including hand-drawn (cel) animation, Stop-motion (such as Wallace and Gromit™ Claymation), and 3D computer animation. In hand-drawn animation, an animator creates key poses, or "key frames," to establish an important frame, by drawing the extreme poses. The frames between these key poses are later filled with in-between drawings. Imagine the Karate Kid (KK for short) practicing his high kick on the pole. An animator would create keyframe drawings by drawing KK with great concentration, just before he launches himself to kick. Then he or she will draw KK finishing his smooth kick. Later, another artist will fill the gaps between the two keyframes by drawing in-betweens. 3D computer animation is basically the same process, with two big differences. First, you set keyframes of KK's move, but instead of hiring some poor souls to do in-betweens for you, the computer churns out in-betweens by a process called interpolation. Filling the blank space between two keyframes is now done by a machine, which doesn't usually complain about performing endless, tedious tasks.

> Interpolation can be tweaked in many ways using the animation editor, to create the most satisfying in-between; see Chapter 11 for more information.

Second, 3D computer animation can create 3D sets and characters that enable an animator to light and compose the scene any way he or she desires, and change it at any time. Let's learn how to keyframe in XSI and start cranking out the animation!

# The Animation User Interface

The timeline is the tool that lets you move through time, by scrubbing along a range of frames. It looks like a slider bar with numbers, at the bottom of the interface. The red line on the timeline is called the playback head or the time slider, and it indicates the current frame. You can move the playback cursor by either clicking on the desired frame on the timeline, or by click-and-dragging it there. You can also use the arrow keys to change frames. The right arrow will move to the next frame, and the left arrow will move to the previous frame. The numbers in the boxes at the left and right of the timeline indicate the first and last frame of the timeline. You may type a number directly in these boxes to specify the range of your animation in frames. When you have animation on a selected object, you'll see red tick marks in the timeline at the nearest frame to the keyframe. These animation ticks give you feedback about animation timing (see Figure 5.2).

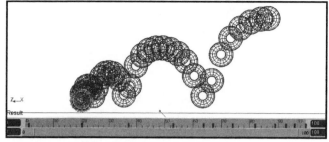

**Figure 5.2**
The timeline also shows keyframe ticks.

## *Playback Controls*

The playback control panel is for previewing your animation, using controls similar to a VCR, shown in Figure 5.3. Let's look at each icon from left to right.

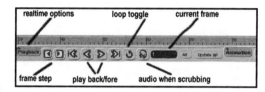

**Figure 5.3**
Playback control lets you preview your animation

◆ The button labeled Playback contains a drop-down menu with various playback option settings, most of which are found elsewhere in the playback control panel, such as First Frame (left playback arrow) and Play All Frames (the tiny button that toggles between All and RT for real time). The Playback button (or menu) also contains the Flipbook entry, which launches the Flipbook application for viewing rendered images or sequences of images.

◆ The pair of smaller arrows to the immediate right of the playback menu moves the current frame backward or forward.

◆ To the right of the next/previous frame arrows is a set of four larger arrows. Clicking on the first or last arrow (the ones with the vertical line next to them) will take you to the first or last frame, respectively. The inner two arrows are like the Play button on a VCR, except that one is play forward and the other is play in reverse.

◆ The icon with a thin, curved arrow is for loop play mode. If loop play is highlighted, when the animation reaches the end of the timeline, it simply goes back to start and plays all over again, until you manually stop it. The range of frames that will be looped is indicated with two yellow bars in the timeline. You can drag these loop end points to different frames to change the loop.

◆ The button with the headphone icon will toggle sound on and off while the animation is played.

◆ The dark gray box is very useful for hopping instantly to an exact frame. Instead of clicking on the timeline to select the frame you desire, you can just type the number in the box and press the Enter key.

◆ The button labeled All toggles between playing all frames or real-time playing. If you click on it, the icon will change to RT, for real-time, meaning that XSI will play the animation back at the speed you set (default is 30 frames per second), even if it has to skip frames to play that fast. The default is All, which means XSI will display all the frames, no matter how long it takes to update each frame. All is useful for checking the motion of your animation, while RT is useful for checking your timing.

◆ Using the Update All button, you can choose what kinds of objects will update during playback. Clicking this button toggles between Update All and Update Selected.

## The Animation Panel

The Animation panel is the strip of screen real estate directly to the right of the playback controls. It contains a number of buttons and menus to ease animation tasks. Let's take a tour through the Animation panel, from left to right (see Figure 5.4).

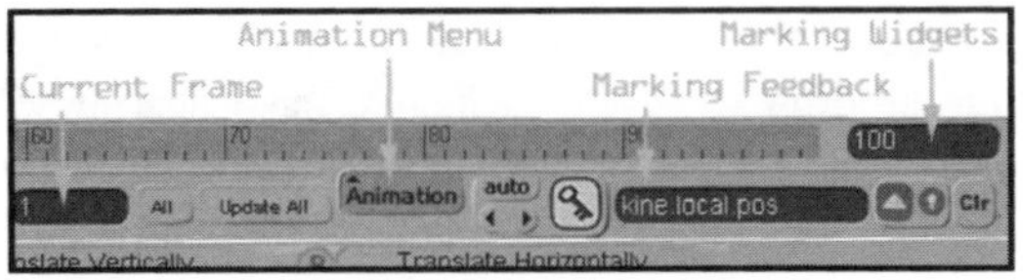

**Figure 5.4**
The Animation panel.

◆ The Animation button in the Animation panel opens a menu with many common animation commands, such as Set Key, Remove Key, Remove Animation, and Copy Animation.

◆ The auto button toggles the AutoKey function on and off. This function automatically sets a keyframe when you change any parameter on an object. It can be a timesaving device when you have to edit keyframes, but because it will set keys on its own, you'll probably end up with keys you don't want. Professionals leave this feature off.

◆ The two arrows below the AutoKey button will skip to the next and previous frame where the selected object has a keyframe already set on the currently marked parameter.

◆ The large button with a key icon is called the keyframe (or simply key) button, and it's used for adding a keyframe at the current frame. The key button won't be available until you select an element's animatable parameter or parameters. The key button can be four different colors, depending on the situation. If the keyframe button is gray, then there are no keyframes for the selected parameter. If it is green, there are keyframes for the selected parameter, but not at the current frame. If the key button is red, the current frame is a keyframe. If it is yellow, a change has been made to the selected parameter, but it has not yet been keyed. Simply click the key button to set a keyframe. (It will turn red.) Clicking the key button on an existing keyframe (where the button is already red) will remove the keyframe.

◆ The dark gray bar next to the key button is called the marked parameter display box, and it will show which parameter you have selected to keyframe. For example, if you selected the Local Transformation X parameter of the object, it will display kine.local.pos.posx. It looks confusing at first, but it will be very useful, as you become more familiar with it. If there is more than one parameter selected, it will display MULTI.

◆ The button with the triangle icon, to the right of the marked parameter display, is called the Marking List button. To mark a parameter, first you need to select an element you want to animate. Second, left-click on the Marking List icon, and a Property Explorer window will open, allowing you to choose which parameter you want to keyframe, such as the Pos (position) folder icon for translation or the Ori (orientation) folder icon for rotation. Just like in the Explorer view, left-click on the + and - signs to look for the property you want to keyframe. Left-click on the name of a parameter to mark it. You can click one more time to cancel the mark on a property. If you hold Shift, you can select multiple parameters to keyframe at once, which can be very convenient. An empty green box next to a parameter means that that parameter doesn't have keyframes set. As soon as you keyframe the parameter, the previously empty box will have a curve in it. It's a very quick way to distinguish which parameters have keyframes, and which don't.

◆ The button with the keyhole icon is for locking the marked parameter, so the particular parameter you want to keyframe stays marked. This tool is very useful to keep certain parameters marked even when you use the transformation menus (which would otherwise automatically become the marked parameter). To unlock the marked parameters, simply left-click on the keyhole icon again.

◆ The Clr button will clear any marked parameter, so no parameter is selected. If parameters are locked, the clear marked parameter icon simply doesn't work. Unlock parameters before using Clr. This icon only unmarks parameters; it won't delete existing keyframes.

The easiest way to mark parameters is to highlight the corresponding transformation cells in the MCP, which automatically marks that parameter to be keyframed. The only drawback to this method of marking parameters is that only scale, rotate, and translate have these large transformation cells. If you want to keyframe a more complicated parameter, such as material color or shape, you need to use the more complex methods of marking parameters, detailed.

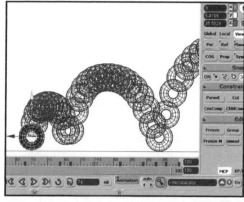

Figure 5.5
You can key with the Key icon.

# Keyframe Animation with XSI

To create animation in XSI, you need to set at least two keyframes on a parameter at different points in time. When a parameter has different saved values at two or more points in time, XSI will interpolate between the values, smoothly changing the parameter from one key to the next.

## Keyframing the Transforms in the MCP

To set simple keyframes on the scale, rotation, or translation of a selected object, just activate the transformation you want to key by clicking on the S, R, or T icons in the MCP, drag the timeslider to the point in time where you want to save a key, and click on the key icon in the Animation panel below the timeline (see Figure 5.5).

The hotkey shortcut for the key icon is K. Tapping K sets a keyframe on all the marked parameters (like scale, rotation, or translation) for the selected object or objects.

## Keyframing in a Property Page

You can also use the Property Editor to add and delete keys. You will notice that each Property Editor has, at the top of the PPG, exactly the same keyframe icon, auto-keyframe icon, and next/previous key icon (see Figure 5.6). Each animatable property also has a green box next to it, which is called the animation divot. You can click on this animation divot to add and remove keyframes.

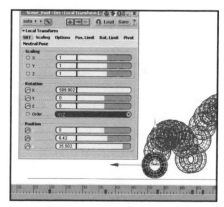

Figure 5.6
The same key icons are in each PPG.

You can keyframe using two different methods in the Property Editor. The first method, named marking, starts with highlighting the name of the parameter by left-clicking on it in the PPG (not the green box, but the name itself). The keyframe icon at the top right of the PPG lights up to indicate that properties are marked.

**99**

You may move the timeline to where you want and change the value of the parameter to your liking, and then just click on the keyframe icon, either in the PPG or the timeline at the bottom of the screen, to set a key at your current frame.

The second method is clicking on the green animation divot to the left of a property in the PPG. Clicking on the animation divot keys the parameter next to it at the current frame on the timeline. The green box will turn red with a curve inside it to indicate that a key exists at that frame, on that property of the selected object. By clicking one more time, the keyframe may be removed.

Each animatable parameter has a complete animation menu that applies only to itself. To see the Animation menu for a specific parameter, right-click on the green animation divot next to the parameter name. To open the Animation editor for a parameter (if it already has some keyframes), right-click over the animation divot and choose Animation editor from the context-sensitive drop menu.

## Clearing Keyframes

There are a few different ways to remove keyframes and animation. To remove a single keyframe, select the object in your scene, and mark the property that is animated with the Marking List icon. Or if you want to remove a transform key, just activate the appropriate transform. Move the timeline or use next/previous keyframe buttons until you come to the frame with the keyframe you want to delete. The keyframe icon at the bottom of the screen should be highlighted red to indicate that there is a key on that object, on the marked parameter at that frame. Click on the Animation menu button in the Animation panel and select Remove Key (Shift-K) from the menu. Voilà, that particular keyframe is removed!

If you choose Animation > Remove Animation > From All Parameters instead of Remove Key, it will remove all the keyframes of the marked property, in addition to expressions. The Property Editor also lets you remove individual keyframes and animation.

If you open a Property Editor, you can use the Next/Previous triangles at the top-left corner of the PPG to scroll through all the frames where there is a key on any one of the properties in the PPG. You can also scrub in the timeline to get to a specific frame, watching for the key icon in the PPG to turn red, indicating that a key exists on a parameter in that PPG. Right-click on the keyframe icon at the top of the Property Editor. Choose Remove Key to remove each of the keys on the parameters at the current frame, or choose Remove Animation to remove all keyframes from all the properties in the PPG. The keyframe options under the key icon at the top of each PPG apply to all parameters in the PG and do not require that the parameters be marked first (see Figure 5.7).

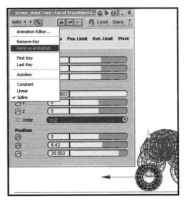

**Figure 5.7**
You can remove the animation from a marked parameter.

# The Keyable Parameters Layout

XSI has a nice, convenient user interface element that groups all your keyframing tasks into one convenient place, called the Keyable Parameters Layout. At the bottom of the MCP on the lower-right corner of the UI there are two buttons, one marked MCP and the other marked KP/L. These toggle back and forth between the Main Control Panel and the Keyable Parameters Layout (see Figure 5.8). Click the KP/L button to hide the MCP and show the KP/L.

When you select an object, the KP/L shows a list of keyable parameters, with their names and their animation divots organized in a stack.

The stack is divided up by the Property page that the parameters come from, and each of these dividers will roll up and collapse to save screen real estate when you left-click on the title bar. If you left-click into the numeric area and drag left to right, you'll change the value of the parameter up or down. For instance, if you click in the Position X number area and drag left to right, you'll move the object along its local X-axis. You can also directly enter numbers into the KP/L. For instance, if you click once on the Position X cell, type a number 0 into it, and then press Enter, the selected object will return to 0 along the global X-axis. You can also click on the left- and right-pointing triangles on either side of the numeric input area to increment or decrement the values.

**Figure 5.8**
The Keyable Parameters Layout.

If you left-click on a number and drag up or down three or more rows, you'll marquee-select a number of keyable parameters, and then numeric entry will apply to all of them.

This is an easy way to set all the scales to 1 or all the positions to 0.

You can, of course, also use the KP/L to set keyframes. If you left-click on the animation divot next to a parameter name, if behaves just as the animation divot does in a Property page. There are even auto, next/previous, and a keyframe buttons at the top of the KP/L, just like in the Property pages (see Figure 5.9).

One area where the KP/L is very different from the Property pages is in what properties are *in* the KP/L. While you have no control over what properties are in the prebuilt PPGs, you *can* determine what properties are in the KP/L. By default, the transformations are in the KP/L, but you can add to the list by clicking on the Parameters button at the top left of the KP/L and choosing the Keyable Parameters Editor option near the bottom of the pop-up menu. This displays a floating dialog box with a list of all the possible keyable parameters on the currently selected object or objects on the left, and the list of those parameters currently in the KP/L on the right. As you select items on the left side and click the Add button to add them to the right pane, they appear in the KP/L for you to animate with.

You can also mark multiple parameters in the KP/L by clicking on their names and then perform other animation tasks, like removing animation or locking values, through the KP/L Parameters menu.

**Figure 5.9**
More animation features are available from the KP/L Parameters menu.

# Practice Time

Let's practice using these tools by keyframing some simple movements.

1. Click on File > New Scene to clear up your previous work.

2. Click on Get > Primitive > Surface > Sphere to create a NURBS sphere, or Get > Primitive > Polygon Mesh > Soccer Ball if you are more adventurous. Close the property window (if it pops up) by clicking on the X button at the top right of the window.

3. Switch the right-side UI from MCP to KP/L with the little view switchers at the bottom-right side. If the sphere is selected, you'll see a stack of parameters labeled Local Transform, with Position, Rotation, and Scaling listed underneath. Mark the position of the sphere by Shift-clicking on Position X, Position Y, and Position Z. All the names will all turn yellow and stay yellow. You may also mark the position parameters by activating the Position transformation tool, by holding or tapping V on your keyboard (see Figure 5.10).

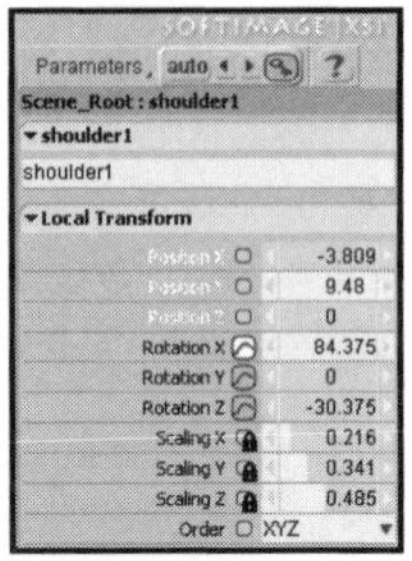

**Figure 5.10**
In this example, Pos (Position) is marked. kine.local.pos appears in the marked-parameter display.

4. Set the current frame to 1 by typing 1 in the box below the timeline (to the right of the headphone icon), or simply click-and-drag the red line on the timeline to the far left.

5. Click on the keyframe icon, either in the timeline or at the top of the KP/L, to key the position of the sphere at frame 1. You noticed the keyframe icon is now colored red. That means there is a keyframe for the marked parameter (local translation, in this case) at the current frame. A red tick mark will also appear in the timeline at the first frame to show you where the key is.

6. Move the current frame to 30. The key icons turn green; this means that a keyframe exists for Position, but not at the current frame.

7. Move the sphere by typing 5 in the Position X box of the KP/L, or just activate the Translation manipulator with V on your keyboard and drag the ball to the right manually. The key icon now turns yellow to indicate that the parameter has been changed since the last keyframe.

8. Let's key again, but this time use the hotkey K on your keyboard.

9. Change the timeline to frame 60, and set a new keyframe, this time using the Property Editor. Switch back from the KP/L to the MCP. Open a Property Editor for local transformation, either by clicking on the Selection button in the MCP and choosing Local Transform, or by right-clicking or Alt-right-clicking the soccer ball in Explorer or Schematic view and selecting Properties > Animation.

You will see that the Position parameters X, Y, and Z all have a green divot with a curve. Click on the green divot to the left of the X-axis slider. The X-axis position parameter is now keyframed. You can key more than one parameter at a time by marking the parameters to key. Left-click on the name (as opposed to the animation divot) of the Position in X parameter (the small x in the PPG) and then Shift-click the Position Y and Z parameters to add them to the marking list; their names now highlighted in yellow.

Left-click once on the keyframe icon at the top of the Property Editor. Now the Y- and Z-axes are keyframed. X, Y, and Z in the Position column should have a red box (see Figure 5.11). Use any of the previous methods to set keys for the position of the soccer ball at several different frames along the timeline.

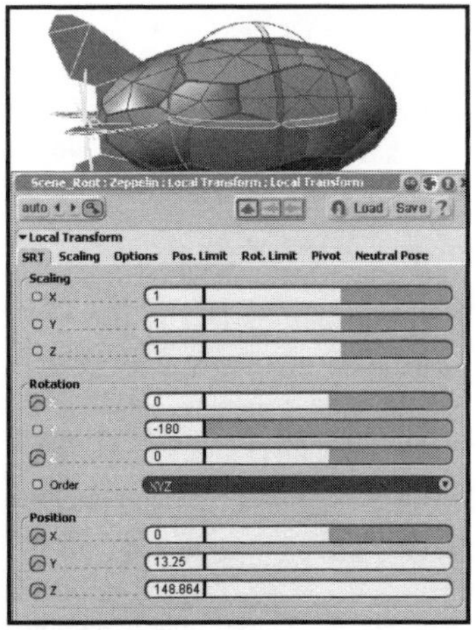

**Figure 5.11**
The animation divot with a curve means that parameter has keyframes set. This object has keyframes set for its position in the X-, Y-, and Z-axes.

Congratulations! Try playing your first animation. To view this animation, you need to use the playback control. Do you see the sphere moving? Change the last frame to 60 by typing 60 in the box on the far right of the timeline, and click on the loop button. Then click the Play Forward button to see your animation play over and over again. Click the same Play Forward button again to stop when you are tired of looking at a ball move.

## The Nautilus: At A Glance

Now, it's time to assemble a simple model with moving parts and animate it. We will put together the Nautilus from Jules Verne's *20,000 Leagues Under the Sea*, adding propellers and flying it through an undersea canyon. This tutorial will make you familiar with various animation tools in XSI (see Figure 5.12).

You'll learn how to:

◆ Assemble a hierarchy for animation

◆ Set keys on the sub using the MCP and timeline

◆ Set keys on the sub using the Animation panel (KP/L)

◆ Preview your animation using the playback control

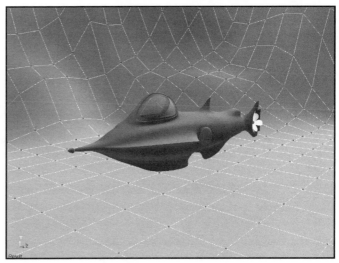

**Figure 5.12**
The finished Nautilus submarine.

## Tutorial: The Nautilus

We are going to assemble a submarine with a rudder and spinning propellers. The hierarchy technique we learned in the previous chapter will help our animation tremendously.

### Assemble the Nautilus

The Nautilus is a simple model constructed of four parts: the hull, the rudder, a prop shaft, and propeller blades. Your first steps will be to assemble these parts into a hierarchy so you can easily animate the whole sub, just the rudder, swinging back and forth, or just the prop blades spinning.

#### Step 1: Clear the Slate and Load the Start Scene

Open the nautilus_start scene from the courseware that accompanies this book. Take a look at the objects in the scene. The hull of the sub is named Nautilus_Hull. The rudder for the sub is a separate object, and the propeller shaft and propeller blades are separate objects. We'll need to get all of them into one hierarchy in order to animate it.

**103**

## Step 2: Assemble the Pieces Into a Hierarchy

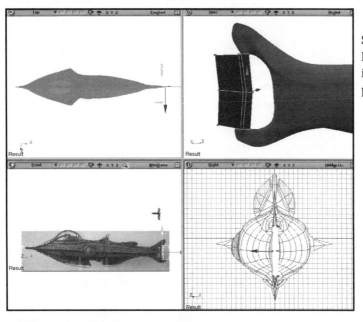

Select the rudder, and place it where it should be, in the tail area of the Nautilus. Select the rudder and rotate it around the local Y-axis, verifying that it swings back and forth as you want it to. When you like it, make the hull the parent of the rudder with the Parent button.

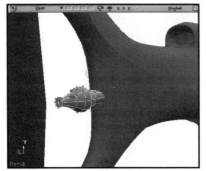

Now move the prop_shaft to a proper spot sticking into the hull and behind the rudder. Move the prop blades, too, to match the images.

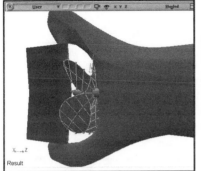

Now simply build the pieces into a workable hierarchy, with the prop blades children of the prop shaft, and the Nautilus_hull the parent of both the shaft and the rudder. You can use the Parent button in the MCP, or you can drag and drop one object onto another in the Explorer.

## Maiden Voyage

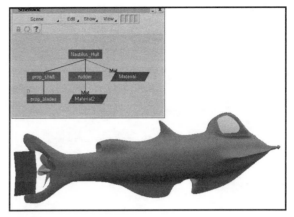

**Figure 5.13**
The finished Nautilus hierarchy.

Once the Nautilus is set up with a proper hierarchy (see Figure 5.13), animation can begin. Keep in mind that to select a node and all its children, you use the spacebar and the right mouse button. Select the Nautilus in Branch mode and move it to the beginning of the underwater canyon.

Our game plan for the animation will be to lay down parts of the animation one at a time, like laying down musical tracks. First we'll set just the translation keys, moving the sub through the canyon. Then we'll add keys on the rotation of the sub, so it aims correctly as it negotiates the twists and turns. Finally we'll add some rotation keys on the propeller.

Make sure that the hull is selected, and that the Translation cells are illuminated in the MCP. Also ensure that the timeslider is set to the first frame of the sequence. Then click the Key button below the timeline.

Change the timeslider by dragging the red current frame indicator to frame 10, select the Nautilus, and move it a few sub lengths down the canyon, aiming for the low spot. The easiest way to do this is to frame the sub in the top view and use the View mode of the Transform tool. This way you can freely drag the sub where you want it to go.

**105**

Set another keyframe, this time with the K hotkey.

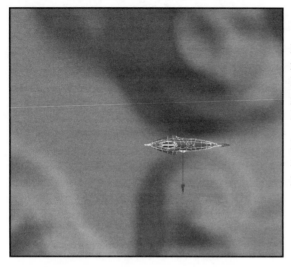

Proceed onward, moving the timeslider, moving the Nautilus, and then setting a key, in five-frame increments. Keep on moving the sub all the way through the canyon to the end. Play back the animation, watching the progress of the sub in the top view. For extra credit, you can get a new camera, place it behind the sub, and then make the camera root the child of the hull. Now when you view the animation through the camera, you will follow behind the sub.

If you see the sub crossing into the floor or walls of the canyon, drag the timeslider to the nearest key, indicated in red on the timeline. Drag the sub to a different position, and then press the K hotkey again to save the change.

## Step 3: Add Rotation

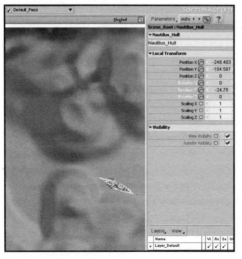

You'll note when you play back the animation that the sub looks odd because it does not turn to face in the direction it is moving. You can correct this by setting keys on the rotation of the sub. We'll want to do this in the top view, and we'll use the Keyable Parameters Layout, or KP/L for short.

Switch to the KP/L with the switcher at the bottom of the MCP, and maximize the top view.

Since you cannot see the rotation menu cells when you are looking at the KP/L, you'll have to use the transform hotkeys—X, C, and V for scaling, rotation, and translation. Select the Nautilus hull in Branch mode (or you'll leave parts behind). Then hold the C hotkey, and point the sub in the direction it is traveling in by rotating it around the Y-axis. Then mark the rotation parameters—Rotation X, Y, and Z in the KP/L—by Shift-clicking on the names. This tells XSI to set keys on these parameters when you click the Key button. Click the Key button at the top right of the KP/L, or click on the Parameters menu and choose the Key menu option.

Drag the timeslider further until you think the sub needs to make a turn, use the C hotkey to change the orientation, and set a new key.

Repeat until the Nautilus reaches the end of the trench. You can always set individual keys on parameters by clicking on the tiny animation divot next to the name of the parameter you want to key in the KP/L.

## Step 4: Spin the Prop

You can now add the final touches to the animation by keyframing the prop rotation. Change one of your viewports to the User view mode, and at frame 1, zoom in on the prop blades by selecting them and using the Frame All hotkey, Shift-F.

Switch back to the MCP, and with the prop blades selected, activate the rotations. Then click on the Add mode button under the transform cells. The Add rotation mode has two benefits. First, with Add mode you can rotate the prop more than 360 degrees. Second, and even better, you can keyframe a single rotation axis, which in this case was Rotation X. Click just the red Rot X button in the MCP, and set a keyframe on the prop.

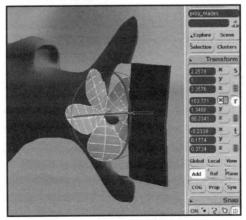

Drag the timeslider to the last frame of the animation. Verify that you have just the Rot X marked, and set the X rotation to 5000 degrees.

Set one last key.

Play back your work.

## Conclusion

You learned basic keyframe animation principles using XSI's animation interfaces. You chose which parameter to keyframe by highlighting a transformation parameter in the MCP and in the Keyable Parameter Layout (KP/L).

# Animation Techniques and Terminology

We owe a lot to the Disney animators of the 1940s and 1950s. There at the Disney studio, extremely talented animators applied real-world physics to their animation and sharpened the acting skill of characters to tell stories effectively. These techniques are still very applicable to 3D computer animation. Let's discuss some of them so you can use them later in your animation.

You can try to apply these theories right away, but when you become more familiar with the animation tools of XSI, especially the Dopesheet and Animation editor that you will study in Chapter 11, these principles will immensely improve the quality of your work.

A list of books to further study technique follows this section.

## The Law of Inertia

Even if you are creating cartoon-style animation, it is vital to follow the basic physical law of inertia to suspend the disbelief of your audience. The law of inertia states that objects in motion tend to stay in motion, and objects at rest tend to stay at rest. Imagine you are on a subway train. When the train leaves the station, your body will try to remain still, so you have a feeling of being pushed backward. When the train stops, your body remains moving and will tip forward. The same law applies to a human body. If you animate Bruce Lee punching Mr. T in the face, you won't animate Mr. T's whole body being punched back at once, because his body will try to remain at the same position. First his head will be punched back, his upper body will follow, and finally his lower body will be pulled away by the upper body.

## Squash and Stretch

Squash and stretch is exaggerating the change in shape of a moving object, while keeping the volume of the object constant. A ball bouncing is a good example. When a ball hits the ground, it will squash flatter to the ground to show that the mass of the ball is pushing itself down, deforming the ball. When it bounces back up, it will stretch to show the elasticity of the ball pulling it back to the original shape. In fact, it will overshoot its original shape to briefly become taller and thinner than normal (see Figure 5.14).

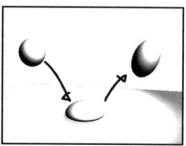

**Figure 5.14**
Exaggerated squash and stretch.

## Anticipation

Anticipation happens when the action requires a shift in the center of gravity. Imagine a warrior with a huge war hammer, that he is trying to swing over a goblin's head. To deliver a powerful blow, he can't just swing the hammer from above his head. He must draw back and then swing the hammer forward using his whole body. The backward motion is called anticipation. It helps to emphasize the action by charging up potential kinetic energy, as shown in Figure 5.15.

**Figure 5.15**
Anticipation helps create more believable motion.

## Overlapping Action

When a character moves, no parts should arrive at the new spot at once. For example, if a character raises his hand, his arm will reach above his head first, and then his hand will straighten up. It's because the movement of his arm is motivating the motion of his hand. The law of inertia is at work here. This multiple movement is called over-lapping action. Delay in the action is called secondary action, discussed next.

## Secondary Action

Secondary action refers to the delay in the overlapping action of a secondary object that is following the animation of a primary object, such as a picture frame tilting when a door slams, or a little girl's pig-tails bobbing as she skips down the street. Secondary actions are the details that make animation realistic and convincing.

## Follow-Through

Follow-through is a close relative of anticipation. It is the motion after the action, where anticipation is the motion before it. When our burly warrior's war hammer makes contact with the poor goblin's cranium, the hammer doesn't just stop. Again, the law of inertia is at work. The hammer tends to stay in motion until the friction of the surrounding world (the warrior's pull, the goblin's head, the ground, etc.) is enough to stop it.

## Silhouetting a Strong Pose

When you set up a keyframe pose, make sure that pose could be easily read if the pose were converted to a silhouette. You want the audience to immediately recognize your character's current action, so it is very important to create visually strong poses (see Figure 5.16).

## Timing

Without good timing, you will not be able to create convincing animation. Good timing can only be achieved by daily study of movies, sports, theatre, and simple everyday life all around you. When you have a good chunk of time to kill, carry your sketchpad and stopwatch and time how long certain actions take. You can time how many seconds it takes a person to walk onto the train, take a bite out of a hamburger, wave at a taxi, or anything else you can think of.

**Figure 5.16**
Silhouetting is a good way to check if a particular pose is easily read.

Studying pantomimes like Charlie Chaplin extensively will also enlighten you as to how the great actor communicates with his audience through timing and exaggerated and expressive poses.

# Conclusion

In this chapter, you learned some basic principles and terminology of animation and several methods of setting keyframes in XSI. You learned a whole new set of tools, such as the Animation panel, the timeline, and the playback control, to keyframe and preview your first animation. Comprehension of the tools and principles covered in this chapter will be very important later, when you work on more complex animation sequences.

## *Bibliography and Suggested Reading*

Blair, Preston. *Cartoon Animation*. Laguna Hills, California: Walter Foster Publishing, Inc, 1994—Greatest exercise book about cartoon animation. Lots of theories and techniques are discussed in this visual treasure.

Culhane, Shamus. *Animation from Script to Screen*. New York: St. Martin's Press, 1988—Insightful book about the animation process. Lots of text, but extremely well-written.

Thomas, Frank and Ollie Johnston. *Disney Animation: The Illusion of Life*. New York: Abbeville Press, 1981—This is the most important book to get.

White, Tony. *The Animator's Workbook*. Watson-Guptil Publications, 1988—Wonderful practical book for working animators from the guy who did the Pink Panther, among much other work.

# Chapter 6
# Materials, Lighting, and Rendering

In this lesson, you will learn:

◆ How to apply materials (surface shader) to objects

◆ What shading models are

◆ How to use render region to preview only one section of your scene

◆ How to light a scene effectively

◆ How to set up the camera for rendering

◆ How to render a file, and render settings

◆ How to use Flipbook and Image Clip Editor

## Introduction

To make your scene realistic or just to give it the look you want, you have to add light, color, and texture to your characters and sets. In this chapter, we will discuss various tools to create surface color, edit characteristics such as transparency and shininess, and add basic lighting techniques, to really make your

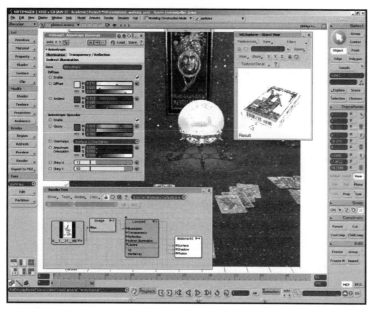

**Figure 6.1**
Tools you'll use.

scene come alive. We will also explore rendering techniques to region-render, create a single picture, and then create successive rendered images. In the end, we will discuss how to preview those images as a movie. Let's begin with coloring an object (see Figures 6.1 and 6.2).

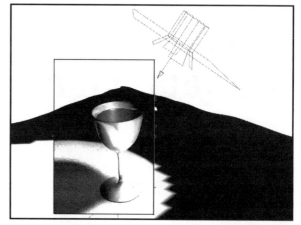

**Figure 6.2**
Ready to render?

## Surface Shader

When you want to color a 3D object, you will apply a surface shader to it. A shader is simply a description of what the surface should look like (see Figure 6.3). A shader can be as simple as the Constant shader, which makes the entire surface one solid color, or more complex, including transparency, reflectivity, and self-luminance. New shaders are written all the time to describe certain surfaces more accurately. For instance, special shaders exist to make accurate metals, gemstones, or even shimmering nebulas of light and energy.

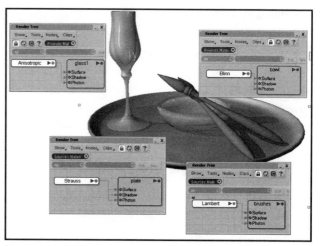

**Figure 6.3**
Shaders determine the surface appearance.

XSI ships with a useful variety of surface shaders, including the aforementioned constant, Lambert (good for dull objects), Phong (good for plastics), Strauss (good for metals), and a lot more. Each shader has options to vary the results. By opening up the Material PPG, you can assign different values to surface shaders to represent different colors, and other characteristics such as shininess, transparency, and reflectivity. We will discuss how to edit shader attributes later.

Surface shaders also consider the light sources in the scene, to give surfaces characteristics depending on where lights are relative to an object and which way the object's normals are facing (see Figure 6.4). You can see the surface normals, which are represented by thin blue lines, by selecting an object and choosing Show > Normals (that's the Eye menu) in the top menu bar. The blue lines' direction indicate which direction the surface is facing. The area of the surface facing more directly toward lights will be brighter than the areas facing away from the lights.

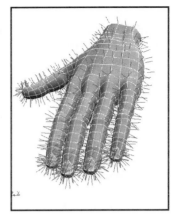

**Figure 6.4**
Surface normals indicate which side is facing out.

## Default Surface Shader

Newly created 3D objects start with a default surface shader. As soon as you create any primitive object, it has a shiny gray color when rendered or viewed in Shaded mode. This one default shader is shared by *all* objects that don't have their own material, so changing the color of one object with the default shader changes the color of all of them.

You can take a look at this surface shader by selecting an object and clicking on the Selection button on the MCP. There will be a property called Scene_Material, and cascaded under that, folders for Surface, Shadow, and Photon. Under those properties, there is a default surface shader called Phong. Clicking on the Phong node in the Property Explorer will prompt you to create a new copy of the Scene_Material s urface shader just for the selected object instead of editing the default Phong node that is shared among all new objects in the scene (see Figure 6.5).

By copying the default shader, you can change the color or other characteristics without having to worry about affecting other objects. Generally speaking, it is not a good idea to edit the default Phong node, since that is the color inherited by all newly created elements.

Therefore, let's try the next method to view and edit a Shader property page.

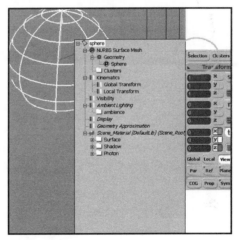

**Figure 6.5**
You can edit shaders using this window.

## Creating a New Surface Shader

You can create a whole new surface shader by selecting the object and choosing Get > Material in the toolbar at the left. The Get > Material menu has different material shaders that are appropriate for different uses. Those uses are enumerated later in this chapter.

Since all the shaders except for the Real Time shaders (not covered in this book) must be rendered to be seen, draw a render region around the selected object, by holding the Q hotkey and dragging a rectangle from top left to bottom right around the object. This invokes the mental ray renderer, and uses the shader on the object and the lights in the scene to draw an accurate image to your screen. As you edit the shader properties, the render region will refresh, showing you the changes.

If you have the preference for auto-pop-up property editors on and then choose the Get > Material > Phong menu command, a Shader property editor will open. This will allow you to change the many characteristics of the surface shader (see Figure 6.6). If you need to manually open the Shader property editor, you can choose that property from the Selection Explorer, but it may be easier to use the Modify > Shader button in the Render module, which achieves the same result.

The Shader property page has a keyframe tool like any other property editor, at the top left. It has an Undo button and Load and Save Presets buttons at the top right. There are three property tabs for all the types of material shaders—Illumination, Transparency/Reflection, and Indirect Illumination—which will be discussed following an explanation of how to set color values.

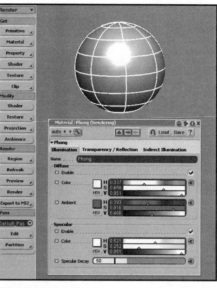

Figure 6.6
Basic Phong shading model.

## The Illumination Tab

Diffuse color controls the color of the surface that is illuminated by the lights in your scene. If you want your object to be red, set its diffuse color to red. One thing to keep in mind is that if the color of the light is something other than white, the final render will mix the color of the light and the diffuse color of the object. This is mainly what you will see in your rendered scene.

Ambient color is the shadowed area of an object. XSI sets a default ambient value of 0.3 (30% gray). Frequently, you will want to set the ambient color darker than that, to create a crisper shadow area (see Figure 6.7). An advanced technique is to set the ambient color to a different hue than the diffuse color, with a darker value and a greater saturation. This makes more complex, subtle colors across different areas of the surface.

Figure 6.7
Keep your global ambience very low.

Specular color is the hot highlight area found on shiny objects. One parameter unique to specularity is the Specular Decay slider. The higher the Specular Decay value, the smaller the shiny spot. Non-metallic shiny materials, such as plastic and porcelain, tend to have smaller specular spots compared to rough metal, which has a broader specular area. Different shaders treat specularity in different ways. The Lambert shader has no specularity at all, the Phong shader makes perfectly round specular dots, and the Anisotropic shader can make specular highlights that follow the contours of the surface. Humans use the shape of the specular highlight to tell more about the shape and texture of the surface. Water and glass have very sharp, hard, shiny specular highlights that follow the curves of the surface. Skin has little or no specular highlight.

## Editing Color Boxes

You can change colors by dragging the sliders on the color bars. The default method of selecting a color is by editing individual RGB (Red/Green/Blue) values. This method is not particularly intuitive, and there is no easy way to make the color lighter or darker after you choose the hue. Instead, you can use the HSV (Hue/Saturation/Value) editing method, by clicking twice on the RGB button to the left of the slider (see Figure 6.8). The HSV method can achieve a desired color faster and more accurately than the RGB method.

Hue is the color's location in the spectrum, from red to violet. Saturation refers to the intensity of the color. For example, sky blue and powder blue are approximately the same hue, with different levels of saturation. Value is how light or dark a color is.

You can also edit a color by clicking on the color box to the left of the slider, which opens a small window with a color chart and various tool buttons. You can click on any color in the editor to choose a color. You can also pick any color from your scene by using the color picker (eyedropper button) located on the bottom left of the window. The ... button expands the window, giving you more selection options, tools, and feedback.

Another great use of the color boxes is that you can copy a color from one color box to another simply by click-and-dragging the color chip (colored box) you want to copy on top of the box you want it copied to.

## The Transparency/Reflection Tab

Transparency controls whether you can see through the object and exactly how "see-through" it is. When you are in HSV edit mode, you can make the object more transparent simply by dragging the V (value) slider to the right. If you are editing in RGB mode, you can actually control how transparent each color component is. If you are using the RGB color system, you can change all three sliders by holding Ctrl while dragging one slider.

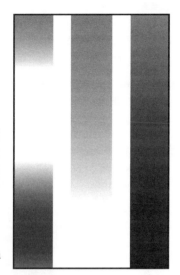

**Figure 6.8**
Hue/Saturation/Value is a natural way to describe color.

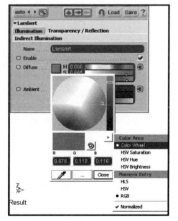

**Figure 6.9**
You can use the color wheel to pick colors.

**115**

Diffuse color and other surface characteristics are lost if you make the object too transparent. Transparency value 0 is a totally opaque object, and value 1 is an absolutely transparent object (see Figure 6.10). You need to render or preview to see the transparency accurately.

Index of refraction controls the refractive property of the object. Refraction is the bending of light through a transparent object. When you put a straw in a glass of water, it appears to bend at the point where it enters the water. Water is denser than air, causing the light to travel through it at a different angle. The default refraction index is 1, which is the density of air (see Figure 6.11). The refraction slider is very sensitive, so you probably won't need to slide it very much to get the desired effect. 1.3 approximates the density of water. Diamond has an index of refraction of 2.2. XSI calculates refraction by casting additional rays (secondary rays) from the point on the surface where the initial ray first hits it. This can create very accurate results, but accuracy requires that you increase the ray depth from the default of 2 to the number of surfaces you want the ray to bend through (usually 4 will do). You can set this in the Render module, in Render Options under the Optimization tab. Increase the raytracing depth refraction, and then make sure that the maximum ray depth is equal to or greater than the refraction depth you set.

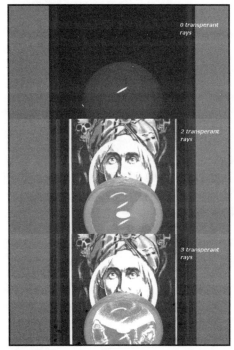

**Figure 6.10**
Make your objects transparent.

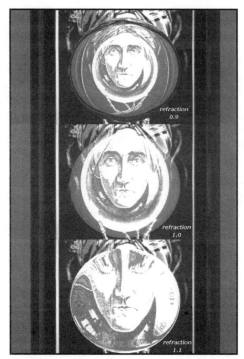

**Figure 6.11**
Refraction bends rays that travel through objects.

Reflection controls how reflective an object is. When an object is not at all reflective, the color of the surface is taken entirely from the Diffuse, Ambient, and Specular color. As the object becomes more reflective, the color of the surface becomes blended with the color of the objects surrounding it. When the slider is 1, the object is completely reflective, like a pristine mirror. XSI calculates reflection by casting at least one additional ray from the surface to the rest of your scene (see Figure 6.12).

Be aware that use of transparency, refraction, and reflection can increase rendering time considerably, since XSI will have to cast many more rays to accurately pick up all the detail from the surrounding objects. In XSI, objects are self-reflecting and refracting for additional accuracy.

## The Indirect Illumination Tab

Translucency adds a thin, silk-like surface appearance. By moving the Translucency slider to the right, you add diffuse color to the far edge of the ambient color, creating a semitransparent look. The translucency changes with the direction and distance to the lights. If you put a light directly inside a translucent object, it will glow beautifully.

Incandescence gives the appearance of a light source within the object, even if no lights are in the scene. You can specify a color, and the Intensity slider will control how much internal glow the object has. Incandescence simulates an object that is self-illuminating, like a fluorescent tube or a firefly. If you want glowing buttons, this is for you.

The Global Illumination/Caustics/Final Gathering portion of the PPG is for adjusting illumination levels in indirect lighting situations, which is not covered in this book.

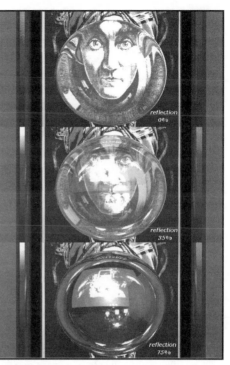

**Figure 6.12**
Reflection bounces rays to reveal the surroundings.

**Figure 6.13**
All the material shaders include indirect lighting.

**117**

## Shading Models

There are eight basic material shaders available in the Get > Material menu. Let's look at the characteristics of each shader and what they are frequently used for (see Figure 6.14).

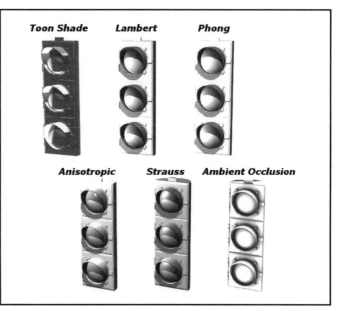

**Figure 6.14**
Various shading models for different surfaces.

◆ **Constant** has only diffuse and transparency parameters. Objects with a constant material color tend to not to have a three-dimensional appearance, since ambient (shadow) coloring is not present. Constant material works well for a backdrop object, such as a sky texture, since your lighting does not create a highlight or shadows on it. Any texture applied to an object with a constant material will be displayed as-is, with no shading.

◆ **Lambert** has diffuse and ambient colors but no specular highlight. That is, it simulates a matte surface, such as cotton clothing or tree bark. Lambert is used for most objects that are not shiny or glossy, and it works well for skin.

◆ **Phong** is used as the default surface shader. It has three basic characteristics: diffuse, ambient, and specular. It's very versatile and easy to edit. Phong can be used for any smooth, shiny object, but it ends to make objects look like plastic.

◆ **Blinn** is similar to the Phong shading model. It has diffuse, ambient, and specular colors. However, sometimes it offers better quality when simulating metallic surfaces, thanks to more accurate and complicated algorithms. It works especially well for a metallic object with sharp edges.

◆ **Cook-Torrance** creates a smooth surface with a somewhat subdued specular highlight. It does not have a specular decay slider to control the size of the specular area. When its Roughness value is above 0, it loses specularity.

◆ **Strauss** is the perfect solution for a frosty metal surface. Instead of Ambient Color or Specular Decay sliders, it has Specular Smoothness and Metalness sliders. Smoothness controls the size of a specular highlight, 0 being a large specular area. However, you will lose diffuse and specular color when the slider is set to 1. The Metalness slider controls the balance between diffuse and ambient color. Setting Metalness to 0 will differentiate between diffuse and ambient color, so the surface will look like very frosty, shiny metal. Setting Metalness to 1 will make the object more glass-like, since the diffuse and ambient colors will be the same.

◆ **Anisotropic** simulates objects with tiny grooves such as a CD or brushed metal. The Glossy slider controls the smoothness of transition between diffuse and specular, and it can create a long streak of specularity, using either U or V coordinate mapping.

# Previewing the Scene Using Render Region

You may have noticed that the regular view ports do not always display shaders accurately. Transparency, refraction, and reflection do not show up at all in these windows. That's because these displays are created with an OpenGL accelerated video card. While this display mode offers extremely fast interaction, it does not support transparency, refraction, reflection, or even smooth shading of specularity. To accurately view how your scene looks, you need to display it using a software renderer. XSI's mental ray renderer offers highly realistic and speedy software rendering.

To quickly and interactively view your scene, we are going to use a tool called render region, shown in Figure 6.15.

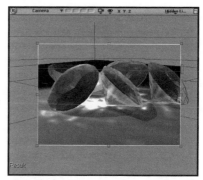

**Figure 6.15**
The render region tool lets you interactively preview the scene.

To activate render region, first enter the Render module (hotkey 3), and click on Render > Region > Region Tool; or you can use the Q hotkey. Render region mode is activated, and the mouse pointer becomes a transparent arrow attached to a white square with a black sphere inside. Left-click-and-drag to draw a marquee box around the region you want to render, in the viewport of your choice. A yellow box with blue control points will appear where you drew the marquee box. Immediately after you release the mouse button, mental ray starts and renders an image of the selected region. This render is truly interactive, meaning that if you change any value, such as diffuse color, or placement of the object or light, render region automatically updates to the change.

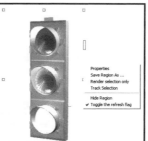

**Figure 6.16**
The render region has an onscreen UI.

The blue squares on each edge and corner of the yellow box are control points. You can left-click-and-drag on them to resize the render region. If you left-click-and-drag on any of the yellow borders, you can translate the render region around its view port. The rectangular blue box at the top-right modifies the sampling level of the render region. If you hover the mouse pointer over the box, it becomes a slider bar. Lowering the slider gives you a less detailed, faster render. If you move the slider up, the render is smoother and more detailed but slower to update (see Figure 6.16).

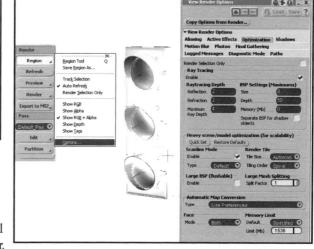

**Figure 6.17**
Or set options in the Render > Region menu.

The Region menu offers a few more tools. If you turn on Render > Region > Track Selection, the render region will automatically move and resize to frame any object you select. If you toggle on Render > Region > Render Selection Only (see Figure 6.17), then, only that object will be rendered in the region. This option speeds up the region considerably.

The Render > Region > Auto Refresh menu command automatically refreshes the render whenever something is changed in the scene that affects the selected area. The default is on, but if the constant updating is slowing you down too much, uncheck Auto Refresh. You can refresh the render by moving the camera or redrawing the render region.

You can also view only the color or alpha channels of the render by checking the corresponding menu option on Render > Region. The default is Show RGB, which looks best when you are looking at transparent items, smoke, fire, glows, etc. If you prefer to see your render region on top of the wireframe, check on Region > Show RGB + Alpha, which draws the rendered pixels on top of a transparent background so that the wireframe shows around the rendered parts.

The Render > Region > Options menu command lets you edit various settings for the render region tool. This is where you need to turn on Caustics and Global illumination if you want to see these effects in your render region, and where you can turn other effects on and off to further speed up the region.

## Fortune Teller: At a Glance

In this tutorial, you will get hands-on experience on how to apply a shader to an object and how to use the render region to interactively adjust materials (see Figure 6.18).

You'll learn how to:

◆ Apply shaders to objects
◆ Edit shaders to create the desired effect, using the Shader property editor
◆ Work with specularity
◆ Use transparency and refraction
◆ Adjust the index of refraction
◆ Add translucency to glass
◆ Use the render region tool to render interactively

## Tutorial: Fortune Teller

So far in this chapter, we've learned the basics of what a shader does and how to edit one. We've also learned how to use render region to accurately see what a shader will look like in the final render. Let's apply this knowledge to create a fortune teller's crystal ball. We will use Shader property editors to tweak a sphere's diffuse color, ambient color, specularity, transparency, refraction, and reflection. While we edit shaders, we will turn on the render region tool, so we can predict the results of our editing.

**Figure 6.18**
What do you see inside the crystal?

## Step 1: Load the FortuneTeller Scene

From the courseware accompanying this material, load the FortuneTeller scene. Examine it closely. There is a crystal ball sitting in a ring holder on a table that is covered with a draped cloth, over a wooden floor.

The curved legs are in a hierarchy called legs, while the rings are in a hierarchy called upperring. The ball itself is named crystal. Looks like a great model, but why is it all gray? Because *you* are going to color it in!

## Step 2: Add a Shader to the Crystal Ball

Press 3 to enter the Render module.

Add an Anisotropic shader to the crystal ball. Select crystal, then choose the Get > Material > Anisotropic menu command. Open the property page for Material > Surface > Anisotropic with the Selection button on the MCP, or with the Modify > Shader button in the Render module menu stacks.

Let's change the color of the ball to a greenish hue. Click twice on the RGB button to the left of the slider for the Diffuse color property so it says HSV. Crank up the S (saturation) slider. The Hue bar will display the color spectrum; move the slider to green. If you haven't already, change the Perspective viewport to Hidden Line mode.

Why can't we see any green on the ball? Because the Hidden Line mode doesn't show color. You could switch to Shaded mode, but it won't display well either, because the lights are too complex for the hardware shading to handle. What's the solution? We need to see how it will render.

## Step 3: Draw a Render Region

Activating the render region tool is a snap. Just press the Q hotkey! The arrow cursor will change to an outline of an arrow, with a box at the bottom of it.

Left-click and drag to draw a marquee box around the crystal ball. The area inside the marquee box is now rendered by the mental ray.

The mental ray software renderer can do much that the hardware shading cannot. Mental ray can accurately cast shadows, show transparency and refraction, show specular shape, and much more (see Figure 6.19).

Try dragging each blue box at the corners of the render region to resize it. Drag on the yellow border to move the render region.

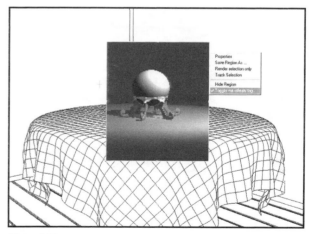

**Figure 6.19**
The render region properly displays transparency, unlike the Shaded view mode.

## Step 4: Edit the Render Region Tool

Let's tweak the sampling level to see smoother rendering. Hover the cursor over the rectangular box at the top right of the render region, and a vertical slider will show up. Drag the slider to the top, and the render is much more detailed but very much slower. Drag the slider to the bottom, and rendering is really quick, but the picture looks very blocky.

> What this slider really does is adjust the number of rays cast per pixel. When the image looks chunky, the renderer is casting one ray for a group of pixels. When it looks smoother, it casts one ray per pixel. When it looks really smooth, it is casting more than one ray per pixel. This is called anti-aliasing.

When you are working on the scene with render region on, you will need to find the best balance between speed and quality to clearly see what you are editing, while not being bogged down by the interactive rendering. For now, keep the slider around the middle.

Choosing Render > Region > Show RGB will make the background black.

## Step 5: Finish Up the Material Coloring on the Crystal

The shadowed regions of the ball look a bit weak, and the specular dot is too bright and not interesting enough. Back in the Anisotropic Material PPG, drag the green tile from the Diffuse sliders over the gray tile of the Ambient sliders, and let go to copy the color from one to the other. Now make the Ambient green darker and more saturated (see Figure 6.20).

Drag the Diffuse tile onto the Specular Glossy color tile, and shift the hue to the blue side to change the color of the specular dot. The specular highlight is too regular and round, however. Drag the Shiny V slider up to make the dot shiny in the V direction, and change the Shiny U slider, too. Make the Shiny U value about 10 and the Shiny V about 30.

As you make these changes, the render region will keep re-rendering the area you chose, so you can see the results.

> There is some ambient light added in by the renderer. To change the amount and color of this 'garbage light' use the Modify > Ambience menu cell in the Render module.

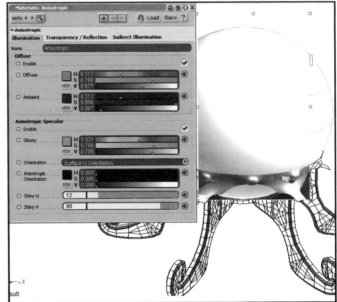

**Figure 6.20**
Ambient controls the color of the shadowed area.

## Step 6: Adjust the Transparency of the Crystal Ball

Let's make the Crystal Ball more glass-like by increasing its transparency, as shown in Figure 6.21.

Click on the Transparency/Reflection tab on the Material property editor.

Change from RGB mode to HSV mode for the Transparency Mix Color property by clicking on the little square next to the color bars that is labeled with the color space that the bars display: RGB, HLS, or HSV.

The Value slider in the transparency mix color controls the amount of transparency. The higher (whiter) the value, the more transparent the object; slide it to about three-quarters transparent (0.75). There is another slider there, named Scale. It also modifies the transparency. The final transparency of the object is a multiplication of both the Mix color and the scale. Leave the scale all the way up at 1 so you that can create transparency effects with just the Mix color.

What happens if you leave the Transparency Mix color in RGB and adjust the sliders that way? It is possible then to make certain color ranges of the object more transparent than others. For our simple purposes, HSV is easier because the Value slider controls the transparency of the entire object evenly.

## Step 7: Add Refraction to the Crystal Ball

A transparent objects rarely looks believable without refraction, because it doesn't look like it has volume (see Figure 6.22). The reason for this is simple: The default value of the index of refraction is 1, which is the density of air.

Slide the Index of Refraction slider in the Transparency/Reflection tab. The crystal glass index of refraction is around 1.2. (Of course, if you don't know the index of refraction of the substance you are working with, you can just keep adjusting the slider until it looks good.)

## Step 8: Add Reflection to the Crystal

Another way to add realism to the scene is by making the ball reflective, so it will show a bit of the surrounding props.

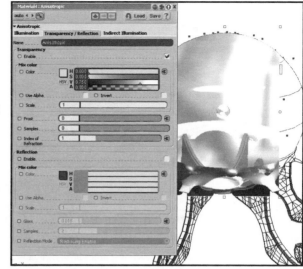

**Figure 6.21**
You can see through transparent materials.

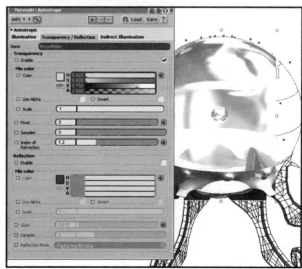

**Figure 6.22**
Refraction makes your crystal ball more realistically transparent.

**123**

Like transparency, the Mix color V (value in HSV) slider of the Reflection tab controls the amount of reflection. Set the crystal ball's reflectivity to about 0.2. Now you can see the props reflected on the surface of the crystal ball (see Figure 6.23).

### Step 9: Add Glossiness to the Crystal

Right now, the ball is just too clean. It's too perfect and too shiny. In real life, glass has imperfections. XSI can add back some of these imperfections by throwing more rays at the ball and jittering them around. In the Transparency tab, turn up the frost a bit (.02 maybe) to add the jitter, and then turn up samples to 1 or 2 to throw more rays. This is a lot slower to render, but it looks good, as shown in Figure 6.24.

You may do the same with the reflections if you wish, using the Gloss and Samples sliders.

### Step 10: Add Some Self-Illumination to the Crystal

Right now, the ball is illuminated by the spotlight in the scene. It might look cool if the ball seemed to glow from some of its own inner light. Switch to the Indirect Illumination tab of the Anisotropic shader PPG. If you pick an Incandescence color and then adjust the Incandescent Intensity slider (to about 0.3), the ball will have some of that color added evenly across its surface. You can make it glow purple, for instance. However, since this effect is added very evenly, it is not as visually interesting as the Translucency effect.

Drag the Translucency slider all the way up to 1. Now the ball will be illuminated by the inner light that is inside the ball, in a more complex way than the simpler incandescence. You can choose how much translucence and how much incandescence you think make the crystal ball look best in the render region.

### Step 11: Add an Environment Shader on Top of the Glass

Currently, when a ray bounces off the glass, it shoots off into space and returns complete blackness. An Environment shader wraps another imaginary image all around the scene so that reflective materials have something else to reflect if there are blank parts of the scene. The result is that the glass will look more complex and realistic.

With the ball selected, choose Get > Shader > Environment > Environment Map from the left-hand menu stack. When the PPG for the image to use pops up, click on New > New From File and locate the Shrineclose.tif from the Pictures directory of the courseware. Choose that image and click OK to complete the effect. This is a frame from an HDRI

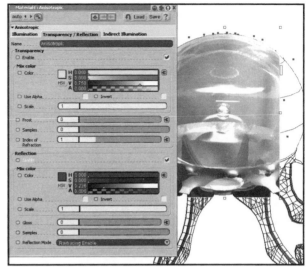

**Figure 6.23**
Reflection shows the ball's surroundings.

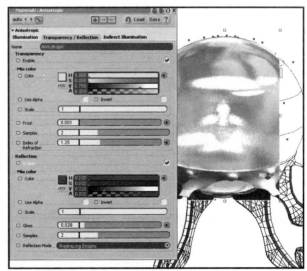

**Figure 6.24**
Glossiness and frost make glass better by making it worse.

image of the Mesmer shrine to obsolete technology. It will now be reflected in the glass, as if the computer and the candles were behind the camera in the same room as the crystal ball.

### Step 12: See How Ray Depth Changes the Look

Open the PPG for Render > Region > Options and turn to the Optimization tab.

Currently, the render region is set to follow reflective rays for three bounces and refracted rays for six bounces, although no one ray may take more than six total bounces. This is because the glass is both reflective and refractive. XSI must follow the rays around for this long to get an accurate rendition of glass. To see what happens when the ray limits are too low, set the maximum ray depth to 1. Now rays die off after just one reflection or refraction. It doesn't look as cool, does it? Remember to increase these ray limits when using transparent and refractive materials.

### Step 13: Add a Shader to the Metal Legs

Select the legs as a tree (spacebar and RMB) so you know that the material you add will be applied to all of them. Use the Get > Material > Strauss command to add a Strauss shader to them all. The Strauss shader is perfect for imitating metallic surfaces. In fact, instead of having different colors for Diffuse, Ambient, and Specular, it has just one Diffuse color and two sliders for Smoothness and Metalness. Set the color to a very dark red-orange hue, and make the surface very metallic and not very smooth. In the Reflection tab, dial up just a little bit of reflection. You should see the changes update in the render region.

Now select the rings as a branch, and apply another Strauss shader. Eedit it to look like beaten gold, with a slight reflection. If the feedback in the render region is too slow to be effective, in the Render > Region > Options, toggle on the Render Selection Only option to isolate only the rings in the render.

Adjust the Smoothness and Metalness low, for a soft golden look. A little bit of red-golden incandescence helps the gold look as well.

### Step 14: Preview the Whole Scene

To see the whole scene render into one interactive render window, use the Render > Preview > All Layers command. When the preview is completed, if you want to save that image for later viewing, use the Save As button in the top of the window.

You have learned how to add a material shader, and edit each parameter of shaders in the property editor. You also learned how to interactively preview the result of editing by using the render region tool. A very important thing to remember is that those shaders don't just control the color of objects, but all the surface characteristics of an element, such as reflectivity and transparency. In the future we will learn how to put a picture on the surface, which is called texture mapping.

## Lights and Good Lighting Technique

When you see diffuse, ambient, and specular color on that crystal ball, what you are seeing is interaction between the shader of the ball and the lights in the scene. Without a light, you wouldn't even be able to see the ball. The color of the surface is blended with the color of the lights that shine on it, depending on their distance, their brightness, and their angle of the object surface to the light. This is called Shading.

Lighting is the most important aspect of rendering. No matter how hard you work on tweaking a shader or how beautifully you paint and apply a texture map, bad lighting will make it look, well... bad.

## What's in the Get > Primitive > Light Menu?

You can create a light by choosing Get > Primitive > Light. It would be a good idea here to "tear off" the Get > Primitive > Light menu so you can see the options and rapidly add other lights to your scene (see Figure 6.25).

**Figure 6.25**
Try to tear off the Light menu.

There are five types of lights available in the Light menu cell. All of them are useful, depending on the situation. Let's take a look at each light and what it is used for.

### Infinite

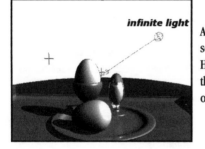

An infinite light is like an abstracted sun: It exists infinitely far away from the scene, and it illuminates the entire scene evenly and from the same angle. Because it is "infinitely distant," moving it won't actually have an effect, However, you can change the direction that the light is coming from, which determines the angle of the light rays in the scene. A hidden default infinite light is created when you create any new scene. You can unhide it with Shift-H on your keyboard.

### Spot

A spot, as its name implies, is like a spotlight. It shoots out light in a cone shape, pointing at a null called its interest, which is created automatically along with the light. You can control the position of a spot light, the position of its interest, the angle of its cone, and the distance away from the spot that the light will travel (called falloff or attenuation).

## Point

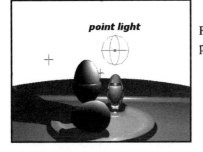

Point lights act like a bare light bulb: They cast light in all directions, out from a single point. You can control their position by translating them. Like spot lights, point lights have a falloff parameter.

## Light Box

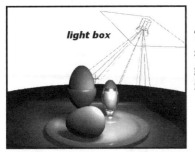

This type of light simulates a film studio's light box. It creates a nice, soft, and diffused light, for a more real, less computer-generated look. This is really just a point light with area lighting turned on.

## Neon

If you want to simulate fluorescent or neon light, a neon light is the way to go. It works just like a point light, except that it has a longer and wider light source, creating a softer shadow and less harsh, focused light.

This also is an area light, with a very long and narrow shape. (Check out the Area tab of the Light property editor.)

## *Editing Lights' Properties*

Let's examine the property pages of a light. Build a floor for the spot to shine on, with a primitive grid. Choose Get > Primitive > Light > Spot, select the spotlight icon, and open the Spot property editor (see Figure 6.26).

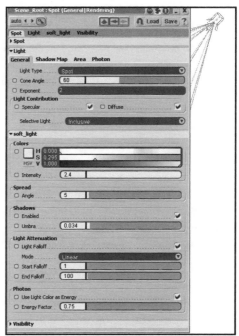

**Figure 6.26**
Edit the light properties.

127

Lights can be changed to spot, point, or infinite on the fly, by selecting Light Type.

There are two important tabs in the Spot PPG, each addressing a different aspect of lighting. The Light tab determines the type of light, cone angle, falloff exponent, and whether or not the light is selective (shines only on some objects). The Soft_Light tab is the actual light shader. It has the settings for everything else, notably the light color, shadow settings intensity, and much more. Start with the Light tab, and draw a render region so you can see the spotlight shining on the floor you made. Now adjust the Light tab controls to see the effect interactively.

Cone Angle controls the width of the beam on a spot light. Spread Angle controls how diffuse the outer edge of the beam is. A lower spread angle creates a more focused beam of light, and a high spread angle creates a more faded, diffuse light. It is extremely useful to turn on Display > Attributes > Cones in the top menu bar if you have spot lights in your scene, which will show the cones in all the views, or use Show > Cones in one view to only show cones there.

Now click on the Soft_Light shader tab of the Spot PPG to look at the light shader settings.

You can set the color of the light with the Color slider, the same way you edit Material shader colors. An important thing to remember if you use HSV mode is that the Value slider controls how intense the light is. You can type directly into the Value box to "overdrive" the light's intensity to greater than 1.

Intensity also determines the strength of the light. The higher the intensity, the brighter the light. This control is multiplied by the light color to determine the final brightness. If you are using HSV color editing, you don't need to use this property. Instead, you can adjust the total intensity by overdriving the value property, but intensity is necessary if you are using the RGB color space for your light (not recommended).

Lights don't cause objects they illuminate to cast shadows unless you check the Shadows Enabled box in the Soft_Light tab of the Light property editor. Umbra controls the darkness of the shadows cast: The smaller the number, the darker the shadows. The default shadow type is raytraced shadows, which create highly accurate, but harsher-edged shadows. Alternatively, you can use shadow mapping, which is often called depth map shadow mapping. This type has a control to make shadows softer, and renders faster, but it is not as accurate as raytraced shadows (see Figure 6.27). You can enable shadow map by clicking on the Shadow Map tab at the top next to General and checking the Use Shadow Map box. Resolution controls the quality of the shadow map. A higher resolution gives higher quality but slower render time. To view the shadow map in render region, you need to change settings in the option box. Choose Render > Region > Options and click on the Shadows tab. Check the Enable box under Shadow Map.

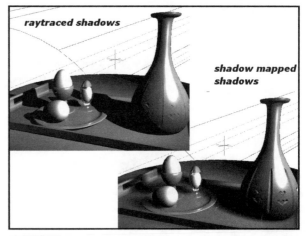

**Figure 6.27**
Raytraced and shadow map shadows.

Light attenuation, also called falloff, is used to determine at what distance a light diminishes in brightness. To use falloff, you need to check the Light Falloff box, set the Light Attenuation mode to Linear, and set Start and End Falloff values. Start Falloff is the distance at which light starts to lose its brightness, in SOFTIMAGE units, and End Falloff is the distance at which the light has faded completely. The Start Falloff is generally set to near zero, while the End Falloff should be close to the width of the scene (see Figure 6.28).

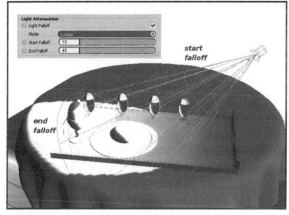

**Figure 6.28**
Falloff determines how far a light shines before it loses its intensity completely.

Changing the Falloff mode to Use Light Exponent will let you set the rate at which the light falls off relative to the distance traveled. The default light exponent is 2, meaning that the light will fall off as the square of the distance (distance raised to the 2nd power). This makes for really rapid falloff, and you will need very intense lights to see the results. A light exponent of 1.2 makes it easier to control while still falling off in a more accurate fashion. Advanced lighting enthusiasts may experiment with Exponent and Intensity to create fantastic and intense lighting effects.

In the following tutorial, we'll practice what we've learned by creating some lights and editing their properties.

## Three-Point Lighting: At a Glance

We learned what kinds of lights are available to us and how to control them using the Property Editor. In this tutorial, we will create a three-light setup, as a starting point of good lighting technique (see Figure 6.29).

You'll learn how to:

◆ Create lights, and place them in basic three-light set-up

◆ Edit several parameters of lights

◆ Add shadows and explore different kinds of shadows

◆ Create a negative light to produce a mood

### Materials Required

LightingScene tutorial scene

**Figure 6.29**
Good lighting technique can have a tremendous impact on the quality of your images.

# Tutorial: Three-Point Lighting

Without good planning, lighting a scene can become very time-consuming. In this tutorial, we will learn the three-point lighting technique used widely by lighting designers to create a basic light setup that enhances the three-dimensionality of the stage or character on the stage set (see Figure 6.30). The three lights are named the key light, the fill light, and the back light. Of course, this setup does not work on every occasion, but it is a good, organized way to start lighting your scene. We will also create a negative light, a light that casts darkness, to obscure part of the scene.

## Step 1: Create and Place a Key Light

Load the lightingscene file from the courseware with this tutorial.

Have three orthogonal (Top, Front, Right) and one Camera view on your viewports. Examine the scene. There is a central tube object with a body in it. We'll want to illuminate this central portion properly. Put a render region around the tube to see it rendered.

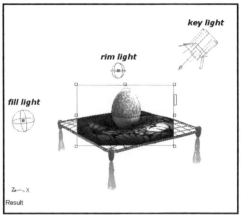

**Figure 6.30**
Simple three-point lighting is the place to start.

First, we will create a spotlight, which will be the key light. The key light is the brightest of the three lights, and it casts shadows. Choose Get > Primitive > Light > Spot.

We need to move the spotlight to illuminate the scene correctly. Imagine that you are looking straight through the camera at the object. The camera direction will be front, and the lights will be at some angle to that direction, both from side to side and up and down.

Make sure the light is shining on the mannequin in the tube, by translating its interest to the center of the tube.

Now move the body of the spotlight up in the Front view, and to the right in the Top view. The purpose of the key light is to shine down from the top-right side of the object, as if the key light were the sun in the early afternoon. In general, the key can be 45 degrees off to one side of the camera and 60 degrees above the camera.

Alternatively, you can change one of the viewports to Spot Lights > Spot to see through the spotlight as if it were a camera. Aiming the light can be much easier using this technique; just track, dolly, and orbit around the scene to change the light's direction. Don't forget to switch back once the light is where you want it, though.

You can view the changes interactively in your render region.

## Step 2: Edit the Key Light

Let's give the spot key light characteristics. Open its property page and change its cone angle to about 40. This will narrow the beam and focus more on the target (see Figure 6.31).

We will make the light a little brighter using the Intensity slider. Move the slider all the way to the right (1). You can directly type in a higher value like 3 if you wish.

Enable shadows by checking the Enable box, and lower the umbra to somewhere around 0.3, so the shadows will be darker.

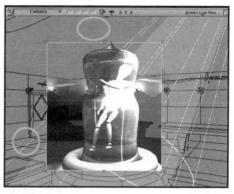

**Figure 6.31**
The three-point lighting technique is a good foundation to build on.

Light attenuation is next. Check the Light Falloff box to enable falloff. Oops, where did the light and shadow go? Because default Start Falloff is 1, light starts to lose its brightness only 1 unit beyond the spotlight and falls off at a rate of 1 divided by the square of the distance ($1/d^2$). Adjust the Start Falloff and End Falloff so that the scene is sufficiently illuminated, yet the light is gradually diminishing in intensity. If you have View > Cones or Show > Cones turned on, there will be rings indicating the Start and End Falloff drawn on the spot's cone, which is extremely helpful when editing attenuation. You can also adjust the Light Exponent, currently 2, to make the light falloff at a slower rate. Try setting the Fall off Exponent to 1.1, increasing the Intensity of the light to 8, and then adjusting the start and end falloff parameters to get a good key light.

Change the color of the key light to be slightly yellowish or yellow-orangish.

## Step 3: Create a Fill Light

Choose Get > Primitive > Light > Point to get point light to use as a fill light. The purpose of a fill light is to smooth out the harsh shadow area created by the key light. Often when you observe a photo shoot, an assistant is holding a large reflector panel to cast light opposite the main light source. This way, the shadow made by the main light source does not obscure the subject's shape (see Figure 6.32).

Move the fill light. It should be placed about 45 degrees from the key light. Also, it does not need to be as high as the key light. In fact, it can be even with the side of the tube.

Lower the fill light's intensity to about 0.5; you don't want it to overwhelm the key light.

The fill light doesn't need to cast shadows. Rather than having to go to great lengths to minimize shadows, we can simply not check the Enable box.

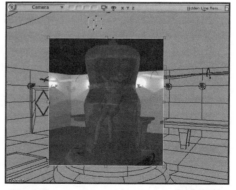

**Figure 6.32**
Only the fill light now illuminates the back of the tube.

The fill light also doesn't need to cast a specular highlight, which would give away its position. In the Light tab of the Property Editor, check off the Light Contribution Specular check box.

Make the color of the fill light slightly bluish.

## Step 4: Create a Rim Light

A rim light (or back light) is used to create an outline on the subject. It produces a more three-dimensional illusion by separating the subject from the background (see Figure 6.33). The light is even weaker than a fill light, and it doesn't cast a shadow.

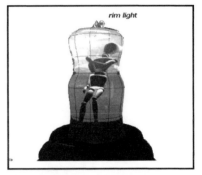

**Figure 6.33**
The rim light outlines the target.

Choose Get > Primitive > Light > Point to create a point light.

Translate the back light so that it is placed behind the target object in the scene (the mannequin in the tube) and slightly above it. If the target were a person, the light would be just above and behind the person's head. Name it rimlight.

Lower the rimlight's intensity to be even weaker than the fill light, around 0.4. Make it a color complementary to the color of the edge of the target object, like a light purple, so it shows the contrast between the object and the background.

Give the light a short falloff distance with a linear falloff profile, so it does not change the lighting in the rest of the scene, and it turns off its specular contribution.

You may want to edit the placement, intensity, and color of the lights to experiment with different effects. Another great technique for lighting is called negative light. Frequently, you won't want to illuminate everything in your scene. In SOFTIMAGE|XSI, you can cast darkness by using negative light, which is a technique unique to computer animation.

## Step 5: Create a Negative Light

Create a spotlight. We use a spotlight because it is easy to aim and control.

Translate the spotlight and its interest so it's aimed at the back corner of the room.

To create negative light, you need to type in a negative value in the Value slider. Change RGB mode to HSV mode, and type -1 directly into the box next to the V slider. Intensity should still be 1.

You can help create a more dark, mysterious mood by using several negative lights to conceal the edges of the room. A very wide spread (like 25 degrees) on this spot will help the effect.

You just learned how to light a scene in an organized manner using the three-light setup. It is a good idea to plan what kind of lighting you will use in a particular scene. Lighting can create a mood and suspense if used wisely. It is highly recommended that you pick up a book that deals specifically with lighting techniques for cinema or photography to study this subject further. The next section will deal with framing a camera and rendering a sequence of images, so we can see fully rendered moving pictures.

# Setting Up a Camera

Another very important aspect of rendering is camera setup. The images you render are defined by where the camera is looking in the scene. Choosing how to frame a shot—what to include and what to leave out—is called composition. Good composition can make a simple scene look elegant and evocative, while bad composition will make the best scene look dull.

Here are some simple composition rules of thumb.

- ◆ Don't try to show it all in one shot. Wide angle fisheye shots are dull.
- ◆ Draw the attention of the viewer to the foreground.
- ◆ Leave the background indistinct, perhaps blurry or darkened.
- ◆ You don't have to center the shot around the foreground object. The foreground elements can be off to one side, so the camera looks past it.
- ◆ Use framing devices in your scene, like doorways and windows to include or exclude the viewer.
- ◆ If you must animate the camera, keep it simple. Avoid flying the camera around wildly.
- ◆ Never animate the camera in a way that would be impossible in real life (until you've mastered the basics).

The most obvious indication of rookie computer animation is sloppy cinematography. Your goal should be for the camera to be irrelevant to the viewer. The viewer should never say anything about the camera, especially "why is it shaking around," or "why am I feeling ill," or "what drugs were the camera crew on?" The camera presents a window to the scene that the viewer looks through. That's all.

In particular, do not succumb to the temptation to put the camera body on a path, or animate it doing anything but moving slowly and gracefully in a straight line, until you have a great deal of experience in 3D graphics.

Let's discuss the different controls built into cameras that you can use to compose your shots.

## *Creating and Editing a Camera*

Choosing Get > Primitive > Camera > Perspective creates a camera that resembles the default camera. You can create an unlimited numbers of cameras, as you desire. Other camera types include telephoto, wide angle, and orthographic.

The default XSI camera rig always has three parts: the rig root, the camera body, and the camera interest. The rig root is the parent of the camera body and the interest, so when you need to pick up the entire camera and move it through the scene, you can do so (see Figure 6.34). If you needed to attach the entire camera to something animated in the scene, you could use the rig to move both the camera and the interest at the same time.

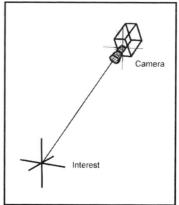

**Figure 6.34**
A camera and its interest.

133

The camera body is the part you look through. It points at the interest at all times, so you can pan the camera just by moving the interest. The camera body also has an up vector constraint, so no matter what you do, it will remain at the same degree of rotation around its central axis. If you want to make the camera roll around its central axis, you must use the Camera roll property.

To look through the new Camera, choose a view. In the View name drop menu at the top left, click on the Cameras submenu option to see your new camera listed. Select your Camera from the list to set the view to look through it.

## Editing a Camera

Most of the parameters used to define a camera can be found in the camera's property page. Select the Camera in the 3D views or in the Explorer, and use the Selection button in the MCP. Alternatively, if you have a view looking through the camera, click the Camera-shaped icon in the top of that view menu bar and choose the Properties command to open the Camera property editor (see Figure 6.35).

You can rename a camera by typing in its Name field.

The Camera Primitive property page has the controls most useful to the beginning CG camera man.

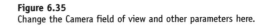

**Figure 6.35**
Change the Camera field of view and other parameters here.

The Format area of the PPG controls what picture resolution and aspect ratio the camera records. If you are planning to output to video in North America, and you want to preview exactly what the final render will look like, you want to set Format Standard to NTSC D1. By clicking the down arrow at the right, you can select other standardized formats for the camera, or manually set a custom aspect ratio in the Picture Ratio field.

Field of View determines what lens angle your camera is using, and how much of the scene you see through it. The default is about 53 degrees, but a better setting to start with is 41.5 degrees, which is about the same as a 35-mm lens. Moving this slider has the same effect as zooming in or out with the Z hotkey in a perspective view.

Clipping Planes tell the camera to stop displaying objects that are beyond (or closer than, in the case of Near Plane) a given distance, in SOFTIMAGE units (see Figure 6.36). If you want to find out the distance

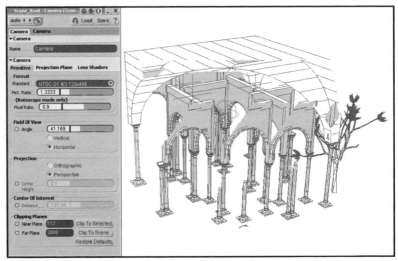

**Figure 6.36**
Clipping planes slice through the scene.

between a camera and an object accurately, find out the name of the camera from which you want to measure the distance, such as Camera1, choose Render > Options, and click on the Format tab. Choose the correct camera name in the Output Camera field and click on Display > Distance to Output Camera in the top menu bar. Now you will see the distance between the output camera—the camera that does the final render—and selected objects in any viewport.

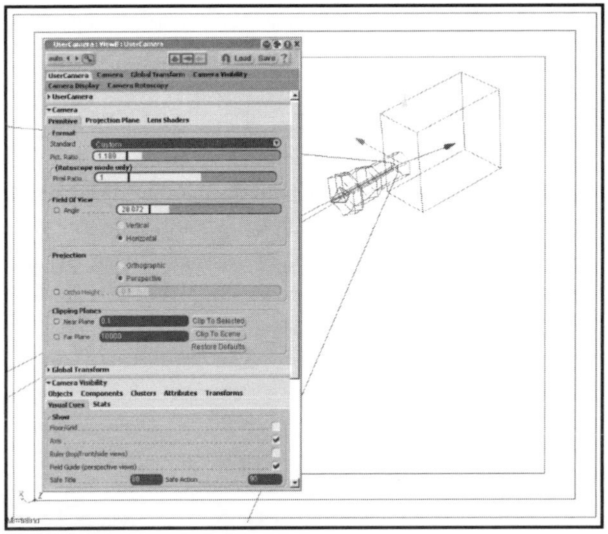

Another important tool is the field guide. Objects close to the edge of a camera's field of view run the risk of getting distorted or cut off when viewed on a television monitor, and the field guide will help you avoid cutting or distorting anything important. You can activate the field guide by clicking the Show menu (eyeball icon) of the Camera viewport you are using and selecting Visibility Optionor by pressing the Shift +S hotkey—and then selecting the Visual Cues tab and checking the Field Guide box (see Figure 6.37).

The Camera view will display three black rectangles. The outermost box is exactly the resolution you have selected (usually NTSC, which is 720×486); anything outside this rectangle will definitely be cut off. The second, middle rectangle is the Safe Action box (also called action safe). Anything outside this box still has a chance to be cut off or distorted, so be sure any important action is inside this rectangle. The innermost rectangle is called the Safe Title box (called title safe). If there is anything in your scene that absolutely cannot be distorted or cut off, such as text, it needs to be inside this rectangle.

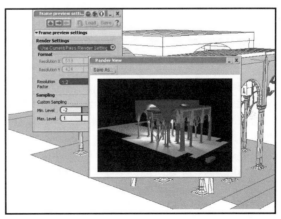

**Figure 6.37**
Camera property editor, and the field guide.

## *Previewing Your Shot*

After you have a camera set up correctly, you might wish to see what the render will look like from that point of view, at the current frame.

The Preview function does just that (see Figure 6.38). Simply switch modules to the Render module, and choose Render > Preview > Active Camera. The resulting floating window will show you the current frame, rendered with the camera in the currently active render pass. You may need to expand the Render view by dragging the lower-right corner to see your whole image. The preview is dynamically linked to the scene, so as you make changes, it updates.

Leave the floating window up, inspect your camera properties again (try Show > Properties from the top of the Perspective View window), adjust the field of view to see the preview update, and evaluate your changes.

**Figure 6.38**
Set up a preview of your scene.

You can save the preview image to disc for later use with the Save As button in the title bar of the Preview window.

# Rendering the File

There's one more subject to cover before we are ready to actually render pictures and view them with the Flipbook tool: setting the render properties. These options are collected by XSI and then passed to the mental ray renderer, which uses your choices to determine how to render the image, at what size and aspect, how to name the resulting files, and where to put them, among many other potential options. You do not have to understand everything in the Render options to render nice images.

Choose Render > Options from the left-side menu stack of the Render module, and we'll look at a few of the important tabs (see Figure 6.39).

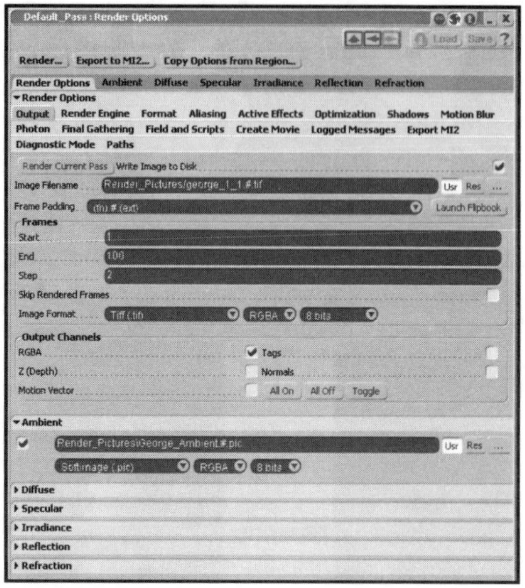

## *Output Tab*

You need to tell XSI where to save images and what to name them by entering a path in the Image Filename field in the Output tab. It's a good idea to render the frames into the Render_Pictures directory in your project. XSI defaults to saving images in this folder of the default project, which you can set in the File > Project Manager dialog box (see Figure 6.40).

Frames determines the start and end frame that mental ray will render. If you want to render a 30-frame animation starting from frame 1, you set Start to 1 and End to 30. If you only want to render frame 30 as a single image, you would enter 30 for both Start and End frames. You can use the step number to skip frames while rendering, to get a quick overview of your work before completing the final render.

You can select what type of picture file you want to produce by choosing one from the Image Format menu. The default is a SOFTIMAGE .pic file, but if you want to use a different program to edit or composite the movie, you might wish to set it to a more standard format, such as .tif or .tga. Some of the formats, notably .sgi, can also store more than one channel width, which means the number of bits used to store each of the R, G, B, and A components. While 8 bits per channel is standard, you'll want to use 16 bits per channel for broadcast TV or film work.

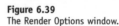

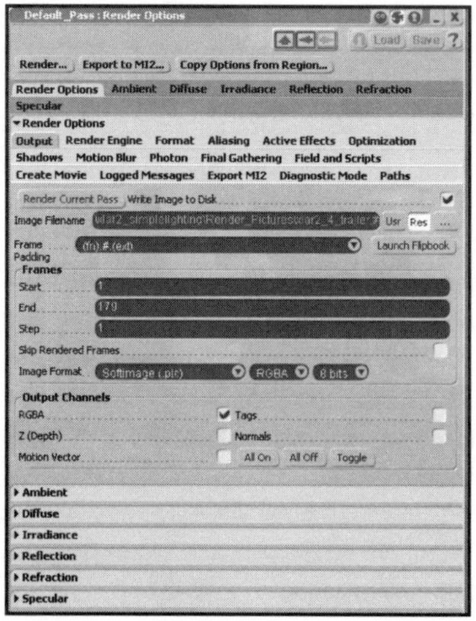

**Figure 6.39**
The Render Options window.

**Figure 6.40**
Tell XSI where to save your finished frames.

## Pass Channels

An important new aspect of the mental ray rendering system was added in XSI version 5.0, called the Pass Channel system. This is an advanced rendering feature, but it will be helpful to understand it so you know why those pages of the Render Options PPG exist. Historically, a render engine would look at the scene and render a single image that described all the light contribution in the scene, much like a photograph does.

However, in animation and special effects work, it is common to render each frame in multiple passes, each describing just a part of the illumination of the scene, for instance a pass for diffuse color, one for reflection, and one for specularity. Then these layers are combined later, in a compositor. Deferring the compositing from the render engine to a compositor allows a human operator to make quick aesthetic decisions, reducing the reflection and blurring the specularity, or color-correcting the diffuse, to meet the artistic goals of the shot. This has always been possible in XSI using the Render Pass system (mentioned briefly at the end of this chapter), but it was accomplished by rendering the scene many times, once for each pass required. This is inefficient in large productions, because the scene must be read and parsed, new files generated, and then the rendering done multiple times. The new Pass Channel system allows for many of the most common render passes to be generated at the same time, within a single render, and written out to separate image files (see Figure 6.41).

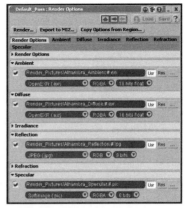

**Figure 6.41**
Pass channels save more than one image for each render.

To use it, just toggle on the check box under the pass channel labels (Ambient, Diffuse, Specular, Irradiance, Reflection, and Refraction) and then set a file path, name, and file type for the resulting image to be saved in.

## Render Engine Tab

You can choose to render your work in different render styles here. Perhaps you just want a hidden line render to check animation timing. Maybe a screen capture of a shaded, textured version like you would see in a finished real-time game is what you need. For finished ray traced, fully rendered work, choose the mental ray render engine.

## Format Tab

You need to tell XSI which camera you are using to make the final render by choosing one from the Output Camera menu. If you have more than one camera, make sure to check this carefully. I've thrown out many a render from the wrong camera.

Picture Standard is similar to the Picture Format camera property. If you are producing content for the North American video standard, it needs to be set to NTSC D1, or perhaps to HTDV. If you set Picture Standard to Custom, you can enter your own image resolution and pixel aspect ratio.

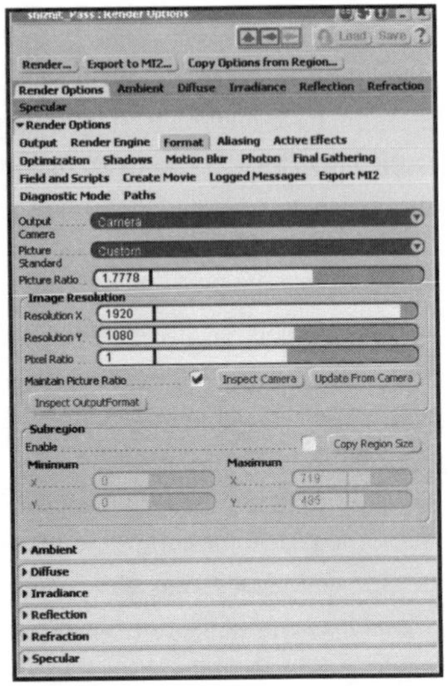

Image Resolution controls the actual size of the image file. You can type in the value directly to create smaller rendered images for testing animation, or larger images for high-resolution stills. This setting overrides Picture Standard. The Pixel Ratio setting makes it possible to render as if the final pixels are intended to be viewed as rectangles and not squares (as they are in NTSC). For web, multimedia, film, print, and most uses other than TV, the Pixel Ratio should be 1.0, meaning the pixels are square (see Figure 6.42).

## Aliasing Tab

Anti-aliasing smoothes the edges of rendered images, as shown in Figure 6.43. The higher the sampling level, the smoother the edges will be, though rendering time will be increased, too. The sampling level determines how many rays will be cast to each pixel. Because the rays arrive at different places on a single pixel, casting more rays will produce a more accurate color for the pixel.

Some pixels will need more samples than others. For instance, a solid black background will look the same whether one sample per pixel is cast or 16, but the pixels along a curved edge between a character head and the sky need enough super-sampling to blur the edge. Setting a lower number of samples for Min Level and a higher level for Max level lets mental ray choose the best sampling at render time for each pixel. An aliasing (sampling) level of -1 casts one ray for every other pixel, 0 shoots one ray per pixel, 1 gives you four rays per pixel, 2 gives nine samples, 3 gives 16 samples, and so on. The greatest difference you can set between Minimum and Maximum Sampling is 3.

Jitter makes anti-aliasing less artificial, by randomizing the location of the samples.

The sampling threshold sets the allowed difference between samples. If the two samples (let's say from adjacent pixels) are more different than the sampling threshold, mental ray goes back and casts more samples to get a more accurate result. If the two samples have a difference that is less that the threshold, mental ray figures the result is good enough and moves on to the next pair of samples. The default values of .2 are too high. Because you can adjust the sampling threshold differently for each color channel (in the RGB color model), you can take advantage of how human eyes have different perceptual accuracy in different color ranges. Humans don't see reds too well, so you could set the red threshold to .1, blue to .075, and green (where humans see lots of differences) to .025. In this case, colors in the green range would end up creating more samples than reds, given a similar coverage in the scene.

Filtering further improves picture quality by averaging the multiple samples for one pixel in different ways to come up with the single color value that can be stored for the final pixel.

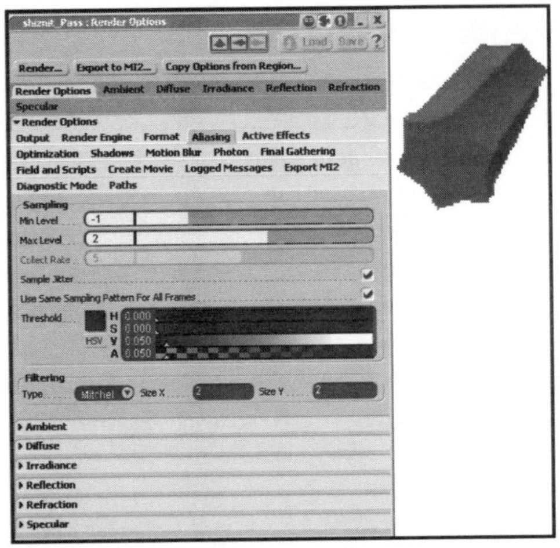

**Figure 6.42**
Set the render picture size and aspect.

**Figure 6.43**
Anti-aliasing smoothes out renders by concentrating on edges.

## Optimization Tab

You will need to modify the settings in the Optimization tab in two circumstances. First, when rendering glass or other transparent and refractive materials, you will need to increase the ray depths for reflection rays, refraction rays, and, of course, the total max ray depth for both together.

When you are rendering a large scene with hundreds of thousands of polygons, and your computer is slowing to a crawl, you can get your renders back on track by adjusting the BSP tree settings and memory consumption settings. A discussion of the BSP is included in Chapter 13, "Hair and Fur." The general idea is to get a stopwatch and change one BSP setting at a time while recording the times it takes to render a single frame, find an optimal setting, and then move to the next setting. A good BSP starting point is Size = 8, Depth = 60, Memory = 128 (see Figure 6.44).

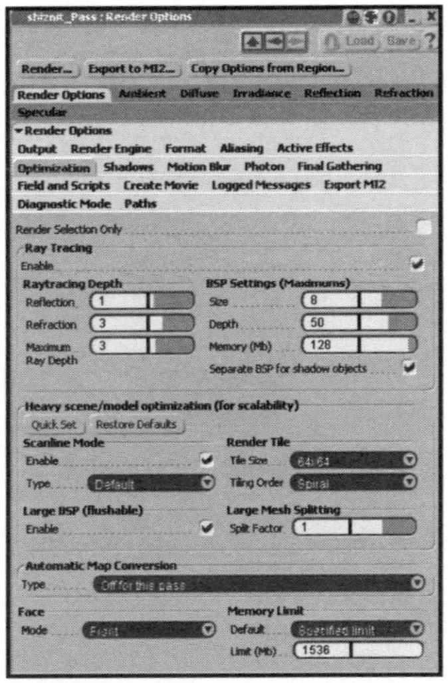

## Shadows Tab

The default setting (regular) will create shadows by raytracing. However, if you are using the shadow map method, you need to turn it on by checking the Enable box (see Figure 6.45).

Once all the parameters have been set, you can start rendering your sequence by choosing Render > Current Pass.

## Logged Messages Tab

The Logged Messages tab switches the verbosity level of the mental ray renderer, so that it reports more or less detailed information back to you, the user, through the XSI Script Editor. If you set the verbosity level to Progress, and then open the Script Editor (the little scroll icon next to the Playback menu at the center bottom of the screen), and then start a render, you will see reports on the render settings used, the images opened and used as textures, the memory consumed by the process, the contribution of each processor and machine to the final result, and the path and file name of the resulting images written out. This information can be invaluable when debugging render problems (see Figure 6.46).

**Figure 6.44**
Optimization settings speed up your renders.

**Figure 6.45**
Different kinds of shadows.

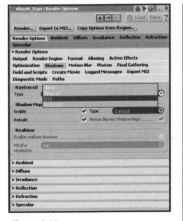
**Figure 6.46**
Get feedback about your render.

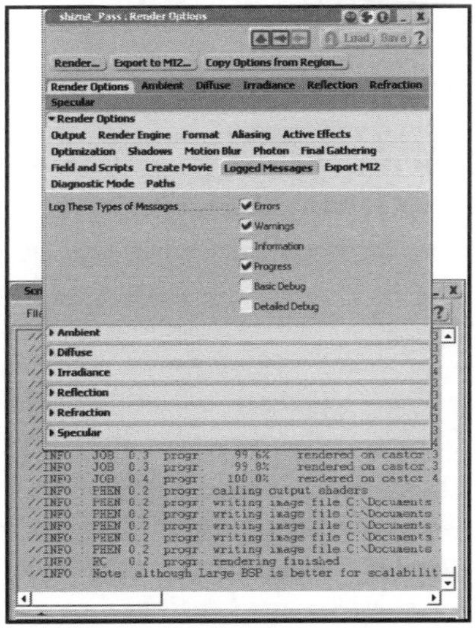

# Nautilus 2: At a Glance

Using what we learned in this chapter, let's render a sequence of images to create a small movie of the Nautilus we made in Chapter 5. We will add lights and cameras and set render options. Finally, we'll set up three passes to render each portion of the animation from a different camera, and then render the final work (see Figure 6.47).

You'll learn how to:

◆ Create multiple cameras in a single scene

◆ Set up passes

◆ Edit render properties

◆ Render a sequence of images

◆ View animation using the Flipbook tool

**Figure 6.47**
Let's view the rendered submarine animation.

## Materials Required

nautilus_done tutorial scene

# Tutorial: Nautilus 2

In this tutorial, we will create a final render of the Nautilus animation. Lights, cameras, and passes need to be set up. Then, after the rendering properties are set, images will be rendered frame by frame and we will view them as a movie using the Flipbook tool.

## Lights

### Step 1: Load the Scene

Open the animated version of the Nautilus traveling through the underwater canyon that you saved after Chapter 5, or just use the nautilus_done scene in the courseware. The Nautilus should be traveling through the canyon, but we don't yet have good underwater lighting or cameras to capture the action as the sub navigates the treacherous depths.

### Step 2: A Spotlight for the Sub

The scene is currently very evenly lit. We'll change that. Get a spotlight from the Primitive menu and translate the spot root and its children to the front of the sub, either manually or with the Transform > Match Translation command. Select the spot body, and lower the spotlight slightly below and in front of the hull so it can shine forward (see Figure 6.48).

**Figure 6.48**
Place a spotlight under the sub as a headlight.

Change one of your viewports to look through the spot light and make minor adjustments, ensuring that it points straight ahead and is zoomed in fairly tight on the seafloor.

Make the Nautilus body the parent of the spot root, and verify that when the Nautilus moves, the spot goes with it.

In an Explorer, change the Explorer filter so that it shows only lights. Use that view to open the lights one at a time, and dim their intensity. Check the sea floor with a render region periodically to see that you get a deep blue glow on the seafloor.

## Cameras

We can add some dramatic cinematography to the animation easily and simply with a few camera cuts. The easiest way to cut between several camera points of view is to create several cameras and render a different frame range from each one. We'll make three cameras, one located behind the sub as it starts out, one traveling with the sub in the middle of the animation, and one in front of the sub as it arrives at the end.

### Step 3: Set Up Camera 1 for the Rear Angle

Get a camera from the Primitives menu, and position it in the trench, just behind the Nautilus on the first frame of the animation. Widen the zoom to about 60 degrees. Change the name of the camera to Rear so we can easily find it again. Look through this camera in one of your viewports to make sure that the shot is framed to show the back of the Nautilus and is looking down the trench (see Figure 6.49).

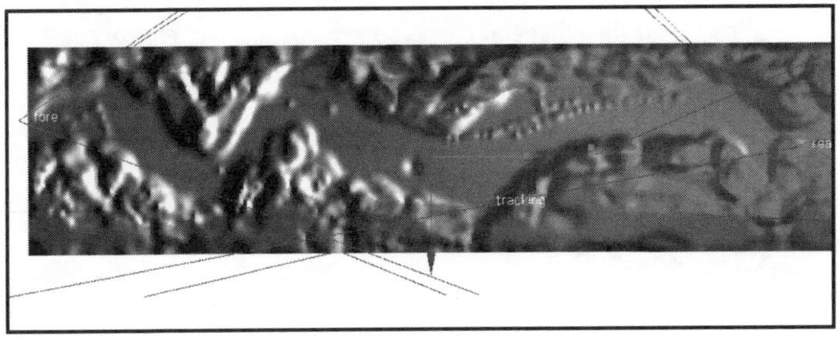

**Figure 6.49**
The Camera field of views overlap.

### Step 4: Set Up Camera 2 Tracking the Sub

Get another camera, and position it midway through the trench, slightly above the Nautilus, and in a position where the camera will see the sub coming and going. We can make the camera track the sub with a constraint on the camera interest. Select the interest, choose the Constrain > Position command from the MCP, and pick the body of the Nautilus. This pops the interest to stay with the Nautilus no matter where it goes.

Scrub through the animation to see that the camera follows the Nautilus, and look through the camera to get a feel for when the Nautilus comes into and out of the camera views. Mark down the frame that the Nautilus appears and disappears from view, and change the camera name to Tracking.

### Step 5: Set Up Camera 3 as the Sub Arrives

Add one last camera at the end of the trench, facing into the scene, where the Nautilus arrives at the end of the animation. Name this camera Fore and look through it to frame the shot.

Finally, write down on a piece of paper the frame ranges that you plan to use for each camera. In other words, starting with the rear camera at frame 0, how long is the Nautilus in view of each camera? To avoid needing to edit, we'll render with the same file name for each camera. To make this work out, there should be no overlaps or gaps in the camera frame ranges.

Note your answers on a sheet of paper like this:

Rear start: frame 0 end: frame 26

Tracking start: frame 27 end: frame 64

Fore start: frame 65 end: frame 100

## Passes

Now we'll set up the passes to render each of these three ranges of frames with a different camera. We'll set up the first pass as we want it, and then duplicate it for the other two passes so we save time and ensure consistency.

### Step 6: Make the First Pass

Start by opening a floating Explorer (hotkey 8) and changing it to the Passes scope with the hotkey P inside the Explorer. Rename the Default_Pass to Rear and open the Render properties by clicking on that small icon.

Set the output path to your local project and name the file Nautilus_Render. Change the frame range to match the range you wrote down for the rear camera in the step prior to this one. In the Format tab, choose a render image size to your liking from the Picture Standard drop list (see Figure 6.50).

Also in the Format tab, choose the Rear camera as the camera to render in this pass, as demonstrated in Figure 6.51.

In the Aliasing tab, set the Min Level to -2 and the Max Level to 1, with the Threshold set to .05 for each of RGB and A (or each of HSV and A). Set the Filtering Type to Gaussian, and the Size X and Y to 1. This is a good setting for quick preview renders at reasonable quality in a short period of time.

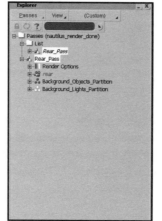

**Figure 6.50**
Name your passes properly in the Explorer.

**Figure 6.51**
Each pass will have a different output camera.

## Step 7: Duplicate the First Pass to Make the Rest

In the Explorer, select the pass by clicking on the name Rear, and use Ctrl-D to duplicate it. Duplicate it again, so you have now three passes (see Figure 6.52).

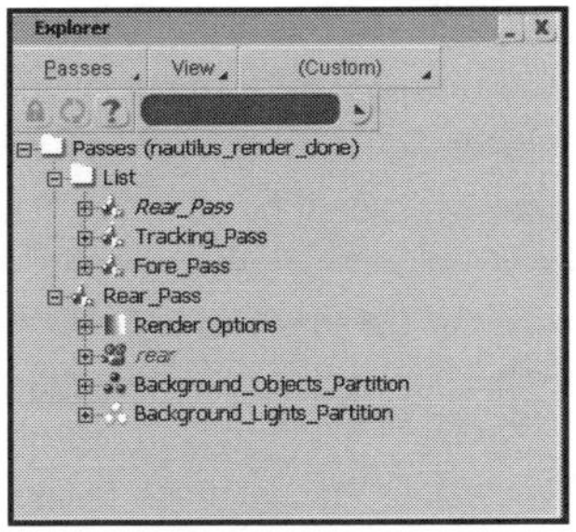

Change the name of the second pass to Tracking, open the render options under that pass name, and change the frame range to match the range you wrote down for the Tracking camera. Verify that the location and name of the Image Filename is the same as in the template pass. If they do not match, change the filen ame to be the same: Nautilus_Render. In the Format tab, be certain to change the output camera to the tracking camera.

Select the remaining pass, name it Fore and change the frame range and output camera as above. Be certain to check (again) the output file name, and make it match the output file name used in the other passes.

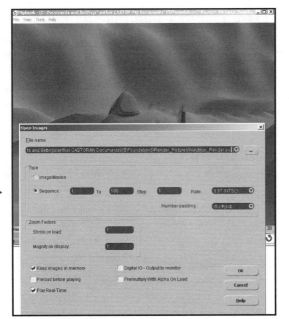

**Figure 6.52**
Now you have three similar passes with different frame ranges and output cameras.

## Render

The penultimate step is to render all the frames from the three passes.

## Step 8: Render All Passes

This is the best part of computer animation: making the computer do all the hard work. Be sure to *always* save your scene before rendering, because rendering is a good time for the computer to crash and take away all your hard work.

After the scene is saved, choose the Render > All Passes command in the Render module, and take a break!

## Watch the Frames

Finally, when the rendering is done, you can watch the results at full speed (see Figure 6.53).

To open the Flipbook, choose the Flipbook menu command from the Playback button below the timeline. Whether or not XSI is running, you can also start the Flipbook from the Windows Start > Programs > SOFTIMAGE Products > SOFTIMAGE XSI 5.0 menu.

Click the ellipsis button (…) from the top of the Flipbook window and navigate to the rendered images. The fastest way to do this is with the Paths button in the top-right corner of the dialog box. Inside your project's Render_Pictures folder, there should be a file named Nautilus_Render [1…100] (or whatever you named your sequence). The range of frames should read 1 to 100, so that each camera contribution is loaded in sequence, because they all have the same render file names.

**Figure 6.53**
View your handiwork with the Flipbook.

Highlight the line with that name and click OK. If you double-click the file, you will be able to see individual frames, but opening individual frames won't let you view the entire animation. After you select the frame sequence you want to view, you will be returned to the Flipbook user interface. There are three toggles at the lower-left corner, for Keep Images in Memory, Preload, and Play Real-Time. Play Real-Time should be toggled on, and Preload and Keep Images in Memory should be off unless you are loading images from a slow network. Click OK to load the frames.

Click on the Play Forward button from the play controls at the bottom of the Viewer window to display the animation. Click on the Loop button to play the animation again and again until you stop it. The frame rate maintained by the Clip Viewer is printed above the timeline.

You can use the Flipbook to check the alpha channel (and other channels) of your renders with the Flipbook > View menu. You can also use the Flipbook as a file converter, with the File > Export command. Poke through the other Flipbook menu commands to see what else it can do!

When you tire of watching the animation, make a note of the things you would like to change. Then close the Flipbook, make changes to the scene, and rerender until you are satisfied with the results.

> An even easier way to open the Flipbook and load it with your rendered images is to open the Render Options PPG. In the Output tab, click the Launch Flipbook button, which runs the Flipbook with the path and file name chosen in the render options.

## Extra Credit: Using the Clip Editor to View Animation

You can also drag and drop images into the Image Clip Editor. In the main XSI UI, change one view to be a browser, and find some other images to look at. Change another one of your View windows to the Image Clip Editor. Click on an image in the browser with your left mouse button and drag it to the middle of the Image Clip Viewer and then let go. It loads into the viewer! You can drag and drop all kinds of image files, including AVI and QuickTime movies, into the Image Clip Editor. The only problem is that these image sources and clips are now stored as part of your scene, which slows down loads and saves, especially if the originals of the files go away. You can clear out these unused clips and sources with the Render module Get > Clip > Delete Unused Image Sources and Clips command.

# Conclusion

Congratulations! In this long and complex chapter, you learned how to add surface shaders to objects, preview using the render region tool, add light to the scene, create and edit the camera, and render a single picture and sequence of pictures by editing render options. In the end, you learned how to play the sequence of images with the Flipbook and the Image Clip Editor. These techniques are still basic, and there is much you can add to each step. Some people spend their entire careers making a study of just cinematography or lighting, and the same principles can be applied to computer graphics. The workflow covered in this chapter will certainly enhance the speed and quality of your work.

# Chapter 7
# Path Animation

In this lesson, you will learn:

◆ How to animate objects on a path

◆ How to save keys on path

◆ How to use orientation and tangency to control an object's movement

## Introduction

Path animation is another useful animation tool. By simply drawing a curve and adding a constraint, you can animate any object, camera, or light along a path. In addition, you can adjust how the object travels through space by moving the control points of the curve, animate the orientation of the object along the path, and change the timing of path animation (see Figure 7.1).

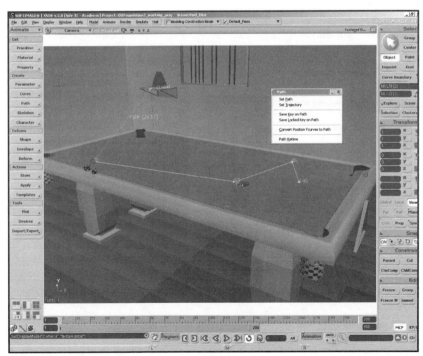

**Figure 7.1**
Tools you'll use.

# Setting Path Animation

Path animation is a type of constraint. You can imagine the path as having a magnetic attraction to the animated object. The object can be moved along the path, but not away from it, and if you move the path curve, the object is drawn along with it (see Figure 7.2).

There are two ways to set path animation. The first method is by drawing a curve, and then attaching an object to that curve. The second way is by setting translation keys on an object and telling XSI to create a path based on that movement. Let's try the first method.

## Animating on a Path by Picking

First, either draw a curve using Create > Curve > Draw Cubic by CVs, or choose one of the pre-defined curves under Get > Primitive > Curve. Make sure you are using an orthographic view port, rather than a perspective-corrected one, when drawing a curve, and avoid any particularly small, tight kinks or twists. Then, select the object you want to animate along the path. You can also branch-select the root of a hierarchy, for a more complex object with children to attach to the path.

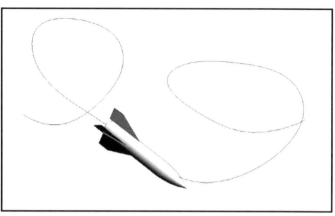

**Figure 7.2**
Path animation can be very useful.

Next, switch to the Animation module (hotkey is 2) and select Create > Path > Set Path. A dialog box will pop up, and you will be prompted to enter the start and end frame of the path animation. There are two check boxes under the Start and End Frame slider. By checking the Linear box, the object will travel on the path at a constant velocity, meaning no ease-in or ease-out, which can be very useful.

For example, if you path-animated a camera around a model to show a 360-degree view of the model, and you wanted to loop the animation for several revolutions, you wouldn't want it to slow down and stop every time it finished turning around, so you would check the Linear toggle On. The Tangent box keeps the X-axis of the object aligned to the curve, so it stays pointed forward on the path. You should toggle this option on unless the orientation of the object is not important.

Click OK to accept these values and move forward to the last step. Note that the mouse pointer is now in a pick session.

Finally, pick the curve you created. The object that was selected (or hierarchy of objects) will jump to a position on the path you picked. Now, when you scrub the time slider, you should see your object animating along the path (see Figure 7.3).

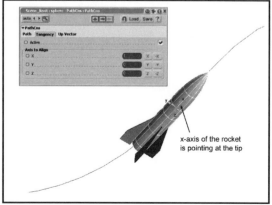

x-axis of the rocket is pointing at the tip

**Figure 7.3**
There are many variables in setting a path.

To modify the path animation, select the animated object and open the PathCns property editor with the Selection button in the MCP. You will have to click on the small plus sign next to the Constraints folder to open up the Constraints properties and see the PathCns property.

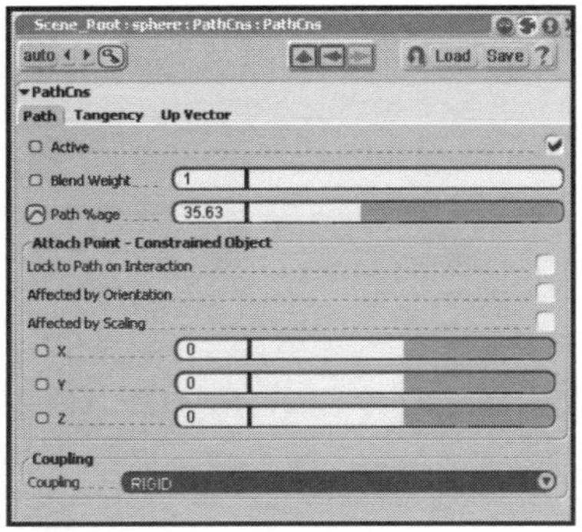

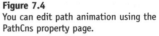

Click on the square icon to the left of the PathCns property to pop its properties into a Property Editor (see Figure 7.4). The Path Percentage slider tells you where on the path the object is; 0 is the start of the path, and 100 is the end. The Path Percentage property is automatically keyed at 0 and 100 for the start and end frame, respectively, that you chose earlier, but you can set Path Percentage keyframes at any time to change the animation's timing.

Under the Tangency tab of the Property Editor, you can toggle Tangency on and off to align one axis of the object to the direction of the path. Which axis that is is determined below, by the Axis to Align text boxes.

**Figure 7.4**
You can edit path animation using the PathCns property page.

Examine your object to find out which axis you want to align to the path by selecting the object and clicking on the Translate menu cells so that the Manipulator icons show up. Observe the orientation of the manipulator and figure out which axis you want aligned with the path. Then put a 1 in the Axis to Align section of the PathCns property page that matches the axis you want aligned, and a 0 in the other boxes. This tells XSI which axis to line up. You can also click the small buttons labeled with the axes, like X and -X, which do the same thing.

The Up Vector tab has a similar arrangement designed to control which axis is facing up (or pointing at another axis). You can also animate the roll of an object here.

## Setting Keys to Create a Path

Alternatively, you can save keyframes and create a path according to the motion created by that animation. First, move the time slider to the frame you want to start animation, and translate the object to the place you want to start the animation. In the Animation module, select Create > Path > Save Key on Path. The selected object's translation is now keyframed at its current position and frame.

If you go to a different frame, move the object, and Save Key on Path again, you will see a curve between the two places you set keys, which can be adjusted to alter the object's interpolation between the two points. This method is very useful when you need an object to be at a specific location at a specific frame (see Figure 7.5). This is also a great place to use the Menu-Memory feature in XSI. When you middle-click on a menu item, the last command you chose will be executed again, without dropping out all the menu items. This makes it faster to run the same command over and over.

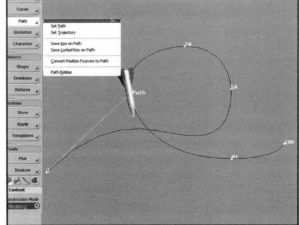

**Figure 7.5**
Setting keys on a path is another way to create path animation.

You can also use Save Locked Key on Path. The difference is that when you use Save Key on Path, any modification to the curve will change the timing of the animation. For example, if you move the last point on the path curve, the objects will end up at in a different location than where you set the keyframe. Save Locked Key on Path will make the object always pass through the point where you keyed, at the frame you keyed, even if you edit the curve. Both methods are useful, depending on what you are doing.

# Editing Path Animation

Since the objects are glued to the path, you can edit the curve's shape any way you like, and the object will just follow the new path. You can edit a path by adding or deleting points, moving points, or modifying the path's properties. Check out the Modify > Curve menu in the Model module for these and other path-editing tools.

## Viewing a Path

You can display the controls for a path animation by selecting Show > Relations in the view port in which you want to view the controls. The numbered white squares are saved keys on the path. Clicking on the dotted white line and pressing Enter will open the PathCns property editor for the selected curve.

## Removing Path Animation

If you want to delete path animation altogether, select the object with the path animation constraint and choose Constrain > Remove Constraint from the bottom right of the Main Command Panel.

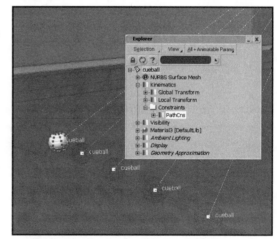

You can also select the item, open the Selection explorer in the MCP, locate the PathCns property, click just once on its name to select the property, and then delete it with the Delete key on your keyboard. You can also see and remove constraints using the Schematic view. Just open the schematic, select the constrained object, and look for the green constraint link arrow. Select that arrow and delete it with the Delete key. If you do not see the green arrow while the constrained object is selected, use the Show menu to make sure that Constraint Links is toggled on, making constraints visible in the schematic, as shown in Figure 7.6.

**Figure 7.6**
Path animation is actually a constraint.

# Tutorial: Smart Bob

We will model a rocket and a target, and draw a curve between them. The animation of the rocket hitting the target is achieved by path animation on the curve (see Figure 7.7).

You'll learn how to:

◆ Create path animation
◆ Use tangency
◆ View and edit path animation

Let's create a rocket named Bob and hit an outhouse precisely using the path animation tool. We will also use the tangency tool to keep Bob's head pointing toward the curve.

## *Making the Models*
### Step 1: Model the Rocket

Choose File > New Scene to clear the slate.

Since we'll be doing modeling first, enter the Model module.

We are going to create a profile curve of Bob and revolve it around the Y-axis.

In the Front view, draw a profile of the rocket, using Create > Curve > Draw Cubic by CVs. Make sure to draw the curve from bottom to top, or the resulting revolution will be inverted (see Figure 7.8).

In Model mode, select Create > Surf. Mesh > Revolution Around Axis. Pick the curve.

Open the Revolution property page, and choose Revolve Around Y in the Revolution Axis menu.

If the surface of the rocket is dark (in shaded mode), it's probably inside out; show normals to check. If it is inside out, choose Modify > Surf.Mesh > Invert Normals.

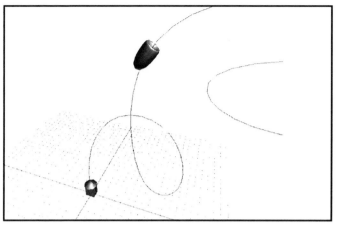

**Figure 7.7**
Let's Bob it!

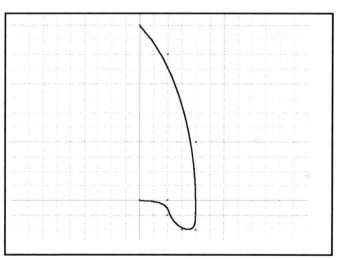

**Figure 7.8**
Draw profile curves bottom to top, or you'll end up with an inverted surface. (You could use Modify > Surface > Invert Normals, but why not save yourself the trouble?)

Name the rocket Bob.

### Step 2: Model the Outhouse

Select Get > Primitive > Polygon Mesh > Cube to get the polygon cube.

Scale and translate the cube, so it's a bit smaller than Bob.

Rename the cube outHouse.

Add a roof using Get > Primitive > Polygon Mesh > Cone.

Again, scale and translate the cone, so it fits on top of the cube.

Name it roof and make it a child of outHouse.

### Step 3: Create a Ground Plane

Create a grid using Get > Primitive > Surface > Grid.

Scale the grid in X and Z to cover the ground surface.

Name the grid ground.

## *Implementing Path Animation*

Now that the objects are created, let's examine how to get them moving.

### Step 1: Creating the Path Animation

Zoom out in Front view, so you have enough space to draw a curve for Bob to travel along.

Select Create > Curve > Draw Cubic by CVs, and draw a curve starting about 50 units to the right of the outHouse. That's where Bob will be launched.

Add more points. Be sure to make it fun! Bob can do a few loop-de-loops or other aerobatics on the way to his target. As long as there are no extremely tight corners or kinks in the curve, he will follow it smoothly. End the curve at the center of outHouse.

### Step 2: Put Bob on the Path

Select Bob, and change to Animate mode (hotkey 2, or F2 in SI3D mode). Select Create > Path > Set Path. Keep the defaults on the window that appears, click OK, and pick the curve as prompted.

Preview the animation. Oops, Bob is not heading toward the curve! We need to constrain Bob's tangency to the curve.

Open the PathCns (path constraint) property page, and click on the Tangency tab. Remember, whenever you need to find a specific property page on a selected object, you can use the Selection explorer, which is the Selection button mid way up the MCP on the right side of your screen.

Check the Active box, and Bob's direction (tangency) is constrained to the curve. Preview the animation.

That's a little better, but it still isn't right. Bob's tangency is constrained to the curve, but the wrong axis is facing forward. Back in the PathCns property page, under the Tangency tab, change the value for X to 0 and Y to 1, and then preview the animation.

### Viewing and Editing Path Relations

You can view a path constraint by choosing Show > Relations (from the eyeball menu above any view), and selecting the object traveling on the path. The white rectangles with numbers next to them represent the location and frame of where you set a key, and a dotted white line connects them.

Select the dotted white line, and then press the Enter key. This is an alternate way of opening the PathCns property editor.

Under the Path tab, the Path Percentage slider will let you move Bob back and forth on the curve. Let's create additional keyframes using this property page.

Move the time slider to frame 20 and drag the Path Percentage slider to 0. Click the keyframe button next to the slider. You just added an extra keyframe. Bob remains at 0 percent of the curve translation, so he won't start his launch until frame 20.

Let's make him Bob slower in the beginning before picking up speed. Move the Time slider to frame 50, and change the Path Percentage to around 14 percent. Click on the keyframe button next to the slider.

Now when you play the animation, you'll notice an extra white rectangle added to the path at frame 50. Bob is flying slowly when he starts out.

One of the most useful aspects of path animation is that you can make changes to the path after you constrain an object to it, and the object will follow the new curve. You can experiment by editing Bob's path curve. Hold down the M hotkey and drag points of the curve around to see this in action.

> You can add points to a curve at any time with the Modify > Curve > Add Point Tool in the Model module and menus.

Great! Now Bob is flying really smartly, and dead on target!

## Conclusion

In this chapter, you learned how to create path animation, with the Set Path command and also by converting translation keyframes into a path with the Save Key On Path command. You can edit animation by editing points on a curve or adding another key on the path. Path animation is often the most intuitive way to set motion to an object.

# Chapter 8
# Building Sets and Models

In this lesson, you will learn:

◆ The terminology of modeling in XSI

◆ How to look around you to find inspiration for modeling shapes

◆ How to organize your work so that you are most effective and productive

◆ How to build and modify NURBS curves

◆ How to make revolutions, extrusions, Llofts, and four-sided patches

◆ All about converting curves to faces and solids

◆ How to work with imported EPS artwork

## Introduction

Because SOFTIMAGE|XSI is an integrated package, including all aspects of the computer animation process, you will find a high degree of synergy between the modeling tools, the animation tools, and indeed all the other modules. In XSI, you may mix and match animation and modeling as you create your scene, by animating the properties of the modeling tools to create animation effects, and by using animation tools like Animated Duplicate and Spline Deformation to create new models. While the ability to go back and forth so easily is empowering, it can also become overwhelming and lead to a lot of down time as you explore new interactions in the program. It is good workflow policy to organize your project into discrete stages and stick with the plan. Usually, that means that modeling is the first step. Enter the Model module or tear off the Model menu to get ready (see Figure 8.1).

## Modeling

Everything you use in your 3D scenes first has to be made somehow and by someone—usually yourself. That's one of the first cold hard truths in 3D animation. Traditional artists have asked me, "Can't you just, like, get some premade stuff?" I usually respond, "Sure, but would you paint using color by numbers? Or design using only clip art?" Some high-quality 3D models are available for purchase or download, but most of the time you'll need to build your models from scratch to fit the needs of your specific scene. That means that everything in your storyboards that the camera will see must first be made. The process of making objects, set pieces, props, and characters for your production is called modeling.

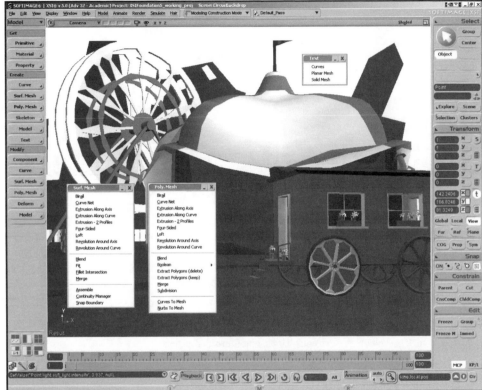

**Figure 8.1**
Tools you'll use (Model menu).

Modeling is defined as the action of creating all the objects that will form the set for your production. Each object that will be seen in your finished animation has to be manufactured in the computer before you can use it. That means that the walls and windows must be designed and constructed; the glasses, plates, and silverware must be made; and the light switches, light fixtures, and light bulbs have to be modeled. In short, everything you want to see, you must first make.

Since there are many different kinds of objects with many different shapes out there in the world, you will have to develop a variety of different techniques, and use a variety of different tools within XSI to build them all. The tools and techniques discussed in this chapter are in no way a complete and exhaustive set. More modeling tools are developed, and other methods of using them are discovered, every year.

Regardless of the modeling tools and techniques you develop and practice, there are certainly some standard and very helpful ways of organizing your work. If you don't bother to organize your modeling tasks and instead jump right on a workstation and start rubbing the mouse, you are likely to find that after bleary eyes and many hours of contemplating the screen, you really don't have much done.

# Planning Your Scene

Scenes can generally be broken down into three parts: the environment, the props, and the characters. Examine your storyboards, and make a list in each of the three categories, determining what you will need.

## Environment

The environment is the area surrounding the action. It gives place and context to the action. Generally, it is a very good idea to keep this as simple as possible, since the actual world is a huge place and the effort that would go into modeling a realistic world would be immense. Ask yourself, "What needs to be seen to validate the action?" If you are doing broadcast logo development, the answer is probably that you don't need an environment at all, since the on-air graphics will be composited on the backgrounds later. The next time you go to the theater, the opera, or a play, pay attention to the sets used. The sets are the environment for the action, and due to the constraints of the stage, set designers are generally quite talented and innovative in their reduction of complexity. In many productions, the environment can be a blank stage, with a black curtain and darkened wings. This setup concentrates the attention of your audience on the area of the action.

Often while modeling your environment, you will be tempted to keep extending the complexity further and further away from the area of the action. One good way to limit this crawl is to light only the areas you want people to look at. You will have no need to build an environment past the limits of the pools of light you use to illuminate the action.

**Figure 8.2**
The environment is the set where action takes place.

A great way to add ambience and a sense of place to your environment is to find a suitable image and texture-map it onto a plane or cylindrical wall as a backdrop. If you blur the image first (using the XSI image editing tools, or another program), your viewers will understand that this blurred backdrop is intended to set the time and place, but it can be ignored beyond that.

If your scene takes place indoors and you must create an architectural setting, draw out the floor plan on graph paper and get the dimensions of the space right before beginning work. Whenever possible, research a similar building plan, and crib from the dimensions there by roughly estimating, using ceiling tiles (usually one-foot square) or by walking it off in strides (usually about three feet). Getting the proportions of a space right is tough, and if you get it wrong, your characters will look out of place in the environment.

The environment could include pillars and supports, fences, trees, bookcases, desks, flower vases, and other set dressings you will need to make the space look lived-in (or not) and believable.

### The Props

Within the environment, your characters will probably interact with other objects: sitting in a chair, opening a blind, throwing a ball, flipping cards, etc. (see Figure 8.3). Each of these objects must be modeled separately and stored for later use in the scene. It's lousy workflow to wait until you actually need a model to go back and make it. Start by creating a list of all the props you will need, eliminating non-essential ones and brainstorming about how to make the ones you keep more interesting.

### The Characters

If you are doing character animation, then you'll need to model or otherwise acquire your characters. Characters can be as simple as a primitive cube or as complex as a fully developed human character with clothes and hair (see Figure 8.4). Keep your characters as simple as you can. Simple characters are actually more effective at creating the suspension of disbelief necessary to pull off successful stories, because they have a wider range of expressive possibilities than real human characters, and because creating realistic human figures is so darned difficult. Representing the human form in painting or sculpture is a lifetime achievement for a classical artist, requiring a solid understanding of human form, proportion, anatomy, and movement. (Note: Think about how much work must have gone into Michelangelo's statue of David the next time you get a hankering to create a realistic human figure. And he was naked...)

All the most effective animated characters in the world (Beavis and Butthead, Ren and Stimpy, Wallace and Gromitt) have been very simply designed, yet capable of incredible acting range and emotion. Remember also that any object can be made into a character using XSI.

## Deconstructing Your Surroundings

The first step in mastering the art of modeling is to observe. Look at the objects that surround you and inspect their construction. In general, greater attention to detail will make your work more interesting visually. For instance, a room detailed in 1960's Spartan cubist furniture will often look less appealing and more "computery" when rendered than a drawing room outfitted in Victorian fashion with an ornate fireplace and grandfather clock. One drawback to detail is that good modeling requires skill and time to complete. Another is that as you model in more detail to your scene, you generally increase the amount of polygonal and patch geometry, and your computer becomes less responsive and takes longer to render images of that scene.

As an artist, you will have to choose where to add detail, where to skimp on detail, or where to add detail with texture maps.

**Figure 8.3**
The characters interact with the props.

**Figure 8.4**
Characters act out the scenes.

When you are working on an important project, it is often a good idea to do some real-world research about the items you'll be modeling. The easiest (and most fun) way to do this is to get a cheap digital camera or Polaroid and go on a scavenger hunt, looking for the items on your modeling list. When you find objects that fit both the descriptions of the item and the style to fit your scene, snap a picture. Then, back at the production studio, you can tape up all the images as reference to guide you in deconstructing them into constituent parts. Another great source of ideas for props is the Ikea furniture catalog, which has thousands of items that are generally attractively designed, yet simple in construction.

Examine each object on your modeling list to see how it can be broken down into smaller components. This works best if you can see a real version of that object to examine how it was constructed. For instance, a light bulb can be broken down into the glass bulb, the metal base, and the wire filament. A floor lamp can be broken down into the base, the pedestal, the bulb, the wire guard for the bulb, the switch, and the lampshade (see Figure 8.5).

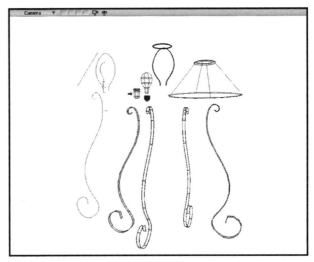

**Figure 8.5**
The individual parts of a floor lamp.

Each of those parts was manufactured or created in a certain, usually simple, way. Examine each to get an idea of how it was done, giving yourself clues about possible modeling techniques in the process. Was the shape stamped out of a flat piece of metal? Was it lathed out of a piece of wood? Molded out of plastic? Extruded from a metal tube?

After going through this exercise a few times, you will find yourself automatically deconstructing the ordinary objects you come in contact with throughout your day.

In general, objects that are round or circular about one axis can best be made with a modeling revolution. Objects made of pipe or with a consistent cross section can be extruded. Plastic parts with complex organic surfaces can be lofted, and parts stamped out of a flat sheet of metal or cut from fabric can be made with the four-sided tool.

For each object in your modeling list, conjure a mental picture of its component pieces and how you will make each of them. The final bits and pieces can easily be stuck together in a hierarchy and then modified together for final scale. One of the great things about XSI is that once a model is built, it takes no effort to duplicate that base model into as many different shapes, sizes, and colors as you wish (see Figure 8.6).

## Saving Models Externally for a Model Library

After you have exhaustively planned all the different items you will need to make, and planned the construction process for each part of each item, you will be ready to get started making them. Since you will want to re-use your models many times

**Figure 8.6**
The finished lamp, with different modeling methods used for different parts.

**157**

throughout the scenes you make, it's a great idea to start creating your own model library. The best way to do this is to create a library scene in XSI that will have certain default elements that are useful for making models.

In your reference library scene, start by creating several elements that will provide a sense of scale while you work. Create a default floor rug area about 10 units by 8 units (8×10 feet), a yardstick 3 feet high standing in the middle of your scene, and a pyramid representing a human form that is 5 feet, 8 inches tall—a standard average human height. These elements will give you a visual reference for the size of individual objects as you model, so you can make all your models to the same scale.

There are also a few things you can do to make your modeling work easier. They all involve turning on feedback options so that you get better information about what you are doing and can make better decisions.

◆ The default gray lighting doesn't show contour or direction of the surface very well. Create three point lights: one bluish, one yellowish, and one red-dish. Imagine a circle lying on the floor grid of your scene. Place each light at thirds around the circle so it forms a triangle about 50 units from the center. Since you made the lights and placed them in the top view, they all lie at 0 in Y. Take the yellowish light and elevate it 50 units up in Y. This simulates the sun. Leave the blue light where it is, and lower the red light 20 units to light the bottom of objects.

◆ Turn on some feedback options in different view windows. In the Camera view, in Show > Visibility Options (the bottom menu command of the Eye menu), look for the Attributes tab. Under the Selected Objects area, turn on Normals, so you can see the direction the surfaces are facing.

◆ Turn on NURBS Boundaries. Curves have a beginning and end and a direction from start to finish along their length. Normally you cannot see this information, but it sometimes becomes useful. The start of the curve is a colored red/green section of the curve when viewed in wireframe. It's a good idea to leave this on all the time so you know which direction your curves are going.

◆ In the Unselected Object side, turn on Name, which will show the names of unselected objects in the Camera view. We'll assume that if the object is selected, you know what it is.

◆ Change one of the views to the Schematic view. The schematic should be your constant companion, useful for organizing your work, naming, and selecting objects.

◆ Use Show > Points; if you can't see the vertices or control points that make up an object, it will be pretty hard to manipulate them. If you select an object but still don't see points at the intersections of the surface edges and parameters, look to the top of the window you are working in, and toggle on Show > Points.

Then, as each object is completed and parented together into a hierarchy, you can create a "model" out of it with the Create > Model > New Model command (see Figure 8.7).

A model is like a tree in the hierarchy, except that the elements in a model have a unique namespace, and these models can be saved individually to disk so that you can pull them back in later. A model can contain objects, animation, expressions, and constraints. In the Model property page (which appears automatically when you create a model, unless you have disabled the auto-PPG feature in the user preferences), you can choose whether

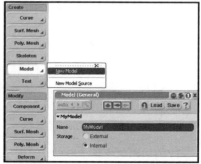

**Figure 8.7**
The Create > Model menu cell.

the model is stored internally or externally. Internally means that the model is bound into the scene file like everything else, while external means that the model is saved separately to disk and can be easily reloaded into another scene.

There are two kinds of models: Regular (static) models and Referenced (dynamic) models. Both are stored the same way, with File > Export > Model, but they differ in how they are imported.

When you use the regular File > Import > Model, the modeled object you import becomes part of your scene and will never change.

If you use File > Import > Referenced Model, the model retains a link to the original model that you exported to disk. Should you need to, you may go back to the original and modify it any way you wish. When you are done modifying it, re-export it to save the changes, and then in the scenes where you imported the referenced model, use the Model > Update Referenced Model command to bring the new changes into each scene.

That way you can share one base model between many scenes, and later make changes at will that ripple through many scenes in your animation.

## *Drawing NURBS Curves*

XSI uses NURBS curves as the basic elements in patch modeling (see Figure 8.8). You can draw NURBS curves in any window, using several different tools, all located in the Model module, under the Create Curve menu cell.

If you choose Create > Curve > Draw Cubic by CVs, you can point to an area of the screen and click the left mouse button to drop the first control point. Point somewhere else and click again to drop the

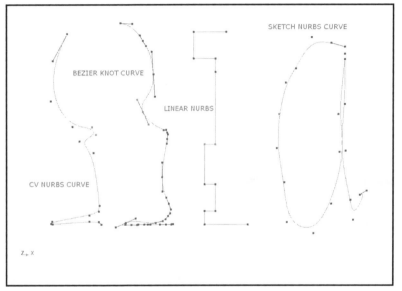

**Figure 8.8**
The different kinds of NURBS curves and the shapes they make.

next control point. Four control points are required to define a CV NURBS curve, so if you drop less than four points, XSI will add some for you. The control points, also known as control vertices or CVs, influence the curve, but the curve does not have to pass right through them. The NURBS curve is sort of a best fit through the points you lay down. This method makes controlling the placement of the curve and the tangency of the curve very easy, and it always maintains a smooth, gentle arc.

While you are laying down points, you can keep the mouse button down and drag to see the curve update dynamically, before you commit to a point location by letting up on the button. If you click with the middle mouse button, you can add a point to the middle of the curve wherever you click. If you click with the right mouse button, you can select other curve commands from a context-sensitive menu, like adding a point to the beginning of the curve, closing the curve, or ending the curve drawing session.

If you choose the Draw Cubic by Knot points tool (it used to be called the Interpolating NURBS tool) from the Create Curve menu cell, a different method is used to lay down points. When you click the second point, a full set of four NURBS CVs are created. As you create more points, the location in space of the curve is modified. Both methods are equivalent, so you can use either tool to create curves; they are provided to give you a personal choice in what you prefer.

The Create > Curve > Draw Linear option draws straight-line NURBS.

You can constrain the placement of a point to snap to the grid by holding the Ctrl button while dropping points, which can make it much easier to achieve precise results.

You can also use the Ctrl snapping hotkey to snap to other objects, lines, midpoints, surfaces, and much more by modifying the options of the Snap menu in the MCP. If you want to snap to a plane, like the default grid, you can click on the Plane button in the MCP to activate a new plane reference to use for snapping. You can right-click on the Plane button to change the properties of the reference plane used in the snapping.

## Adding Bézier Curves

Some people are more comfortable with adjusting Bézier-type curves, which are curves that have a control point and two floating control handles that adjust the tangency in and out of the control point. It is usually easier to control sharp corners using this type of curve.

You can draw Bézier-style curves with the Create > Curve > Draw Cubic by Bezier Knot Points command in the Model module. If you go to edit a Bézier-type curve, you'll note that when you click on the ends of the control handles, you can make them longer or shorter and change their angle relative to the control point. You can click on the smaller circular part of each handle to change the angle of the tangent handle without changing its length. Gently and slowly mouse over these handle areas with the M hotkey (Tweak tool) active to see them light up.

## Adding and Deleting Points

After a curve has been drawn, you can go back to it and add more points to either end, or in the middle. The Modify > Curve > Add Point Tool performs this magic. With the command active, the status bar informs you that the left mouse button adds points to the end of the curve, the middle mouse button adds points to the inside of the curve, and the right mouse button displays a context-sensitive menu with additional options, like adding points to the beginning of the curve and closing the curve. This command can also be used to add detail to a patch surface that has already been created. The Modify > Curve > Delete Point Tool command will remove points from a curve.

## Inverting Curves

Since curves have a start and an end, it must be possible to swap those ends. This is called inverting the curve. If you have a car that must travel down a path you have drawn, but the car drives in reverse, you can simply invert the path curve that you drew. To do this, use the Modify > Curve > Inverse command.

## Moving Points and Tweaking Components

Individual CV points on a curve (or surface) can be moved interactively by choosing the Modify Component > Move Point Tool command. With this command active, when you click on a specific point in one of the view windows, you can drag the point to a new location. This only works with CVs, not Bézier handles, Knot points, and other curve manipulators. For these, there is a better tool, called the Tweak Component tool.

Because the Move Point Tool command is so useful, it has a hotkey assigned to it: M, called the Tweak hotkey. You can also hold down the Ctrl key while dragging to make the point snap to grid intersections, assisting in accuracy. When you have the Tweak tool (M) in use, various editable parts of the curve appear, including Knot points, which are junctions between spans of the curve. You can tweak (move) all these visual cues to adjust the shape of the curve.

In production work, you will want to keep your menu command picking to a bare minimum, since it takes your eye off the object you are working on. Practice holding the M key with your left hand and picking and transforming vertices until it is second nature. Currently, XSI logs each move you make as a separate Move Component operator, under the geometry mesh operator of the object. Freezing the operator stack will cook all these move operators down into a base mesh, when you want to simplify your scene.

If you want to avoid creating a lengthy operator stack altogether, you can toggle on the Immed button in the MCP, which turns on the Immediate mode. While in Immediate mode, all changes you make will be added without creating an operator in the stack.

## The Modify > Curve Menu

There are so many possible things to do to the curves in XSI that there is a menu dedicated to holding all the tools, called the Modify > Curve menu located in the Model module. Tear off the Modify > Curve menu while working on curves to have easy access to these functions (see Figure 8.9). In addition to the aforementioned Add Point and Delete Point and Knot tools, this menu has options for aligning Bézier handles, converting between CV Knots and Bézier control points, inserting a corner, and more.

## Tagging Points

Sometimes you will want to operate on more than one point at a time. Tagging points is a method of selecting multiple points at once, that can all be moved, rotated, and scaled together, relative to the center of the selected object. You must be in Point Selection mode to operate on these points. If you use the T hotkey, XSI will automatically place you in the Point Selection mode, but you can do it yourself by clicking on the Point button in the top section of the MCP, just under the large selection arrow. Now the transformation controls such as scale and translate will apply only to the points that you have selected.

## Proportional Modeling

Proportional modeling solves a tremendous problem in organic modeling. Often, an object will have hundreds of points, making some types of editing difficult and tedious. For example, simple changes in the facial expression of a complex model could require manual manipulation of each of dozens of points. As a modeler, it would be great if you could grab just one point and have the other points in

**Figure 8.9**
The Modify > Curve menu.

the area stretch to follow the selected point, like grabbing the edge of a rubber mask to distort the features. Proportional modeling accomplishes this feat (see Figure 8.10). When you move one point, all the points in vicinity (set by you) are also affected. Nearer points are affected more than distant points, and the rate of falloff can be changed with a spline curve profile. This feature works for polygonal meshes and for NURBS models. By default, on NURBS and Polygon meshes, the area of influence is measured in 3D space, along all X, Y, and Z axes.

You can toggle on proportional modeling with the Prop button in the MCP. If the Prop button is grayed out, it means that you need to activate a transformation (any transformation) to make the button visible. You can also toggle on proportional modeling in the Modify > Component menu.

Now each move operator in the Operator stack will have a proportional operator underneath it.

XSI gives you some feedback while you are using proportional modeling, to show you the area of the surface that will be affected. That feedback is a circle that moves with your cursor over the surface, showing the radius of the effect.

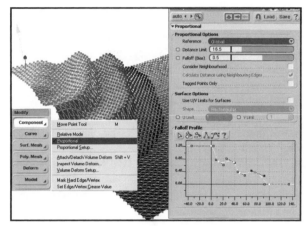

**Figure 8.10**
The proportional modeling menu cell, and a property page showing the falloff graph.

Proportional modeling works in Tag mode with all the transformations. You can tag selected CVs or vertices, and then use the scale, rotate, and translate menu cells. The proportional modeling operator will also change the points surrounding the ones you have tagged in a smooth, gradual falloff. The area of the falloff will be graphically shown to you as a region of fading color from the red tagged points at the center to the black points at the limit of the effect. You can also use proportional modeling with the Tweak tool (M) on meshes, but not curves.

You can examine and manually change just how the Proportional operator works by inspecting the Proportional PPG with the Modify > Component > Proportional Setup menu command.

The Distance Limit is the radius of the effect, while the Falloff Profile curve describes how the effect gradually lessens over the range of the radius.

If you are working on a NURBS surface, the effect of the proportional modeling can be set to Use U/V Limits, which measures distance in U and V rather than the XYZ system, to calculate how much a point's neighbors are affected.

## *Copying Curves*

You can also create a curve from another curve, or even from a NURBS surface that already exists in the scene. If you choose the Create > Curve > Extract Segment command, and then pick a starting and ending position on a curve, a new curve will be created that is identical to the other curve, trimmed to the points you picked. Additionally, if you open the Extract Curve Segment property page for the new curve, you can modify the starting and ending points of the curve (with the Curve Point Adaptor sliders) so that you end up with a different portion of the original curve (see Figure 8.11).

You can pull a curve off of the surface of an existing NURBS object with the Extract from Surface command.

After you choose the command, click and hold down the left mouse button while you move your mouse over the object. You'll see a red feedback line indicating the U isoline exactly under your mouse. When you release the mouse button, a new curve will be created. If you don't want the U curve, but rather want the perpendicular V curve, then choose the V Isoline filter from the Filter drop menu in the MCP (the little triangle above the Name edit box) before running the Create > Curve > Extract From Surface menu command.

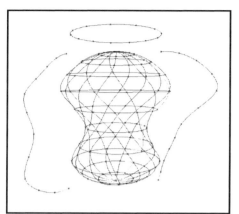

**Figure 8.11**
The Extract tools make a new curve either from a surface or from another curve. The copied curve matches the contours of the original perfectly.

Using the filters, you can also extract curves based on selected U and V knot curves. You may also use the tool in a different way, by selecting a U or V knot curve or Isoline (or many of them) first, and then running the Extract From Surface command.

This feature is very useful for matching one shape to another while modeling. For example, if you have modeled the hood of a car, you could extract the base of the hood to get the starting curve of the windshield.

If you didn't get the curve you wanted, remember that the Extract Curve property page for the new curve allows you to change the location on the original object that the new curve is extracted from.

You can also go back from polygon mesh objects to curves by selecting edges on the polymesh and turning them into a single NURBS curve. Just select the edges with I (select edge by raycast) and use Create > Curve > Extract from Edges.

Each of these modeling tools retains a relational operator connection to the original curve. If the starting surface changes, your extracted curve will also change. You can freeze the operator stack of the new curve to disconnect this relationship.

## Connecting Curves

You can make a new curve out of two smaller curves with the Create Curve > Merge command. You'll need to tell XSI which ends to snap together, like this:

1. Select one curve.

2. Choose the Create > Curve > Merge command.

3. The initial curve goes into component mode, to remind you to pick an end. Drag a rectangular marquee selection around the end you want connected to the other curve.

4. XSI is still waiting for more input. Drag a pick marquee rectangle that touches the second curve. It turns orange. Drag a marquee around the end of that second curve that you want connected to the first.

5. Now that XSI has all the information it needs to complete the command, a new curve is created that joints the two original curves.

The property page for this operator also offers controls for picking which end snaps to which end.

## Creating Curves from Animation

You can also create curves from the paths taken through space by ani-mated objects or even tagged vertices in your scene. As an example, imagine a fighter jet twisting and corkscrewing through the sky, leaving trails of vapor from the tips of its wings. This feature is located in the Animate Module and is called Tools > Plot > Curve (see Figure 8.12). If you have an animated object selected, the curve will be generated using the center of that object as the reference. If you are in Point mode and have one or more vertices selected, a curve will be generated for each vertex. The dialog box that pops up after you choose the com-mand offers you the chance to name the curves, the ability to set at which frame the curve starts and stops being generated, and how often a control point is placed (Step). You should also note that if your object isn't moving at a constant speed, perhaps due to the natural ease-in and out of spline interpolation, the control points won't look evenly distributed in space, and will bunch up at the beginning and the end. You can fix this in the animation editor by making the function curve linear before you plot the motion.

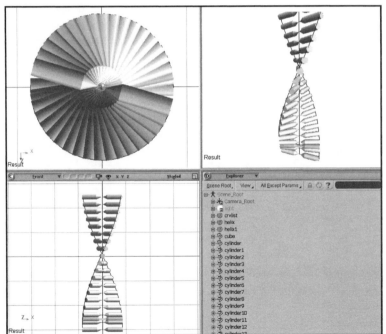

**Figure 8.12**
This helix was made by animating the center crossbar and then plotting the ends with Plot > Curve.

## Resampling and Cleaning Curves

You can dynamically clean up curves that have either too many or too few control points by cleaning the original curve or by fitting a new curve to it with a new number of points.

To create a new, matching curve with a different number of points, use the Create > Curve > Fit on Curve command in the Model module. In the property page for this command, you can interactively determine how many points the new curve has. If the new curve has too few points, it may not perfectly match the original curve.

You can add a Modify > Curve > Clean operator to an existing curve to clean it up, reducing its complexity and simplifying its shape. This feature is tremendously useful for patches, too, and allows you to better control how much detail you are modeling into a surface.

## Opening and Closing Curves

An open curve is one where the beginning and the end do not meet. Many surface shapes will require using a closed curve as a construction element. Imagine creating a garden hose from a circular profile curve. If the circle isn't closed, the hose will leak. The Modify > Curve > Open/Close command simply opens or closes the selected curve by moving the point of the end to the same position as the point of the beginning and ensuring that the correct continuity is preserved so that the seam is invisible. You can toggle this operator on and off through its property page.

# Making Surfaces Out of Curves

Working with curves is one way to build NURBS and polygon models in SOFTIMAGE 3D. The concept is simple enough: By drawing curves and connecting them, surfaces can be created. Because of the rich variety of curve shapes, an infinite number of unique surfaces can be made with this method. There are four major categories of surfaces created from curves in XSI, described by the method of creating them: revolutions, extrusions, lofts, and four-sided patches. Each curve modeling tool has a different style and works better for certain kinds of models, but they all rely on curves as a basic construction element.

Each modeling tool can make either a NURBS object or a polygon mesh object, depending on whether you called the tool from the Create > Surf. Mesh menu or the Create > Poly. Mesh menu (see Figure 8.13).

When you make a surface from a curve, the resulting surface is related to the generator curve with an operator, so that if you then change the shape of the curve, the shape of the surface made from it will change. This relationship is profoundly useful, because it means that you can refine the shape of your surfaces after they have been made, when you can see whether or not they look like what you had in mind when you drew the curve.

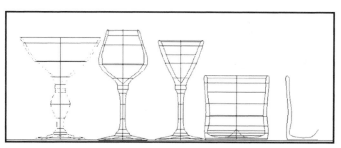

**Figure 8.13**
Each glass was made by modifying the same curve. Then each glass had its operator stack frozen, severing the connection to the generator curve.

In 3D modeling, the more iteration you make between the design and the completed shape, the better the model is going to look. It also means that in real life when your art director or client comes in to look over your work, and wants to make changes, you don't have to start from scratch. This concept is called relational modeling, and it makes your life easier.

SOFTIMAGE|XSI can keep a complex chain of relational links between different operations, so that the results of changes at any step are automatically sent down the chain to the finished model.

For example, if you drew a curve, revolved a surface from it, extracted a curve, inverted it, and extruded a third curve along the extracted curve, all those steps would be stored in a relational hierarchy. You could go back to the original curve and change it, and the results would ripple through the revolution, the extraction, the inversion, and the extrusion to change the final product.

Relational modeling is also a potent animation tool. If you were to save different shapes for that original curve at different points in time, the resulting modeled surface would animate over time.

The best part of relational modeling is that it is the automatic behavior of XSI for almost all modeling operations. In fact, you only have to know that it is on when you want to disable the relationship between a surface and the curves that generated it. To do this, just select the surface and click the Freeze M button in the bottom of the MCP, or use the Edit menu from the MCP and choose the Operator > Freeze Modeling item. (Both are the same.) The relationship of the surface to the other curves will be deleted, and the surface will become a stand-alone object in its own right, with no relation to the curves that created it.

> If you have a hierarchy of splines used in creating a model, and the model blows apart like an exploded view diagram when you move the hierarchy, you will need to freeze the operators used in the modeling. This is because the surface is getting double transformations when you move it. It moves once, and the curves used to generate it move. Therefore, the surface moves away from the curves and the model comes apart.
>
> It's also a good idea to freeze the operator stack for an object when relations when you are done modeling the object and are reasonably certain that you won't want to make further changes.

# Vive La Revolution!

The first surface creation tool to master is the revolution. A revolution is a surface that is symmetrical around a central axis, but where the surface can change how far it is from the axis as it goes. Think of a revolution as the kind of surface that would come out of a lathe. Because the revolution modeling tools are descended from NURBS modeling tools, all the surfaces they create are composed of perpendicular rows of U and V edges. You draw one curve, and all the others are created from there.

## Revolving a NURBS Curve

A NURBS curve can be drawn in any view and then revolved around either a global axis or around another axis that you draw with a NURBS curve.

To revolve a curve around a global axis, use the Create > Surf. Mesh > Revolution Around Axis command. If you wish to draw your own axis of revolution, you can use the Create > Surf. Mesh > Revolution Around Curve command. Most often you'll draw your revolution profile close to a global axis (usually the Y-axis) and use the Create > Surf. Mesh > Revolution Around Axis command. XSI will by default choose to revolve around global Y, but you can change the axis used for revolution in the Revolution PPG if you need to use a different axis.

To perform a revolution around the global axes, select the revolution profile curve and execute the Create > Surf. Mesh > Revolution Around Axis command. You can also do it in the opposite order—execute the command with nothing selected, and then pick on the revolution profile (see Figure 8.14).

If you want to specify the axis of revolution with another curve, you can draw that with a two-point linear spline, select the original profile, run the Revolution Around Curve command, and pick your own new custom axis with the left mouse button (see Figure 8.15). Now the revolution will be made relative to the curve you drew.

I tend to build my revolutions in the front view, next to the global Y-axis, and revolve them around Y. Revolving a shape in the front view around the X-axis can make other interesting shapes, like car tires.

Open the Revolution operator from the Selection button in the MCP to adjust which axis is used, how far around the revolution extends, how many U and V subdivisions there are, and whether the resulting shape is open or closed in U and V. The Revolution Angles determines how far around the object is lathed. If you choose 360 degrees, it will be completely circular, and the edges in the U direction will become closed together. If you revolve less than 360 degrees, the U parameter will be open.

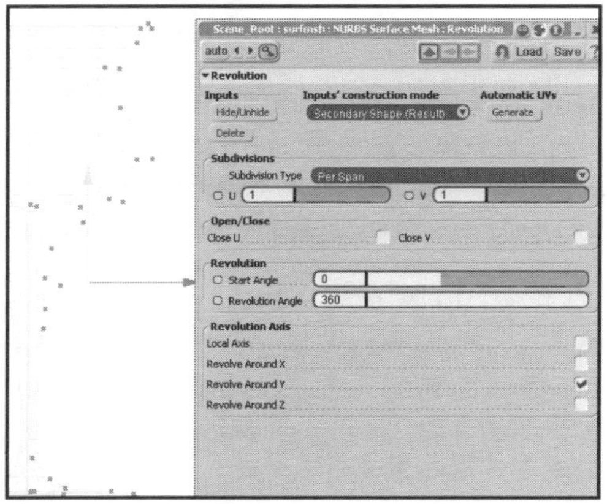

The level of detail in the resulting revolution is not limited by the resolution of the curve you drew. You can use the Subdivisions portion of the Revolution PPG to increase or decrease the resulting density of the model. When the Subdivision Type is set to Per Span, the U and V sliders multiply by the original curve spans (sections between knot points) to arrive at the final detail. When Subdivision Type is Absolute, you can specify exactly how many spans you want in the resulting model, which, if you are using a Poly Mesh operator, determines the model poly count.

By default, all modeling operators are relational and therefore dynamic. If you change the curve that you originally drew to create the revolution, the revolution itself changes. You can change that here in the Revolution PPG by clicking the Delete button in the Inputs section, which freezes the model and removes the original curve. There is not much reason to do this, since you may be able to reuse the curve later, and you can always freeze the revolution manually.

You can set shape keyframes for the revolution profile and cause the resulting shape to animate over time.

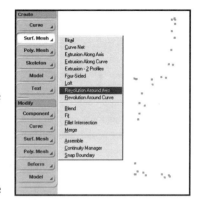

**Figure 8.14**
A revolution curve and the menu cell.

**Figure 8.15**
The revolution property page.

Revolved objects are extremely easy to create and are quite commonly found in the real world. Keep an eye out for objects made of revolutions as you go through your day, and when you find one, consider the axis it was revolved on and what the cross section would look like if it were sliced open (see Figure 8.16).

# All About Extrusion

The next most useful surface creation tool in the Create menu is the Create > Surf. Mesh > Extrusion command (and the identical poly mesh version, Create > Poly. Mesh > Extrusion) (see Figure 8.17). Extrusion takes a generator profile and extends it into the third dimension along an axis or another curve, to create a surface. Extrusions can also be made along two different paths, so that the resulting shape stretches between both rails. Extrusions can be performed on open and closed curves.

The extrusion process is easy to think of as a pasta machine (or a Play-Doh machine if your inner child is still stronger than your inner yuppie). The shape of the extrusion profile determines the shape of the object that gets pressed through it. Keep in mind that, like pasta, extrusions in SOFTIMAGE|XSI do not have to be rigid—they can follow curved extrusion paths.

Look around you right now and analyze the objects you see. Those that are symmetrical around one axis make good candidates for extrusion. Try looking at objects end-on from different sides to see if you can visualize the extrusion profile. The most overused extrusion example is flying text, but rain gutters, tube metal, wires, pipes, and electric cords are all good examples of extrusions.

## Extrusion Along Axis

Start by drawing a NURBS extrusion profile in the front view. (Try something simple, like a swirling curve.) Then with the first profile selected, choose the Create > Surf. Mesh > Extrusion Along Axis command from the Model module, open the Extrusion property page created by the operation, and look at the new shape that was created in your scene, as demonstrated in Figure 8.18.

The Extrusion Axis determines the direction that the profile is pushed to create the shape. If you choose X, Y, or Z, the extrusion will be a rigid object symmetrical around that axis.

The Length slider can make the extrusion taller in one axis, but you can change this later by scaling on one axis. You don't have to worry about getting it right at the moment.

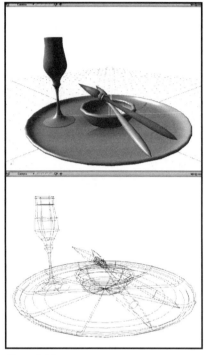

**Figure 8.16**
A variety of revolved surfaces.

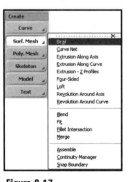

**Figure 8.17**
The Surface menu cell and Extrusion command.

**Figure 8.18**
The Mesmer logo, before and after simple extrusion.

The Subdivisions sliders allow you to add just the right amount of detail to your extrusion, and the extrusion shape can be either open or closed.

Like the Revolution operator and many other modeling operators, the Extrusion PPG has controls to hide and delete the profile curves used in the extrusion, and a Subdivisions section where you can determine the final detail or resolution of the extrusion result model.

## Extrusion Along Curve

You can also create extrusions that meander along a path, keeping their profile shape.

You'll need to draw two curves: one for the profile and one for the path it will follow. The Extrusion operator isn't smart enough to match the starting rotations of the profile and path, so you should make sure that the profile is rotated to the correct angle for the start of the path. To make the extrusion, select the profile, run the Extrusion Along Curve command, and finally pick on the extrusion path. A new object will be created. Select it and inspect the Extrusion property page, which is similar to the Extrusion Along Axis PPG, but it also has two new toggles for Snap to Profile and Rotate Profile. If Snap to Profile is checked on, the new object will begin in space exactly where the extrusion profile still is, instead of building it at the beginning of the extrusion path. If Rotate Profile is toggled on, the extrusion will try to be tangent to the path at all times.

The Length slider can be animated to grow the extrusion along a path.

## Birail Extrusions and Two Profile Extrusions

Birail Extrusions are extrusions that stretch between two curves. The resulting cross section gets bigger as the curves get farther apart. XSI chooses the positions on the cross section to attach to each of the two profile curves, so controlling the results can be a bit tricky. If the extrusion cross section is open, XSI just uses one end of the cross section curve for each rail of the extrusion. If the curve is closed, like a circle, it may guess or be unable to get a solution. When the tool cannot make a new surface, it creates a small spherical icon in the middle of the screen.

# Making Tracks: At a Glance

The prototypical use for guided extrusions are roller coaster tracks. In this tutorial, however, we'll throw in a curve ball: The tracks will be animatable so that they build themselves dynamically. The tracks will extrude themselves along the guide rails, while the cross bars in between them pop into existence at the same time (see Figure 8.19).

You'll learn how to:

◆ Extrude along one axis
◆ Extrude a profile along a curve
◆ Attach objects to a path

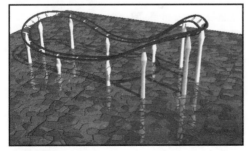

**Figure 8.19**
The completed set of tracks.

◆ Animate the visibility of an object

◆ Make changes with the modeling operators

# Tutorial: Making Tracks

Here's the short game plan next will follow detailed instructions. You'll draw a center curve for the overall shape of the tracks. Then you'll create a central cross bar, and animate it down the central track. You will tag the ends of the cross bar, and use a Plot function to make new curves for the left and the right track exactly where the ends of the tie travel through space. You'll draw a cross section of the rail, and use a guided extrude command to make the tracks, setting keys so that the tracks grow into existence right behind the animating railroad tie. Then, using Duplicate Multiple, you'll make 50 of the cross members, keeping them live on the path. For extra credit, you could animate the scale and visibility of these cross members, so that they seem to appear and grow into position as the animation progresses.

## Step 1: Draw the Outline of Your Tracks

Using the NURBS curve drawing tools, plot out the shape of your tracks in the overhead (Top) view window. The tracks can follow whatever shape you want.

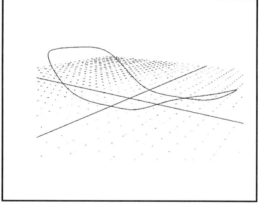

Unless you want your riders to plummet off the track at the end, use the Modify > Curve > Open/Close tool to make the track a closed circuit, or do the same by right-clicking after you drop the last point and choosing Open/Close from the context-sensitive drop menu.

In the front and side windows, raise some of the points of the curve to make hills and drops in the track. (Use Show Points in a View title bar to make points visible.) See Figure 8.20.

## Step 2: Make a Cross Member for the Track

**Figure 8.20**
A camera view of the track path.

Next you'll design a cross bar that will link the two tracks. Get a primitive polygon mesh cylinder, and in the Geometry property page, adjust the number of V parameters to 4, so we have some detail on the cylinder to model with.

Tag the points at the top and at the bottom of the cylinder, and scale them smaller in X and Z by holding down just the left and right mouse buttons as you scale, so the tips of the cross bar are narrow.

Untag the points, select the cylinder again as an object, and scale the whole cylinder until it looks like it will be the right size and shape for the curve you drew in Step 1. (Remember, you can make it thinner by holding just the left and right mouse buttons, and you can scale it uniformly by holding the Shift button.)

## Step 3: Attach the Cross Member to the Track

You want the cross member to be attached to the path that runs down the center of the tracks, animating along the length of the path from the beginning to the end.

Now with the cross member selected, enter the Animation module and choose the command Create > Path > Set Path. In the dialog box that pops up, leave the animation Start at 1 and the End at 100, and check on the Linear and Tangent boxes.

Click OK to dismiss the dialog box, and finish the command by picking on your path. The Linear option will remove the ease-in and ease-out so that the cross bar moves at a constant rate along the path. The Tangent option will make the cross bar rotate as it follows the curve around.

Open the PathCns property page if it didn't pop up automatically (click on the Selection button in the MCP and look under Kinematics/Constraints/PathCns), as shown in Figure 8.21.

Click on the Tangency tab. When Tangency is active, the cross section changes orientation at different points along the path to remain correctly oriented between the rails. The Tangency command can align any axis of the cross section to the track, so in the Tangency tab of the property page, type a number 1 in the axis you want aligned, and a 0 in the two others to let XSI know which axis to align. If you want to know which is correct before trying it turn on Show Centers, and zoom in on the cross section. Look at the colored arrow that you want to be aligned to follow the curve: red, green, or blue. If you want the red axis aligned to the curve, put a 1 in the X text box of the Tangency section. If you want green, put the 1 in Y, while for blue you would use Z (RGB = XYZ). The correct axis here is the X-axis.

Now that your cross section is aligned to the path, check that it is facing up in the right direction. If it isn't, you can go to the Up Vector tab of the PathCns property page, and check the Active box to enable the Up Vector. The axis with a 1 in the entry area will be the axis aligned up in global Y. You can modify this by changing the numbers (Z up is what we need—put a 1 in Z and a 0 in X and Y) and by adjusting the roll.

When you use the Create > Path > Set Path command in Animate mode, the cross bar will be stuck on the path you made, and the point of attachment will be the local center of the cross section. That's what we want in this case, but it's nice to know that you can change where an object is stuck onto a path. Just move the center in Center mode with the translate keys, or you could just tag all the vertices of the cross section and use the Move Center to Vertices command, located in the Transform menu of the MCP.

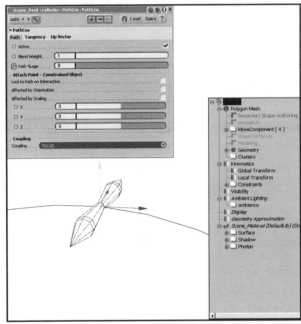

**Figure 8.21**
The Path Constraint operator and property page.

Back in the Path tab of the PathCns property page, see that the Path Percentage is animated. This is what actually moves the cross section along the path. Scrub in the timeline to see the cross section move and the values change.

## Step 4: Make Some Paths for the Rails

We need two more paths for the rails to follow: one inside of the center path and one outside. We can't just duplicate the original, because then the rails would overlap. We can't duplicate and scale the original, because then the rails might not maintain a constant distance between themselves. What we can do is use the animated cross bar to define two more curves that follow the ends of the cross section as it moves through space. This is called plotting (see Figure 8.22). XSI can plot the position of objects from their centers or from tagged points, creating a path by dropping a new point in space at intervals in time.

Zoom in really close on the cross bar, and tag just one point on each end of the cross section. (If you tag more than one point, you'll make more curves than you need, since the curves will be drawn from the tagged points.)

Now with the two tags still active (showing in red), in the Animate module, near the bottom under the Tools section, choose the Plot > Curve command. Leave the Start and End Frame properties at the defaults, and change the Step Value to 5, so that a point is created on the curve every 5 frames. Click OK to execute the command.

Do a Modify > Curve > Open/Close on each of the new curves, so they form an unbroken loop.

## Step 5: Draw the Profile of the Tracks

In the right view, draw the cross sectional profile of the rails that your roller coaster will run along. Imagine that you just cut a slice out of the tracks, and imagine the shape of that slice. Keep the shape of the profile fairly simple, with less than eight points. The complexity of the shape will have a huge impact on the complexity of the final tracks, and complexity will mean a slowdown for your computer.

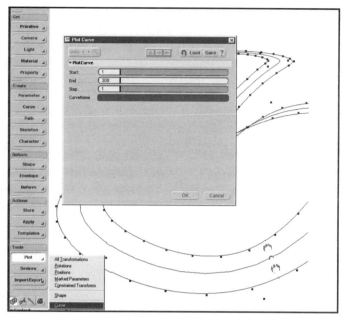

**Figure 8.22**
The new rail guides, after plotting.

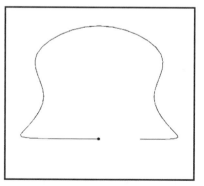

**Figure 8.23**
The cross section of the rails. Note the point where it will attach to the curve.

Make sure that you create the curve in the Right view. Also, it is good to know that the Extrude command will place the extrusion on the path using the center of your profile for placement, so if you want the rail to run above the middle of the path, you should enter Center mode and offset the center of the cross section below the rail cross section curve.

## Step 6: Make the Path Extrusions for Both Tracks

With the track profile selected, execute the Extrusion Along Curve command from the Create > Surf. Mesh menu.

Pick one of the two new track curves created in Step 4. Open the Extrusion Property page if it did not open automatically, (If the tracks are dark, maybe they need to be inverted. Check the normals: if they seem to point inside the surface, invert them.) You can make the tracks curvier by increasing the number of subdivisions per span if you wish.

We want the track to grow out, starting small and reaching all the way to the beginning at the last frame. The Extrusion End Position slider in the Extrusion property page accomplishes this. Set the slider to 1 at frame 1, and click on the small green animation divot to the left of the property name End Pos to set a key.

Move the time slider to frame 100, set the End Pos to 100 (meaning 100% of the length of the curve), and set another key. You may also adjust the U and V span subdivision to make a smooth track if you need to. Keep the subdivision as low as you can to avoid slowdowns in interactivity, while having enough subdivisions to be able to maintain the shape of the curve. You can also animate the number of subdivisions, so that the number grows as the track does.

Repeat Step 6 for the other curve created in Step 4. You now have a set of two tracks!

## Step 7: Make More Cross Sections

Back in the Path tab of the PathCns property page for the cross bar, the path Percentage slider controls where along the path the cross bar is. Since we want 50 of them, all at different places along the path, we won't really want this one animated along the path, but rather we'll want it stationary at the beginning of the path (see Figure 8.24).

Drag the timeslider to frame 1, and then click with your right mouse button over the animation icon to the left of the Path percentage slider. When the pop-up menu appears, choose the Remove Animation option. Now when you scrub in the timeslider, the cross bar should remain stationary at the beginning of the path.

We want 50 (total) of the cross sections, so we need to make 49 more, all at different points on the path. Fortunately, XSI will do this for us automatically, so we won't have to do the same thing over and over, 49 times.

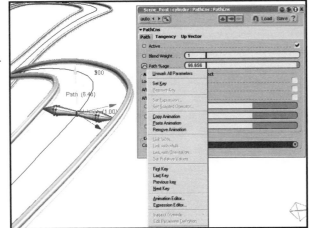

**Figure 8.24**
Removing the animation from the End Position parameter in the Path Cns property page.

A simpler way to create multiple cross bars at different points along the middle path would be to use the Duplicate from Animation option. However, the point of doing it this way is to use a formula inside of a property page. This technique can be applied to almost any property, so it's more flexible than Duplicate from Animation.

Go to the Duplicate/Instantiate Options item in the Edit menu at the bottom of the MCP, and make sure that the Constraints property is set to Copy & Share Input. When we duplicate the cross bar, this will ensure that the path constraint that we set is duplicated along with it.

Now select the cross bar, and from the Edit menu at the bottom of the MCP, choose Duplicate/Instantiate > Duplicate Multiple, and make 49 more copies, with no changes to the size, placement, or rotation. The result is that all 49 new cross bars should lay in the same place on the track.

With all 49 new cross bars selected (they should still be selected, unless you have clicked on something else after making them—if they are, the selection box will say MULTI(49)), open the property page for the Multiple Selection > Kinematics > Constraints > PathCns using the transient selection explorer in the MCP. (Hint: Expand the Kinematics property page to see the Path Constraints.) See Figure 8.25.

Now any changes we make to the Path Constraint will be applied to all of the selected cross bars.

What we really want is for each cross bar to have a different position along the path, starting at 2 and going up to 100. Click directly into the text entry area of the Path Percentage slider (where the number is) and type the formula $L(2,100)$, which means "Make this value different on each cross section, changing linearly from 2 to 100." Press the Enter button to execute the change. All the cross sections should be in different places, evenly spaced along the center curve! If they don't seem to change, force a refresh of the scene by dragging in the timeline.

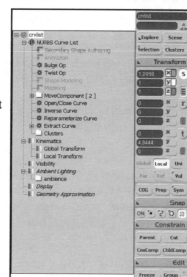

**Figure 8.25**
This is the transient selection explorer (the Selection button in the MCP) showing a curve with a bunch of operators on it.

Try animating the length of the extrusions and then making the cross sections become visible as the tracks build past them for extra credit. The roller coaster is an example of flexibly using both axis extrusions and path extrusions to construct a set. Since the modeling tools are dynamic, they can also be used to animate the construction of the path.

# Lip Service: At a Glance

Let's make some lips, using a variation on the Extrusion tool (see Figure 8.26).

You'll learn how to:

◆ Perform a Birail extrusion

◆ Use the Guided extrude

# Tutorial: Lip Service

Other forms of extrusion along a curve are the Birail and Extrusion—two profiles commands. Both use an extrusion profile and two extrusion paths, one for each side of the profile. As the profile extrudes along the two paths, the profile gets bigger or smaller as needed to connect them. This differs from the standard extrusion, which follows one profile. Birail extrusions are great ways to make boat hulls, bananas, saxophones, and other shapes where one profile changes size as it sweeps along two guides. Here we'll use Create > Surf. Mesh > Birail to make a set of lips.

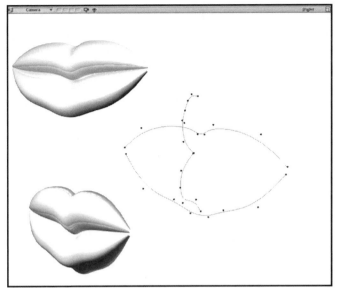

**Figure 8.26**
The completed lips.

## Step 1: Make the Spline Guides

Run your finger along the top edge of your lip, and then draw that shape with a NURBS curve in the Front window. This shape will become the top extrusion path.

Trace your bottom lip edge, and draw that, too, starting from the same side as before. Your splines should now look like an outline of a pair of lips. In this case, the two curves—one for the top and one for the bottom—do not need to have the same number of control points. If you want perfectly symmetrical lips, you could draw only the top curve, duplicate it, and scale it in negative Y to make the other curve (see Figure 8.27).

The final method is to use the Symmetry tool when drawing the curves. Right-click on the Sym button in the MCP and choose XZ, to set the symmetry plane to XZ, which will mirror each point in positive Y with another in negative Y. The Sym button should remain lit up, showing that Symmetry is on. Draw the top lip curve again, in the Front view, above the origin. As you draw, XSI will mirror your work, creating the other lip curve. Tap the Escape key when you are done to end the command and turn off Symmetry.

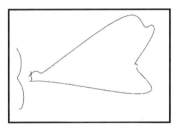

**Figure 8.27**
The contours of the lips are the two guide splines.

### Step 2: Make the Lip Shape Cross Section

Move to the Right view. Now, using the lines you just drew to help with scale, draw a cross section of your lips at their middle, fullest, tallest point. This will be what is extruded, with the scale modified to fit between the two guides.

The cross section should be drawn in the Right view, so that it is perpendicular to the guides (see Figure 8.28).

The scale of the cross section piece doesn't matter. XSI will scale it down so that the starting end of the profile runs along one guide, and the ending point runs along the other guide.

### Step 3: Make the Lips

With the single cross section selected, execute the Create > Surf. Mesh > Birail Command and then pick on the top and bottom lip profiles. The pair of lips is made!

You can open and adjust the detail in the lips with the Birail operator on the object, under NURBS Surface Mesh in the Operator stack, to make smoother lips (see Figure 8.29).

### Step 4: Tweak the Results

If the surface of the lips is dark, it may be inside out; show normals to check. If the normals are facing the wrong way, choose Modify > Surf. Mesh > Invert Normals.

You can interactively adjust the lips by modifying the curves and changing the curves' position or shape (including the cross section).

When you are happy with your lips, you can select them and go to Operator > Freeze Modeling from the Edit menu to remove their dependence on the profile curves. Birail is a simple tool that is very powerful and useful. Plant leaves also make great candidates for Birail extrusions.

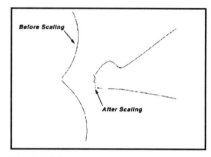

**Figure 8.28**
The cross sectional curve describes the contour of the lips.

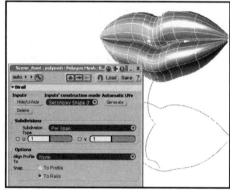

**Figure 8.29**
The Birail menu and property page.

# Lofted Surfaces

Some shapes in the real world aren't symmetrical around any axis. Revolving or extruding a profile curve can't make these shapes. However, they can be made by drawing a series of cross sections slicing through the object.

To visualize this, imagine a stick of celery. Lay the mental vegetable down on an imaginary cutting board, and starting at the top, cut it into slices about a half-inch thick. Each slice is a cross section. When the celery is all cut up, imagine carefully stacking the slices back together and wrapping a sheet of plastic tightly around them (see Figure 8.30). That's what a lofted surface is: a spline patch stretched over a series of cross sections.

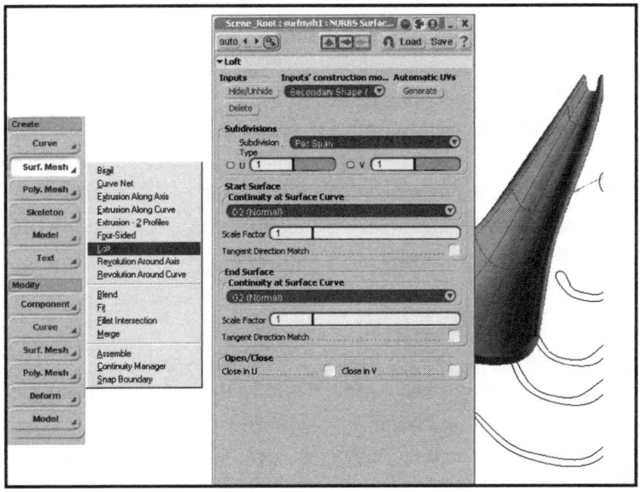

Another good visualization of a loft (or skin) is the roof of your house. First, the cross-sectional ribs of the roof are constructed out of two by fours, and then a waterproof skin of tarpaper and shingles is lofted over them to form the roof.

Human shapes can also be made from skinning cross sections. Visualize the cross sectional shape of your leg, starting at the thigh and moving down the leg about six inches at a time. A skin made from circles made to the shape of the cross sections of your leg would look just like the real skin stretched on your frame (see Figure 8.31).

Lofts can be created from at least two NURBS curves with any number of control vertices. Although the cross sections don't have to share the same number of points, it's often good workflow to start with one cross section (called a rib) and then duplicate and modify it for the next, the next, and so on.

When you have a few cross sections, and you have placed them apart from one another in space, choose the Create > Surf. Mesh > Loft (or Create > Poly. Mesh > Loft) menu cell to activate the command. You must now pick each of the cross sections in order, from first to last, with the left mouse button. If you accidentally pick one out of order, press the E key to cancel the command, select the first one, and do it over. If you forget which mouse button does what, look at the status bar to see how to choose the cross sections. When all the cross sections are picked, use the right mouse button to finish the command and bring up the Skin dialog box. You can also use the new Freeform tool (hold down hotkey F9) to select the profiles in order, by drawing one line with the tool through them all, from start to finish. The order is important. If you loft some members out of order there will be a strange pouch in the lofted skin. If you make a mistake when selecting ribs for a loft, use the Esc key to cancel the Loft tool without creating a loft, and do it over again.

After the loft is complete, open the Loft property page in the Property Explorer from the MCP to adjust the subdivision, continuity, and other properties.

If the surface is dark, it's probably inside out. Check by showing the normals. They should point outward from the surface. If they do not, use the Modify > Surf. Mesh > Invert Normals command to flip them.

**Figure 8.30**
The celery cross sections change shape as they go.

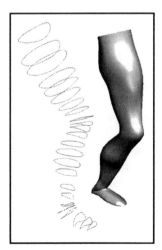

**Figure 8.31**
A human leg and the curves that made it. A drawing of a leg was used to match proportions.

## Getting a Head in XSI

Skinning is also a great way to make human faces. Walk into a room with a mirror, and imagine drawing lines from the center of the top of your head down your face and under your chin, about a half an inch apart. Then turn these curves projected onto your face sideways in your mind so you can look at them in a side view. The shape of each line is the contour of your face at that longitude, with the top of your head and under your chin being the poles. Another method is to locate one of the poles inside your mouth and the other at the rear of your head, and imagine the contour lines coming from inside your mouth and over the top of your head to the back (see Figure 8.32).

## The Four-Sided Tool

The four-sided patch tool is the most useful and least utilized of all the XSI NURBS modeling tools. It is designed to create a surface from four different splines that represent the four sides of resulting surface. Each one of the splines can be a different shape and can even have a different number of control points (although it's a good idea to make opposite sides have the same number of points). Why is this important? Imagine that you are modeling a human character and have divided the chest area into squares for the pectoral area and the stomach area. The bottom edge of the pectoralis needs to exactly match the top of the abdominal section, and the edges need to line up over the kidneys. You could draw simple surface curves over a polygonal shape to define these areas and then use the four-sided tool to turn them into NURBS surfaces prior to binding them together in a surface mesh.

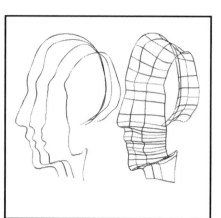

**Figure 8.32**
A human face can be drawn using contours as loft curves.

Using the tool is easy. Draw the four sides out of separate splines, and try to get the end of one side at least close to the start of the next curve, so that XSI can correctly guess which end of the curve to connect to the next curve. The direction you draw the curves is not important.

Finally, choose the Create > Surf. Mesh > Four Sided command from the Model module, and pick each of the four sides in a consistent order, clockwise or counter clockwise. If you pick the sides in the wrong order—i.e., one side, the opposite side, and then the next pair of opposite sides—the patch will be mangled.

When you pick the last (fourth) spline boundary, the surface is completed! Open the property page to modify the U and V subdivision, making the four-sided surface follow the contours of the splines more closely.

Modeling is an art form, and these tools are just the basic elements you will use to practice your craft. Each can be combined with other, more specific tools in SOFTIMAGE XSI to perform unique functions. Some techniques work miracles in some circumstances and don't work at all in others.

As the artist, you should experiment with all of them to find the tools that work best for you.

# Psycho: At a Glance

In this tutorial, we will create a part of a bathroom scene, using many different modeling tools to create and assemble the pieces of a bathtub and shower curtain (see Figure 8.33).

You will learn:

◆ How to use the Four-Sided tool

◆ Further application and practice on the use of extrusions and revolutions

# Tutorial: Psycho
## Step 1: Create the Floor and Walls

We need to create some simple floor and wall area for our scene. For the floor, use Get > Primitive > Surface > Grid to create a floor plane. Type 2 in all three scale axes' entry boxes to make the grid twice as big.

We want only two walls that will be the back of the tub and shower arrangement. In the Top view, choose Create > Curve > Draw Linear, and holding down the Ctrl button to enable the grid snap, place five points along the edge of the grid in an L-shaped configuration (see Figure 8.34).

Now extrude this linear L-shaped segment up in Y to make the walls, using the Create > Surf. Mesh > Extrusion Along Axis command.

By default, it will extrude in the wrong direction, so in the Extrusion property page, check only the Extrude Along Y box (check off the others) and make it snap to the placement of the L spline by checking the Snap to Profile option. You can make the walls shorter with the Extrusion Length slider, or taller with the Scale in Y menu cell. Change the U and V subdivisions if you want to. Make the floor the parent of the walls, and change their names in the schematic view to keep the scene organized.

## Step 2: Model the Bathtub

The tub will be a revolution for the basic shape, with some simple tagging and moving points to make it squared off. In the Front view, draw a cross section of a tub using Create > Curve > Draw Cubic by CVs, including the inner and outer walls, as if you sawed through the tub with a hacksaw (see Figure 8.35).

**Figure 8.33**
The completed, assembled tub scene.

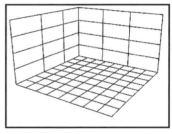

**Figure 8.34**
The grid floor and the extruded walls.

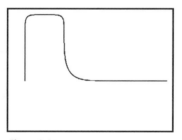

**Figure 8.35**
The revolution profile for the bathtub. The Ctrl key made the points snap to the floor, keeping the line straight.

**179**

Make the outside of the spline end straight down at the floor height. Make the inside end stretch towards the center Y-axis, with four or more control points so the floor of the tub will have some detail. Leave the last point just shy of the Y-axis, so there will be a hole in the middle of the tub (at the Y-axis) for water to drain through. Again, you can use the Ctrl key to drop points right on the grid so that the tub has straight sides and a level floor.

Make the tub with the Create > Surf. Mesh > Revolution Around Axis command. If you drew the profile in the front view, it should be revolved around the Y-axis, so open the Revolution PPG and make sure that Y is the axis of revolution. If the surface is dark, it may need to be inverted, using the Modify > Surf. Mesh > Invert Normals command.

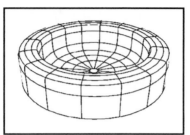

**Figure 8.36**
The tub after revolution, with more U subdivisions.

Open the property page for the new NURBS surface. Make the U Subdivisions 16 so we have a smooth tub, with enough points to sculpt (see Figure 8.36). Check the Close U box to seal the tub all the way around.

Now we'll sculpt the tub into a more rectangular shape by tagging points and moving them in space. In the Top view, show points and tag one-half of the tub (using the T hotkey), minus the two rows of points around the middle hole.

With the points tagged, drag them in global Z only (which will keep the tub straight) to elongate the tub into a nice shape.

> Are you a perfectionist? Tag the points around the hole and translate those down in Y slightly, so the tub will drain correctly.

With the same points selected, scale the tub in X only to make the foot of the tub slightly thinner. If you wish, you can make the head of the tub a bit taller than the foot. Tag the points in the front half of the tub, deselect all those at floor level, and tag the remaining points up in Y only (see Figure 8.37).

Untag those points, and tag only those points near the floor of the tub. Carefully holding both the left and right mouse buttons, scale the bottom of the tub inward slightly to make a graceful shape.

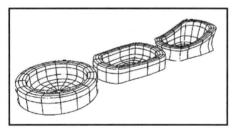

**Figure 8.37**
The tub in different stages of tagged and moved points, sculpting its shape.

When you are done sculpting the tub, use Edit > Operator > Freeze Modeling (or the Freeze M button) from the MCP to get rid of the Move components and simplify the tub geometry.

The tub probably isn't in the right place or the right size for the floor and walls. Scale it down and place it in the corner. (Remember, Shift constrains scale to work uniformly so you don't dent the tub accidentally.)

## Step 3: Model the Shower Rod

The shower rod is a circular tube of metal that should follow the curves of one-half of the tub and hang above it to hold the curtain. We'll grab a curve from the tub as a guide and use an Extrusion Along curve to make the tube.

First, with nothing selected, run the Create > Curve > Extract from Surface command. Pick on the tub shape to select the tub and pick on an edge you want to extract running on the lip of the tub. If you clicked over more than one curve, a list of curves will be presented. Choose one of the knot curve options to create a new curve on the tub. If the curve is running in the wrong direction, delete that curve and try again. If it's too hard to pick the curve after activating the tool, you can pick the curve first, with the V knot curve filter (with the tub selected, the little triangle in the MCP).

Look in the Camera view to see the new curve. In the Extract Curve operator property page, adjust the Position slider to pick a position along the top inside of the tub, so the curtain will hang inside the tub and prevent water damage. You can also scale the curve as you wish to fit inside the tub (see Figure 8.38).

When you're happy with the curve, translate it in Y to the top of the walls. There are two problems, however. We only need half of the curve, and it needs to be straight across, all at the same height.

With the curve selected, run the Create > Curve > Extract Segment command to get a new curve that is just a portion of the original. The command will wait for you to click on the base curve to define where you want the beginning and the end of the new segment to be. Pick points on the curve along the outside of the tub, away from the walls. If the tool chooses exactly the wrong half to keep, open the Extract Curve Segment PPG and adjust the Position sliders on the two Curve Point Adaptor tabs, which define the start and end point.

To make the curve level, change the scale in Y to be 0.

Name this curve rodTop.

Finally, select Get > Primitive > Curve > Circle, scale it to an appropriate cross section size for the shower rod, and use the Extrusion command, picking the half-tub curve as the extrusion path.

Adjust the size of the circle as needed, and invert the surface if it's dark (see Figure 8.39).

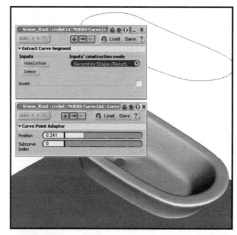

**Figure 8.38**
The extracted curve after moving it up in the air, and the property page that created it.

## Step 4: Model the Shower Curtain

If we make the shower curtain out of a four-sided patch, using the same curve as the rod for the top and bottom, we'll be able to animate various effects and keep the curtain flowing.

Copy the rodTop curve and name it rodBottom. Move it down into the tub.

Draw another curve with five or so points, in the Front view, stretching vertically from the top rod curve to the bottom rod curve.

In the Top view, translate it to one end of the two rod curves, and name it leftEdge.

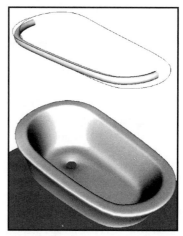

**Figure 8.39**
The final rod, made from an extrusion along an extracted, modified path.

**181**

Duplicate the left edge and name it rightEdge. Then translate it to the opposite end of the rod curves (see Figure 8.40).

Choose Create > Surf. Mesh > Four-Sided, and pick each of the four curves, in order. (It doesn't matter which curve you start with, but continue clockwise or counter clockwise. For example: left, top, right, bottom works, but left, right, bottom, top does not.)

A four-sided surface is created. Adjust its position so it hangs from the bottom center of the rod. You can also move points on the curves you used to create the curtain, to make it wavy.

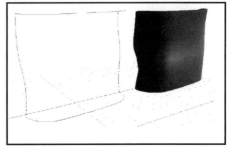

Want to have more control over the appearance of the curtain? Well, the curtain is too straight because it doesn't have many points along the top and bottom. You could go back and use the Create > Curve > Fit On Curve tool to make new top and bottom curves with more points. Then you could run the Four-Sided command again, and move these points back and forth in the Top view to make more ripples in the curtain.

**Figure 8.40**
The four sides of the curtain, and the resulting four-sided surface. Try moving the points on the curves after making the surface!

## Step 5: Model the Shower Curtain Clips

Shower clips look a bit like rings that don't connect all the way around. A simple way to make them is to get a primitive circle, move it off center from the global Y-axis, and revolve it not quite all the way around so there is a gap for the curtain.

Select the circle you used as the Extrusion profile for the curtain, duplicate it, and name it clipcircle.

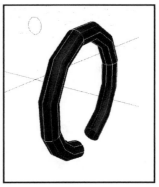

Translate it in Y one half-unit, and revolve it with the Create, Surf. Mesh, Revolution Around Axis tool. In the Revolution property page, set the Revolution Axis to X (only—uncheck Y), the Start Angle to 200 degrees, and the Revolution Angle to 330 degrees (see Figure 8.41).

Move the resulting shower clip to a position on the shower rod so you can see what it looks like. Select the circle it was revolved from and adjust it, scaling it smaller and moving it along the Y-axis to change the dimensions of the clip until you are happy.

Make 8 or so more clips and position them along the top rod to hold the shower curtain, and rotate each of them in Y so they face the right direction (perpendicular to the rod).

**Figure 8.41**
The clip is an incomplete revolution of a curve offset from an axis. Adjust it by modifying the size and height of the revolution circle.

## Step 6: Showerhead and Handles

The showerhead is a great object to revolve. Draw a revolution spline like the picture, revolve around Y, and then either bend the head manually by tagging points, or use a Bend deformation, adjusting the Bend Angle, Radius, and Offset in Y to make the showerhead bend so that it can come out of the wall but still spray down into the tub (see Figure 8.42).

When you're finished, rotate, scale, and translate it into place on the wall.

The knobs could be simple revolutions, or perhaps a revolved center stalk with four revolved knobs parented to it. Examine the parts diagram, make the parts, parent them together, and then duplicate the finished knob hierarchy for the other side.

## Give Yourself a Hand: At a Glance

In this tutorial, we will learn how to create a realistic humanoid hand model using a couple of powerful NURBS tools built into SOFTIMAGE|XSI.

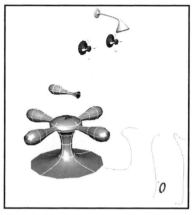

**Figure 8.42**
The showerhead is a revolution that has been deformed with a Bend operator.

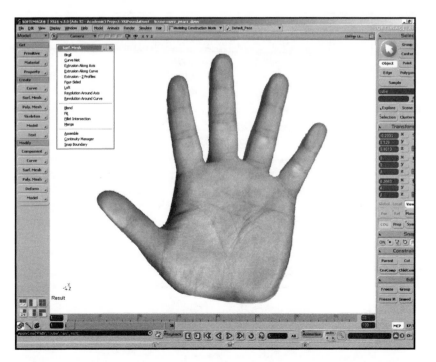

We will learn how to:

◆ Use the Rotoscope view to create an image plane to use as a modeling reference

◆ Use the Revolution command to create fingers

◆ Use the Fillet Intersection to fillet between the fingers and the palm, creating a smooth blend

# Tutorial: Give Yourself a Hand

Unless you have a photographic memory, it can be hard to model something as complex as a human hand from scratch. Especially when modeling human body parts, the proportions of the model are difficult to get just right. One way to make your job a lot easier is to import an image into XSI and use that image as a backdrop to model over. This technique is called rotoscoping. There are many picture formats you can import to XSI. In this example, we have used the BMP format.

## Step 1: Create an Image Plane (Rotoscope)

Scan your hand on a flatbed scanner, or use the picture from the project for this book included on the CD-ROM.

In the Top viewport, click on the view style button in the top-right corner (it says Wireframe if you are in Wireframe mode), and select Rotoscope to put the view into the Rotoscope mode. The Rotoscope Options page will appear. Using this option page, you can tell SOFTIMAGE|XSI what image file you want to use as a background in the View window.

Click on the New button and select New from File to load an image. Browse to the picture of the hand you are using, and select it. Close the Rotoscope Options page.

When you zoom or track in Rotoscope view, you will notice that the picture does not change size or placement with the grid (and objects in the scene). Let's track the camera, so the middle finger stays right on top of the center Z-axis line.

Hold the Z key, and using the left mouse button, align the center Z-axis line to the middle finger. This step is important because we want to revolve a NURBS curve along that axis.

> You can scale, offset, and otherwise edit the actual image you imported by clicking on the Edit button. This is also the same as right-clicking in the clip window to show the context-sensitive options and choosing Clip Properties. If you closed the Rotoscope window and want to open it again, you can get it from Wireframe > Rotoscopy Options.

> Since the backdrop picture does not zoom or track, it is important to align the View window using the rotoscope to your satisfaction, and then discontinue using zoom or pan in that window. To make sure you do not accidentally change the scale of the model relative to the scale of the roto image, you can click the aspect lock icon (looks like a magnifying glass) at the top of the roto view.

## *Step 2: Create the Fingers*

Maximize the Top view so you can really see what you are making. (Left-click on the resize viewport button at the top-right of the view.)

Make sure your toolbar on the left is in Model mode. Select Create > Curve > Draw Cubic by CVs.

Plot about 15 points starting from the tip of the finger toward the root. Make sure to add more points around the joint areas of the finger so that it will bend well when animated.

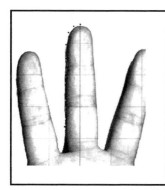

Select Create > Surf. Mesh > Revolution Around Axis, and then right-click to end picking. (We're going to revolve around an axis, not a curve.)

Oops, it looks strange! Don't be alarmed. Open the Revolution property page, and select Revolve Around Z (and uncheck any other axes that are marked) at the bottom of the Revolution Axis menu. Close the window.

Using your finger as a reference, edit the finger to your liking in the Right view. You can use the M hotkey to move points one at a time, or use the T hotkey to tag multiple points, and scale, rotate, and translate them in Point mode. You can check the overall appearance of the finger in the Camera view. Use the Top view to make sure the finger fits with the image plane. When you like the way the finger looks, you are done.

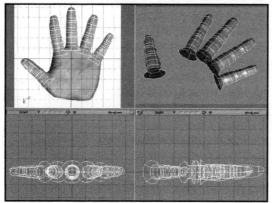

Switch back to Object selection mode, and choose Edit > Duplicate/Instantiate > Duplicate Single from the top menu bar. A duplicate of the finger is created in the same place as the first.

Translate the new finger in the Top view so it's lined up with the index finger on the Rotoscope image. Scale, rotate, and edit tagged points so the index finger is the correct size and shape. Repeat this step for the ring finger, pinky, and thumb. Be sure to check the Front, Right, and Camera views during this process to make sure the fingers look accurate from all angles, not just the Top view.

**185**

## Step 3: Create the Palm

Choose Get > Primitive > Surface > Sphere to get a NURBS sphere.

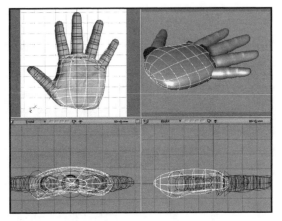

Open the property page for the sphere, change the Radius to 3, and add more detail by changing the U and V subdivisions to 12 each. Close the Sphere property page.

We want to have one pole of the sphere at the wrist, so we can connect it to the arm later if we want to. We have to rotate the sphere to make this happen. Rotate the sphere 90 degrees around the X-axis. You can type 90 directly into the entry box for the X-axis in the rotation menu cell if you wish.

Move the sphere and scale it to approximately the size of the palm, using the image plane in the Rotoscope view as a guide. Also check the thickness of the palm in the other views, and scale on one axis at a time, as necessary.

Tag and move points to conform the sphere to the shape of the palm in the image.

Make sure that the edge of each finger extends into the palm sphere surface at least a little, so we can create a good fillet.

Getting close is good enough, because the fillet will hide the details in the joint. But if you wanted to be really precise, you could extract the curve from the open edge of the finger, project it onto the sphere, and rebuild the finger to extend to that new projected curve.

We are going to create a fillet intersection, so that the finger surfaces and the palm surface will connect seamlessly. A fillet is a curved section of surface that connects two parts smoothly, like caulk running between a floor and a wall. The fillet in the hand will make the surface of the fingers appear to seamlessly transition into the palm.

## Step 4: Create a Fillet Intersection

Deselect everything by holding the spacebar and clicking an empty area.

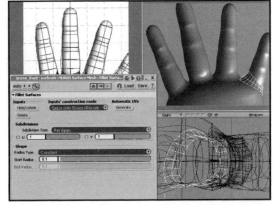

Make sure you are in the Model mode, and then choose Create > Surf. Mesh > Fillet Intersection.

The status bar at the bottom prompts you to pick the objects you want to create an intersection between. Pick the index finger, which will highlight white. Then pick the palm, and right-click to complete the Fillet Intersection command.

A fillet will be formed between the index finger and the palm.

Open the property page for the fillet intersection, and change Radius Type to Cubic, and Start Radius and End Radius to 0.3. You can adjust these to see the effects on your hand.

Repeat the fillet procedure for the other three fingers. For the thumb, set Start Radius and End Radius to 0.5, for a broader transition.

# Turning Curves into PolyMeshes

Since drawing a curve is such an easy way to rough out a shape, it would certainly be useful to be able to generate polygon mesh surfaces from curves. You could use this function for basic polymodeling, for filling in curves (sometimes called a face), and for creating extrusions based on spline shapes. In the real world, this technique is used every day for creating 3D logo artwork from 2D logo art created by graphic designers.

XSI has an operator that will convert a NURBS curve to a filled surface mesh. This tool can also take multiple curves as input. It will even interpret inner curves as holes, and make the mesh appropriately.

The operator that does this is called, appropriately enough, the Create > Poly. Mesh > Curves to Mesh operator, and can be found in the Model module.

There are a great many options in the Curves to Mesh PPG, and we'll explore most of them in the following examples.

## *Simple Closed Shapes*

Open the scene called MesmerIcons from the courseware that accompanies this material.

You'll see a variety of different shapes, representing glyphs in the Mesmer language system.

Since they are just curves, they won't render. Let's turn them into polygon mesh surfaces that we can apply materials to and render in 3D.

1. At the bottom left, there are two hands, each with three fingers, where the middle finger points to a dot. The simplest case is to fill a closed curve.

2. Select the leftmost dot and choose the command Poly. Mesh > Curves to Mesh. The dot will now be filled in. View it with the camera in the shader view.

3. You can do more than one curve at a time. Select the three shapes next to the filled dot, using Shift and the spacebar to extend the selection. With all three selected, use the Polymesh > Curves to Mesh command to fill all of them in (see Figure 8.43).

**Figure 8.43**
A simple closed curve, converted to a polygon face.

If you select one of the new filled-in-shapes (called faces when they are perfectly flat like this), you'll see that it is composed of a single polygon. You can adjust how closely the polygon matches the original curve. With the face selected, open the Curve to Mesh Converter PPG. In the General tab, the Step Contour slider determines how many edge vertices are added between each control point on the original curve. More contour steps makes for a more accurate shape (see Figure 8.44).

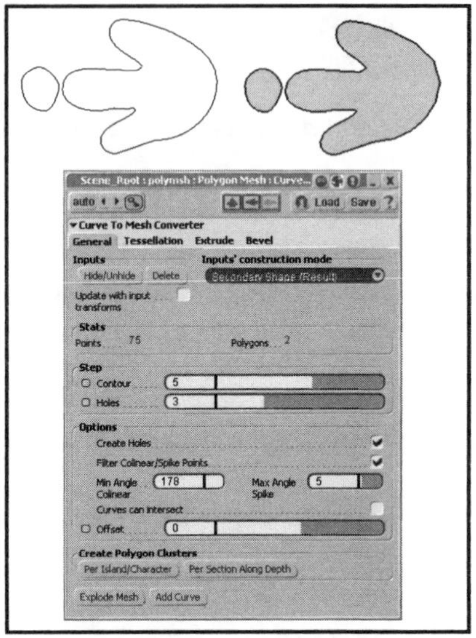

## Compound Shapes

The next shapes over look like four fingered hands with a minus sign or a plus sign in them. This is a more complex shape, because it contains negative space. The Curves to Mesh command will automatically figure this out correctly. When you select one curve and then select another curve within the first, XSI interprets the inner curve as a hole.

The curves don't have to be selected in a particular order, or be in a hierarchy. It's a good idea for them to lay in the same plane.

Select the outer hand and the inner negative space (the minus sign). Use the Polymesh > Curves to Mesh command. A new polygon mesh will be created with a hole correctly placed in the middle.

Okay, fine, you say, but how smart is it? Can it have a hole within a hole, and mix and match positive and negative space? Yes, it can. The far-right hand has a hole in it and then a dot inside that hole. It also has a dot outside the hand, showing that XSI interprets outlaying curves as positive space. Select all these curves at once with the Shift-spacebar method, and run the Polymesh > Curves to Mesh command (see Figure 8.45).

## Tessellation

Right now, XSI is making polygons that don't have any interior detail. This is only one method, called Minimum Polygon Count. Depending on what you plan to do with these shapes, you might want more detail on them. For instance, if you tried to deform these icons, they wouldn't look very good because there would be large flat polygonal faces that wouldn't bend well.

You can ask XSI to chop up these new polygon meshes in different ways. This is called tessellation. Select the last hand shape you made, and open the Curve to Mesh converter. Tab over to the Tessellation tab.

**Figure 8.44**
The contour value determines how similar the polygon is to the original curve.

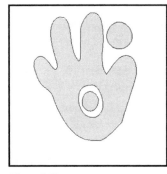

**Figure 8.45**
The Converter treats concentric curves as holes in the face.

Under Method, choose the Delaunay tessellation method, which creates only triangular polygons by stitching back and forth between adjacent vertices. While this doesn't look as clean as the Minimum Polygon Count Method, it would work better if the object flexed or deformed. You can modify how the tessellation works for your specific object with the Delaunay options (see Figure 8.46). Try toggling on Maximum Area and setting that slider to 10.

The Medial Axis option works well for objects without internal holes and objects that are more rectangular in shape.

## Extruding Imported EPS Art

Many times in the real world, you'll be asked to use someone else's art instead of making your own. For flying logos, for instance, it's important to have precise art so that the client doesn't complain that your version of the logo isn't quite right.

The best way to do this is to ask for encapsulated postscript art from the client or a designer. EPS files are very common, and XSI will import EPS from FreeHand, Illustrator, QuarkXPress, and other programs (see Figure 8.47).

Try this out yourself. Use the command File > Import > EPS File. Then browse to the Pictures directory of the course material and choose the Meslogo.eps file. XSI will import this PostScript file and create one big compound curve out of it.

Select the Mesmer line art, move it above the icons, and scale it up.

Finally, run the Create > Poly. Mesh > Curve to Mesh command on it, and pull up the Curves to Mesh Converter PPG.

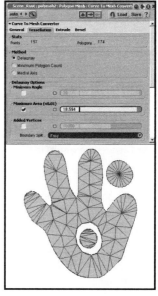

**Figure 8.46**
Delaunay tessellation makes triangles

Up until now, all the polygon meshes we've made have been flat, but that is not necessary.

We can also use the converter to extrude and bevel imported line art.

In the General tab, reduce the Step Contour to 1, making the resulting mesh much less dense. Now switch to the Extrude tab. Enter the number 1 in the Length slider and examine the results in the Camera view. The Mesmer logo art has been extruded along an axis! The extrusion has three components: a front, back, and middle tube. You can toggle any combination on or off to get a different look with the Parts check boxes. After trying out the parts, check them all back on (see Figure 8.48).

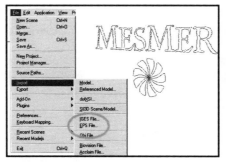

**Figure 8.47**
Import .eps art from FreeJand, Illustrator, Quark, or other design programs.

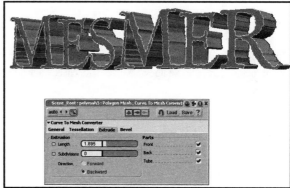

**Figure 8.48**
Extruding the EPS makes a nice 3D logo.

Logos often look better with a softer edge, called a bevel. The converter can do this, too.

Switch to the Bevel tab. To make the operation faster, first uncheck the Sides Back toggle, so only the front will be beveled. Then reduce the Sampling Step to 1.

Now drag on the Depth and Height sliders to add a beveled edge to the extruded logo. Try setting both Depth and Height to .25 SoftImage units. Then render the results in the render region.

When you are done creating the extruded logo art, freeze the object to remove the Curves to Text operator (see Figure 8.49).

## The Text Creation Tool

If you don't want to create logo typography in a different design package, you can certainly create text within XSI, with the Create > Text menu in the Model module.

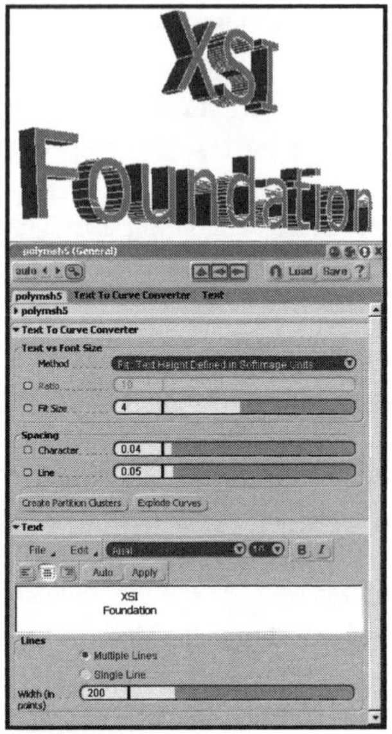

**Figure 8.49**
Beveling rounds the edges of the extrusion.

**Figure 8.50**
You can create 3D text without leaving XSI.

The text creation tool is another operator that takes installed fonts and creates NURBS curves from them, that can then be made into 3D renderable geometry with the Curves to Polymesh tool (see Figure 8.50).

Try this first with the Create > Text > Curves command. Open the Text to Curve converter operator on the 3D Text object that is created.

In the Text tab, you can enter any text you like, make font and style choices, determine whether to break onto multiple lines, and determine the text alignment method for multiple lines. Changes take effect when you click the Apply button, or constantly if you toggle on the Auto button.

The Text to Curve converter tab has other commands to adjust kerning and leading, called character space and line space in XSI.

You can also make text as flat faces with the Create > Text > Planar Mesh and Create > Text > Solid Mesh commands, using the same controls as are found in the Curves to Mesh operator.

## Conclusion

In this chapter, we have covered the basic modeling tools in XSI, along with some strategies for using them fruitfully in real-world applications. There is a great deal more to learn about modeling in XSI, including more sophisticated patch modeling, surface meshes, and the continuity manager, but these tools will get you started in the right direction. Don't forget to plan out your modeling work carefully and use good workflow habits!

# Chapter 9
# Working with Layers

In this lesson, you will learn:

◆ How to create new layers to organize your scene

◆ How to move objects in your scene to one layer or another

◆ How to turn layers on and off

◆ How to select using layers

◆ How to render only certain layers

## Introduction

After just a little bit of time working with XSI, you will doubtless be creating fairly large scenes, with hundreds or even thousands of objects. Although we've already looked at scene-wide organization tools like the Explorer and the Schematic view, there is still room for more productivity-enhancing organization tools. The Layer View and Layer panel are intended to help you with that (see Figures 9.1 and 9.2).

**Figure 9.1**
Layers are the L in KP/L.

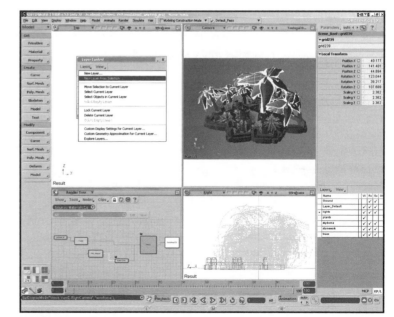

**Figure 9.2**
Tools you'll use.

# Using Layers

Using the Layer Control panel, you can group your work into separate layers according to any scheme you devise to fit your scene. If you were building a car, you could put the wheels, tires, axles, and chassis into one layer, the engine block into another, and the body into a third. Then you could easily turn off the layers you were not working on at the time, to better focus on the layer you are working with.

If you are working on a special effects composite shot, you could place the backgrounds into one layer, the geometry into another layer, the glowing elements into a third, the particle effects into a fourth, and so on, separating your work so you could easily turn on or off any combination of the effects for preview or rendering.

If you are working on a character, you might have a complex IK skeleton, a system of controls for the rig, a low-res skin for working with, and a high-res skin for rendering. Each could be on a different layer.

Once your scene is organized into layers, you can easily hide everything you are not working on, color-code elements within each layer, or quickly set certain layers not to render.

## The Layer Menu and the Current Layer

At the bottom of the Main Command Panel on the right side of your screen is the view switcher for the Keyable Parameters Layout (KP/L) panel. There in the KP/L you will find the Layer tools. The Layers menu in the KP/L is where the commands are located for adding, removing, and managing the layers that exist in the scene. If you want to edit layers while also using tools in the MCP, you can open the Layout panel in a floating window with the hotkey 6 (see Figure 9.3).

## The Layer Control Panel

When you choose View > General > Layer Control from the top menus (or tap 6), the Layer Control panel is displayed (see Figure 9.4). You are free to move the Layer Control panel around the screen to any comfortable location. You can also resize it by clicking and dragging on a bottom corner of the box, to make it larger or smaller as needed for your layers.

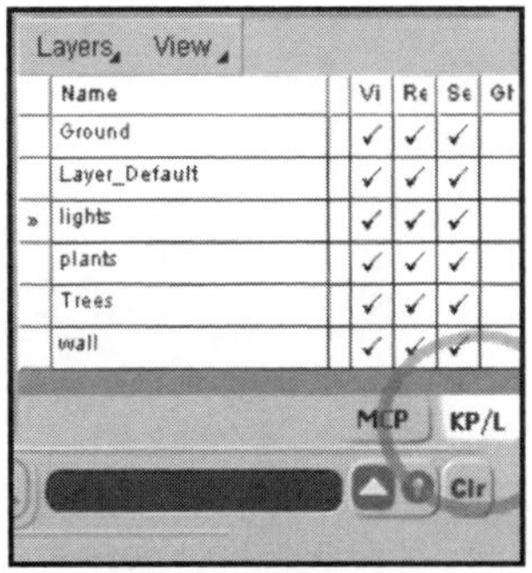

**Figure 9.3**
The Layer menu in the KP/L panel.

**Figure 9.4**
The Layer Control panel.

The Layer Control panel is a small floating dialog box divided into rows and columns (see Figure 9.5). Each row is a layer. Each column is a box for a check mark. The columns are Color, View, Render, Selectable, and Ghost. You can check or uncheck each column box for a given layer. Checking View toggles the layer visibility in the scene, marking Render makes it renderable or un-renderable, clicking Sel makes the layer selectable or unselectable, and clicking Ghost makes it possible to see animation ghosting for that layer. You can have any combination of the four aspects for each layer.

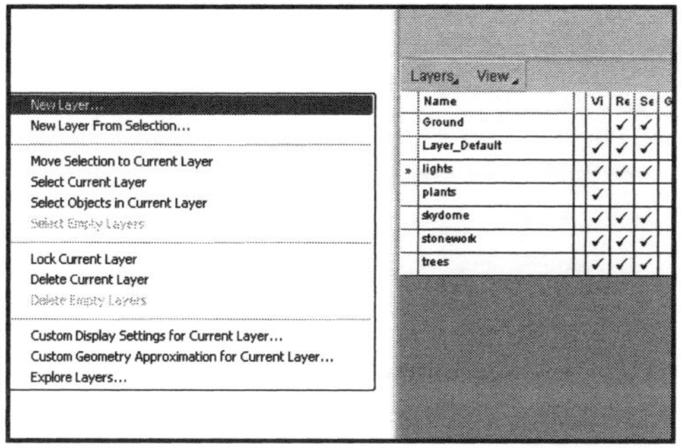

### Choosing the Active Layer

If you click on the button at the left side of each layer name, that layer becomes the active layer. All new objects that you create are placed by default into the active layer. You can select the entire contents of a layer by right-clicking on a layer name and choosing Select All Objects in Layer. When a layer is active, that is the layer that objects will be moved to if you choose the Move Selection to Current Layer command. That layer will be highlighted in a minty green color in the Layer Control panel.

**Figure 9.5**
Layer commands are in the Layer context sensitive menu.

> Layers can be viewed in the floating Explorer. Use the top-left Filter menu in the Explorer, or just type an L in the Explorer view.

### Adding Objects in a Scene to a New Layer

To create a new layer, just select the objects you want added to the new layer, and choose the Layers > New Layer From Selection command. A new layer will be created with the selected objects as members. To change the name of the layer, double-click on the name in the Layer Control panel, and then edit the name and press Enter when you are done.

### Moving New Objects into an Existing Layer

When you already have a defined layer and you just want to add some objects to it, make the target layer the active layer, select those items you want added, and use the Layers > Move Selection to Current Layer command.

The best way to move objects from one layer to another layer is to use the Explorer view, showing layers (hot-key L), and then expanding the layer to see the list of objects within it. The objects can then be dragged and dropped to the new layer (see Figure 9.6).

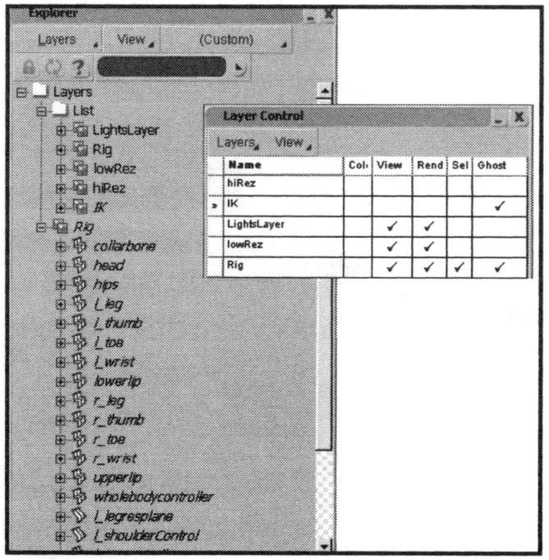

## Organizing a Character: At a Glance

In this quick and easy tutorial, you will use the Layers commands to organize a character into layers for easy animation.

**Figure 9.6**
You can show the layers and their contents in the Explorer.

You'll learn how to:

◆ Add high-res and low-res skins to an object, and then show only what you want

◆ Move all Inverse Kinematic skeletal chains to a layer so they can be easily hidden

◆ Make the control hierarchy selectable and everything else unselectable

◆ Make the control hierarchy invisible to the renderer, but visible to you

## Materials Required

The Julian_layers.scn scene (available from the CD-ROM courseware that accompanies this book)

# Tutorial: Organizing a Character

Open the Julian_layers scene from the XSIFoundation5 project, and examine the contents. The Julian monkey character has both a high resolution and a low-resolution mesh. We're going to want to work with the low-res version, but we'll keep the higher-res version around for later, higher-quality renders. We also need to make the controls selectable so you can use them but invisible during the render. We need the other stuff to be the opposite—unselectable and perhaps invisible during working, but renderable for the final effect.

## Step 1: Put the High- and Low-Res Meshes on Separate Layers

Show the Layers Control panel, in the KP/L. Make one view an Explorer view, and press the L hotkey to show the layers list.

Select the higher-resolution version of Julian, and carefully place it on top of the lower-resolution version, checking all three views.

Place the high-res version on a new layer, by making sure it is the only object selected and choosing the Layers > New Layer from Selection command. In the New Layer Name dialog box that pops up, call this layer HighRes.

Make the high-res version un-selectable, un-renderable, and invisible by unchecking all three columns in the Layer Control panel.

Select the low-res mesh, and using the same commands, put the mesh on its own layer.

Name that new layer lowres.

> Later on, you could bind the high-res to the Inverse Kinematic. When you do that, the mesh must be selectable. Weighting the envelope also requires that the mesh be selectable.

Make the low-res layer visible and renderable, but unselectable.

## Step 2: Put the Inverse Kinematic Skeleton in a Separate Layer

You will want all the Inverse Kinematics (IK) on a separate layer so you can easily make them unselectable, since you'll be manipulating them with the control objects.

Switch back to the MCP. Using the selection filter, which is the small diagonal triangle in the top portion of the MCP, choose Chain_Element. This will limit the selection tools to select only IK chain parts.

Now, holding down the spacebar and Shift to get a multiple selection, drag a rectangle around everything in the whole scene. All of Julian's IK should be selected, and nothing else.

Switch back to the KP/L or view a floating Layer panel with the hotkey 6. Place this skeleton on a new layer, setting the name of the layer to IK, and make it unselectable and invisible. Also make it Ghostable, so you can see animation ghosting (trails) on the IK as Julian moves around.

Click on the Object button in the MCP to turn off the filter, and select the other parts of Julian that you want grouped with the IK, like the skull, the diaphragm, the hips, and the collarbone.

Add them to the IK layer with the Move Selection to Current Layer command.

### Step 3: Make a Layer for the Controls

Select all the control elements (the cones and spheres outside the Julian model), and make them into a new layer.

Name the new layer controls.

These control elements need to be selectable so that you can set keys on them easily, but you don't want them to be rendered. Change the check marks in the Layer Control to make the controls visible and selectable, but not renderable.

Now you have the elements of your scene organized into layers so that you can easily select the controls without accidentally selecting the mesh or the IK bones. You also have the power to make sure that the controls don't render, but the skin will!

## Conclusion

The Layer menu and Control Panel are not too hard to figure out, but they can make a fantastic impact on productivity. You can find many more innovative uses for the layers system. Try placing special effects on their own layer in a scene to make managing renders easy.

# Chapter 10
# Deformations and the Generic Attribute Painter

In this lesson, you will learn:

- ◆ How to use various deformers
- ◆ How to edit Bend, Bulge, Shear, Taper, and Twist properties
- ◆ How to deform by Curve, Surface, Spine, and Lattice
- ◆ How to view and edit the Operator Stack
- ◆ How to use the Push Deformation and Weight Maps
- ◆ How to paint weight with the Generic Attribute Painter
- ◆ How to use weight maps from one model to another with GATOR

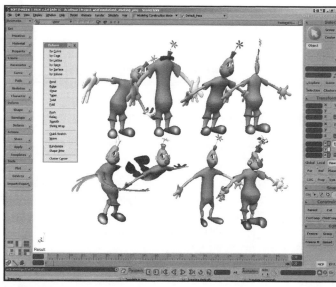

**Figure 10.1**
Tools you'll use.

## Introduction

Deformation tools can provide a great amount of freedom to modelers and animators alike. The primary function of deformers is to give you a very easy-to-use control to deform an object. You can deform all kinds of objects, hierarchies, and even clusters. You can also animate properties of deformers to create animated deformation effects such as a wiggling snake or rippling water.

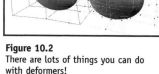

**Figure 10.2**
There are lots of things you can do with deformers!

## The Deform Menu Cell

You can find the deformation tools in the Modify > Deform menu cell in the left toolbar of the Model module, and under Deform > Deform in the Animation module. As usual, it will be convenient for you to tear off the Deform menu so it stays open while you read this chapter.

The basic deformation tools are extremely easy to use and edit. Each of them only requires you to select the object you wish to deform, and choose Modify > Deform > *Any deformation tool*. You can also get a Property editor for the operation in the usual way, through the Selection button in the MCP, to edit every aspect of the deformation. Many of these deformers are perfect for creating cartoon-like physical effects or modeling complex shapes.

You can apply a deformation on one shape at a time, but you can also use deformations on hierarchies of objects, on multiple selections of objects, and even on groups of objects.

## Fundamental Deformation Tools

Deformation tools are operators, and they will be added to the properties of the objects they affect. To see the operator stack, select the object in question and click the Selection button on the MCP. The gear icons indicate operators, which can be modified the same way as any other property, using the Property editor (see Figure 10.3).

Deformers can be edited interactively; any changes you make will be displayed immediately, even if there are several deformations applied to the object.

If you have deformed an object to your liking, and you don't plan on animating the deformation, it's a good idea to freeze the operator stack. Freezing the operator stack will save the object's current shape and remove all the operators, freeing up some RAM and CPU load.

In XSI version 4.0, the operator stack was divided into four modes: Modeling, Shape Modeling, Animation, and Secondary Shape Modeling. All this means is that there are categories in the operator stack. You could choose to put the deformations in the Modeling category, in the Animation category, or the other categories. You can choose to freeze some of your operators but not others. The Freeze button in the MCP applies to whatever the current construction mode is. You can set the current construction mode with the Construction Mode menu at the middle top of the UI (see Figure 10.4). Try it out by switching the construction mode, adding a deformer to any object (even Move or Tweak actions are operators), and then looking at the stack in the Explorer. The deformation operator will go into whichever construction mode you had selected.

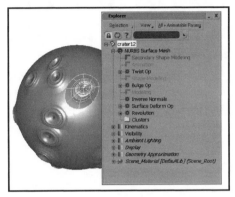

**Figure 10.3**
The operator stack lets you edit your deformations after they are applied.

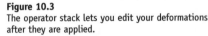

**Figure 10.4**
The Construction Mode menu.

To freeze the current operator stack, select the object and click on the Freeze button at the bottom of the MCP. You can also choose Edit > Operator Freeze Selected from the main menu or the MCP to freeze the current Construction Mode operator stack.

> Advanced users may try to freeze just individual categories of the operator stack. As of this writing, if you select a construction mode in the Explorer and choose Freeze Selected, if will be frozen—and all the operators below it will be frozen, too.

## Bend

Just as the name suggests, Bend bends objects (see Figure 10.5). The Bend property page is a little bit complicated. In the Direction area, you can set both the Bend Direction and the axis of the effect. In the Amplitude area, Angle controls how much the object is bent. Radius determines how big the area of the bend is, with a small radius resulting in a sharp bend and a large radius resulting in a more gradual bend. Offset displaces the "center" of the bend along any axis.

**Figure 10.5**
The Bend deformation.

**Figure 10.6**
The Bulge deformation.

## Bulge

Bulge pulls points outward to make the object look inflated (see Figure 10.6). You can change which way an object bulges by checking on the Deform Along check boxes. Amplitude controls the extent of the deformation tool. The Amplitude Modulation Profile is a spline graph that gives you finer control on how this deformation influences the object, depending on how far away points are from the center of the deformation.

## Shear

Shear pulls points at the top of the object, while pulling bottom points in the opposite direction (see Figure 10.7). It resembles a cartoon character's anticipation before running like hell. The Shear property editor is extremely similar to the Bulge deformer's. You can change which way it shears and which axis it uses. One difference is that there are only two points on the profile curve.

## Taper

Taper "pinches" one end of an object on one or more axes (see Figure 10.8). Deform Along controls which sides of the object are pinched. Axis controls which direction the deformation is pinched toward, and Amplitude determines how much the object is deformed. Like Shear and Bulge, there is an Amplitude Profile curve you can edit.

**Figure 10.7**
The Shear deformation.

**Figure 10.8**
The Taper deformation.

## Twist

Twist successively rotates rows of points to wring the object like a towel (see Figure 10.9). Its Property Editor looks a bit different from the previous three deformers. Angle controls how much the object is twisted, while Vortex is an effect that gradually dissipates the twist as it leaves the vicinity of the object's center, creating a shape more like a tornado or whirlpool than a wrung towel.

## Fold

The Fold deform operator gives you an axis to displace the points in, creating a crease in the plane of the other two axes (see Figure 10.10). For instance, if you pick Y as the Normal fold axis, the crease of the fold lies in the X-Z plane. Where it lies in the X-Z plane is controlled with the Angle and Offset sliders. Angle causes the fold to rotate around, swinging 360 degrees through the plane, and Offset moves the center of the fold. The distortion slider make a four-way fold. If Fold Type is Linear, the crease is sharp. If Fold Type is Spherical, the fold is made in a rounded fashion. If you increase Fold Angle past 360 degrees, you can create a rolled-up tube like a cigar. Adding Distortion shrinks the ends to make a joint shape. Enjoy.

## Push

The Push deformation displaces points of the surface outward, in the direction of its normals (see Figure 10.11). This deformer is very useful when used in conjunction with the weight painting tool. You can add weight interactively with strokes of the mouse to push and pull surfaces. We will discuss this in greater detail later in this chapter.

## Randomize

Randomize moves points randomly, in the axes you specify (see Figure 10.12). This deformation is great for creating landscape geometry or other irregular surfaces with lots of bumps.

# Advanced Deformation Tools

There are four more advanced deformation tools. These tools require a little bit of preparation, but they create stunning modeling and animation effects fairly easily.

**Figure 10.9**
The Twist deformation.

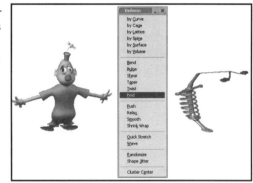

**Figure 10.10**
The Fold deformation.

**Figure 10.11**
The Push deformation.

**Figure 10.12**
The Randomize deformation.

Let's take a look at each.

## Deformation by Curve

Keyframing something like a huge, slithering anaconda or a powerful great white shark swimming would be extremely difficult. However, Deformation by Curve can achieve these effects quite easily.

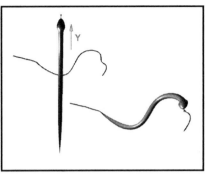

**Figure 10.13**
Deformation by Curve can deform an object along a curve.

Deformation by Curve will deform an object by moving the object's Y-axis along the U direction of the curve you create. The object will try to bend to follow the curve's shape. (How successfully it does this depends on the level of detail on the object and how sharp the turns in the curve are.) You can animate the object's Y translation to make the object move from the beginning to the end of the curve and animate the control points on the curve itself to change the object's shape (see Figure 10.13).

Creating a deformation by curve is easy:

1.  Although you can choose which axis will be along the path later, it's a good idea to figure out ahead of time what you want. Generally, you should create the model or hierarchy facing up in global Y, and whatever is up will then be forward along the curve.

    If your object is not at the global origin, then the object won't deform along the curve properly, but will be instead offset from the curve by the distance between the local center of the object and the origin. It is also good form to move the object and the origin before deforming it.

    It is a good idea to zero out the transforms of the object before deforming it with Transform > Freeze All Transforms from the MCP, to avoid confusing yourself or XSI.

2.  Create a curve. The Draw Cubic by Knots curve tool is especially useful since the curve will go exactly through the places you drop a point.

3.  Select an object to deform. You can also select a hierarchy, model, or even a group. Choose Deform > By Curve from the Deform menu at the bottom of the Model module.

4.  The mouse cursor will turn into a pick cursor. Pick the curve you drew. Your model should have snapped to the beginning of the curve (though if it doesn't, there is a way to fix that, mentioned later).

5.  Open the Curve Deform property page under the Surface Mesh object. The three sliders in the Scaling section will let you scale the deformed object in three axes relative to the curve. Roll lets you rotate the object around the curve, along its local Y-axis. The Translation section controls the movement of the object. Along Curve will move the deformed object from the beginning of the curve to 20 units forward and backward. If you want to go farther each way, you can type a number directly into the box at the left of the slider. The other two sliders move the object up and down and side to side (away from the curve).

6.  The Constraint tab has a special tool just in case you haven't frozen the transformation of either the object or the curve. If you moved the object and didn't freeze it before using Deformation by Curve, you need to click on the Constrain to Deformee check box. It will snap the deforming object right onto the curve. The Constrain to Deformer check box is used when you have moved the curve and haven't frozen it. If both of them were moved prior to using Deformation by Curve, you need to check both check boxes.

We will use Deformation by Curve later, in the tutorial. Let's move on to the next deformation tool.

## Deformation by Surface

If you want to conform one surface to another surface's shape, Deformation by Surface can achieve it. For example, you could wrap some extruded text around the surface of a globe or make a drop of water slide down a leaf.

Whereas Deformation by Curve aligns the chosen axis of the deformed object to the U parameter of a curve, Deformation by Surface aligns the X and Z axis of an object to the U and V parameter of a surface (see Figure 10.14). In other words, you do not have a choice of orientation when using the Deformation by Surface tool. You need to choose which axis you want perpendicular to the surface, and rotate the object so that axis is facing in global Y (up). Then freeze the transformations to keep it that way, and also freeze the operator stack for good measure to remove the center operator.

Here is how it's done:

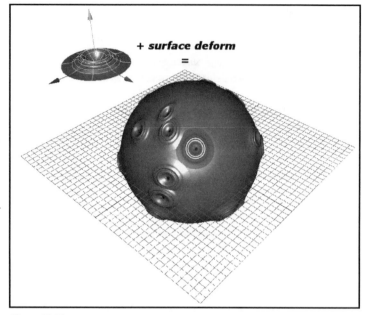

**Figure 10.14**
The Deformation by Surface tool wraps an object around a surface.

1. Create a base surface on which the object will deform. A polygon object cannot be a base surface, since it lacks U and V parameters. You can have another deformation tool already applied to the base surface; the two will work together.

2. Select the object to be deformed. It can be a hierarchy, model, or group. Unlike the base surface, this object can be a polygon mesh. However, you may need lots of subdivisions for the object to deform correctly. Make sure the side you want facing out from the surface is facing up in global Y, and freeze the object's rotation. Lastly, freeze the object's stack.

3. With the object selected and the toolbar in Model mode, select Modify > Deform > by Surface.

4. The mouse cursor will turn into the pick tool. Pick the base surface you will deform the object on.

5. You may see your deforming surface extremely (improperly) deformed, but don't be alarmed. Open the Surface Deform property page, and simply scale the object down by sliding Scaling X and Z axis to the left. You can move, scale, and rotate using the sliders in the window. The Constraint tab works the same way as the Curve Deformation property editor. If you don't create (or freeze) your objects at the global center, the controls here can fix the deformation to look correct, but it's better to get it closer to right the first time.

## Deformation by Lattice

Lattices are very effective if you want to pull on part of an object or squash and stretch an object.

A lattice is a bounding box, like a cage, that surrounds another object to take control of its entire geometry (with less control points). The only thing you need to do is edit the points on the lattice, and the geometry under it will change accordingly (see Figure 10.15). It's a perfect solution for simple modeling or animating an object with lots of detail, since a simple lattice can control complex geometry underneath. The level of detail on a lattice can be changed to suit the resolution you want to work with. You can either apply a lattice directly to an object or create a lattice first and then apply it to something.

Here is how to apply a lattice. It's actually easier than curve or surface deformation:

The first method uses the Get > Primitive menu cell to create a lattice, instead of the Deform menu cell.

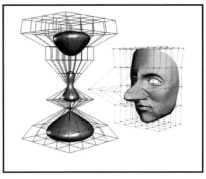

**Figure 10.15**
Lattices have many uses.

1. Select an object, hierarchy, model, or group. There is no particular requirement on how this object is placed or oriented, unlike the other deformers.

2. Click Get > Primitive > Lattice. Done! A lattice object is created around the selected object.

3. Open the lattice deformation property page. Set its subdivision to the resolution you want to work with. More subdivisions mean more detail, but lots of points to deal with. Too many subdivisions may mean it's not that much different from picking and moving the original object's surface points, losing the benefit of lattice deformation. Interpolation controls how points on the deforming object are weighted to the lattice. Curve will create nice smooth weighting, but if you want to have sharper edges with more detail, Linear is the way to go.

4. Move, scale, and rotate the points on the lattice, and the underlying object should deform along with the lattice points. You can animate the movement of the lattice points to create animated deformation.

The second method involves creating a lattice first, and then applying it to an object.

1. With nothing selected, create a lattice using Get > Primitive > Lattice.

2. Select the object you want to deform and choose Modify > Deform > by Lattice. Pick the lattice you want to use.

3. The Property editor looks very different from the first method. Deformation Scope deals with how the object's points are influenced by the lattice. All Points (SI3D) will affect all points of the deformed object. If the Falloff Relative to Lattice's BBox option is chosen, only the points of the object that are inside the edited lattice are influenced. (So, for instance, you could make the lattice into a funnel shape and animate the object passing through it.) Scaling will let you decide if you want to treat the scale of the lattice as a deformation factor. The default for the option uses the lattice's center for scaling the object; Apply Scaling to Geometry (SI3D) will scale the object using its own center.

You can also use *any* object (though usually a polygonal object) as a deformer very like a lattice with the Deform by Cage deformer. A cage is simply a lattice that does not need to be an evenly spaced cube of points. You can, in fact, model a polygon cage to exactly fit the deformation needs of your model. This tool is covered in more detail in the *XSI Illuminated: Character* book (Mesmer, 2002).

## Deformation by Spine

This last deformer can deform a surface using a curve, without putting the object on the curve. The curve will have a zone of influence as soon as the spine deformation is applied. Like a magnetic power, the deforming object's points are attracted to the curve as long as points are within the curve's zone of influence. This means the curve should be fairly close to the surface. The only thing you need to do to deform the surface after that is to move the curve itself or the points on the curve.

Here is how to use it:

1. Create a curve you want to deform a surface with. The curve should preferably be in close proximity to the deforming surface, because you need to make sure its zone of influence is actually influencing the target points of the surface.
2. Select the object, hierarchy, model, or group you want to deform.
3. Select Modify > Deform > by Spine. The mouse cursor becomes a pick cursor. Pick the curve you created to deform the surface.
4. The deformed surface should now have clusters (points) that are displayed in blue.
5. The Spine Deform property editor has only a mute control. More controls are in the Spine WeightMap Operator, which is located in the Clusters folder, under the DeformBySpineWeightCls and the Envelope_Weights weightmap. Cascade all these out to find the Spine WeightMap operator, and open it. Falloff Amplitude controls how the curve influences the object's points. The left column controls the weight of the points: 1 means 100% weight, or total attraction to the curve, while 0 is "unaffected." The bottom row is the percent of the zone of influence: 0.0 is exactly on the curve, and 100 is the edge of the curve's influence. Radius sets how much the magnetic power of the curve will influence the object. Moving this slider to the right adds more influence radius, thus deforming more of the surface. Longitudinal controls the influence of the curve lengthwise, allowing you to control how much of the curve affects the surface.
6. Move, scale, and rotate the curve; the points close to the curve should follow its transformations.

## Shrink Wrap

The Shrink Wrap deformer takes one model and projects all its points in space to follow the contours of a different model, called the target model. The Shrink Wrap deformer uses three objects to get the job done: an outer wrapper, and inner copy of the wrapper, and the target object in the middle. If, for instance, you wanted to shrink a balloon around an animated character so that it looked as if the character were struggling to get out of the balloon, you would need the larger outer balloon, the target character, and a smaller inner balloon to project the outer one. See Figure 10.16.

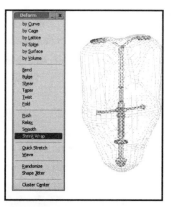

To see the Shrink Wrap deformer work, you would choose the outer wrapper that is the model that the deformer goes on, run the Deform > Shrink Wrap command, pick the target object, and then pick the inner wrapper object. Each vertex on the outer wrapper will move toward the matching vert on the inner object, stopping only when it reaches the surface of the target. You can open the Shrink Wrap operator PPG on the outer wrapper and adjust the Amplitude slider to blend from the deformed version back to the original version of the outer wrapper.

**Figure 10.16**
The result of the Shrink Wrap deformer.

Advanced users can try using the Shrink Wrap deformer with just two objects: the outer wrapper and target. Start with the outer wrapper selected. Then run the Deform > Shrink Wrap command and pick the target. Righ-click to terminate the command before picking an inner object. Open the Shrink Wrap PPG and try out the Closest Vertex, Closest Surface, and Closest Surface (Smoothed) options, new in XSI 5.0.

### *Relax and Smooth*

The Relax and Smooth deformers are really the same thing, just with different settings. These deformers take each vertex on the model and average its position with the surrounding vertices. This can create effects like melting, where the sharper features of the object are smashed down, erosion effects and, most commonly, rounding effects (see Figure 10.17). Just select the object to be smoothed and apply the deformer. Then adjust the Strength slider in the PPG.

## Muting Deformers

You can mute deformers to temporarily remove their effect from an object (see Figure 10.18). On the property page of most deformations, there is a Mute check box. You can check or uncheck this box to toggle the deformation without deleting it. You can also set keyframes on the Mute check box. If you expand the Mesh property in the Explorer to see the deform operators, you can right-click on an operator there in the Explorer and choose Mute from the context-sensitive pop-up menu.

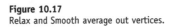

**Figure 10.17**
Relax and Smooth average out vertices.

## Clusters

When you created a spine deformation, you may have noticed that the points on the surface had two colors: blue and green. What do these colors represent?

The colored groups of points are called clusters. Clusters are groups of a component of an object, such as CVs, vertices, and faces. Clusters can be user-defined. Doing so can allow you to quickly and easily select and animate a specific portion of a model, without having to painstakingly select a group of points every time you want to change them.

In case of the spine deformation, XSI automatically created two clusters. The blue cluster is weighted 50% or more to the spine deformation.

**Figure 10.18**
Muting a deformer turns it off temporarily,

You can view and select clusters by selecting an object that has them, and clicking on the Cluster button at the top of the MCP, below the Select menu.

To create a cluster, select the points you wish to group, and click on the Cluster button at the bottom of the MCP, below the Edit bar. Name the cluster using the Property editor. Note that the cluster's name is displayed at the top of the MCP, immediately below the name of the object.

## Push Deformation and Weight Maps

A weight map is a property that is added on surfaces and clusters. It can affect the way deformations behave.

The color of the weight map changes how much a deformation will affect the surface. You can paint your own weight maps to build more complex deformation effects (see Figure 10.19).

There is an easy, automated way to sculpt models with the push operator, but it will make more sense to you once you have done it the long and hard way.

To paint weight on a surface by connecting a weight map to a deformation, follow this procedure:

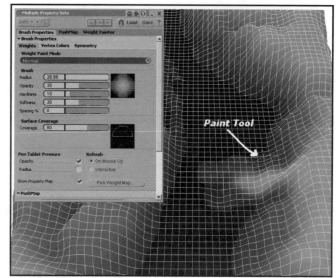

**Figure 10.19**
Pushing and pulling a model using a weight map and the Generic Attribute Painter (GAP).

1. Select an object. If you want to sculpt the whole surface, just select the object in Object mode. If you want to affect only certain parts of a surface, tag just those points.

2. Choose Get > Property > Weight Map. A weight map is created for the whole object or selected points. A cluster is created automatically, prior to generation of the weight map, because weight maps are actually stored on clusters. To find a weight map, use the Selection explorer in the MCP while in Object Selection mode (with an object selected), and then open up the Clusters folder. Under each cluster, you will find a Weight_Map, and under that a Weight Map Generator.

3. You can't see weight maps by default. Make sure Weight Maps is checked in the Show menu (eyeball icon) of the view port you are using, and change to Constant Shading mode.

4. Open the Clusters > WeightMap > Weight Map Generator property page from the Selection button in the MCP. Several parameters here are very important.

   Weight maps can be made with a default pattern of values. You can change this pattern with the Weight Map Type drop-down menu. Leaving it at Constant is a good idea to start.

The Base Weight is the starting default value of the weight map. It indicates just how much the weight map can drive a deformer to start with. Base Weight defines what "blank" is, on the weight map. If you plan to paint on the map, set this to 0 so there's no weight (and therefore, no effect) unless you paint it there.

Weight Value Range controls how much weight can be painted (and also "unpainted" if the Min value is negative) on the map. When you move on to using the Generic Attribute Painter, left-clicking will paint positive weight, and right-clicking will paint negative weight.

The Minimum and Maximum Weight Value Range sliders set the possible minimum and maximum influence of the weight map on other deformers. For instance, if you have a Bend deformer, you might want the weight map set to have a range from -90 degrees to 90 degrees. In contrast, if you are using a bulge operator, you might want more subtle control, and could set the Min to -.5 and the Max to +.5.

5. Now the only thing you need to do is to switch to the painting tool. You can either get the paint tool from the Property > Map Paint Tools > Paint Tool in the Model Module, or simply use the W hotkey.

6. As mentioned before, left-clicking paints weight and right-clicking removes it. Middle-click and drag to change the size of the brush interactively.

Now you are painting on the weight map, coloring it to suit your needs, but it is not yet hooked up to anything, so the object is not changing shape. Before we connect the weight map to a deform operator, let us talk about weight painting options for a short while.

## The Generic Attribute Painter

The Generic Attribute Painter (GAP) allows you to paint values on a 3D surface. The brush size and other attributes can be customized to suit your workflow. Choosing Get > Property > Map Paint Tools > Brush Properties, or using the Ctrl-W hotkey, will summon the Paint Properties editor (see Figure 10.20).

Radius controls the size of the brush. You can also change the size of the brush on the fly by dragging with the middle mouse button while in GAP mode.

Hardness and Softness let you determine how much of a feathered edge you want.

Opacity controls how much of the value is added when you paint, similar to the pressure control on the airbrush tool of most paint applications. 100 means 100% of the maximum weight will be painted with every stroke. It's a good idea to set this value low, which gives you more control and lets you gradually build the surface.

If you have a really fast computer and a fairly simple weight map to paint, you can turn on Interactive Refresh to see the results as you paint value onto the weight map.

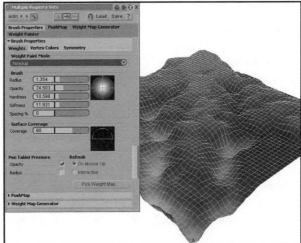

**Figure 10.20**
You can edit your brush using the Paint Options property page (Ctrl-W).

**207**

# Using a Weight Map with a Deformation

You can use a weight map to modify the strength of any deformation across an object.

You must have a weight map created and have a deformation on the same object. To hook up the weight map to the deformation, open the Property Editor for that deformation and click on the plug button to the right of the Amplitude slider. Choose Connect from the drop menu that appears. A Property Explorer will pop up. Expand Polygon Mesh (or NURBS mesh), Clusters, and then WeightMapCls to find the weight map you created, and finally click right on the name of the weight map to select it. It will become highlighted in purple. Click anywhere out of the Property Explorer to close it (see Figure 10.21).

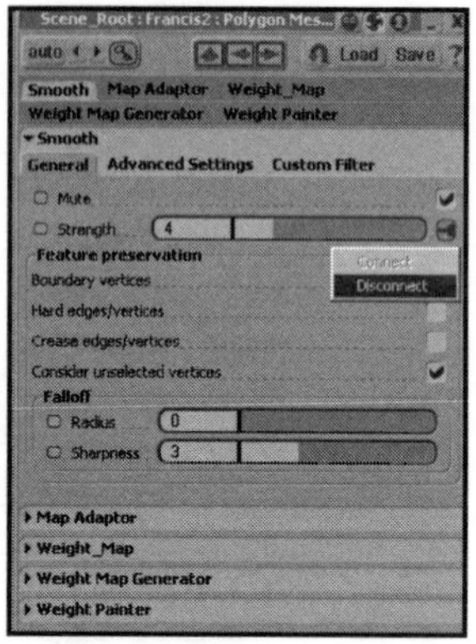

Now the Deformation operator and the weight map are connected, but nothing will happen to the surface until you start painting. It's worthwhile to note two things—that the Amplitude slider of whatever deformation you used is actually multiplied by the value of the weight map at each location to give the final effect, and that you can use one weight map to drive many deformations.

**Figure 10.21**
The weight map connection spot.

In our simple example, select the object you added a weight map to, and add a Deform > Bulge Operator. (If your object was a grid, choose a twist instead, because grids don't bulge very well, being so flat.) Open the Bulge PPG if it is not already open. The Amplitude slider controls how much the bulge changes the shape of the object, and the weight map plug to the right of the slider will modify it. Click the Amplitude plug icon and choose Connect; then open WeightMapCls by clicking the plus icon. Finally, pick the weight map itself. Suddenly the bulge is modulated by the weight map.

# Organic Sculpting with the Paint Push Tool

Because all polygonal mesh objects and patch surfaces are defined by the vertices and control points that make them up, you can, of course, change the shape of the object by moving those points around. This fundamental concept is the basis of organic modeling. When you simply push and pull points on the surface to create the shape you desire, you have the ultimate degree of control over what you come up with. Although the experience is different, organic modeling is just like sculpting with clay, in that your talent and dedication are all that stands between you and a masterpiece.

Since polygonal meshes are usually composed of a great many vertices, sculpting in this way is pretty hard, unless you are building low poly game characters. NURBS surfaces usually have many fewer control points, and form very nice smooth shapes, making sculpting them much easier and more productive. You will want to start with a NURBS surface (or polygonal mesh) that has enough subdivisions for the detail you want to model into the object but not more than you need, since too much detail tends to be confusing and difficult to work with.

Now you can do it the easy way. XSI has a tool designed to make sculpting easier and more intuitive. The Paint Push tool from the Property > Map Paint Tools menu cell in the Animate Module can be used to sculpt the surface of an object into whatever form you desire. You could use this to model a human shape, paint in the valleys and mountains of a landscape, or model the creases and folds into a pair of digital blue jeans.

Select your object, and inspect the geometry PPG, turning up the U and V subdivisions until you have plenty of detail to work with—usually 24 points in U and V or more.

Next, with the object to sculpt selected, choose Get > Property > Map Paint Tools > Paint Push Tool, which will automatically add a push operator and a weight map and activate the Paint tool. You can now start painting on your object, but let's make some changes that will make it easier.

Select your object again; then pull up the Paint options with Ctrl-W or the Get > Property > Map Paint Tools > Paint Properties command. Set the opacity quite low, around 10%, so that you can work gradually, and adjust the brush softness to get a smooth, gradual fade of the brush shape. Click the key icon of the brush PPG to lock it open so you can make changes while you work (see Figure 10.22).

The Paint Push tool should still be active, showing you a circle tangent to the surface of the object you have selected. If it is not, activate it again from the menu, or hold down the W button, the hotkey for Paint Weights. A circle appears on your surface, following the contours as you roll your mouse. The size of the circle is the size of the brush. It can be adjusted carefully by holding down the middle mouse button and dragging left to right.

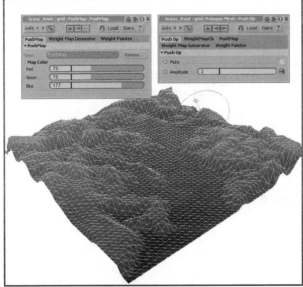

Now click your left mouse mutton to paint positive values on the weight map, which changes the value of the push operator at that point on the surface, and displaces the surface mesh right there, under your mouse. The surface will update when you let up on the mouse button, so practice sculpting with short strokes.

**Figure 10.22**
This is a grid, deformed with a Push operator, modified by a weight map.

The left mouse button will pull out, and the right mouse button will push in. The total push and pull available can be changed by looking at the PPG for the push operator.

## Toro the Ravenous: At a Glance

You learned about many deformers in the previous section. Let's practice applying them. We'll create a deep water environment with a lot of seaweed, add a fish, and swim him with a curve deformation (see Figure 10.23).

You'll learn how to:

◆ Modify a seafloor with the Push and Randomize deformers
◆ Place seaweed with the Surface deformer, and animate it with a Wave deformer

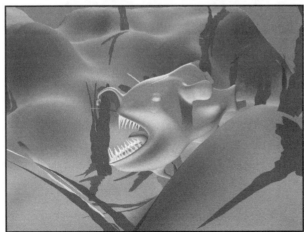

**Figure 10.23**
Toro is on the prowl!

◆ Draw a curve and wrap it to the seafloor with the ShrinkWrap deformer

◆ Curve-deform the fish to a path, so he swims convincingly

# Tutorial: Toro the Ravenous

Deformations are quick and easy ways to modify existing geometry and to create new animations based on those new objects. Let's start by opening the starting scene, which has the seaweed and fish models hidden, and adding the seafloor.

## Step 1: Open the Toro_start Scene

Look at the Explorer, and see that there are hidden objects: a fish, some seaweed, and a sample seafloor.

## Step 2: Create a Seafloor of Your Own

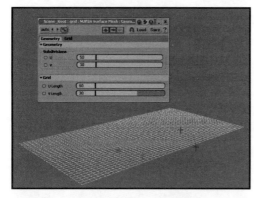

Hide the seafloor if you unhid it, and get a surface grid. It must be a surface, meaning a NURBS object, not a polygon, in order to deform the seaweed to it. Open the grid geometry PPG, and change the U and V subdivisions to 50 and 30, respectively. Also change the U Length and V Length to 30 and 50. Frame the grid in your camera view and maximize that view.

## Step 3: Add a Push Deformer

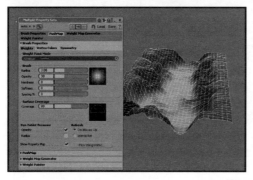

With the grid selected, use the Property > Map Paint Tools > Paint Push Tool command from the Animate module or menu. This adds a weight map and an attached Push deformer. Open the Paint Tool properties with the Ctrl-W hotkey, and change the Opacity to 30 so you lay down paint more gradually, making fine changes possible. Verify that Weight Paint Mode is Normal, and close the PPG. Hold W to start up the Paint Push tool, and click with your left mouse button and drag to paint a positive push on the surface. Click-drag with the right button to paint a negative push. You can toggle on the Show (eyeball) > Weight Maps option to see a color representation of the weight map even when you do not have the W key held down.

## Step 4: Randomize the Seafloor

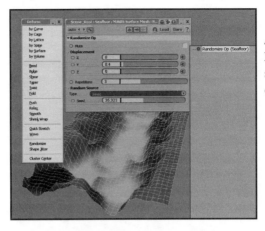

Add a bit more interest to the seafloor by selecting it and adding a Randomize deformation from the Deform > Deform menu in the Animate module. Open the Randomize operator that is now on the seafloor, and adjust Displacement, setting X and Z to 0. This way the randomization is only in the Y or height direction.

## Step 5: Plant Some Seaweed

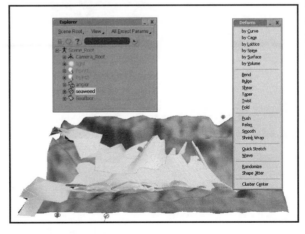

Open the Explorer, find the seaweed, and unhide it. We need to plant many copies of this seaweed object, but let's start with a single one. Select the seaweed, and then choose Deform > By Surface. XSI enters a pick mode. Pick on the seafloor. The seaweed will be squashed onto the seafloor, but it won't look so good until you scale it properly.

Select the seaweed geometry and open the Surface Deform Operator PPG. Look for the Transform tab, and set the scaling X and Z to about .02, meaning two percent of the scale of the grid.

You can move the seaweed by very gently dragging the Translation X and Z sliders in the same Surface Deform PPG. Translation X moves the seaweed along the U parameters of the seafloor grid, and transform Z slides the seaweed in the V parameter. The range of both U and V goes from -.5 at one end of U or v to a max of .5.

## Step 6: Make a Lot of Seaweed

You could repeat the previous process many times over, but there are some simpler automated tools we can use to plant seaweed that take advantage of the fact that duplicating an object with a deformation (or a constraint) keeps the constraints and deformations. To see this, select your deformed seaweed, and choose Edit > Duplicate/Instantiate > Duplicate Multiple. This opens a modal dialog box where we can make some choices about what we want. Change the number of copies to 100, and verify that the Duplicated Items > Constraints option is still set to Copy and Share Inputs. Click OK.

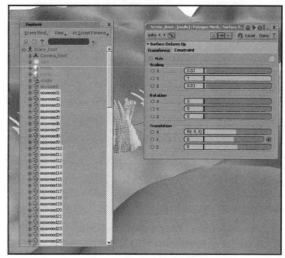

This makes a lot of seaweed, but it's all in the same place, which is no good. There is a trick we can use, however. Open the Explorer, select the first seaweed, and show the Surface Deform PPG. If you Shift-select the other seaweed objects, all their Deform operators will be loaded into the same PPG. Click on the next to Translation X and type R (-.5,.5). This sets each seaweed to a different random value in X. Repeat this for the Translation Z value, but set this to R (-.2,.2) so that the seaweed mainly lies along the bottom of the seafloor trench.

## Step 7: Add a Curve for the Fish to Swim Along

In the Top view, draw a CV NURBS curve, swinging down the middle of the trench in a fishy manner. We want this curve to follow the topography of the bottom you created, so with the curve selected, use the Deform > ShrinkWrap command and pick the seafloor. To finish off the shrink wrap, select the curve, examine the ShrinkWrap PPG, and change the Projection Type to Closest Surface. You should now see the curve follow the terrain. Select the curve and translate it in Y up a bit so the fish won't be swimming through the seafloor.

## Step 8: Add the Fish to the Curve

Find the fish named Angler in the Explorer, unhide it and make sure it is selected, and choose the Deform > By Curve menu option. Pick the curve you shrink wrapped to the seafloor. This puts the fish on the curve, but is he attached to the curve, facing the right way? No? We can change that. Inspect the Curve Deform PPG on the Angler, and in the Constraint tab, click the Constrain to Deformer toggle. This makes the fish hop to the start of the curve. Frame the fish in your Camera view, and in the Curve Deform tab, experiment with the Axis drop down to find which way the fish should face. Next, adjust the Roll slider to let the angler swim right side up. For extra credit, you can come back to the roll and set keyframes.

### Step 9: Swim!

The angler isn't moving, because his position on the curve is static over time. We can change that by setting some keys on the Translate Along > Curve parameter in the Curve Deform PPG. At frame 1, set a key by clicking on the Animation divot. At the last frame of the animation, start dragging up the Translation Along > Curve parameter. See the fish slide along the curve! The last problem to overcome is the limited range of that slider. You can set it manually to something like 70 and set a key so that the fish reaches the end of the curve.

## Conclusion

Deformation tools can be extremely useful for modeling and animation. They often provide a very quick and easy method of doing something that would otherwise be very complex. The various deformations, even the malleable ones such as by Lattice and by Weight Map, are fairly specialized; the trick is to know which tool works for your project. It would be a good idea to experiment further with the different deformations, to explore their full capabilities.

# Chapter 11
# The Animation Editor

In this chapter, you will learn:

◆ A bit about traditional animation: Anticipation, Action, and Follow-through

◆ The importance of poses and pauses between actions

◆ How to preplan the animation process using a Dopesheet

◆ How to view and understand the graphs of animation in the Animation editor

◆ How to add more animation and edit existing work in the Animation editor

◆ How to play back your work in several different ways, and evaluate it

◆ How to refine your animation until it looks good

## Introduction

SOFTIMAGE|XSI is different from other, less powerful animation tools. SOFTIMAGE|XSI was built as a tool for artists to communicate visually with other people. The number-one goal of good animation is to connect with an audience, to articulate and communicate a story, an emotion, a feeling. Without that emotional connection to the audience, 3D animation is ultimately just unfulfilling eye candy, the visual equivalent of junk food. SOFTIMAGE|XSI makes it easier for creative professionals to express themselves to other people through animation.

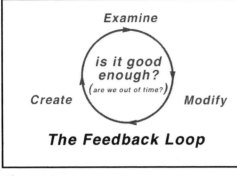

**Figure 11.1**
The feedback cycle is crucial to creating good work.

Expressive animation is not just a change in the shape of a mouth, although it might begin there. Expressive animation captures subtlety and nuance through careful timing and precise control over the action. Getting your work to this stage is always the result of much iteration: trying it out, seeing how it looks, correcting the movement and timing, and doing it over until it looks right. This process is called the feedback loop (see Figure 11.1). The more immediately your animation tool can show you how your work will look, the better your revisions can be. The more revisions you can go through, the better the final product.

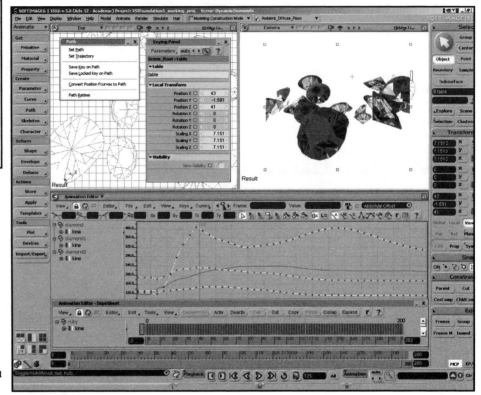

**Figure 11.2**
Tools you'll use.

The SOFTIMAGE|XSI Animation editor has accuracy and control over every animated parameter in the environment, and the speedy feedback loop required to edit and perfect great animation.

# All About Timing and Its Effects on Animation

In SOFTIMAGE|XSI, all time is represented by frames. How long is a frame? It's however long you want it to be. By themselves, frames do not have special relationship to real-world units of time measurement; they are relative to the speed at which they are played back.

In the United States, televisions display 30 frames per second. In Europe, it plays at 25 frames per second. Motion pictures play at 24 frames per second. Some traditional animation is run as slow as 12 or 15 frames per second (so the animators don't have to draw quite so many frames by hand). You need to decide before you start animating how you will be planning to view your animation. Generally, that determines how the SOFTIMAGE|XSI frames translate into real units of time (see Figure 11.3).

**Frame rates from around the world**

| | Format Name | Details | Frame rate |
|---|---|---|---|
| U.S. Television | NTSC | interlaced, 2 fields per frame, Odd field dominant | 30 frames per second |
| European Television | PAL | interlaced, 2 fields per frame, Even field dominant | 25 frames per second |
| Film | | Single frame | 24 frames per second |
| HDTV | 1080i | interlaced, 2 fields per frame, Odd field dominant | 30 frames per second |
| HDTV | 1080p | single frame | 24 frames per second |
| SDTV | 480p | single frame | 60 frames per second |

**Figure 11.3**
You must know your frame rate before you begin.

A side effect you need to think about is that running your finished animation at different speeds has the effect of slowing down or speeding up the action within. This means that the timing that looked perfect when you were previewing your animation onscreen might not look so great on video or on film (see Figure 11.4). Make sure you preview your work and perfect the timing at the same frame rate that you will use for your final output (which is 30 frames per second (fps) most of the time).

> You can specify the speed that XSI uses to play back frames when it is keeping timing by going to the File menu, choosing Preferences, and going to the Time PPG, which shows the frame format to be NTSC (29.97 fps) by default.

After you have the correct timing chosen for your specific work, you need to plan out the timing of the action in your animation. Working out the timing prior to beginning work is an essential component of good workflow. If you wait to figure out how long things will take until you are in front of the computer setting keyframes, you are guaranteed to get it wrong, and your animation will look lousy.

Animation timing is the study of how long each action of a character really takes in real life and how that real-life version can be changed to accentuate the effect you are looking for in animation. For instance, if your character is dribbling a basketball and then putting up a shot, it's crucial that the dribbling of the ball is believable. If you make the dribble cycle too slow, it will look like your character is moving underwater. If you make the shot too fast, it won't seem to obey the correct laws of gravity.

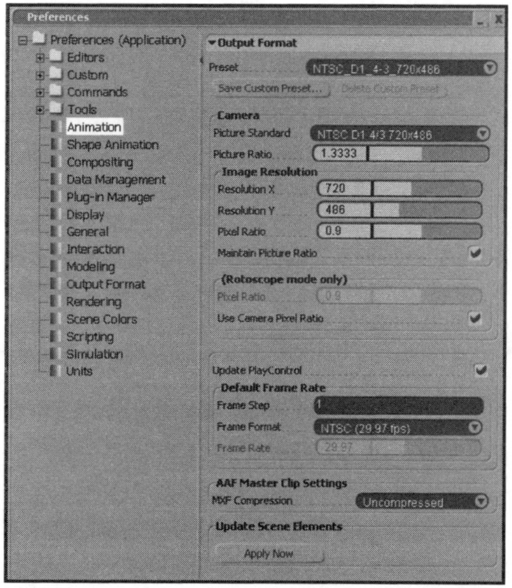

**Figure 11.4**
Set your frame rate in the User Prefs Output Format PPG.

The speed with which a character performs an action also determines how the audience will perceive the intent and emotion of the character. The same action, say, a simple walk cycle, will impart a different emotion depending on how long the character takes for each step. If the character walks fast, it's a vigorous happy walk. If the walk takes twice as long, it's a slow, languorous or depressed walk. Figure 11.5 has the secret you need to collect all of this information.

There is only one way to determine correct timing for your specific need: Act it out with a stopwatch, convert the time on the stopwatch to frames, and log the timing information you develop on a timing sheet (known as a Dopesheet in traditional character animation—see Figure 11.6).

If your character needs to cross a room and open the window, and then stick his head outside, act out the scene yourself, holding the stopwatch. Practice the scene, developing the feel that you want it to have in the finished work. If you aren't acting really silly and dramatic, your finished character won't either. If you can't act out the timing and the action you want with your body, you won't be able to do it onscreen by setting keyframes, which is a million times harder. Collect timing information for each part of the action, broken down. Then convert that stopwatch time to frames by multiplying by the frames per second at which you plan to output your animation. Break down repeating motions into time per cycle. This formula will help.

**Figure 11.5**
Your secret weapon—cost: $5-10.

Number of frames = Time for action / Number of cycles * Frames per second

For instance:

Crossing the room in three complete angry strides = 1.65 seconds. 1.65 seconds divided by three strides = 0.55 seconds. 0.55 seconds times 30 fps = 16.5 frames per angry stride.

Throwing the window open = 0.8 seconds = 24 frames.

Sticking head out the window = 1 second, 30 frames.

Extending hand, yelling = 2 seconds, 60 frames.

Now, when you go to set the actual keyframe animation, you'll have a personal, kinesthetic feel for the motion of the character based on your own acting of the event, and you'll have an accurate record of how long each part will actually take. All that is left is to actually pose the character and set the keyframes.

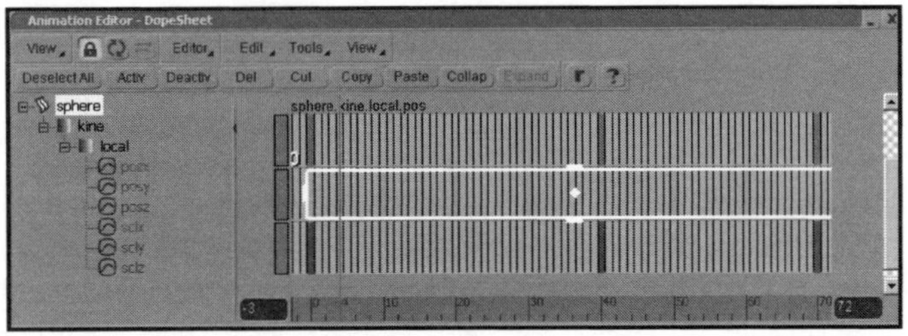

**Figure 11.6**
The Dopesheet is your planning tool.

If you don't use a stopwatch, your animation will almost always be really slow, as if the character were underwater. Your audience, accustomed to half-second edits and quick-cutting MTV-style visual feedback, will become bored.

## Three Parts to Each Motion

When you are performing character animation (or just about any animation at all), it's useful to break down each action of the character into three parts: the introduction, the action, and the result of the action. The proper names for these are Anticipation, Action, and Follow-through (see Figure 11.7). Optimally, you would use the stopwatch to determine the timing of each one.

During the anticipation phase, the character telegraphs to the audience that he is about to do something important. Ren pulls back his hand and holds it for several frames before smacking Stimpy, in a classic example of anticipation. The audience watches the hand, since the animator provided the visual language to tell people what was going to happen next.

In the action, the hand descends rapidly, often in an arc (arc of motion), and contacts Stimpy's fat head. This portion happens very fast, and is barely perceived.

In the follow-through, Ren pushes his hand through to the other side of Stimpy's face (which animates as a result of the action) and holds the hand in the fully extended follow-through pose.

Of the three portions of the action, the middle part is the least important because it's the least interesting. The audience holds its breath during the anticipation and relaxes during the follow-through.

Failure to pay attention to this simple rule of cartoon animation will make your job harder and your work less successful.

> After you learn the ropes using the classical methods, you are free to experiment with your own styles, the same way that John Kricfalusi did when he adapted standard cartoon timing to create the Ren & Stimpy effects. Just pay attention to the basic rules first.

**Figure 11.7**
These three frames show anticipation, action, and follow-through.

## Pauses and Holding Poses

Your character does not have to be in motion at each frame of your animation. There is, however, an almost irresistible urge when animating with 3D tools to set keyframes so that your character is always doing something—easing into one action or easing out to something else. The effect of this rookie mistake is that your characters look drunk or palsied. Powerful animation technique makes use of pauses between actions to focus the attention of the audience on what has just happened or what's coming next. Pauses can indicate reflection on the part of your character, or decision making, or puzzlement. Try not to have each movement of your character blend into the next needlessly. Changing the amount of pausing between actions and poses can also effect the pacing of the story. Often, the first portion of the script calls for slower, more reflective pacing while characters are developed and motivations are explored. When the earlier portions have used a more measured pace, later sections can occur with more active timing, shorter shots, and quicker editing to enhance the level of excitement during crucial conflict scenes.

Examine the fine work of Nick Park and Aardman Animation (notably, the Wallace and Gromit series) for examples of excellent pacing, with effective changes of timing between different scenes.

## The Animation Editor: Infinite Control

Keyframing is only the beginning in SOFTIMAGE|XSI. To define how a value changes over time, SOFTIMAGE|XSI generates an equation based on the value of the keyframes you set and at what frame you set them. With this equation, XSI can determine what a value should be at any point in time, not just the points you set explicitly. The equation is a spline (a curve) and can be seen as a graph with the value being changed on the vertical axis and time in frames running along the horizontal axis. The official name in XSI for this kind of graph is an Animation Curve. (Formerly Function Curve, or Fcurve, in SI3D. The term Fcurve is still used in places in XSI.) See Figure 11.8.

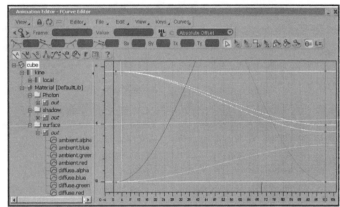

**Figure 11.8**
One set of animation curves, for the color of a light changing from green to red.

The Animation Curve isn't just to help you visualize animation, however. The Animation Curve is a potent way to create and edit animation. Each object in your scene can have a separate Animation Curve for each animatable parameter, creating hundreds and hundreds of Animation Curves for you to work with. After you set keyframes on an object to change something about an object over time (like its color, or position, or shape), you can visualize that change over time in a simple graph. The graph is a curve, demonstrating the value that you changed versus time. This graph isn't just a way to see the animation in your scene—you can also change it there!

Using the Animation editor (see Figure 11.9), you can:

◆ Add keyframes

◆ Delete keyframes

◆ Move keyframes

◆ Select groups of keyframes and edit them

◆ Translate and scale the whole Animation Curve

◆ Remove all animation from one property

◆ Create and edit animation cycles

Load the TireBounce_start scene from the project for this book from the CD-ROM accompanying this book to use as reference material while exploring the Animation editor.

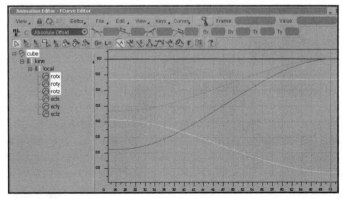

**Figure 11.9**
This is an empty Animation editor.

The Animation Curves for a selected object can be viewed using the Animation editor. The Animation editor can be called up in a number of different ways that are convenient for different uses. To see all the animation curves on a selected object (or a number of selected objects at the same time), go to the bottom of the timeline, click on the Animation button, and choose Animation editor from the pop-up menu there. (The hotkey is 0. See Figure 11.10.) This will pop up a floating window with a collapsible title bar. You can also manually change one of your View windows to show the Animation editor with the Animation editor drop-down menu in the title bar of the view.

To see a single parameter represented as a function curve (which is often much more useful than looking at everything), find that parameter in the property page where it lives, and then right-click on the animation divot (the little round button to the left of the parameter name), as shown in Figure 11.11. A drop-down menu just like the one at the bottom of the screen in the timeline will appear. If you choose Animation editor from the menu, only the curve for that parameter will be shown.

Select the tire object and call up the Animation editor to examine its Animation Curves using one of the preceding methods. There's not much there, huh? Add in some keyframes.

First adjust your views so you can see the tire moving and the Animation editor at the same time. One way to do this is to set the Animation editor to run across the two Top view windows, and set the tire in the Right view to run horizontally across the two Bottom view menus. Remember that you can extend views horizontally or vertically by right-clicking on the resize box in the top-right corner of that view.

> There is a clever layout for people lucky enough to have two monitors that shows the regular XSI UI on the left monitor and the Animation editor and other animation helpers on the right. Try it out with the View > Layouts > Dual-Animation command from the top menu bar.

Start by moving the tire up in the air on the left side, activate the Translation portion of the MCP, and tap the K key to set a keyframe. Move 15 frames later in the timeline, move the tire forward a bit and down to the floor, and set another key. See the Animation Curves grow in the Animation editor? No? That's because there were no curves to show when you opened the Animation editor. Cause it to refresh and reload the new Fcurves by clicking the Recycle button in the Animation editor, which is the circular icon with two arrows at the top left of the Animation editor next to the Lock icon.

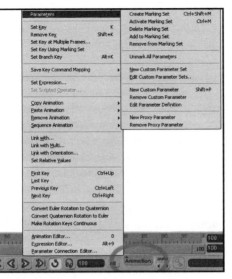

**Figure 11.10**
The Animation menu from the timeline area at the bottom of the screen.

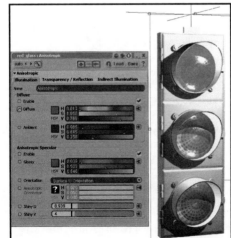

**Figure 11.11**
Animation divots in a property page.

**221**

Move 13 frames later and translate the tire up, not quite as high as before, and forward a bit more. Set another key. Proceed forward, setting more keys closer together with less tire bounce and forward motion until you get bored or the tire comes to a halt, whichever happens first. Examine the curves you created in the Animation editor.

The Animation editor has been scrolling right to left as you have been dragging the timeline from frame 1 to frame 100.

You will doubtless wish to see the whole range of the animation, from frame 1 to frame 100. You can navigate in the Animation editor just as you do in the three-dimensional views, with Z. Pressing the Z key and left mouse button drags in the timeline to show a different part of the curves, Z and middle mouse button zooms in, and Z with the right mouse button zooms out. You can also use the hotkeys F to frame selected curves and A to frame all the curves. Try these out to scale the curves to fit your view, so you can see the whole animation you created.

## Finding the Animation Curve You Want

If the window contains more than one Animation Curve, how do you know which Animation Curve is which? The left panel of the Animation editor contains a hierarchical Explorer view of all the different animation curves present in the Animation editor at that time. You may scroll among them to see what parameters have already been animated on the object (or objects) you had selected when you called up the Animation editor. If a parameter exists but has not been animated, it will show up as a horizontal line in the Animation editor.

Each Animation Curve has a name, made up of the name of the object followed by the name of the property that is being animated. This name is itself a hierarchy that you can read in the left pane of the Animation editor. At the top comes the object name (tire), and under that is how it moves (Kine). Then comes whether the movement is relative to the global center or a local center (Global or Local), and the translation/position (posx, posy, or posz), orientation/rotation (rotx, roty, rotz), or scale (sclx, scly, sclz). Each part of the name is separated by a period (see Figure 11.12). In this way, some valid names for the animation on the tire would be:

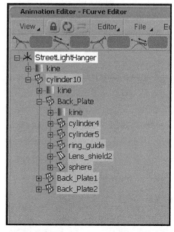

tire.kine.local.posx, meaning where the tire is in on the X-axis.

tire.kine.local.roty, meaning the rotation of the tire around the Y-axis.

These names are represented in the left-hand pane of the Animation editor as individual words in an Explorer-style list, but you can see the actual name in the command line or the script editor (both at the bottom left of the screen) to see what is really happening.

If you click on the name of the parameter on the left, then the corresponding curve will be activated in the right side of the editor. You may also select curves in the right side, by holding the spacebar and either clicking directly on a curve or drawing a selection rectangle that crosses the curve. This will highlight the name of the curve on the left-hand side.

**Figure 11.12**
Here are the names of the animation curves in the TireBounce scene.

It is often hard to see what you want in the Animation editor, either because you are looking at the wrong area of the curve or because the scale of the animation makes the curves very short. Remember that you can frame curves (or tagged keys) by tapping the F hotkey.

What if you have a lot of animation on a single selected object, and you need to limit the curves that display in the Animation editor to make it easier to work with? In this case, the View menu at the top of the Animation editor has settings to help you. To see the differences, first mark the rotation transforms and set at least two keys at different frames on the rotation of the tire, just to clutter the AE (Animation editor) a bit. Click the Recycle icon to load the new Fcurves into the AE.

The View > Animated Parameters command will show you all the Fcurves on the object (everything that has keyframes), though you also may need to use the Recycle button.

If you are looking for the Translate, Scale, or Rotate Animation Curves, you can activate that transformation in the MCP and then toggle on the View > Marked Parameters menu item from the top menu bar of the Animation editor, to view and frame just those curves.

If you want to isolate just one curve, select that curve in the Explorer list on the left side of the AE, and choose the menu command View > Selected Parameters.

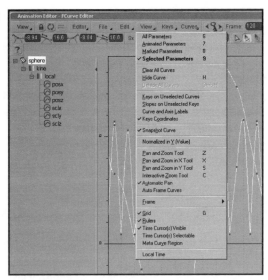

**Figure 11.13**
The View menu helps you isolate just the curves you need to see.

> XSI has a new feature that solves an old problem. When you want to see two different parameters with different scales (like rotation, which is in degrees, and translation, which is in inches, millimeters, or feet), inevitably one parameter or the other is too big and stretches off screen, while the other is too small to see what you are doing. XSI has a feature in the View menu of the Animation editor called Normalized in Y, which will scale all the selected curves so that they fit on the screen, regardless of the unit scale of the curves.

Let's discuss this simple tire example to get more comfortable with the meaning of the curves in the AE. The tire in the Animation.Tirebounce scene was animated to bounce along the floor using local translation. The Animation editor below the ball shows the three Animation Curves for local transformation in X, Y, and Z. The vertical axis of the Animation Curve shows the value of the parameters in XSI units. The horizontal axis shows the time proceeding from left to right (see Figure 11.14). Each Animation Curve tells us exactly where in that axis the object is at each frame in the animation (and even between frames).

## *The Slope of the Curves*

Moving through time, the Animation Curve changes slope as it passes through the control points you created by setting keyframes. SOFTIMAGE|XSI uses a Bezier spline for the curve, which means that the control handles of the curve modify the slope (the tangency of the curve) at every point along

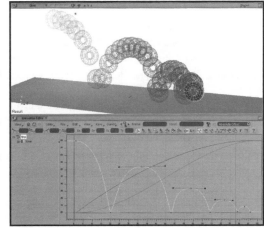

**Figure 11.14**
The tire's path through space is determined by the change in the Animation Curves.

**223**

the curve. By default, XSI eases in from the first point and eases out to the last point. (You can change this in File > Preferences.) Using these Bezier curves avoids jerky-looking animation, because the values accelerate and decelerate at the start and the finish. (Warning: This can also lead to motion that looks too fluid.)

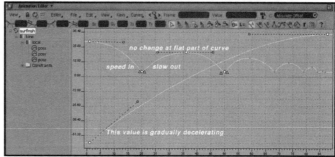

The slope of the curve at any one point is the rate of change in the parameter being animated. Think of this as "how fast it's going." We humans imagine this speed of something traveling at a constant rate (or changing at a constant rate) as a straight line (see Figure 11.15). If the straight line is horizontal, the parameter is not changing at all, or we might say, the object is not moving at all. If the line is near horizontal, the object is changing very slowly. We say then that there is a shallow slope, which means things are not changing very fast. If the slope is steep, the line is going up or down more sharply, and we say the object is changing fast.

**Figure 11.15**
The slope of the curve determines speed and acceleration.

The change in that slope over time (say, from the first point to the second point) is called acceleration, which is easy to think about as "how the animation is speeding up or slowing down." We humans look at this as a curve, rather than a straight line. If the curve is getting flatter, we say the object is slowing down (or the rate of change in a parameter is slowing). If the curve is getting steeper, that property change is speeding up, and the object change is accelerating.

In traditional animation, acceleration at the beginning of a movement is called ease-in, while deceleration at the end of a movement is called ease-out.

## *Editing Animation with Animation Curves*

If you wish to edit your bouncing ball's behavior—say, to make it bounce higher—you do not have to re-keyframe the new motion. You can simply edit the location of points in an Animation curve with the M key, just as you would edit any curve. By holding the M key and dragging a point on the Animation Curve with the mouse, you can change the value of the animated parameter and move the point to a different frame in time.

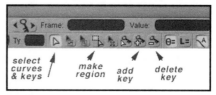

You can add new keys and remove existing ones without using the keyframe techniques, by adding or removing keys directly in the Animation editor. To add a new key to the curve, hold down the I hotkey for insert (or click the Insert Key button—the one with the plus sign—at the top of the Animation editor), point to an area of the curve, and click with the left mouse button. If you click and hold the mouse, you can drag the point to a specific place on the curve before letting go of it (see Figure 11.16).

**Figure 11.16**
These buttons help you edit the curves.

To delete keys, you can simply tag them one at a time or tag a group with the T hotkey, drag a marquee around them all, and then press the Delete key on your keyboard. You can also click on the Delete button at the top of the Animation editor (it has a minus sign) and then click on the keys you want to remove.

The most useful general-purpose button in the top of the Animation editor is the Edit Key tool—represented as a pointer with a key. With this button, you can select curves using the left mouse button, add new keys with the middle mouse button, and remove keys with the right mouse button.

Try editing the height of your tire bounces by dragging (with hotkey M) the top points of the local position in the Y Animation Curve higher in the Animation editor and playing back your animation. Later you will also click the Bezier handles to adjust the curve tangency, which changes how the ball accelerates in and out of keyframes, making the bounce more believable.

You may undo or redo any of your changes in the Animation editor by typing the standard Ctrl-Z and Ctrl-Y hotkeys, respectively. Try it out: Move some points around, and then use Undo until you are back where you started.

# Playing Your Animation

Of course, the first thing you'll want to do after you animate an object by setting keyframes is see how that object moves and changes over time. Seeing your animation on the computer screen is not only the big payoff for the animator, it's what the client pays for. The only way to make sure that the animation you get is the animation you wanted is to check, check, and recheck the playback. You can play your animation in a number of ways, but they all start with an understanding of the Time slider and how frames in SOFTIMAGE|XSI relate to real time.

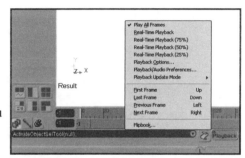

**Figure 11.17**
These buttons play back your animation.

If you want to see the scene play by itself, you can simply click one of the VCR-style Play controls below the Time slider (see Figure 11.17).

## *Improve the Playback Rate*

As your scenes become more and more complex, it will not be possible for XSI to play back each frame at a constant rate of 30 frames per second. However, there are a couple of things you can do to help the playback maintain an appropriate speed.

First, you can reduce the number of View windows that are refreshed each frame by using the Window Lock option. To lock all the windows but one, click directly on the letter in the top-left corner of the window that you want to keep active, which will blank out all other views. The fewer windows that have to be refreshed, the more computational power your system can spend on drawing your animation in the window you care about, and the faster it plays.

## *Rendering Tests*

Seeing a real-time playback of the animation in your scene is critical to good animation during the feedback loop portion of your workflow. If you don't watch it at the speed your consumers will, you can't possibly know what it will look like when they see it. If you don't know what it will look like, it will probably look bad. The solution is to use non-real-time methods of rendering frames, and real-time methods of playing them back.

XSI has a major improvement in how you view your animation work while it's in process. Now, previewing your action is much easier and more flexible than ever before. You can create a preview of your work in any View window, in any view style, at any time. Just choose a view to capture (usually the Camera view), and select Start Capture from the Camera menu in the middle of the title bar of that view window. (It has the icon of a camera, not the word "Camera".) See Figure 11.18.

A dialog box will pop up with options to set the capture size, the picture format, and the compression used. To quickly see your capture, change the drop menu labeled Scale to 1/2 size, leave the other defaults, and click OK. A new Preview window will appear, and XSI will start drawing frames into it, starting from the first frame you have set in the timeline until it reaches the last frame of the timeline. As each frame is drawn, it will be written to a cache on disk. When the process is done, the cached files will be loaded into the Flipbook and displayed (see Figure 11.19). If you chose to save the capture as QuickTime, the QuickTime viewer will pop up instead of the Flipbook, and if you chose .AVI, the Windows Media Player will pop up instead of the Flipbook. All file types can be used to see your animation play back in real time.

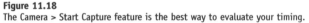

**Figure 11.18**
The Camera > Start Capture feature is the best way to evaluate your timing.

It's a good idea to create a local directory on your computer to store the capture files in, rather than writing them across your network all the time, which imposes quite a bandwidth load and is slower for you and everyone else on your local network segment. In Windows, the C:\WINNT\Temp directory is a good place to put the files. In Linux, the /tmp dir will suffice.

The improvement is that this method writes the image files to disk for later perusal. After closing the Flipbook, which will empty the RAM cache, change another View window to the Image Clip Editor. Now use the File > Load command or drag and drop the frames from a browser into the Clip Editor. This stores the Capture for later in the clip list. (It also makes it available to be used as a texture map on another object.)

If your preview does not play back in the Image Clip Editor at a consistent speed, it may not be possible for your computer to retrieve the frames from the disk rapidly enough. (This will happen if you skimped on buying that SCSI drive.) In this situation, XSI must cache the frames in RAM memory, which is much faster than normal PC hard drives. Right-click on the clip and choose Cache

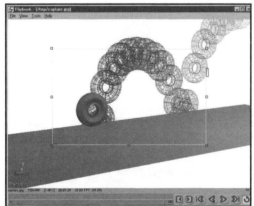

**Figure 11.19**
You can play your tests any time in the Image Clip Editor.

Properties, scroll down the clip property page, and toggle on the Frame Caching option (see Figure 11.20). This loads the frames into memory on the first round and then plays them back, keeping the timing you set in the same clip property page. You may also increase the amount of RAM allocated to the cache if you have a lot of frames to preview, and a lot of RAM in your computer.

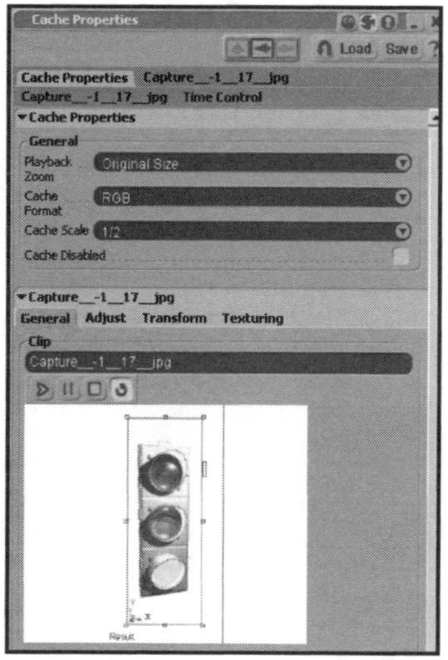

### Common Capture Styles

While the Wireframe style is the fastest method for rendering frames into the capture buffer, sometimes it is difficult to make out the action in your scene through all the criss-crossing lines of the wireframe. One way to make the view easier to comprehend is to use the Hidden Line Removal rendering style. In Hidden Line Removal, only front-facing surfaces are rendered, and objects in front obscure those behind them.

Another neat trick is to draw a render region in the view you plan to capture, and then initiate a Camera > Capture session. The mental ray will render just that portion, and the view style will be used for the rest of the frame (see Figure 11.21).

**Figure 11.20**
Toggle on the cache to store frames in RAM during playback.

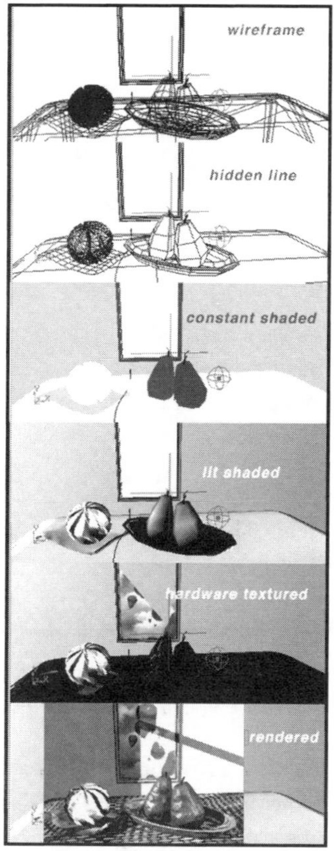

Now back to the Animation editor.

# Intermediate Animation Curve Editing Techniques

Swap and Snapshot enable you to experiment without fear of screwing up your animation. Think of Swap and Snapshot as controllable Undoes (see Figure 11.22). If the option named Snapshot Curve is toggled on in the View menu (and it is by default), when you edit an Animation Curve the previous state of the curve is saved into the swap buffer, and a thin black line shows you what the Animation Curve used to look like. This thin dashed black line is called the snapshot.

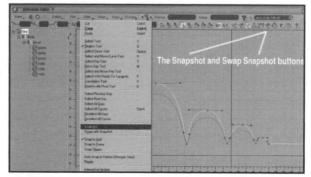

The Snapshot and Swap Snapshot buttons

**Figure 11.21**
Some styles are slower to capture, but easier to see.

**Figure 11.22**
Swap and Snap are like another level of Undo for your animation.

If at any point in your work you decide that the old Animation Curve was better, simply click the Swap with Snapshot button (it looks like one dashed curve and one solid curve with two triangles) to recall the old curve and place the new one in the swap buffer. If, while you are editing, you decide that you wish to save an intermediate Animation Curve before exploring further, click the Snapshot button (it looks like a curve, with a camera icon above it). This button replaces the saved Animation Curve in the buffer with the current one, but it does not replace the current Animation Curve as the active one.

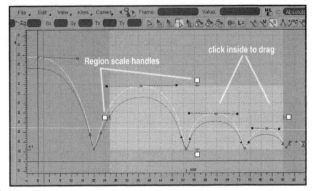

## Working on Groups of Points: The Region Editor

XSI has a new method of changing a large number of keyframes, perhaps on many different animation curves, all at the same time. This new feature is the Region editor. When you have a region defined, it encapsulates all the keyframes within it, and the whole group can be scaled along the value axis or the time axis, or moved in either direction (see Figure 11.23).

**Figure 11.23**
The region surrounds all the keys.

To use the region, select those curves that you want to work with (you may multi-select curves with Shift-select), click on the Region button at the top of the Animation editor (it has an arrow drawing a box), and drag to define the region (see Figure 11.24). The hotkey for drawing an animation curve region is Q, just like drawing a render region. A box appears as you drag, surrounding the keyframes you will be modifying. Small, square handles on the edges of the region scale it in four different directions. You can move the entire region by clicking in the middle of the region and dragging it around within the Animation editor.

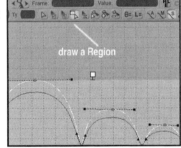

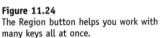

Translating a region of an Animation Curve in the X-axis has the effect of moving the whole animation in time, either earlier or later depending on which way you go. By looking at the frame values on the X-axis, you can easily synchronize action in the Animation Curve with a specific frame.

**Figure 11.24**
The Region button helps you work with many keys all at once.

Translating the whole Animation Curve in the Y-axis has the effect of changing all the values in that Animation Curve by the same amount.

For instance, in your tire scene, you can make the ground plane that the tire bounces on higher or lower by dragging a region over the entire kine.local.posy (the Y position) Animation Curve and then moving up the region in the Y direction.

Scaling the region has the effect of making the action of the keyframes more or less pronounced.

You can make all the bounces taller, leaving the floor level where it is by selecting the Local Position in Y Animation Curve and then dragging a marquee around all the highest points (the peaks of the bounces). Then you can drag the top-middle handle (a small white square) of the region up in Y twice as high as is was. During playback, your ball should bounce twice as high and hang a little longer before crashing to earth.

As of XSI version 4.0, there is another neat tool that is really an extension to the Region concept, called the Stretch with Pivot tool. It acts like a region for scaling selections of keys, but rather than scaling them to the sides of the region, you can select the center point around which all the points scale. It is easy to use. Just select some curves and tag some points. Then activate the tool in one of three ways: from the Edit menu (Edit > Stretch with Pivot Tool), from the button in the AE toolbar that looks like a mouse pointer with aiming crosshairs, or with the B hotkey. Now your mouse is a pointer for the center of the scaling operation. Point where you want the tagged keys to scale to, and drag with the left mouse button. You can choose to scale horizontally or vertically relative to the pivot with the middle and right mouse buttons, or just according to which direction you drag first with the left mouse button. Try it out.

## Directly Changing Key Values

In XSI, it's fantastically easy to precisely set the values of one or more keyframes. For instance, if you know that a wheel has to rotate exactly 175 degrees at a certain frame, you can select the key by dragging a marquee around it, type a number in the numeric entry Value box at the top of the Animation editor, and press Enter. You may also set values on more than one key at a time. You can make a number of keys match the same value. For instance, you can set the local Y position of a character's feet so they hit the floor at the same level, make a tire bounce exactly at the same floor height. Just select all the individual key points in the Animation editor with a selection marquee and type a number in to the Value box at the top middle of the Animation editor. That value will be assigned to all the keyframes when you press the Enter key (see Figure 11.25).

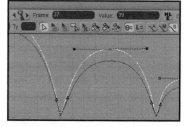

**Figure 11.25**
Just select a key and type a value into these boxes to set it precisely at a given frame.

You can also directly enter frame numbers to make sure that a key happens on a specific frame. Again, just select the key by dragging a marquee around it with the spacebar, and this time enter a frame number in the Frame numeric entry box at the top of the Animation editor.

You will also notice numeric entry boxes for the precise values of the tangency handles, should you need to precisely set those.

If you want all your changes to result in keys that are snapped to exact keyframes in time, there is another clever option hidden in the Edit menu. Toggle on the Auto-Snap to Discrete Time option to make sure that when you change keys they end up exactly on a keyframe and not in between. This will ensure that all keys land on a specific frame, even if you scale a region of keys or make some other modification. You can also do this after the fact by selecting keys and using the Move Keys to Nearest Frames command.

## Working with Keys and Slopes

Slope is a critical tool, because it controls a parameter's rate of change in and out of keyframes. This is a fancy way of saying that it controls the timing of the actions being animated—how quickly things change. Because the normal functions of the Bezier control handles keep the two sides even (with the same tangency), the default Bezier curve is not suited to any motion that changes from acceleration to deceleration (or changes direction entirely) at a single keyframe (see Figure 11.26).

A good example of when you might want to use this option is when your tire bounces on the floor. As the tire approaches the floor, it accelerates due to the force of gravity, but at the instant of contact, that acceleration should become deceleration as it bounces up against gravity, slowing down.

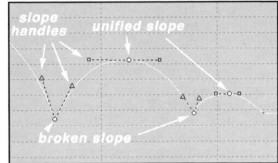

**Figure 11.26**
One key on a curve, showing the slope handles.

Unified Slope Orientation is a fancy way of saying that the two tangency handles are exactly flat to each other, both tangent to the curve. Without Unified Slope Orientation, we say that the slope is Broken.

Try breaking the slope of the bouncing ball Y translation Animation Curve at the point when the ball hits the ground by tagging the point in question and tapping the O hotkey. That action toggles the Unified Slope Orientation property from the Keys menu (see Figure 11.27). Now you can use the M key to change the tangent handles independently for that point.

With the slope of the curve broken at that point, you can adjust each tangent handle of the point separately. The handles should be moved so that the curve changes direction abruptly at the keyframe, just like the tire changes direction abruptly when it hits the floor.

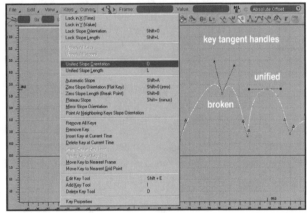

**Figure 11.27**
Use these menu items to break and unify the slope on individual keys.

You can also break the slope of many keys at once by selecting them with a marquee or by Shift-clicking on them and choosing the Keys > Unified Slope Orientation command from the top menu bar of the Animation editor. The Keys > Unified Slope Orientation is a toggle, so it unifies the slope, meaning that the control handles are once again connected in a straight line. Unifying the slope at a given keyframe with the O hotkey makes the Animation Curve interpolate smoothly in and out of that keyframe, preventing rash, sudden moves.

In SOFTIMAGE|3D 3.x, the slope handles could not be lengthened, which required additional keyframes for some shapes of the curve. You may now adjust the length of the slope handles to make fatter curves or make all tangent handles the same length with the Unified Slope Length command.

## Interpolation: Constant, Linear, and Spline

The Curves menu Interpolation controls adjust the method of interpolation used between points throughout the entire curve. Because the default Bezier spline curve isn't always the best choice for all kinds of animation, the Animation editor offers some other types of curves that might better suit your specific needs, as shown in Figure 11.28.

Choosing the Curves > Linear Interpolation command causes the interpolation between each point to become a straight line. Linear is an excellent choice for animating lights and colors, where ease-in and ease-out are not so important. Using Linear interpolation on movement creates a mechanical, robotic look.

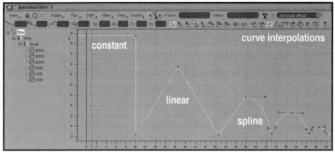

**Figure 11.28**
Interpolation changes how the curve works between keys.

Curves > Spline Interpolation with Keys > Plateau Slope is very useful for character animation, because it retains the ease-in and ease-out attributes of the Bezier curve, but it uses a linear segment between two points on the curve with the same value. Ordinarily, a Bezier curve going through two points adopts a somewhat serpentine path through the keyframes, which can cause backsliding, foot dragging, and other unwanted behavior in characters. Using Plateau Slope means your characters stay where you put them when they are not supposed to be moving between one keyframe and the next, but still move fluidly when they do move. Curves > Constant Interpolation will make the value stay constant from one key to the next, and then jump suddenly to the new value without any interpolation. This is not often very useful.

## Deleting Animation Curves

At this point, you should be wondering how to remove animation from an object—you know, make it quit moving. That seems like a tall order in SOFTIMAGE|XSI, because so much is geared towards adding animation, but it's really quite simple.

If you want to eliminate just one Animation Curve, select the curve scheduled for termination and choose the Keys > Remove All Keys command from the Keys menu within the Animation editor.

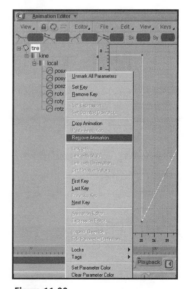

**Figure 11.29**
The Remove Animation commands help you clear out unwanted animation, or just start over.

Each animation divot in the property pages also has an option called Remove Animation located in the menu that cascades down when you right-click on it (see Figure 11.29). This option whacks the entire Animation Curve, in addition to any expressions or linked parameters on that property.

On the Animation menu in the timeline, there is an option to Remove Animation > From Transforms, which will wipe clean all the scale, rotation, and translation Animation Curves on the selected object. This also works for selections of multiple objects.

The Animation menu also has options to remove other specific types of animation, including constraints, expressions, and scripted operators.

If you want to remove all the animation from a marked parameter (say, translation), you can do that from the general XSI interface with the hotkey Ctrl-Shift-K.

## Creating a Cycle

Sometimes you want an object to have a repetitive motion, such as a wheel spinning or the pendulum of a clock swinging back and forth. In the Curves menu, you will find the commands required to accomplish what you need.

When you activate the Curves > Cycle or Curves > Relative Cycle menu commands, all of the keyframes you have set already will repeat endlessly in time, both before the start of the Fcurve segment and after the last frame you have set in the AE (see Figure 11.30). You can see that the cycle repeats endlessly through time by zooming out in the AE. The F hotkey frames back to the actual keys you set.

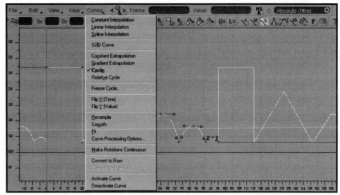

**Figure 11.30**
This basic action has been cycled perpetually.

If the first and last points you keyed do not have the same value, you may see some jumping in the animation as the object snaps from the last frame back to the first. When making cycles, take care to make them smooth by setting the first and last key to precisely the same value using the numeric entry Value box at the top of the Animation editor.

### *Gradient Extrapolation*

Curves > Gradient Extrapolation finds the slope of the last two points in the Animation Curve and simply continues on at the same slope indefinitely. This type of motion is great for objects that constantly spin, like wheels and propellers.

## Ping Pong: At a Glance

You'll learn how to:

◆ Set keyframes a few different ways

◆ Edit and fine-tune the animation

◆ Change timing with the Animation editor

◆ Work with the slope of the Animation Curves

◆ Create Animation Cycles

◆ Add anticipation and follow-through to your work (see Figure 11.31)

## Materials Required

This tutorial uses the Animation_Pingpong_start.scn scene file from the courseware accompanying this book.

# Tutorial: Ping Pong—Animation Editing

During this tutorial, you will set keyframes to create a simple game of table tennis. After setting basic keyframes for the translation of the ping-pong ball back and forth, you'll use the Animation editor to change the timing and slopes of the ball's translation animation curves so that it seems to bounce correctly. Then after the ball is bouncing right, you'll make a cycle out of the movement so that the ball bounces back and forth endlessly. Next you'll edit some of the translation keys so that the ball bounces to a different part of the table on each bounce, at a different speed, adding some interest to the game. Finally, you'll animate the ping pong paddles to meet the ball at the right place and time, and add traditional animation anticipation and follow-through so it looks like a human being is swinging the paddles—not a computer.

**Figure 11.31**
The finished Ping-Pong scene.

## Keep Your Eye on the Ball

### Step 1: Load the Animation_Pingpong_start.scn Scene File

Look into the project for this book and load the Animation_Pingpong_start.scn scene. It contains a simple ping-pong table, with a ball and two paddles (see Figure 11.32). Nothing is animated yet.

Examine the scene, selecting the ball and the paddles to get the feel of the objects.

### Step 2: Set Nine Keyframes on the Ball

Open the Right view and extend it horizontally. Then zoom to frame the scene before setting any keys.

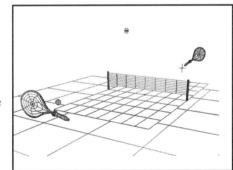

**Figure 11.32**
The starting scene.

The ball needs to start at one end, at the location of the paddle. In the Right view at frame zero, move the ball to contact the paddle on the left and set a key for the local translation of the ball on all axes: X, Y, and Z.

Move the timeline ten frames later in time, and set another key for the ball half-way to the net, on the surface of the ping-pong table. (Remember, in ping pong, your serve has to bounce once before it clears the net.)

Since we can't see a change in the X-axis in the Right view, the keys will have the same X value. That's okay—we want the ping pong ball to travel straight back and forth because we're going to modify that later on with a different technique.

Set another key ten frames later for the ball, directly in the middle of the table, above the net.

Ten frames forward again, set another key for the ball on the table, halfway between the net and the far side.

Ten frames later, set another key at the location of the second (far side) ping-pong paddle.

Ten frames later (try typing 10+, and then enter the current frame text box), the ball should be above the net, on the way back, because on the return the player does not have to hit the ball to bounce before the net.

Keep going. Set keys all the way back to exactly where you started. This should take eight keyframes, so if they start at 0 and are ten frames apart, they should end at frame 70 (see Figure 11.33).

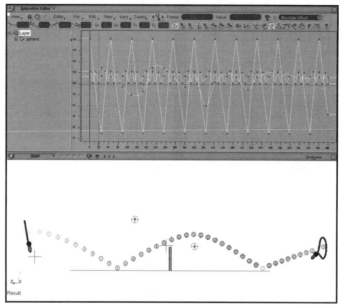

**Figure 11.33**
Eight keyframes in the Animation editor.

To ensure that the last frame is exactly where the first was, try moving the time slider to zero, right-clicking and dragging to frame 70, and then setting a translation key. Right-dragging the time slider doesn't update the screen, so it's a quick way to copy values from one key to another. You can also just tag the first key on an fcurve in the AE, look at the value and copy it, tag the last key, and set it to the same value.

## Step 3: Take a Cold, Hard Look at Your Work

Play back your animation, making sure that you are seeing it at 30 fps (frames per second), just like your customers would if this were a real job. Click on the small button in the timeline that toggles from All (Frames) to RT, which stands for Real Time. You might also isolate the Perspective window so that it is the only window that will refresh, by clicking the letter in the top-left corner. (Click it again to activate the other windows.)

You could also set the last frame to 70 and click the loop button to get a good feel for the looping of the animation (or just turn on looping (next to the headphones icon in the playback area) and drag the end loop indicator 9 (the yellow bar in the timeline) to frame 70.

It looks pretty bad, doesn't it? Make a mental list (or a physical one) of all the things that are wrong with the animation. The ball weaves in and out of the floor. Instead of bouncing, it just goes back and forth in a fashion that is too regular and boring, and it doesn't hang in the air quite right. In addition, the speed of the ball should vary over each hit, starting fast and then slowing down as it nears the other side. In general, the animation is dull and lifeless. Let's fix it!

## Step 4: Open the Animation Editor and Set a Cycle

Change the last frame of the animation to 320 frames, so we can set a cycle and see a few different volleys of the ping-pong game.

Open the Animation editor by selecting the ball and choosing Animation editor from the Animation menu in the timeline at the bottom of the screen, or by using the 0 hotkey.

Within the Animation editor window, use the View > Animated Parameters menu item to show just the animated curves: the local translation in X, Y, and Z.

Select the animation curve for local translation in X (the red one). Remember that we never really changed the X value, so it should be pretty flat, even though it has some keyframes on it. We'll want to remove all the middle keyframes on X, leaving the first and last keys (at frames 0 and 70, respectively). That way, when we cycle it, we only have keys for when the ball hits the first ping pong paddle, which we'll edit to make the game more interesting.

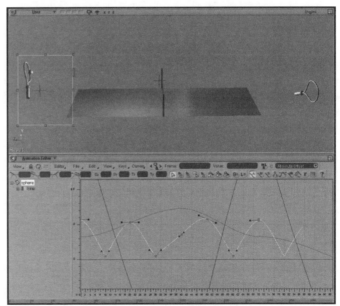

Drag a marquee rectangle, using the tag hotkey (just hold down the T key), around all the points on the red X-axis curve except for the first and last point, and then press the Delete button on your keyboard to remove them.

The Z (blue) curve represents the travel of the ball back and forth down the length of the table. It has redundant keyframes, too, but we need to keep the keys at frames when the ball strikes either paddle. Those are keys at frames 0, 40, and 70 (first, last, and middle). Keep the keys at those frames and delete the others.

Now we'll make a cycle. Select all three curves—local X, Y, and Z—with the spacebar and set a cycle so that they go on indefinitely into the future with the Curves > Cycle menu item (see Figure 11.34).

Turn off Loop if it's on, and drag back and forth on the timeline, or play back the animation, to see that we now have four complete cycles. If you set the end frame of the animation to be even further out in time, we would get even more cycles, but four is probably enough for us now.

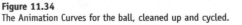
**Figure 11.34**
The Animation Curves for the ball, cleaned up and cycled.

With all the curves selected, look at the menu item Keys > Plateau Slope, and make sure it is unchecked. This menu item would make it tough for us to adjust the tangent handles in the next step. With the curves selected, use the F key to frame up the curves to fill the AE.

## Step 5: Edit the Cycles

Now we can fix some of the problems on just one set of keyframes and see the result on all four cycles—a real time-saver. First we'll change the timing on the ball's travel down the table, which is the local translation in Z.

When the ball leaves the paddle, it should be moving at its fastest rate (the slope of the animation curve should be the steepest) and the ball should gradually slow down just a bit until it hits the other paddle. (The slope should gradually flatten out a little bit—not too much.) Then, at that instant, the ball should suddenly be going faster again as it comes off the paddle and repeat the slowing down process due to air resistance all the way back to the paddle at the other side (see Figure 11.35).

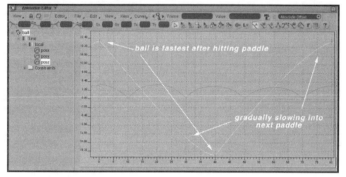

**Figure 11.35**
The ball is moving fastest right after hitting each paddle.

To make the slope of the line change so dramatically at the points where the ball hits the paddle, we need to break the tangent handles for the keys in local Z. Start with the first key at frame 0, select it, and use the menu item Keys > Unified Slope Orientation, or just the O hotkey. Now you can change the tangent handle after the key independently from the tangent handle before the key. In other words, the ball can now change direction or speed instantly at a keyframe, instead of having to ease in and ease out.

Adjust the tangent out key's handle so that the slope of the curve is greatest (steepest) at the instant the ball leaves the paddle, and gently eases into the next keyframe. Then adjust the tangent handle out of the next keyframe so that it is steepest, easing gently back to the next key, the location of the original paddle.

After the orientation of all the keys' tangent handles is broken, a fast way to set the ease-in and ease-out to something close to what you want is to tag the keys and use the Keys > Point at Neighboring Keys menu command.

Play your animation and fine-tune the effect so that the ball seems to slow down just slightly as it moves across the table and then picks up speed instantly as it changes direction due to the hit from the paddle.

The tangent handles leading away from where the ball struck the paddle can be longer than the tangent handles where the ball has just struck the paddle and is leaving it.

Avoid making the changes to the curve too dramatic, or the Z and Y keys won't line up well at the frames when the ball is supposed to go over the net. It might go through it.

Now we'll fix the bounces off the table (see Figure 11.36). Select the (green) translation in Y curve, and tag one of the lowest points in the local Y-axis, which is the ball's height in the air. Look to the top of the Animation editor and note the value of the Y curve at that key. All the bounces should hit the table at the same level, so tag all the lower points in Y and type the value you noted into the same box you read it from and press Enter. All the keys will now be set to the same height.

With only the lower keys still selected, use the O hotkey again to make the tangent handles independent. We need the handles to come together in a sharp V shape, accelerating into the floor, and instantly changing direction and then decelerating out of the floor. Modify each set of handles to look like a V shape, and play back the animation to see the difference. Fine-tune to your liking.

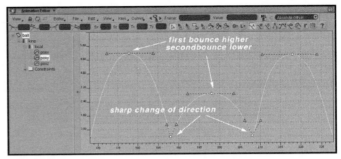

**Figure 11.36**
Gravity slams the ball into the table, slows it down in a gradual arc up in the air, and then back down to the table again.

## Step 6: Freeze the Cycles

We need to freeze the cycles so we can make each one slightly different, adding to the interest of the game.

But first, take a look at the first and last key on each curve to make sure they have the same value. If the curves start and end at the same value, the cycle transition will be seamless.

Now select all three curves and use the Curves > Freeze Cycle command, and enter the first and last frames of your animation timeline (maybe 0 and 400, for instance) into the Freeze Cycle dialog box. Then press the OK button to complete the command. Freezing the curves adds actual keyframes from your first frame to your last frame, so you can edit them and make the cycles nonuniform. Zoom out in the AE to see that the cycles exist as actual curves with actual keyframes.

Currently, the ball travels straight up and down the middle of the table. Let's change that. Keep the Animation editor up but change one of your other views to be the Top view. At frame 40 (where the ball hits a paddle), check to see if there is a key on the X fcurve. If so, great. If not, add one precisely by moving the timeline Current Frame indicator to frame 40 and using the Keys > Insert Key at Current Time command from the AE menus. Either way, use the M hotkey to change the value of the key on the red X animation curve slightly. You must let go of the point to see the change, unless you toggle on Interactive Update at the bottom of the Edit menu.

See that the ball now arrives at a different spot on the table. Also change the other frames where the ball reaches one end of the table, except the first and the last frames, to make a more challenging game for the contestants. We'll leave the first and the last frame so we could still cycle our animation if we wanted to.

Play back your animation using the Real Time playback option, and note how much better it is! Pat yourself on the back.

## *It's All in the Wrist*

Currently, the ball is moving on its own up and down the table. We need to add the illusion that the paddles are driving the ball back and forth. We can also add anticipation and follow-through to the action of the paddles to make the animation seem more lifelike and realistic.

### Step 1: Move the Paddles

Start by matching the position of the paddles in X to the position of the ball when it reaches the ends of the tables.

This is pretty easy—just move the paddles in X to meet the ball—but we need to throw in a twist. The paddles need to get to their position slightly before the ball does, because that's the way humans do it. Arriving before the ball is a form of anticipation.

There is a quick way to do this. Branch-select the first paddle, and at frame zero, set a keyframe for its local translation in X only (by only marking X).

Drag forward in time until the ball bounces across the table and finally comes back to the first paddle. (This should be frame 70.) Drag the paddle in X to meet the ball, and set a keyframe. (Use the K hotkey.)

Now, right-click and drag the time slider about eight frames earlier in time, which will change the time without moving the paddle. Set another keyframe in X. The result should be that the paddle moves to take up position eight frames before the ball gets there.

Follow this pattern each time the ball gets back to the paddle. Set the key for the moment the ball strikes the paddle, and then right-click and drag and set another key a few frames before that. (Vary the number of frames between keys from 5 to 15 so that the person with the paddle has a harder time getting to some shots.)

Repeat for the other paddle, and play back to examine your work.

### Step 2: Add Follow-Through and More Anticipation

The paddles still look like a bad game of Pong—they just don't have any human-ness to their movement. What's missing? Anticipation and follow-through. We'll add that in with some simple rotational keyframes.

As the ball approaches, perhaps 15 to 20 frames before the hit, the paddle should swing back, rotating around local Y, to get ready for the wrist action that drives the ball. It should hang in that cocked position until a few frames before the hit, perhaps 2 to 4 frames. Then it should swing rapidly through the position of the hit and fluidly follow through to a rotation past the original, unrotated pose (see Figure 11.37).

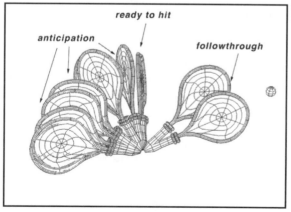

**Figure 11.37**
The arc of the paddle, showing the three phases of the action.

Select the first paddle, and 15 frames before the ball strikes it (about frame 55), rotate the paddle around Y to cock it ready to strike, and save a key.

Right-click and drag the time slider forward to three frames before the hit (about frame 67) and set another rotational keyframe, so that it stays cocked for 12 frames before the hit. This waiting in the cocked position is anticipation.

About 5 to 8 frames after the hit (perhaps frame 78), rotate the paddle through the ball to the other side, as if the weight and inertia of the paddle caused the wrist to over-rotate. Set another keyframe. This over-rotation is called follow-through.

About 30 frames later, return it to the original, unrotated position, and set a keyframe for rotation, so that it is ready to cock again in anticipation and repeat the whole thing again.

Since the Rotation curves have spline interpolation active by default, there will be quite a bit of mushy change that you did not intend. Remove the accidental changes in the rotations by selecting the curves and all the points on them and toggling on the Keys > Zero Slope Orientation option. This will keep the rotations from changing when you don't want them to.

Repeat this pattern for each strike of the ball. Remember: 15 frames before the hit, rotate the paddle to a cocked position. Keep it there until a few frames before the hit, unload on the ball, and rotate through smoothly, ending up approximately eight frames after the hit with another keyframe in the fully rotated follow-through position. One second later, restore the paddle to the unrotated position so it's ready to cock and fire again. You can vary the timing for each one to make it more human and less precise.

After you have all the keys set for anticipation and follow-through, check your handiwork! It should look pretty good.

Whew! What a tutorial. This process of setting lots and lots of keyframes and then adjusting them to fine-tune the results is pretty much what it's like to be a production animator. Also, remember to add the anticipation and follow-through to all your actions, lest they come across as wooden or "computery."

> Extra Credit: Use the Region tool to change the timing of *all* the curves from stroke to stroke, so that some shots are hard (fast) and others are soft (slower).

## Conclusion

Animation is what XSI is all about, and the incredible level of control that XSI provides the animator is what makes it such a fantastic tool. Remember that the Animation editor is often a quicker way of adding the keys you need and the only way to change the ease-in and ease-out of the animation. Don't forget to pay attention to the little things: slope, anticipation, and follow-through.

# Chapter 12
# Working with Images

In this chapter, you will learn:

◆ How XSI loads and stores 2D images

◆ How texture mapping is done in XSI

◆ How to choose the right texture support for the job

◆ How to layer textures in the Texture Layer editor

◆ How to assign polygon (and NURBS) UV information for precise mapping

◆ Why there is a 2D compositor in XSI

## Introduction

SOFTIMAGE XSI is an integrated 3D animation and special effects package. That means that in addition to building 3D models, animating and rendering them, XSI has tools and features for using images created in other applications as texture maps, for painting images (both raster and vector) from scratch, and for compositing

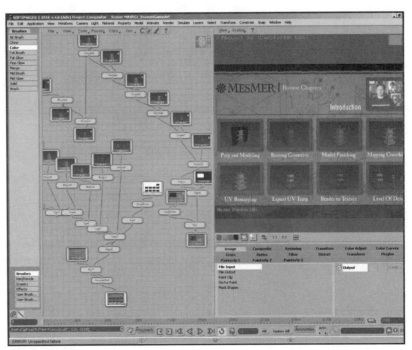

**Figure 12.1**
2D compositing in a 3D package.

endless layers of other images together to create new results. We'll explain the 3D texture projection system and have a brief look at UV layout (see Figure 12.2).

## Sources and Clips Explained

Very often you will want to use images already created from some other source in your XSI work. For instance, you might have a scanned image of a product logo from a client that you need to use, a background image that the product needs to be composited on top of, or practical film footage that needs to be matched in XSI. You can import these different types of images into XSI to work with them by turning the images into Clips and Sources (see Figure 12.3).

**Figure 12.2**
Tools you'll use.

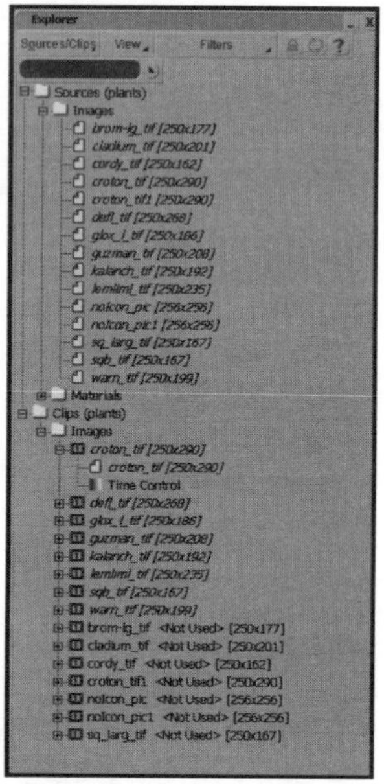

Each image (or image sequence) located on your hard disk or network can be used in your XSI scene by creating a reference to the images. This reference has two parts: the Source and the Clip.

The Image Source is the object that stores the name of the image file or sequence, where it is on disk, how fast you want the sequence to play, how long the sequence is, and a few options related to rendering, as shown in Figure 12.4.

**Figure 12.3**
The sources and clips can be found in the Explorer, at the Sources/Clips level.

**Figure 12.4**
The source properties include the file name and path.

The Image Clip is a new object that is based on an Image Source, but it adds new properties, like the image size, crop, color balance, and more (see Figure 12.5). We'll examine these Clip properties later in this chapter.

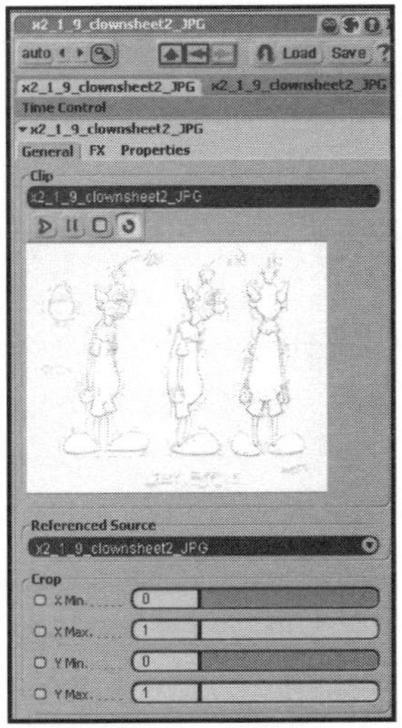

Both Image Sources and Clips can be viewed in the Explorer, at the Sources/Clips scope (hotkey o in the Explorer). There must be at least one Source for each Clip, although there may be many Clips referencing each source. Because the Source is really just the file location of the image on disk somewhere, the images are not really stored *in* the scene file. That means that if you modify them on disk with some other program, you will see the results in XSI. It also means that adding images does not make your scene file any bigger, because the scene just points to where the images are saved.

So while we might say we are bringing images into XSI or importing images we really are just making reference to their location.

## Importing Images with the Image Clip Viewer

It's a good idea to bring all your imagery into your XSI scene at one time, to optimize your productivity and workflow. You do this with the Clip Viewer and the Browser view.

If you open the Clip Viewer in one of your four View windows, you can create Sources and Clips by using the File > Import menu or by opening your browser in another View window and drag images from the browser into the Clip editor (see Figure 12.6).

**Figure 12.5**
The clip properties include cropping and clip FX.

If you have a single image to import, you can locate the image in the browser, drag it to the middle of the Clip editor, and let go to create a Source and a Clip. The image will appear in the Clip editor. When you drag and drop another image into the Clip editor, it is added and shows up in the window. You can use the Clips drop menu to see the images you have imported and to play back sequences.

If you have a sequence of images that you want to use, for instance as an animated texture map, it needs to be named like this: Name.Number.Extension (powerup.1.tif for instance).

**Figure 12.6**
The Clip Viewer shows you all the clips imported into your scene.

When you look at the images in the Browser, XSI will combine all the files and show you only one icon. When you drag and drop it into XSI, only one source and one clip will be created, no matter how many individual images there were in the sequence (see Figure 12.7).

If it happens that you only really want one of the images, you can double-click on the icon in the Browser to drill down into the sequence and drag just one into the Clip editor.

XSI will happily read TIFF, TARGA, JPEG, and even the native Photoshop file format, .PSD. However, if you choose to use .PSD files in the Render Tree portion of XSI, only the first layer will be accessible, as shown in Figure 12.8. (The compositor can extract all the layers, however.)

You can also create Image Sources and Clips a few other ways. The Render module has several features for importing images and making clips and sources in the Get > Clip menu. You can also import a file directly when you need to use it, in an image node, or when using the Texture Layer editor. Some methods are easier in different circumstances.

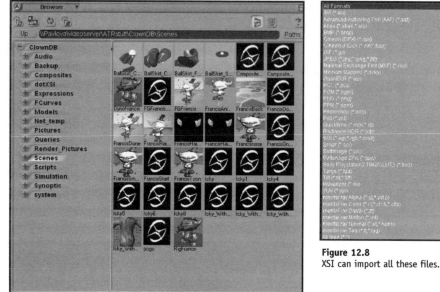

**Figure 12.7**
The browser is just a File dialog box with image icons.

**Figure 12.8**
XSI can import all these files.

I mentioned earlier that the images are merely referenced in the XSI scene. That might lead to problems if you took your XSI scene file somewhere else on a CD-ROM and tried to open it. The images would not be there, because they did not travel with the scene.

You can solve this problem. If you check the box marked Copy External Files Under Project when you save your XSI scene, then during the save, XSI will locate, gather, and move all the referenced images from where you found them into the Pictures directory of the XSI project you saved the scene to. When you transport the entire project, now containing both scenes and images, to the new location, all your images' clips and sources will have the path to the local images and will therefore load properly. This collection feature is extremely convenient.

XSI can also import and work with high dynamic range images, like Cineon, HDR, and OpenEXR images. For a complete list of all the formats XSI can import and use (and, for the most part, write out), open the Image Clip Viewer window and choose File > Import (or use the Compositor File input node) and look at the File Type list at the bottom of the dialog box.

## Updating References

If you open the Explorer, switch to the Sources/Clips scope, open the Sources > Images folder, and inspect one of the clips you have created by clicking on the icon to the left of the name, you'll open up the Image Source PPG and can then see the path to the file.

If at some point it was necessary to swap this image with another, you could manually change the file path here, and the same source would reference a different image. Any Clip you use in the scene that refers to this Image Source would therefore also point to the new image.

## Dynamic Update from Photoshop

You can also use Photoshop to edit a file used by XSI, and you see the results immediately after you save the file from Photoshop, even if both applications are running. The user preference in File > Application > Preferences > Rendering > Misc tab named Reload Externally Modified Image Clips on Focus controls this behavior.

## Removing Unused Clips and Sources

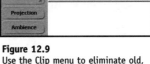

Since Clips and Sources can also come into your scene with Model imports, it sometimes happens after working with a scene for a long time that there are lots of Image Sources and Clips that you no longer wish to use.

Since Clips depend on Image Sources, you can remove the clips without removing the sources, but not the other way around. While you can delete Sources in the Explorer with the Delete key, it's usually easier to use the Get > Clip > Delete Unused Image Sources and Clips command from the left-hand menu stack in the Render module (see Figure 12.9).

**Figure 12.9**
Use the Clip menu to eliminate old, misdirected and unused clips.

You can also view image files used in your scene with View > General > External Files Manager. The External Files Manager also has tools for repathing images when you need to move the file from one drive location to another.

## Using the Clip Effects

Sometimes when you have created an image in some other program, and then imported it and used it, you discover that it is not quite what you needed, and some adjustment must be made. XSI has a solution for the most frequent minor image editing problems, called the Clip Effects. Clip Effects are filters and changes to the image that occur non-destructively, after the image has been read from the file on disk. That means that you can crop or blur or flip your image in XSI without damaging the original file, and without going back to your image editor to make the edit. The Clip Effects are also animatable, which is a neat feature.

The Clip Effects are located on the Clip itself, so you can see them all by locating the clip in the Explorer and inspecting its properties. It is usually faster and easier, however, to use the Clip editor to examine the Clip Effects.

Advanced users planning to render with mental ray standalone or on a render farm should avoid using Clip Effects, because these are changes to the image that XSI itself causes. If you rendered using mi2 files, XSI would no longer be there to do the clip effect processing, and the result would be different.

## Flipping

When mapping a texture to a NURBS patch, the U and V direction of the surface determine the initial orientation of the image on the patch. Sometimes the image is upside down or mirrored so that it appears backward. While you could adjust the texture projection to solve these problems, it is often easier to just flip the image horizontally or vertically with the Clip Effects. You can use the Clip Effect PPG for this, by popping the context-sensitive menu from the Clip Viewer.

The one thing you cannot do with flipping is rotate the image 90 degrees (see Figure 12.10). If the image is lying on its side and you need it to be vertical, you will have to use the Swap UV toggle in the texture projection.

**Figure 12.10**
You can flip but not rotate!

### Monochrome, Invert, and Blur

If you are using Photoshop reference material to bump or displace a surface, you frequently need to adjust the image once you see the rendered result. The Clip Effects are again useful here. Since Bump and Displacement are calculated using the luminance of the image (all the red, blue, green info added together, and clipped to a maximum value of 1.0), it helps to see the image in that way, too. The Monochrome Clip Effect does this.

Perhaps now the Displacement is the opposite of what you want, dipping in where you wanted it pushed out. You can use the Invert Clip Effect here.

If the results of your Bump or Displacement are too chunky and crunchy, perhaps you need a finer displacement Tessellation or a different Bump filter. Or you could in some cases get away with applying a Gaussian blur filter to the original image. The Blur Clip effect helps here (see Figure 12.11).

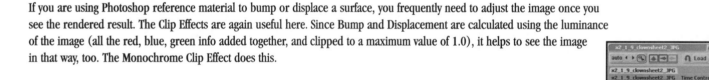

**Figure 12.11**
Color correction and blur.

Since the Clip Effects are animatable, you can use one image file and then animate changes in the hue, saturation, gain, and gamma to change the effect it produces over time.

# Rendering with Images

Generally speaking, texture images are wrapped onto a scene object using a texture projection, which precisely controls what part of the image falls where on the object. Then that texture image can be used in the render tree or the Texture Layer editor as inputs to any number of shaders.

Once the image has been mapped onto an object (stretched across the surface), that image can be used as an input to the rendering system, driving the color of the object, its transparency, the reflectivity, roughness, and displacement of the surface of that object, and much more.

The first step, though, is to understand how the image is mapped (projected) onto the surface of an object in your scene.

## All About Texture Projections

Stretching an image across a surface is actually a big problem in 3D animation software. Because objects can have such different shapes and topologies, there are several ways of mapping an image onto a surface. Some work better than others. The fundamental problem is that most pictures are rectangular, while most objects are not. We need some way to convert the shape of the rectangular image to fit the shape of the nonrectangular object. Imagine that you have a cloth flag and you need to wrap a package with it, making sure that the flag does not wrinkle, does not overlap itself, and completely covers the box. Now imagine doing the same wrapping job with the flag and a more complex shape, like a human head, and you'll imagine the difficulty.

To "wrap" an image around an object in XSI, the object must first have a texture projection that shows how you want the image wrapped.

You create a texture projection by selecting the object and choosing the Property > Texture Projection > Create New Projection command from the Render module (see Figure 12.12). In the dialog box that follows, you can choose exactly what type of projection you want to start with and what it should be named.

The texture projection you create will actually be a new object in your scene, but it will be automatically added in a hierarchy as a child of the object you first selected, so that when you move the object you will also move the texture projection.

What a texture projection really does is match each vertex of your model (which exists in 3D space, with three coordinates, x, y, and z) with a new location in 2D space. This new space is often called UV texture space, or just the texture coordinates. The goal is for each vertex of your model to have a unique location in the image map, so that the map is stretched evenly over the surface. That's why we talk about texture UVs, even on polygonal objects, which have no explicit UVs of their own. The UV's might better be called the XY's, because they really are the X and Y offsets into the flat 2D image.

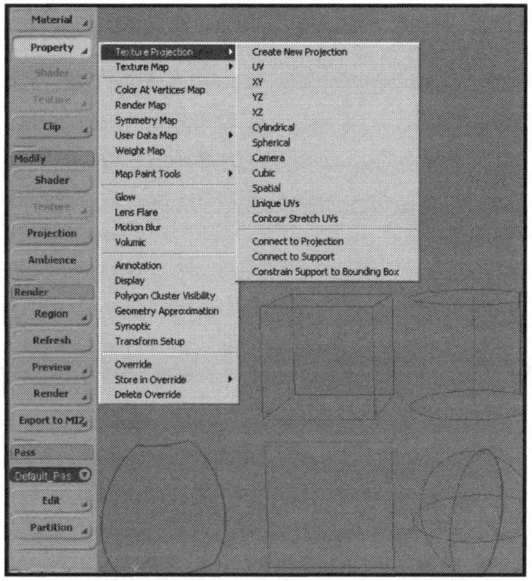

**Figure 12.12**
The Property > Texture Projection menu and some projection icons.

The Property > Texture map is different from the Texture Projection menu. Texture Maps in XSI are only for use in hair, fur, and particle emission.

## Planar Projection

Let's look at a concrete example to make it more plane (pun intended).

1. Start by getting a primitive poly mesh grid.

   Add a point light above it so you can see the texture when we add it. We want to create a new texture projection for this grid. Since the grid is itself flat, it makes sense to use the simplest projection, the planar projection. A planar projection works like a movie projector. It just shines the texture evenly perpendicular to a flat plane. All you need to do is know which plan you want the projection to work best for. Since the grid is flat in the XZ plane, we should use a planar XZ projection (see Figure 12.13).

2. Add the new texture projection.

   Select the grid, and choose Get > Property > Texture Projection > XZ (see Figure 12.14).

   Let's examine the results to see what happened. Open an Explorer, select the grid, and then expand it with the plus sign to see if it has any children. It does in fact have a child: the newly created Texture_Support.

3. Add a new Material to the grid.

   In order to see the result, we'll have to add a material and an image to the grid.

   With the grid selected, use the Get > Material > Phong command to add a new material and shader to the grid.

   Now change the Camera view style to Textured Decal, so we can see the image when we add it to the surface of the grid (see Figure 12.15).

4. Open the Texture Layer Editor view.

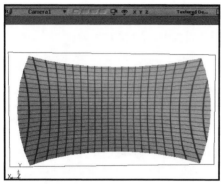

**Figure 12.13**
Planar projections are good for flat things like movie screens and floors.

**Figure 12.15**
See the textures in the Texture Decal view style.

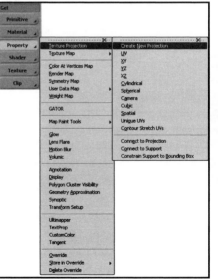

**Figure 12.14**
Use the Get > Property menu to add projections.

The Texture Layer Editor (or TLE, shown in Figure 12.16) is a special interface designed to make adding and layering images on objects simpler. Click on the View menu in the Top view and choose Texture Layer Editor, or open a floating TLE window from the Application > Views menu.

This simple view shows what is happening to the most simple shader parameters. By default, only ambient and diffuse color are shown, which is fine for now. If you double-click on the color chips in the Base Colors column, you can change the ambient and diffuse colors directly.

5. Add a new texture layer.

The idea with the TLE is to add new layers of textures, choosing how they will be applied to certain shader inputs, and making decisions about how they are to be composited on top of one another. Using the TLE is simple.

Start by adding a new blank texture layer, by using the Edit > Add Layer command, by selecting the Add Layer button at the top of the TLE, or by right-clicking over the word ambient and choosing Add Layer.

**Figure 12.16**
The Texture Layer Editor UI.

Each layer has a tile to hold the color (RGB) image you want to add and a tile to hold a different alpha channel image to mask it. The alpha determines what parts of the image show on top of the base color tiles, in the same way that you can "mask" off parts of a house to keep new paint from sticking there, or use a cardboard stencil and a spray paint can to paint in a pattern over an existing base.

6. Add the image.

Right-click on the left-most tile (colored gray), and from the drop menu, choose the Image menu item. In the dialog box that pops up, we have two tasks: Choose the projection we made earlier so XSI knows how to wrap the image, and choose a new image to view.

From the Texture Projection drop menu midway down the PPG, choose the Planar XZ projection.

Now choose an image to view. If you have previously imported image clips, you find them in the Image drop list. If you have not, you can use the New button next to the Image drop menu to choose one from your disk or network.

Choose the Extractchannel.tif image from the project accompanying this book. It has RGB channels and an alpha. You should now be seeing the image mapped flat on your plane!

We'll come back to the TLE later. But first, let's talk more about the other projection methods.

## Cubic Projection

The planar projection method works well for things that are flat and aligned along one plane in your three-dimensional world, but that does not describe very much of what you face in texture mapping a scene. Most objects are more complicated than simple planes, so we need more complex methods of pasting a texture onto them. We need better texture supports. The next simplest texture projection in the XSI arsenal is the cubic projection. When you use a cubic projection on an object, the projection breaks up the object into portions according to which of the six cubic planes (front, back, left, right, top, and bottom) the parts of the object most closely face. This works perfectly for cubes but not so perfectly for other objects (see Figure 12.17).

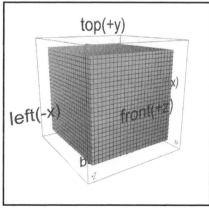

**Figure 12.17**
The Cubic projection is like six smaller planar projections.

You can see the results by getting a primitive cube, using the Get > Material > Phong button to add a new material, and then using the Get > Texture > Image command from the Render module to add an image texture to the cube. In the Material:Image PPG (use the Texture Layer Explorer to get back there if you close the PPG that pops up when you use the Get > Texture > Image command), look half way down and locate the now empty Texture Projection drop menu. The New button to the right of that drop box is a fast way to create a new texture projection. Click the New button and choose Cubic to add a new cubic projection to the selected cube. The cubic projection has a green cube icon onscreen.

From the Image area of the PPG, click the New button next to the Image drop menu to find a new picture to map on the cube.

Now you have a texture cubic mapped onto your cube object, so you can see it either in the render region or by changing your Camera view style to Texture Decal, which displays a single texture image on your models using the graphics hardware in your computer.

A cubic projection makes a lot of sense on an object like a cube, but what happens on a sphere? Try it out!

## Cylindrical and Spherical Projection

If you experimented and tried to use a cubic projection on a spherical or rounded object (like a soccer ball) as suggested above, you noticed that while it did map the image you chose onto the ball, the texture was added six times, and there were obvious seams between them where they met on the ball.

On spherical objects, the spherical orojection or the cylindrical projection might be a better choice (see Figure 12.18). These projections also have a green icon (round and cylindrical, respectively) to show you they exist and how they are oriented.

To see these in action and to assign the projection in a slightly different way, follow these steps.

1. Get a soccer ball model with the Get > Primitive > Polygon Mesh > Soccer Ball command.
2. Assign a new material with Get > Material > Lambert.
3. Assign a new texture projection with Get > Property > Texture Projection > Spherical.
4. Add a texture with the Get > Texture > Image command.
5. In the texture Image PPG, choose the texture projection you just added with the drop menu. It will be named Projection (Spherical).
6. Choose a new or existing image to map on the sphere.
7. Examine the results in the textured decal view and in the render region.

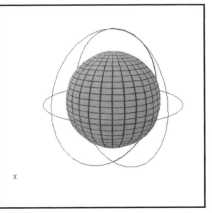

**Figure 12.18**
A spherical projection wraps around an object.

You can change the orientation of the texture, which means how the texture is rotated on the object, by selecting the actual projection object in the 3D viewports and rotating it. Changing the rotation (or translation, or scale) of a texture projection changes how the textures applied with it fall onto the surface under the projection.

If you have a hard time finding the texture projection icon to select in your 3D views, use the Explorer view. Select the object that the projection belongs to and expand that object in the Explorer. (Easy to do in Selection scope, with the E hotkey in the Explorer.) Then look at the bottom of the list. You can select the Texture_Support object in the Explorer and see it highlighted in the 3D views.

## UV NURBS Projection

Okay, so we can wrap textures around planes, cubes, and spheres. But what about objects with organic shapes? This is more complicated, so we need to understand some terminology. The challenge here is that images are inherently rectangular, and organic shapes are not. Imagine trying to find the right place on a dinosaur to line up the top and bottom of a skin texture, and you'll see what I mean. The solution is to give up on projecting an image across the entire shape of the object and begin to think in terms of wrapping a part of that image on each part of the model. The parts of the model are called Samples and the parts of the image are called UVs. We want to match XY positions in the image with the underlying UV positions on the object (see Figure 12.19).

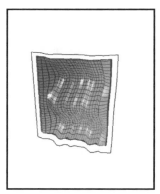

**Figure 12.19**
UVs connect images to each sample (vertex) on the object.

Unfortunately, only surface objects (made out of NURBS) automatically have surface UV information associated with each sample, so we can use automatic UV mapping only on NURBS. We'll examine manually adding UVs to polygons next.

To see how to UV map an image on a complex NURB, follow these steps.

1. Get a NURBS Torus with the Get > Primitive > Surface > Torus command, or use a NURBS surface or your own design.
2. Assign a new material with Get > Material > Lambert.
3. Assign a new texture projection with Get > Property > Texture Projection > UV.
4. Add a texture with the Get > Texture > Image command.
5. In the texture Image PPG, choose the texture projection you just added with the drop menu. It will be named Projection (UV).
6. Choose a new or existing image to map on the torus.
7. Examine the results in the textured decal view and in the render region.

    Look for the green icon of this new UV projection in the 3D views. If you have a hard time finding it, open an Explorer, frame the torus with E, and expand it to show the UV projection. Select it and see how it wraps around the torus.

## Subprojections

All texture projections have a sub-component called a subprojection or a support, which makes it easy to move, scale, and rotate textures once they have been added to an object and have a texture projection assigned. You can see this special subprojection by selecting the full (green) Texture_Projection in the Explorer or the 3D views, and then clicking the Modify > Projection > Edit Projection Tool button (hotkey J). When the subprojection is showing, you will see a rectangular shape with yellow edges and colored axes. You can click to modify the projection directly in your 3D views. It's easy to get confused. Try this on a rectangular NURBS surface first to get the hang of it (see Figure 12.20).

## The Texture Layer Editor

The render tree in XSI is a limitless tool for creating new rendered looks, but for some simple tasks, like adding and layering textures, the render tree is neither easy nor quick to use. So, to improve the workflow for image texture layering, the SOFTIMAGE engineers added a new user interface just for simple texture layering, called the texture layer editor, or TLE for short (see Figure 12.21).

The idea behind the TLE is to build a new layered paradigm, similar to the layers in Photoshop, where images can be added on top of one another, masked to determine what shows through each layer, and the mix between them adjusted with sliders.

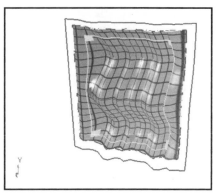

**Figure 12.20**
The subprojection makes it easy to position the image on an object.

The goal of the TLE is to make it easy to set the base color of an object, add a texture on top of the base color, and then add additional textures on top of the rest as needed.

Imagine that each new texture image or procedural shader can be masked, which means that you can use another image to define the areas where that image shows over the top, and the areas where the base coat shows through. This is just like masking off the wood trim around the windows of a house before you paint the walls. The masked areas keep the original color, and the unmasked areas take on the new top layer.

Masks are really grayscale images, with values ranging from black to white. Imagine that black means completely transparent and white means completely opaque, while shades of gray in between mean that the top and bottom layers are mixed.

Now imagine that you can add as many layers over the top of each other as you wish to get a more complex look, and each layer can be blended with the layers below it and masked out with a different grayscale image.

**Figure 12.21**
The TLE is for blending stacks of images.

You can display the TLE by changing one of your view panes to the Texture Layer editor or by popping up a floating TLE with the Shift-7 hotkey.

Along the top of the TLE are the now-familiar Lock and Recycle buttons, as shown in Figure 12.22. By default, the TLE will stay locked on the material assigned to the object that was selected when you opened the TLE. If you want to see a different object's layered textures, you need to select the object and click on the Recycle button. Next to the Lock and Recycle icons are the most important buttons in the TLE: Add Layer with Preset and Add Layer.

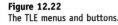

**Figure 12.22**
The TLE menus and buttons.

Since only the base color (ambient and diffuse) show when you first look at the TLE, you have to add a new layer using these buttons before you can add an image or a mask.

The TLE makes great use of the context-sensitive menus. If you click with your RMB (or Alt-RMB depending on your preference set up) in the large gray area in the upper-left portion of the TLE, you may access the port selections. Ports are the parts of the Material shader that you can map with a layer in the TLE. By default, only Ambient and Diffuse show here, but you might want to add Specular or Bump to the layer to get the effect you are after. If you RMB-click on the name of a port, like Ambient, you can remove it from the layer.

If you RMB-click on a Texture layer (after you have added one, of course), you can mute that layer, solo it to see only the effect of the layer, and move it up and down relative to other layers.

The two tiles at the left side of each layer are the Image and the Mask, respectively. Right-clicking over the leftmost tile, the Image tile, pops up a menu where you can choose the image or procedural shader to add to that layer. Clicking on the Mask tile gets you a similar menu that adds and modifies the image or shader used to determine how and where the layer shows on top of the base color and the layers below it.

Perhaps the easiest way to understand how to use the TLE is to jump right into a tutorial and try it out.

## Tutorial: Rocky Start

In this tutorial, you will use the Texture Layer editor to add a series of layered textures to a rock object. Your goal is to understand the layering process, and create a more complex rocky texture out of several image maps.

In this tutorial, you will:

◆ Add layers in the TLE

◆ Use mask images to blend the foreground and background

◆ Invert masks

◆ Use a gradient to blend two layers

◆ Add a new port to the TLE

## Step 1: Open the Rock_Start Scene

Open the Rock_Start scene from the course material accompanying this book. Take a look at the scene, which contains a rock and several lights. The rock already has a set of polygon texture UVs added to it, so you don't have to create your own texture projection. These UVs were made and laid out in the Texture editor, covered later in this chapter. The rock shape is just a cube with a Smooth deformer and a Randomize deformer.

## Step 2: Open the Texture Layer Editor (TLE)

Select the rock and then change your top-left viewpane from being the Top view to being the TLE. Drag a render region around a part of the rock so you can see the color it will have when rendered.

Now double-click on the color tile in the TLE on the line labeled Base Color'under the word "diffuse," which is the diffuse color input. This opens the material shader that's already assigned to the rock. Then drag around the color sliders to test that you can see the color changing in the render region (see Figure 12.24).

Leave the base color a dark red, so when we learn about masking, we'll be able to easily see what is the base layer and what is not. Close the Lambert PPG.

Copy the Diffuse color to the ambient color by clicking on the Diffuse color tile in the TLE and dragging it to the Ambient color tile.

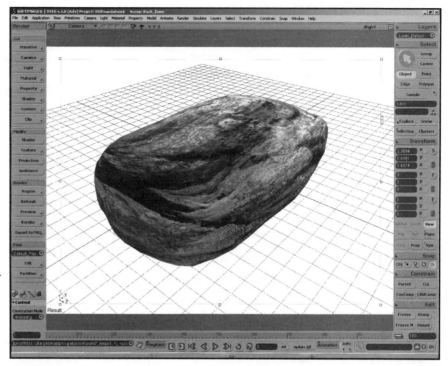

**Figure 12.23**
The rendered rock with complex textures.

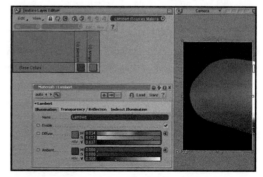

**Figure 12.24**
The rock without textures is boring.

## Step 3: Add a New Texture Layer

The first step toward adding a layered image to the final texture is to add a layer to put the image into. You can add a layer with the Add Blank Layer button at the top of the TLE, or with the Add Layercommand from the context-sensitive menu in the Ambient and Diffuse ports. By default, the left tile on the new layer is empty, showing just gray.

Whatever is in that tile will now be blended over the red base color (see Figure 12.25). Try dragging the Layer Mix slider in the new layer, which is the top bar with a number in the middle of it. The number is the proportion of color that the layer contributes to the mix. If you drag the slider to the right until it reads .85, that means that the gray color is added 85 percent on top of the ports (ambient and diffuse) that are included in that layer.

Leave the slider all the way up at 1.00, which indicates that the Layer Mix is 100 percent.

## Step 4: Adjust the Port Mix Sliders

The Layer Mix slider is like the main volume knob on your iPod or car stereo. Sliding it up and down adjusts the color intensity equally on all the ports included in the layer. The Port Mix sliders are the shorter sliders directly underneath the port names (Ambient and Diffuse, by default.) These adjust the volume of each port within the main mix, and they are analogous to adjusting the faders on your stereo to emphasize the bass or treble of the music. They provide finer adjustment. Play with the two Port Mix sliders to see how they modulate the Layer Mix slider, and then put them back up to 1.00.

## Step 5: Add an Image

Up until now, you have been mixing the gray color on top of the red rock background, which is not terribly exciting. Let's add a rock texture to the layer.

Right-click on the leftmost tile to open up the context-sensitive menu, or left-click carefully over the little drop triangle in the top-left corner of the tile to see the menu. Choose Image from the menu, which means "add an image to this tile" (see Figure 12.26).

The Material:Image PPG should open (double-click on the tile to open it manually), showing you the default noicon.pic rainbow-colored grid. Use the New Image button and choose New from File. Then navigate to your course material, and look in the Pictures folder of the XSIFoundation5 project. Choose the clay.JPG file, and click the OK button.

From the Texture_Projection drop menu in the same PPG, choose Texture_Projection(Explicit) that is there already, and close the PPG.

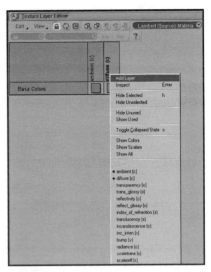

**Figure 12.25**
A new layer in the TLE—ready to blend.

**Figure 12.26**
Click on the triangle for the drop menu in the TLE.

## Step 6: Adjust the Mix

Now in your active render region, you should see the rock texture mapped onto the rock object. It is added on top of the red background color according to the value of the Layer Mix sliders and the Port Mix sliders.

You can also change how the base color is mixed with the image in the Texture layer by choosing new mix methods from the Mix Method drop menu right below the Layer Mix slider.

Experiment with these different Mix modes. Then return the Mix mode to Over and the main layer mix and port mixes to 1.00.

## Step 7: Add a Mask Image

This rock texture is added evenly all across the rock object. That happens to be what we want here, but what could we do if we wanted the rock to be mixed differently in some places than in others? A mask will modulate the blend, so that more of the base or more of the layer can be seen in areas of the rendered object.

To see how this works, first change your Front view to be the Image Clip viewer. From the Image Clip Viewer File menu, choose the File > Import command, and bring in the CheckerMask.JPG file. Look at it in the Image Clip viewer and note that it has areas of white with black squares on top. We'll use this image to mask the rock, so the rock texture shows through in the white areas of the mask, and the red base still shows through in the black areas of the mask (see Figure 12.27).

Let's make this happen now. Click on the little drop triangle from the top-left corner of the mask tile and choose the Image menu item, which adds another Material:Image PPG and opens it.

From the Image drop menu, select the CheckerMask_jpg image clip, which is already in the clip list because you imported it into the Image Clip viewer.

Again, choose the existing Texture_Projection and close the PPG.

Now your render region should show alternating areas of red and rock on the object.

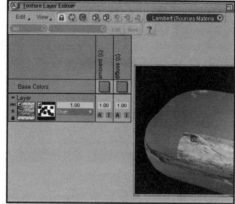

**Figure 12.27**
The mask image lets the rock show through in the white areas.

We don't actually want that to show permanently, so pop open the context-sensitive menu for the Mask tile and choose No Mask to go back to the solid rock texture.

## Step 8: Add a New Layer

This is, after all, the Texture Layer editor, so we should layer more than one texture here. We want to start with adding a mossy pattern on top of the rock.

Add a new layer by right-clicking in the gray space of the first layer (or use the Add Blank Layer button). Then use the image context-sensitive menu to add an image to this new layer. (Remember, it is the Image command from the Image Tile context menu, as shown in Figure 12.28.)

Use New from File to add the Moss.JPG file, and use the same texture projection.

## Step 9: Adjust the Rock/Moss Mix

Now you can adjust the strength and the mix mode of the moss on top of the rock. Try the Bounded Plus mix mode, and the Hide/Reveal (Bounded) mix mode. Try the hard light and soft light controls, with different values for the Main Mix slider.

## Step 10: Add a Layer Mask to the Moss

Now use the Layer Mask tile on the Moss layer to add a new image mask. Try the GradientMask.jpg file from the Pictures directory. The gradient image has a black to white gradient running from left to right. The result of masking the moss with this gradient is that more moss grows on one side of the rock.

Rename the Moss layer by right-clicking on the name of the layer (now Layer1) and choosing Rename from the menu. Name the layer Moss.

## Step 11: Add a Bump Layer

We should add some bump texture to the rock, but there is no particular bump channel (yet) in the TLE. We need to add a new port (channel) and a new layer to make this happen. To add the port, right-click over one of the existing ports and choose bump from the drop menu (see Figure 12.29). A new port, labeled bump(v), will pop into the TLE. The (v) indicates that it takes a vector input.

Add a new layer at the bottom of the existing stack, and rename it bump. Then right-click on the image tab and choose the SurfaceMask.jpg file.

Now in the Material:Image PPG, click on the Bump Mapping Enable check box. Without this checked, nothing will happen.

Close the PPG that opens after you assign the existing texture projection.

We don't want the bump image to change the diffuse and ambient, so we can remove the Port Mix sliders from the Bump layer. Mouse over the Bump layer and right-click over the ambient port. Then choose Remove from Layer. Repeat for the diffuse port.

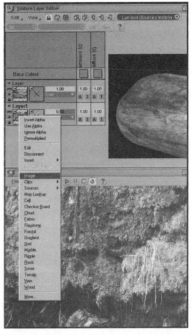

**Figure 12.28**
Now you have a base layer and two image layers in the TLE.

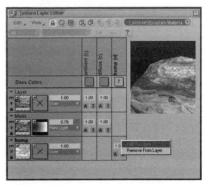

**Figure 12.29**
Bump mapping breaks up the surface a bit.

One last thing is required. The bump port is also empty. Right-click over the empty bump port on the Bump layer and choose Add to Layer.

Now you'll see the surface quality of the rock change as the bump map is added. Play with the Main Mix and Pump Port mix sliders to change the effect.

You can invert the bump map effect by clicking the tiny I button in the bump port of the Bump layer.

### Step 12: Add One More Complex Layer

Add a new layer, and in the image clip, add a new image from the courseware. Choose the longcrack.jpg file, and toggle the Bump Mapping Enable check box on this layer. Also choose the existing texture projection to map the file onto the rock.

Click on the Mask layer and add the crackmask.jpg file.

The crack is black in the mask, which means that the layer will show everywhere except where we want it—in the crack. Right-click on the mask tile and choose Invert to reverse the color of the mask (see Figure 12.30).

As a final experiment, try reordering the layers to see what other effects you can create. To move the last crack layer up the stack, select it by clicking in the name area of the layer, and then use the + button on the numeric keypad (or the Layer context menu) to move the layer's order.

### Conclusion

You can use the TLE to add lots of images to your models, blending the effects with Layer masks that determine what shows through, where, and how much.

You can also blend procedural shaders using the same technique. (Just RMB-click on an image tile and look at the Cell, Cloud, and other shader options there.)

It may also be instructive to you to look at the render tree after building a layer setup to see how the layers are plugged together there.

Happy layering!

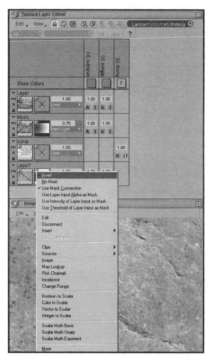

**Figure 12.30**
The inverted crack bump map matches the image.

## Polygon UVs and the Texture Editor

Imagine wrapping a flag around your hand and fingers—it is impossible to do without folding it. One solution would be to cut up the flag into strips, one for each finger, and then wrap the strips onto each finger independently. If you could chop up the flag image into pieces exactly the right size and shape for each finger, you could do a bang-up job of mapping the flag onto a hand.

That is exactly the idea behind the Texture editor. The Texture Editor view (hotkey Alt-7) shows the relationship between three things: the surface of an object, the surface of a rectangular image, and the texture space of the projection on the object (see Figure 12.31).

Another more intuitive way to describe what the Texture editor does is to say that it "pins" parts of an image to parts of a model. The "pins" are called UVs, and they attach a vertex (or sample) of a model to a pixel in the texture.

You can select each of these UV pins and move it around in the Texture editor, to attach a different part of the image to each vertex in your model.

The easiest way to understand the Texture editor and the concepts of building your own UVs is to do it. The following tutorial will lead you through a very simple example, mapping dots on a die.

### Tutorial: UV Mapping Dice

This tutorial will introduce you to the Texture editor in XSI and show you how to carefully match one area of a model with one specific part of a texture sheet. This technique is commonly used to bind textures to characters, props, and other objects in computer game art. You will learn how to:

◆ Get around the TE

◆ Select texture UVs

◆ Move UV islands in the map

◆ Copy and paste UVs in the TE

◆ Unwrap UVs with the best fit

◆ Freeze UVs when you are done

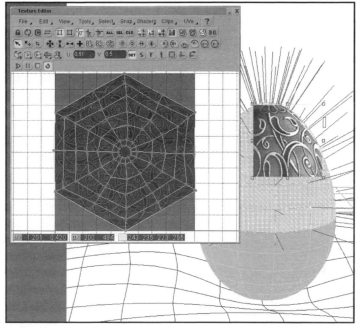

**Figure 12.31**
The Texture editor helps lay out images onto organic surfaces.

**Figure 12.32**
The dots are textures placed on the sides of a cube.

## *Step 1: Add a Material and a Texture Map to the Dice*

Before you use the Texture editor (called the TE in this tutorial) to map parts of an image to parts of a model, you must have some things done. The model must have a material, and the material must have a texture map plugged into one of its color channels. By popular convention, the texture map is most commonly plugged into the ambient and diffuse channels while using the TE. Since the material needs a texture map, it also needs texture projection to support the map.

Which projection is the right one for you? It doesn't matter, since we will be modifying the resulting projection in the TE. You should choose an initial projection that matches the shape of the model being mapped to make your own job as simple and obvious as possible. In our case, since we have a die to map, we'll use a cubic projection.

Open the Dice_Start scene and select the die (see Figure 12.33).

Add a cubic projection with Get > Property > Texture Projection > Cubic.

Use Get > Material > Blinn to add a new material. Then add a texture to the ambient and diffuse channels of the Blinn shader, with the Get > Texture > Image button in the Render module, with the Texture Layer editor, or eith the render tree. Choose the image named DieMap.tif from the Foundation5 project Pictures folder as the image to map onto the die.

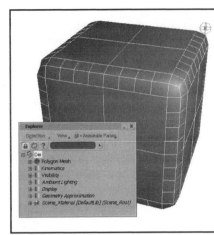

**Figure 12.33**
The dice scene.

Switch your Camera view to Textured Decal mode so you can see the texture map applied to the die.

The texture is on there, but note that the entire texture, all 21 dots, has been scaled to fit on each site. We really want just one set of dots on each side. We can use the Texture editor for that.

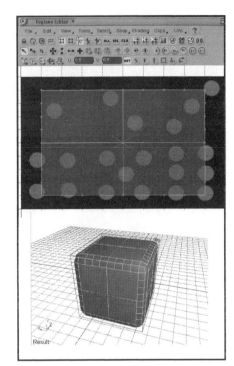

**Figure 12.34**
The Texture editor shows the dice map, the UVs, and the selected polygons.

## Step 2: Open the Texture Editor

With the die selected, change your Top view to be the Texture editor, or if you prefer a floating TE, choose View > Rendering/Texturing > Texture Editor from the menus along the top of your screen. You'll see an image in the background and a pattern of yellow edges and little blue squares on top of it. The yellow edges and blue squares look like edges and vertices in the 3D views, but they represent something slightly different. The blue squares are a value called a UV, which is stored on each vertex and expressed as an offset along the height and width of the image (see Figure 12.34).

Another way to describe the UV is to say that the blue square pins that particular sample or corner of a polygon to the part of the image that lies underneath it.

If you select a component on the model (a vertex, an edge, or a polygon), you will see the UV attached to the selected component highlight red in the TE.

There is actually more than one UV sample for each vertex in the model, because more than one polygon shares each vertex. For instance, if four polygons come together and share one vertex, then there are four UV samples: one for each corner that overlaps.

How do you know when one red UV dot in the TE is really more than one laying on top of each other? Look for a fine red line pointing into the polygons that share the vertex!

> Keeping the UV samples together where one vertex is shared among many polygons is called vertex bleeding and can be turned on in the Select menu of the TE. Keeping all the UV samples for each polygon together is called polygon bleeding.

## Step 3: Set the TE Display Options

You can make changes to how the TE displays the UVs you are working on and the image plane in the background.

First, to see a different image behind the UVs, you can use the Clips drop menu to select from the image clips loaded into your scene. Next, if you have more than one texture projection attached to the model, you can choose which texture projection to base your UVs on by choosing the texture projection you want to use in the UVs menu. You will want to leave the clip set to DieMap.tif and the UVs set to the Texture_Projection you created previously.

You can also dim the image if you are working on a texture that makes it hard to see the yellow lines and UV dots. Use the View > Dim Image command in the TE to make the UV lines and samples easier to see (see Figure 12.35).

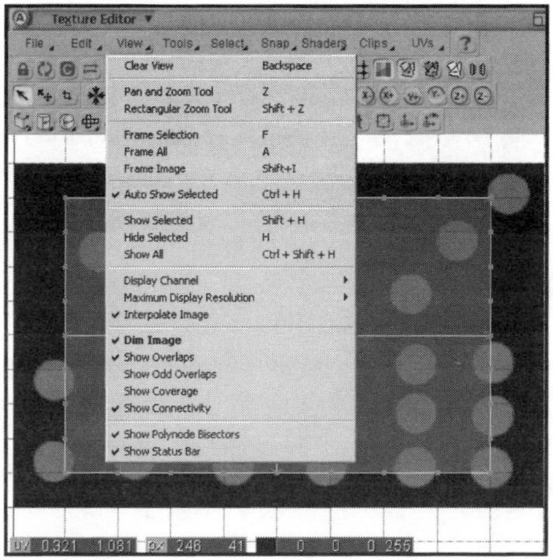

**Figure 12.35**
Use the View menu to choose what you see in the TE.

You may be confused if the TE shows too many UV samples at once. In a larger, more organic character, the UVs might start out as a giant jumbled mass of interconnected dots and lines. It would be a lot easier to see only part of the UVs at once. You can do this by selecting components (usually polygons) in the 3D view and synching up the TE to that selection. Turn on the View > Auto Show Selected option to make this happen automatically.

## Step 4: Freeze the Texture Projection

Keep in mind that the UVs are created in the beginning from the texture support, so if you accidentally transform the texture support while editing the UVs, you will mess up your work. The solution is to freeze the texture support you placed on the object initially. The only purpose of that texture support was to get your texture to show up on the object and to get the UVs into the image map. Once you see the UV samples in the TE, you can freeze the texture support with the Edit > Freeze menu in the TE menu bar, or select the whole model and freez it with the Freeze button in the MCP.

Now your UVs are safe.

## Step 5: Map All the Polygons to Part of the Texture Without a Dot

We want the dots mapped onto the sides, but first we want to make sure nothing is mapped onto the corners. One easy way to do that would be to select one polygon that shows just black on it, and copy the UVs for that one polygon. Those UVs show that an empty area of the texture is mapped on. Then we could paste those UVs to all the polygons so they would point to an empty area of the map (see Figure 12.36).

To do this, just select one blank polygon on the die with select polygon by raycast (U), use the Edit > Copy UVs command from the TE menu bar, select all the polygons on the die (try Y-LMB and drag a rectangle around the die), and use the Edit > Paste UVs command from the TE.

Now all the polygons are mapped with an empty area of the texture.

## Step 6: Map the First Side

We want to start by mapping the single dot onto one side of the cube. Deselect all the polygons, and then select just the four connected polygons on one side of the die. These polygons now highlight in the TE. The problem is that they are all laying over one another. We need them flattened out.

The easiest way to un-pile UVs like this is to use the Tools > Planar Subprojection > Best Fit command, or just click the Planar button in the TE.

The Planar Best Fit looks at the selected polygons and flattens them out to match the size of the complete image (see Figure 12.37).

Now we need to scale down the UVs, which currently cover *all* the dots, so they cover just the dot in the top-left corner of the map.

Look to the top of the TE and note the SRT buttons. These scale, rotate, and translate the selected UVs.

Click the S button and drag the left mouse button to make the UV selection (called an island) smaller. Then use the right mouse button to make the shape of the island square. When it is about the right size, click on the T button in the TE and drag the island so that the center of the island is in the center of the single dot in the top-left corner of the image.

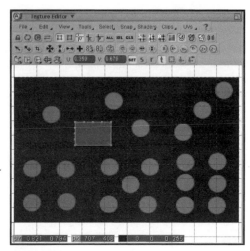

**Figure 12.36**
Start with all the polygons mapped to no dot.

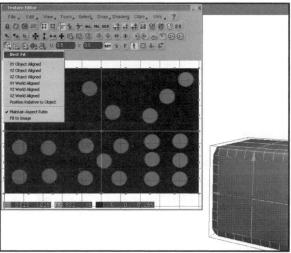

**Figure 12.37**
Planar Best Fit is a simple way of unwrapping UVs.

## Step 7: Map the Next Side

Deselect the selected polygons on the die in the 3D view, and select four on an adjacent side. Repeat the Planar Best Fit and again scale and translate the UVs, but this time fit them to the second group of dots on the image, the top middle group with the two spots.

## Step 8: Repeat for All Sides

After you unwrap and place the UVs for the third side of the die over the group of three dots in the image, try to rotate the UV island. Note that when you rotate the island with the R button, the dots orbit around the side of the cube alright, but the island changes shape in the TE, becoming more stretched out. That's because the UVs are represented as relative to the location of the pixels in the image in height and width, and if the image is elongated, then the image map will seem to distort when the UVs are rotated. Just rescale them back into a square shape when you are done (see Figure 12.38).

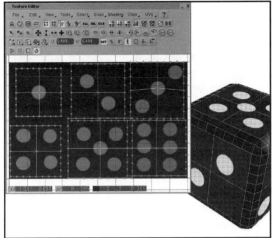

## Step 9: Moving Just One UV at a Time

When you have all the sides done, choose one side with a dot right in the middle (the one side, the three side, or the five side), and select the four polygons that make up the side so you see the UVs in the TE.

**Figure 12.38**
Now all the sides show a different part of the dot image map.

We want to adjust the center UV to be exactly in the middle of the dot.

First, look to the Select menu in the TE and make sure that Island Selection, Polygon Bleeding, and Vertex Bleeding are off.

Now hold the M hotkey (for move), click on the centermost UV, and drag it in the image a ways. Note that it leaves the other UVs underneath it behind, and it creates a tear in the texture mapped to the die.

This is usually a bad thing, so the TE shows you the open edges by adding strong colored lines connecting to the errant vertex.

Undo to put it back, and then use the TE Select menu to toggle vertex bleeding on. Now move the center UV, and see that all the UVs connected to it move with it, preserving the shape of the dot as much as possible.

> If you have disconnected UVs from a single vertex that should be shared, you can hook them back together by tagging them in the TE and using the Tools > Heal command.

## Step 10: Freeze the TE Operator Stack

When you are done moving UVs around, you should simplify the UV information to make modeling and texturing work faster and be more stable. The TE keeps an operator stack as you work with the UVs, just like the operator stack that grows as you perform polygon modeling. To see this stack, select your die, and in the Select Button explorer in the MCP, look for the Clusters folder. Open that and then open the Texture_Coordinates_Auto cluster and the Texture_Projection node to see all the operations you made in the TE.

You may use Freeze M in the MCP or Edit > Freeze in the TE to flatten the Texture Projection node.

## Conclusion

You are done texture mapping the die. You should now understand how texture UV space is a connection between the location of a vertex or sample on a model and a specific pixel location in a texture image. You should be able to open the TE, isolate your view to specific UV samples with the Auto Show Selected functionality, and unwrap parts of the model UVs into flat planar subprojections in the map. Finally, you should know how to move the UV islands in the map, making them bigger and smaller or rotating them to fit the part of the map you want textured onto the selected polygons to which the UVs belong.

# Using the Texture UV Editor to Stamp UVs

Sometimes you will have a model file but not a texture file. You might want to paint on the model, adding makeup or other details, using Gimp, Photoshop, DeepPaint, or another image editor. But in order to paint on the object effectively, you need to know what part of the model you would be painting on, if you were actually painting in 3D. The solution is to stamp the polygon edges from the model directly into an empty texture image in the Texture editor. Then import the file into Photoshop and, in a new layer, paint what you want on top of the stamped file, using the lines of the model as a guide.

After you lay out the polygon UV information (as explained earlier in this chapter), the Texture editor can help by marking the locations of the polygon edges onto an image file.

After you have correctly unwrapped a poly model in the UV Texture editor, you can stamp the polygon edges into any image map file with the Stamp UV Mesh function from the Edit menu of the Texture editor. This adds little paint lines, and saves the file back where it came from.

Now you can open that file in your Image editor and actually see the polygon organization there, so you can more easily paint the features in the right places (see Figure 12.39).

When you save the file from your Image editor and open the model in XSI again, the results will immediately become visible (see Figure 12.40).

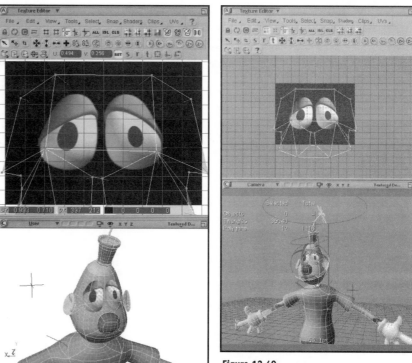

**Figure 12.39**
Icky needs some vision.

**Figure 12.40**
The UV editor, and Ickies eyes.

As long as you don't change the size (in pixels) or the name of the image file, it will be reapplied to the original model file in XSI just exactly as it was when you stamped the UVs into the image file (see Figure 12.41). In that way, the new painted image will perfectly align with the features of the model.

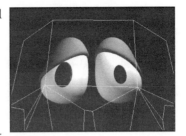

**Figure 12.41**
Now the UVs for Icky's head are stamped into the image.

## Using the Compositor

The XSI Compositor is a bit like a collection of effects that can be chained together, by plugging one into the other, as far as you want to go to achieve a given effect. That tree of connected effects (called operators in the XSI Compositor) is evaluated at each frame, and the results are presented to you in the FX Viewer or saved to disk. In this way, the compositor is dynamic and nondestructive. To understand the difference, imagine that in Photoshop you take a picture of a cherry tree with pink blossoms against a blue sky, select the sky and blur it, apply a Mosaic filter to the whole image and finally flatten the layers. Now you think you might want to go back and make just the sky bluer (see Figure 12.42). You can't do that in Photoshop, because flattening the layers destroys the history of the image. Also, while Photoshop applies filters linearly, one on top of another, the XSI Compositor is a node-based tree structure, allowing for branching, and in certain cases, loops (see Figure 12.43).

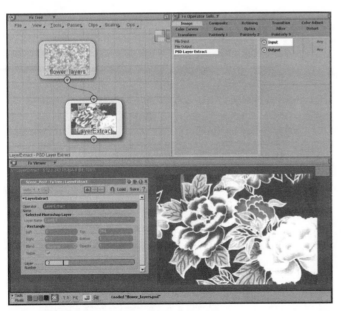

**Figure 12.42**
You can pull layers out of PSD files in the Compositor!

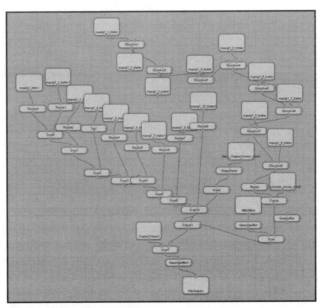

**Figure 12.43**
A Comp with linear and looping branches.

In the XSI Compositor, each filter is run only when you need it, and the original images are never changed. So you could go back to extract the blue sky from the image, color-correct it, and add it back to the original, even after a Mosaic filter was also added.

You can also use the Compositor to extract specific layers from a PSD file, using the PSD Layer Extract image operator.

## Layering Animation Over a Background

The best way to use the Compositor is to open the Compositing Layout from the Application > Layout menu. This layout has the three elements of the compositing UI (FX Tree, FX Viewer, Operator Selector) already opened for you, and a Brush Tool panel on the left side. You can also modify the views in the normal XSI layout to show these views.

The Operator Selector is the library of operators (think filters) you have to choose from, the FX Tree is where you chain the operators together, and the FX Viewer is where you see the results.

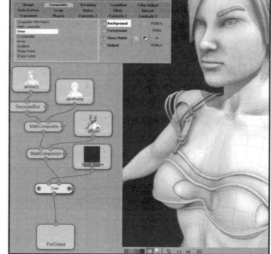

In order to plug together like Legos, each operator must have at least one input and one output. In fact, most operators have at least two inputs: one color input and one mask input. The mask determines in what part of the image that operator will have an effect—just like a selection mask in Photoshop. However, the difference is that you can use another image as that selection mask. That's why there is another input for the mask. If the operator were one that mixed or combined images, there would be one color input for each image it could operate on. For instance, an Over operator layers one image over the other, using the matte to determine which parts of the foreground are transparent (see Figure 12.44).

In this case, we want to layer foreground animation from XSI over an image created in Photoshop.

To import the images into the FXTree, you first make clips of them. Use the File > Import Images menu item in the FXTree to create the clip and the source and to load the image into the FXTree interface.

**Figure 12.44**
Some Overs, and the Over operator selector.

In our case, we want two images: the clown foreground and the stars background.

To combine them, we'll need an Over operator. Open the Operator Selector in a floating window with the View > Operator Selector menu command in the FXTree view.

In the Composite tab, select the Over effect and examine the inputs. The fast way to use the Over effect is to middle-click first on the background image and then on the foreground. Then middle-click in the FXTree where you want the node placed. But in our case, let's do it the long way to reinforce the concepts.

With the Over selected in the Operator Selector, middle-click in the FXTree window to place the node. It needs to have both the background (nebula) and the foreground (Qstretch clown) connected to it. Click on the small triangle dropping from the bottom of the stars image (the output), and drag it to the left-top input triangle on the Over operator. This plugs the output of the stars image into the background input of the operator. Now repeat for the foreground, plugging the Clown output into the Foreground input on the Over. That's it—you are done (see Figure 12.45).

You can test your work by hovering your mouse over each node and clicking the right-bottom V button, which will display the results in the FX Viewer. See how the final Over node combines each original image!

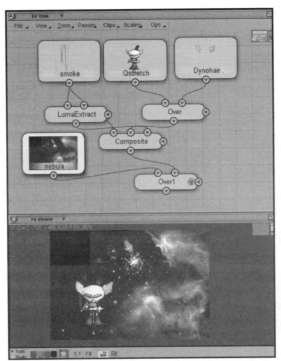

**Figure 12.45**
The completed (simple) composite.

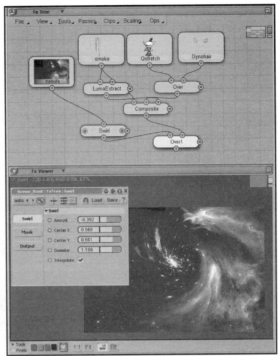

**Figure 12.46**
Now the Swirl operator is stuffed under the clown.

Now let's put a filter on the stars. From the Distort tab of the Operator Selector, choose the Swirl operator, and middle-click to drop it in the FXTree. It needs to be connected after the nebula and before the final Over.

Unplug the Nebula from the Over by right-clicking on the part of the line that enters the Over from the stars.

Now plug the Out of the stars to the In of the swirl, and the Out of the swirl to the background input of the Over. Load the result into the FX Viewer with the V button to see the result, as shown in Figure 12.46.

You can always adjust the properties of an operator. Hover your mouse over the swirl and click the E (Edit) button to see the property page. Adjust the sliders to your liking.

**267**

For extra credit, try applying the Lens Flare operator to the whole stack, and the Glowing Edges operator to just the clown.

### Extracting PSD Layers with the Compositor

Extracting layers from a PSD file for use in XSI also uses the Compositor, but it requires a bit of trickery. Basically we're going to rewire from the Compositor back to the clip, and then use the clip in the rest of the program normally (see Figure 12.47).

We need two clips. One has the layered Photoshop file. The other is a dummy and can be blank. When both are imported into the FXTree, you'll note that clips have two parts: a node called the FromClip that points to the source file on disk, and the actual clip node.

If you add a Layer Extract node to the Photoshop Layer clip (here called flower_Layers), you may pull out any layer that you wish. Then if you plug the output of the Layer Extract node to the input of the dummy clip (here called Clip_Pattern), you would be replacing the input that was coming from disk, and instead using the layer extractor from the Compositor. Then you could use that clip in the render tree, and in fact the image would be coming

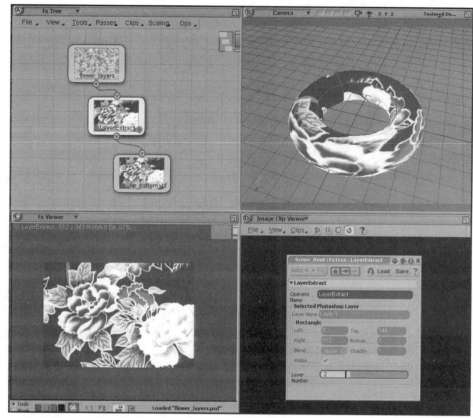

**Figure 12.47**
You can extract Photoshop layers with the Compositor.

from the Compositor, not from the disk. In addition to making it possible to read Photoshop layers, an infinite number of other possibilities present themselves to use the Compositor to modify Photoshop files and then pump them into the renderer.

## Conclusion

Using images in your scenes opens up a gulf of possibilities for texturing, rendering, and compositing. XSI's powerful facilities for controlling how textures map onto models and how textures blend and multiply in the render tree are quite intuitive and easy to use. As you learn what visual detail can be added with textures, you'll save yourself modeling time. As you learn how to use the compositor, you'll save your machine rendering time and find it easier to complete all your work in the time available.

# Chapter 13
# Hair and Fur

In this chapter, you will learn:

◆ How to add texture to your characters with fur

◆ What types of hair and fur exist

◆ How to groom fur and hair

◆ How to apply lighting and shading on hair

◆ How to control the cut, density, and color of fur

◆ How to make fur react to movement and dynamic forces

◆ How to use hair and collision objects

◆ How to use hair in environments and props

◆ How to use the Hair instancing system

◆ How to render and optimize hair

## Introduction

Computer rendering engines have always been pretty good at creating smooth, shiny, hard-shelled surfaces, but generally not so good at rough, fibrous, textured, or hairy surfaces. In XSI, we can add a layer of fur or hair on top of any surface to achieve these effects. Adding the hair to a scene is the easy part, however. The difficult

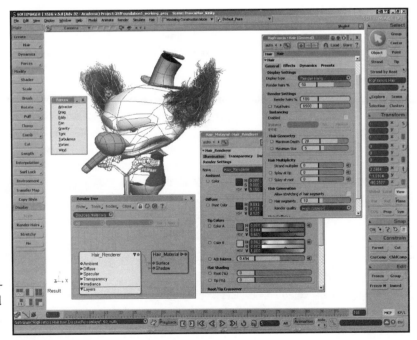

**Figure 13.1**
Tools you'll use.

parts include grooming the hair to look how you want it to, setting up the hair shaders and lights to render nicely, and optimizing the hair so it will render efficiently and quickly.

What can you do with the hair system in XSI? The hair system is terrific for adding hair to humans, fur to animals, and texture to all manner of objects. It's great for vast fields of short grass, it can create rows of waving wheat or long grasses, and it can be used to grow dense foliage like trees and jungles with the hair instancing option. You can use hair to add thatched huts, whisks, top knots, wires, strings, and all manner of other long, stringy objects to your scene. Hair is so useful in XSI that it has its own module, the Hair module, alongside the Model, Animate, Render, and Simulate modules.

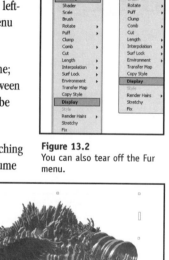

Figure 13.2
You can also tear off the Fur menu.

## Growing Hair and Fur

You can add fur to any Surface Mesh object, any polygon object, or any polygon cluster on a polygon object. Change your left-hand menu stack to view the Hair panel by clicking the top-left module switcher and choosing Hair, or open a floating menu with all the Hair commands by tearing off the Hair menu from the top menu bar (see Figure 13.2).

Both the Hair panel and floating Hair menu shows all the buttons and tools needed to grow hair from objects in your scene; adjust the length, direction, and shape (called the groom of the hair) of each guide hair; and control the interactions between hair and the rest of the environment. But before we grow some hair, let's talk about the three different ways that hair can be rendered in XSI.

Hair is most often rendered as little flat strips, called Geometry Hair Primitives, or as fuzzy little squiggles using a ray marching algorithm (called Volume hair) (see Figure 13.3). The Geometry method works best for lots of long flowing hair. The volume method can be useful for short, cropped, densely matted fur, and the buffer renderer works best for areas with a very high hair count, like fields of grass. Finally, you can use the hair system to extrude guides across a surface that will be replaced with instanced models at render time (called Instancing), allowing the hair system to be used to plant and grow things like flowers, corn stalks, trees, or in fact anything at all that you can model and build in XSI.

When you select an object and use the Create > Hair from Selection command from the Hair panel, XSI adds a hair object as a child of your selected object, with a property called Hair containing all the parameters you will want to adjust to grow your hair and control the cut and groom. This object can be selected in the Explorer or by rectangle-selecting any of the short little guide hairs that are emitted from the surface of your object (see Figure 13.4). These guide hairs

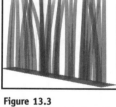

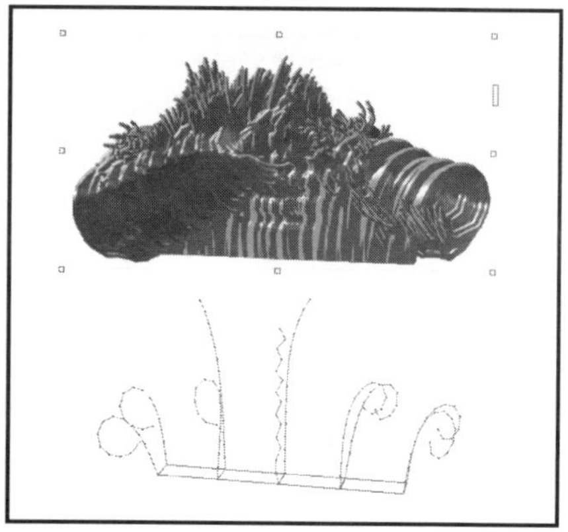

Figure 13.3
Hair is really a lot of small flat strips.

Figure 13.4
Guide hairs define the shape of the Render Hairs.

represent where the hair will go when rendered, but they are not the actual hairs themselves. Rather, since there may be a great number of hairs on your object (potentially millions or more), the guide hairs provide a simpler, easier, smaller number of elements for you to work with. These guides will then control where and how the hair is grown. You can set the number of actual hairs rendered with the Total Hairs slider in the Hair PPG.

## Selecting Hair

You can select the entire Hair object by using the space bar and dragging a rectangle, just like any other object in XSI. With the Hair object selected, you can choose to scale all the hairs to be longer. Just click on the Scale button from the Hair panel, and wait for your mouse cursor to change. Now slowly and carefully drag sideways across your screen, and watch the hair guides grow longer.

When you have a hair object selected, there are some special component selection tools available in the top-right MCP that are designed to let you manipulate just parts of the hair that are influenced by certain guide hairs—Strand, Tip, Point, and Strand by Root (see Figure 13.5).

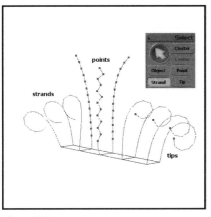

**Figure 13.5**
Selected Tips, Points and Strands.

With the Hair object selected, click on the Tips button in the top of the MCP, and drag a rectangular marquee around an area of hair to see that the tips are selected. You can now translate, rotate, or scale these tips to adjust the shape of the hair.

There are exactly 15 points and 14 segments on a guide hair strand. The first point anchors the follicle where the hair is emitted from the surface. You can select the remaining points with the T hotkey, just like vertices on a polygon mesh, and drag them around to change the groom. The actual number of segments in the rendered hair is controlled by the Segments number in the Hair property page, and the smoothness of the hair curve is controlled with the Geometry Approximation property page Hair options. Each hair can be smoothly curved, even if it has only three or four render segments, by changing the Hair Curve Type to Cubic and the Render Level (degree) to 2 (see Figure 13.6).

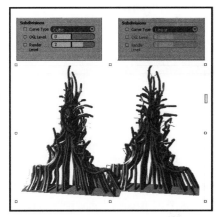

**Figure 13.6**
The Hair Geo Approx property page smoothes hair.

If your hair does not seem to perfectly follow the surface, so that hairs start out growing above the surface of your model, you may need to adjust the Hair emitter Subdivision level in the Hair Generator Operator PPG to match the SubDee level of your characters (see Figure 13.7).

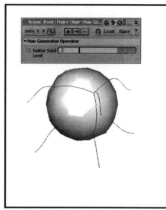

You can reduce the number of hairs rendered to change the look of the result and to work faster while doing initial groom. You can always increase the number of hairs rendered later. Select the Hair object by rectangle-selecting around some of the hair strands, and open the Hair PPG, either with the Property Explorer or with the Enter key.

In the Hair PPG, look in the General tab for the Total Hairs and the Hair Multiplicity sliders. The total number of hairs grown at render time is equal to the number of hairs multiplied by the hair multiplier. Start with a low number of hairs, like 600, with a multiplier of 3, for fast interactive renders. Set the multiplier Splay at Root to .05 and the multiplier Splay at Tip to .1 so that each cluster of three hairs coming out of the same follicle will splay out slightly away from each other.

**Figure 13.7**
Hair can follow a subdivision surface.

## *Grooming Hair*

After you have grown your hair, the next step is to groom it into the cut, shape, and style that fits your character. XSI has many tools for you to experiment with, but a few are shown in Figure 13.8.

You can comb hair in any View window by selecting the hair and choosing the Comb command sub options to pull all the hairs in one Cartesian coordinate direction, one Camera view direction, or normal to the surface. This pulls back the hair tightly in the comb direction. To let the roots of the hair stand up again, adding body and volume to the hair, select all the hair strands and click on the Puff Roots button, and then slowly drag to see the effect.

The Brush tool is an all-purpose groomer that drags, pulls, and twists the hair points within its radius. The left mouse button pulls all the hair points within the falloff radius, the middle mouse button twists up hair within the radius around your mouse cursor, and the right mouse button spreads hairs apart or clumps them together. You can adjust the radius of the Brush tool while it is active by holding the R key and dragging slowly with the left mouse button.

You can also tag points on the hairs using the T hotkey and then transform the tagged group just as you would any other selection of tagged points in XSI. You may also use the M hotkey to drag a single point on a single hair. When dragging a single point on a single hair, the hair behaves as if it is a strand of string and you are pulling on it somewhere in the middle.

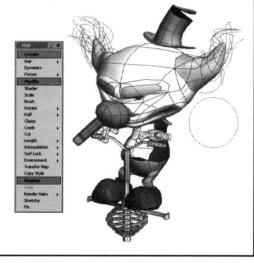

**Figure 13.8**
Grooming tools.

The XSI Move Proportional effect also works on hair. If you enable proportional editing, with the Prop button in the MCP, and use either the T or M hotkeys mentioned earlier, all the points close to the selected points will be affected. You can adjust the radius of the Proportional effect with the R key (see Figure 13.9).

You can also use any of the regular SOFTIMAGE XSI deformers to manipulate the hair points and groom the hair. Remember that hair grooming, like everything else in XSI, creates an operator stack. When you have sculpted your hairdo, remember to freeze the modeling stack to ensure stability and performance.

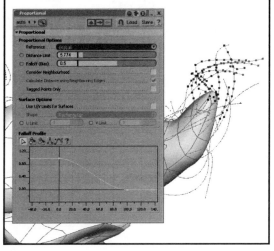

**Figure 13.9**
You can groom hair with proportional modeling.

## Hair Length, Thickness, Kink, and Frizz

Each hair you can render is in some way similar to its neighbors, but at the same time it's quite unique. In real life, each hair has a slightly different length, girth, thickness, and shape. But the variations are not random—the shape and curl of the hair changes gradually in some complex procedural fashion determined by the elaborate dance of our genes, proteins, and enzymes. This tremendous variation coupled with the slow, procedural variation of the hairs generated from one follicle to another is what gives natural physical hair an unbeatable combination of variation and evolving consistency. Our goal is to replicate this in 3D.

XSI has a few controls that will add random variation to our hairs and some procedural variance. If you open the Hair PPG and progress to the bottom of the Effects tab, where you determine the variation in thickness between the root and tip, you will find a slider for variation in length called Random Scale. This value varies the length of each hair from its neighbor. Because this variation is pseudo random, it will not create patterns in the hair and so will add a rough, choppy look. Keep it below .25 for best results, and manually change the length of clumps of hair for more complex and natural styles.

Natural hair may be completely straight (like the author's head hairs) but most of the time human hairs have a certain zigzag shape, called frizz in XSI, and a gradually evolving circular corkscrew shape we call kink (see Figure 13.10). Both kink and frizz are expressed in the Hair PPG as waves, with frequency (period, or wavelength) and amplitude interpolating from root to tip with the Frizz at Root and Tip or Kink at Root and Tip sliders. You can adjust these variables to create everything from gradual slight variations between hairs to tight afro effects. To explore how these variables change the results, simply create a sphere, grow about a thousand hairs from it, and then with a render region open, change the values of the kink and frizz parameters. In the fourth tab of the Hair PPG, the Presets tab, you can set the options for kink and frizz for different hair styles.

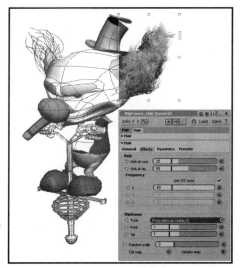

**Figure 13.10**
The Hair PPG has kinkiness.

# Lighting and Shading for Hair, Fur, and Grass

The shape of the hair or fur is only one component of the final look. To be believable, your hair, grass, or fur will also need to have a nice shader. Long strands and fibers generally have a large specular component to their illumination, which is shared between adjacent hairs. This is most obvious in the sheen pattern on long hair, where the sheen extends laterally across many hundreds or thousands of hairs. The final shading of the hair is controlled by three main factors: the hair settings in the Hair properties, the shader you use on the hair and its settings, and the lighting you add to illuminate and shadow the hair.

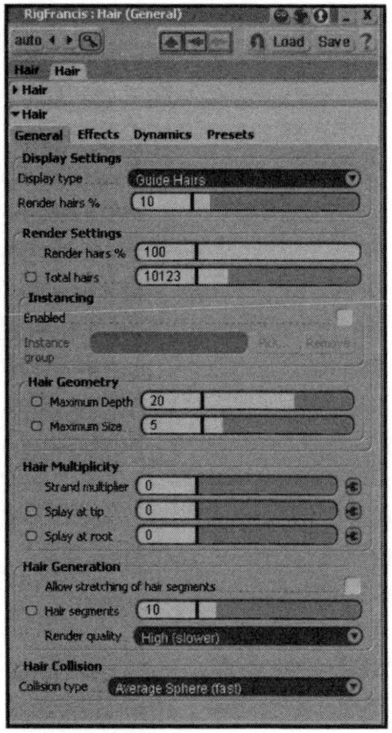

Start with the hair settings. Select the hair and open the Hair property page from the Selection explorer. Now adjust the number of hairs you want emitted, the multiplier,

**Figure 13.11**
Choose the number of hairs you want to see rendered.

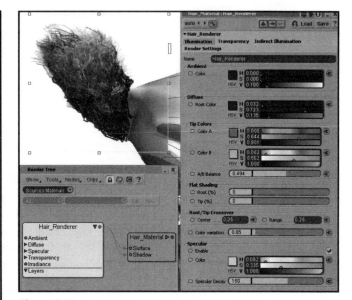

**Figure 13.12**
The hair shader controls the look of rendered hair.

and the number of segments in the hair. The total number of hairs generated on the surface at render time is equal to the number of hairs you select multiplied by the hair multiplier. The multiplier creates small clumps of hairs at each follicle, which deviate from each other according to how much variance you add for the tip and the root. You should never have a hair multiplier without some root or tip variation. The total number of hairs in the scene determines your look, but it also influences render time (see Figure 13.11). Hair imposes two time hits: one for the generation of the hair, and another for the rendering. You can always start small and increase the hair count only after you have tuned the look appropriately.

Next, in the Hair PPG, choose the number of hair segments that makes sense with your specific needs. If you are using the hair to create very short stubbly things like grass or whiskers, you can get away with few segments, like 3 or 4. If you have long, flowing hair with lots of curvature, you'll want to increase the number of segments. Since there are only really 14 segments on the guide hair, the author doesn't think there is much (if anything) to be gained from going above 14. Keep in mind that the Hair Geo Approximation can further smooth the hair without generating more segments. More segments means more hair generation time when you want to preview or render the hair.

Then adjust the shader on the hair. Select the hair and open the render tree (hotkey 7) to view the shader network on the hair (see Figure 13.12).

If you simply want to adjust settings on the default hair shader, you may use the Modify Shader command from the Hair panel or floating menu.

If you are using the Geometry hair method (you can check the Hair PPG to be sure), you can actually add any combination of material and texture shaders that you want to color the hair. By default, however, the Hair_Renderer shader is applied. Just for demonstration and learning purposes, unplug the Hair_Renderer shader and plug a Simple Lambert shader into the Surface socket on the Hair Material node. Adjust the diffuse and ambient colors of the Lambert shader and render your hair with the render region. You'll see a nice shade, but no specular highlight. The hair looks quite solid. Now we'll experiment with the hair texture space.

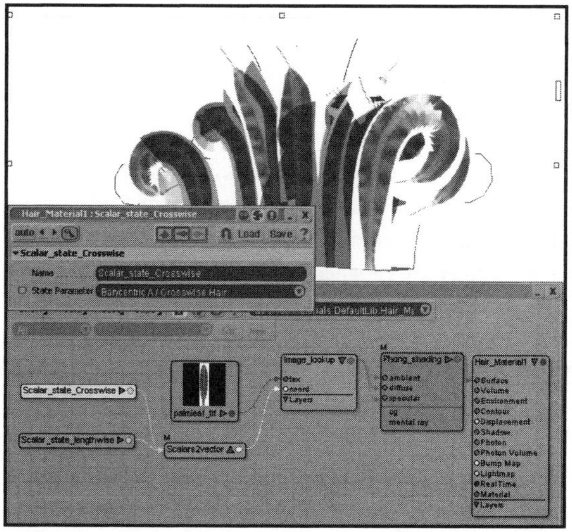

Each hair has two coordinate systems, called the Barycentric coordinates, which map a unique texture space along each hair. You can visualize this space with the Scalar State node from the Nodes State menu at the top of the render tree. If you open the Scalar State node, set State Parameter to Barycentric B (Lengthwise), and then plug that node into the surface of the hair material, you will create a light to dark color pattern along the hair (see Figure 13.13). The Barycentric A (Crosswise) option in the same node shades sideways along the hair. You can use these Barycentric coordinates to drive mix nodes between colors or to drive a Texture Space node to get proper texture coordinates, allowing you to map a texture onto each hair, for instance, to create grass or a dense jungle foliage.

**Figure 13.13**
Barycentric coordinates let us map onto hair.

Now plug the good old Hair shader back into the Surface input on the Material node and open it. From the last tab at the top, the Render settings, choose a hair shading style with the Diffuse Model drop list. Will this be short hair or long hair? Next, add in some Normal Blending (less than .50), so that hairs next to one another share normal information. This creates a sheen. Reducing the self-shadowing factor means that more light will penetrate to the roots of the hair, making it lighter and more visible.

Switch to the Illumination tab of the Hair_Renderer shader. The Hair_Renderer shader allows for a diffuse root color that transitions to one of two tip colors and a specular highlight color on top of that. To illustrate how this works, try setting the Root color to a dark red, and the two tip colors to blue and yellow. Before rendering, set the Root/Tip Crossover to be .33, meaning at the first third of the hair. Then set the transition range to .25 so that the transition from root to tip occurs over 1/4 the length of the hair. Finally, set the specular color to black so you see only the colors for the root and tips. Then render a preview or a render region to see the effect (see Figure 13.14).

**Figure 13.14**
Hair color can fade root to tip.

**275**

After you play with that for a while, dial in some specular color to see how it creates a sheen across neighboring hairs. You can increase the Specular Decay amount to somewhere in the 150–200 range to create a sharper spec highlight. Tab to Transparency, and try adjusting the root and tip transparency amount to see the effect on the look of your hair.

Lights change the look of hair and fur dramatically, because of the high degree of specular sheen found in most hair and fur. If you plan accordingly, you can maximize the look of the hair while minimizing the lighting pass complexity. The general rule of thumb is that you should use a point light with specular off and shadows off to fill in the illumination of the fur, and then one or two spot lights to add the sheen and shadow. In no case should you use Area lights with Geometry fur, since the fur is composed of little flat strands that will not shade differently with Area lights anyway. Your spot may have ray traced shadows on to darken the root areas of the hair (which is self-shadowing anyway). You may use Shadow Maps as long as the shadow map resolution is not too high (nothing over 2,000) and the Shadow Mapped light is close to the character with the fur being lit (no more than 5 to 8 times as far away as the character is tall) so that you maximize shadow map coverage. Shadow maps and volume shadow maps will create soft, deep, fluffy-looking hair, while ray traced lights and shadows will create a harder, more solid look appropriate for brooms, car washes, and the like. Final Gathering should probably be avoided on hair in order to minimize flicker. Ambient occlusion shaders work well (though slowly) on hair.

## Mapping the Cut, Density, and Color of Hair

You will likely want to have shorter hair in some areas, longer hair in others, more hair in some spots, and balder patches in other spots. And perhaps you'll want to pattern the fur so that it grows a different hue in regions like tiger stripes or hash marks on a grass field. You can do all this and more with the hair system in XSI.

Many parameters in the Hair PPG are mappable with weightmaps. This means that you can paint areas of more or less influence directly on your character or hair emission mesh with the XSI GAP (Generic Attribute Painter), and then transfer that weightmap from the emission mesh to the Hair object where you want to plug it in. Most commonly, you will want to map the density and cut of the hair (see Figure 13.15).

### Painting a Cut Map

Select the Hair Emission mesh, and create a weight map with Property WeightMap. If you are growing the hair on a polygon cluster, you can also add the weight map to a cluster of points based on that polygon cluster. (Select the poly cluster, and then use Select Adjacent Points from the top-right Select menu in the MCP.) Once you have a weightmap, you need to change some visibility attributes in your views to see it while you paint. Maximize your Camera view, and from the Visibility menu (eyeball), turn on weight maps. Then change the view style to Constant.

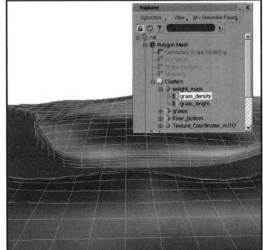

**Figure 13.15**
You control the cut and density with weightmaps.

You should see a pretty turquoise blue color applied to your model. You may now paint directly on the weight map by holding the W hotkey and then clicking the right mouse button to remove weight from the map. Since by default the map is at 100%, clicking the left mouse button can't add anything until you've removed some weight with the right mouse button. Paint away!

It is a good idea to select the weightmap in the Explorer under the Cluster node you applied it to and change the name to reflect what you have in store for that weightmap. Name this one Cut Map. When it is applied to the Hair > Effects > Cut map plug at the bottom of the Effects tab in the Hair PPG, it will adjust the length of the hair. The hair in the lighter, bluer areas will be longer; the hair in the dark areas will be shorter.

## Painting a Density Map

A density map is a weight map just like the cut map, but when it is mapped to the Density parameter in the Hair PPG, it will control the distribution of the hair on the model. Areas with lighter blue will have more dense hair or fur, and darker areas will have a sparser covering.

Build yourself another weightmap, paint a pattern, and name the weight map DensityMap.

## Linking Weightmaps to Hair

The weightmaps you just painted are actually on the model (a character or environment piece, perhaps). The hair is a separate object, so we need a method to get the weightmap from the base object to the Hair object so it can be connected to a mappable parameter on the Hair PPG. The Hair control panel provides this functionality with the Transfer Map button. To use it, open a floating Explorer window and focus it on your model (hotkey E in the Explorer), with the clusters expanded so you can see the weightmaps you painted, underneath the point cluster that was created to hold it named WeightMapCls. Lock that Explorer open so that you can continue to see the contents even when you select another object (see Figure 13.16).

Select the Hair object, perhaps by dragging a selection marquis around some of the guide hairs. Now in the Hair module, choose the Transfer Map command. XSI enters a "pick" session, asking you to pick the map to transfer. Click on the Cut map you created in the floating Explorer you locked open. This creates a new "link" to the weight map on the actual hair object. You can confirm that the map made it over by examining the properties of the Hair object in an Explorer. Expand the Hair > Clusters folder of properties. If you see a WeightMapCls with your weightmap underneath, you have succeeded in transferring a map from the object to the Hair.

Repeat the performance for the density map.

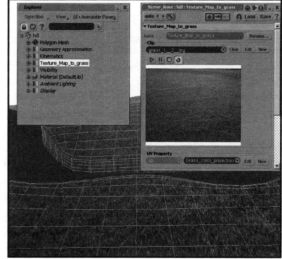

**Figure 13.16**
You can transfer maps to hair emitters.

## Mapping the Hair Parameters

You are now ready to connect the weight maps to the hair parameters. Select the hair object and open the Hair PPG. When you look carefully, you will see that a number of the parameters have a nifty little electric plug icon to their right side. Whenever you see this plug, it indicates that the parameter can be mapped with a weightmap, or texture map.

Scroll down to the bottom of the Hair PPG Effects tab and find the Cut Map and Density Map plugs. Click on the plug icon next to the Cut label, and from the pop-up Explorer, choose the weight map that you transferred. Repeat for the Density map (see Figure 13.17). Now simply render the hair with a render region or a preview to see the results!

## Mapping Hair Color

You can map the color of the hair, so that it varies across the surface of your model or character, using any render tree or texture map. For the sake of efficiency, it's a good idea to render map or reduce the complexity of any render trees you use to drive the hair color to a single mapped color. To use a texture map to drive the hair color, follow these steps, as illustrated in Figure 13.18.

**Figure 13.17**
The plug icon lets you connect a weightmap.

1. Apply the texture map to the base object, making sure you have a good texture projection so the image is mapped where you want it, with the Property > Texture Map menu items. This is different from adding a texture projection to the object, in that it adds a Texture Map property to the object we can pick with the Transfer Map command.

2. Inspect the Texture Map PPG on the object. Choose the image you want to use to drive the hair color from the Clip list, or add a new clip with the Clip New command. Add a UV property (this is important!) so the map is laid out on your model properly. If you already have UVs on the object, you can choose existing ones with the same UV Property portion of the Texture Map dialog box.

3. Grow some hair on your object. Groom it appropriately.

4. Transfer the texture map from the Model object to the Hair object. In an Explorer, frame the Model object and show the Texture Map property. Then lock the Explorer so it does not change when you select the Hair object. Select the Hair object and use the Hair > Transfer Map tool, picking the texture map you have framed in the Explorer, to transfer a link from the texture map on the Model object to the Hair object.

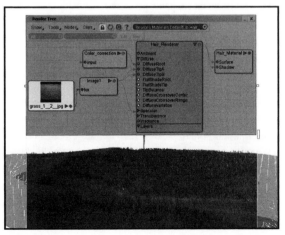

**Figure 13.18**
Drive the color of hair with a map.

5. Drive the colors. Open the hair material in the render tree (select the hair and tap 7), and then double-click the Hair_Render node. Everywhere you see a plug icon, you can plug in a map. Try clicking on the plug next to the Diffuse Root Color. Then from the pop-up list, choose Clips > *Name of the image* you chose in step 2. This connects the image map to the proper parameter on the Hair Render shader, using the UV information you added to the texture map.

You can also do this manually in the render tree by simply choosing an image node, using the UVs that were added in the texture map step, and plugging it in where you will. The important steps to making this work seamlessly are the steps where you added a texture map property to the base model object that you grew the hair on, and then the step where you transferred that to the Hair object.

## Making Fur React to Dynamics and Forces

Just creating visually realistic hair alone isn't good enough for character work. The hair has to move in a realistic fashion to be believable. Fortunately, the XSI hair system has a physically based dynamics system built in. Hair strands can be made to react to changes in the inertia of the model, to collisions with the model or other objects, and to external forces like wind and gravity (see Figure 13.19). These effects will give your hair and fur a sense of life and action.

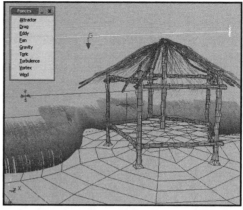

**Figure 13.19**
Hair dynamics means gravity, collision, and forces.

To enable dynamics for hair, select the hair, and in the Hair panel, choose the Dynamics option. This adds a Dynamics operator to the Hair object. Open the Dynamics operator on the Hair object using the Selection Explorer, and take a look at a few of the more important options. The Cache mode governs whether the hair is simulated live on the fly each time the playback head moves to a new frame (the "live" mode), is simulated and then written to a cache file (Read&Write mode), or is read only from an existing cache file (Read Only mode). If you plan to render this work on more than one machine at a time or on a render farm, you'll need to generate a simulation, write it to a network location accessible to all render nodes, and then set the Cache mode to Read Only before you send the scene to render so that all the render nodes pull from the same set of dynamic cache files. The File Name line below the Cache State allows you to choose this common location for the cache files (see Figure 13.20).

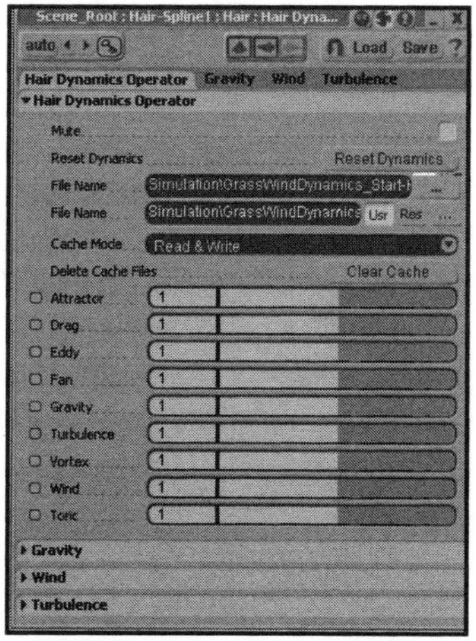

**Figure 13.20**
The Hair Cache mode.

> For advanced render farm management, you may instead wish to write scripts to copy just the used frames of the simulations to each render node in order to reduce network traffic.

With these dynamics enabled on your furry object, try dragging the object around to see how the hair reacts to changes in the object velocity.

## Changing the Dynamic Properties of the Hair

With dynamics enabled, you'll want to be able to change how stiff the hair is. In the Hair PPG, in the Dynamics tab, there are sliders to control the stiffness of the hair at the root, called root stiffness, and also at all the segments past the root, called stiffness. If you set a nice high value for the root stiffness, like .9, and a lower value for the stiffness, like .6, you'll get very fluid hair. Experiment with the settings to get the effect you desire.

You may now want to add some forces to the hair simulation to make it more realistic. You can add gravity to induce the hair to drop down, turbulence to add a bit of ambient noise to the simulation, and wind to suggest airflow from a given direction. To add a force, just choose one from the Hair > Forces menu. The force will be identified by a green icon in the 3D view, initially located at 0,0,0 in global space. Try this out by adding a gravity force. Just because a force is in the scene does not mean that it is affecting your hair. To make certain that the two are linked, select the hair, and choose Environment > Apply Force command to enter a pick session. Then pick on the force you want to associate with your hair. Press the Esc key to complete the pick session. Now if you play back the scene, you'll see the hair react to the gravity by falling limply (see Figure 13.21). The default gravity is almost always far too strong. Adjust the strength of the Gravity by selecting it and editing its properties with the Property Editor. Change the (fact) strength from 98.1 to 5. Run the simulation again to see the effect. If nothing changes, make sure your Dynamics mode is on Live. If it is on Read&Write, reset the simulation and clear the cache with the buttons in the Dynamics PPG. Try adding and testing the Turbulence and Wind forces on your own.

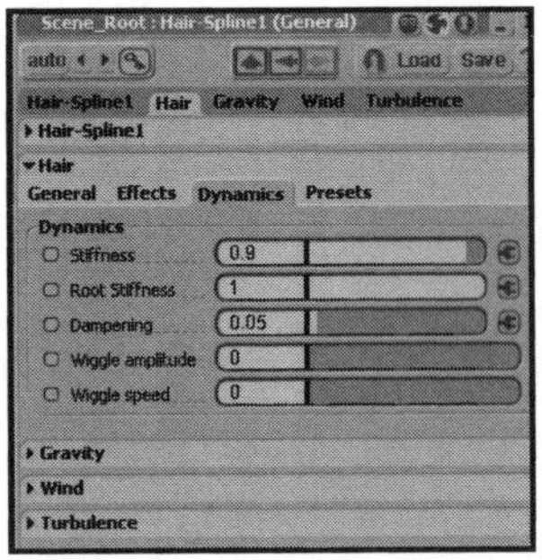

**Figure 13.21**
Adjust the hair limpness here.

# Using Hair and Collision Objects

Because your hair exists in virtual reality, there is nothing initially preventing it from penetrating into another object. In other words, if you rolled a croquet ball through a field of grass made from hair in XSI, the hair would remain motionless, and the croquet ball would pass right through the blades as if it were a ghost. We can change this by assigning a collision object to the hair (see Figure 13.22). When an object is a collision object, XSI checks at every frame to determine whether it is about to penetrate through the hair. If it is, XSI applies a dynamic force to the hair to move it out of the way. We can illustrate how this works by creating a simple example. If you create a grid, grow grass on it, and then create a sphere and animate it moving from outside the grid, across the top of the grid, and off the other side over 100 frames, you'll be ready to create a collision object.

First, select the hair and make it dynamic. Next, select the hair and choose Environment > Set Obstacle to enter a pick session. Then pick the ball with the left mouse button. Press the Esc key to end the pick session. Now play back the animation to see the results. The grass (hair) should part nicely in front of the ball as it passes through!

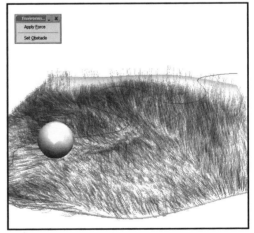

**Figure 13.22**
Grass colliding with and pushing away from the ball.

Now select the ball and look at its properties in an Explorer: There is a new one there called sphere_obstacle. In the rest of the XSI dynamics system, this defines how the shape of the object is considered by XSI at every frame. If the object is highly detailed and has an irregular shape, you can choose the Actual Shape collision option. This yields the most accurate results, but it takes much longer to calculate each frame. Unfortunately, the hair system does not use this control page.

Collision between Hair and Scene objects is handled in XSI a bit differently from collisions between one regular Scene object and another. To make the performance of the Hair collision system acceptable, the hair collides only with bounding spheres. If you have a complex shape that needs to collide with hair, it is a good idea to make a number of smaller spheres attached to the object in areas where there is an obvious topographical feature. Then you can use these small spheres as collision objects. You can examine the options for collision objects by opening the Hair PPG and looking to the bottom of the first tab for the Hair collision options: Average Sphere, Exact (slower) and XSI (fast and rough). Try each collision method, playing back your animation of the ball through the grass to see how they behave differently.

> For complex character and collisions, it will make more sense to create spherical collision objects to use as stand-ins for the actual geometry you want the hair to collide with. This method gives you more control over the number of collision objects, their placement, and the final result.

## Using Hair in Environments and Props

Hair certainly has a great many uses. Think creatively, and look around yourself for examples of thin stringy things that come in rows or bundles. Of course, you can make fuzz, fur, and hair, but you can also make thatched roofs, fly swatters, brooms, tall grasses, all manner of bristles, and much, much more (see Figure 13.23).

### The Hair Instancing System

You can also use the hair system to place, distribute, and deform any other type of model you can make in XSI. Instancing means taking one model and making many copies of it, distributed around your scene, where those instances are created only at render time. You won't be able to see them in the scene until you render. This has tremendous advantages, where you want to build scenes of such complexity that you cannot manipulate the whole thing in a traditional scene. For instance (no pun intended), imagine a field of corn. You don't want to model each cornstalk, and you certainly don't want to animate each moving a bit in the wind. But you could easily grow a field of fur, varying the height and distribution, and then replace the hair with instances of a model (see Figure 13.24).

**Figure 13.23**
Hair props.

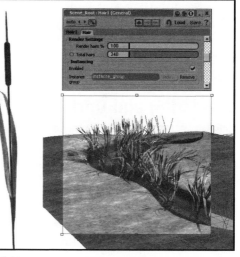

**Figure 13.24**
Lots of cornstalks, instanced by hair.

You can turn any hair emitter into an instance generator, but only groups of objects can be instanced. Just put your single item or any number of different items into a group with the Group button at the bottom right of the MCP, and name that group Instances just for good measure. Then open the Hair PPG, and in the Render Setting > Render Type drop down, choose Instancing. Then in the Instancing section of the PPG below, click the Pick button and select the Instances group you made to multiply through the grass emitter. Finally, choose the number of instances you want in the Total Hairs entry box, and render a render region to see the results.

If you animate the hair using dynamics, forces, or another deformer method, the resulting instances will be animated in the same way.

Try this out by adding a Turbulence force to your hair system. Select the Hair object, either in an Explorer, or by rectangle-selecting with the spacebar around some of the guide hairs. Is there already a Dynamics operator on the hair? Great. If not, you can always add one with the Dynamics command in the Hair menu or module. When you have a hair emitter selected that has dynamics applied to it, you may use the Forces > Turbulence command to add a force to the scene. Because the hair was selected when you created the force, the force will be automatically linked to the hair, and will therefore blow the hairs around. If you did not have the hair selected, or you had many hair emitters that you wanted to be influenced by the force, you could select all the hair objects and then use the Environment > Apply Force command to connect all the selected Hair objects to one or more forces.

To see the effect of the dynamics, select the Turbulence force (it has a squiggly icon), and open the Turbulence PPG. Increase the Amplitude slider to 100, just to make sure you see something happening. Select the Hair emitter again, open the Hair PPG, and change the display Type to Render Hairs, which will draw simple graphical representations of the hair into your real-time display. Now click the Playback button in the timeline, to see the hair blown around by the Turbulence, and adjust the Phase Angle of the Turbulence force. You might need to keyframe the phase angle at a few different points in time to generate a viable turbulence effect. Finally, just reduce the Amplitude during playback, until you achieve the result you are looking for.

# Rendering and Optimizing Hair

The Hair system in XSI makes it very easy to generate really tremendous amounts of work for the mental ray renderer. Imagine, for instance, that if you make a mere 100,000 hairs, with a multiplier of 10 and 15 segments per hair, you have created 15 million hair segments that must be created and rendered each frame. If you use the hair instancing system, you can easily end up with millions and millions of triangles to render. The first step to successful hair rendering is understanding the limits of your computer and working within them. The more hairs you grow, the longer it will take to generate them and the more RAM will be required to render them.

There are two phases to the hair rendering process: the hair generation phase, when XSI actually constructs the hairs in the appropriate shape and passes the data to mental ray, and the rendering phase, when mental ray casts rays at the hair to determine the resulting image.

When you start a render or a render region or preview, XSI begins the first phase. This generation phase will take longer as you increase the number of hair emitters in the scene and the number of hairs per emitter. Because this phase is a linear process and runs only on one processor, it cannot be sped up by using more computers or running it on a computer with more procs or more cores.

The hair system in XSI deals easily with up to one million hairs in the generation process, although making that many hairs may take several minutes.

The rendering phase is highly tunable. The mental ray renderer deals well with at least two to five million render hairs on a 2GB machine. Adding cores and procs will speed up this phase of the render. You can also assist this phase of the render by optimizing the BSP settings for the hair object itself and for the render as a whole.

To tune the Hair object BSP, look in the Hair PPG for the BSP tree settings, and try:

Maximum Depth = Between 8 and 12

Maximum Size = Between 5 and 20

These hair settings will generate fast, efficient hair boxes for up to a million hairs, using a minimal amount of RAM for the Hair BSP. The author's research on a Sun Opteron 64-bit system suggests that you should keep the maximum fepth low and the maximum size low, though just in the Hair PPG BSP settings. Render BSP settings are different. Hair-generation time does not seem to change much with differences in these settings but render memory consumption can be dramatically changed.

To tune your render, try setting the Render > Options BSP settings as follows for a quick start:

Max Leaf = 6

Max Depth = 60

Max Memory = 256

Memory Limit = Three-quarters of the RAM in your machine, i.e., 1536MB for a 2GB machine.

> Make sure you have your render preferences set to unload the render cache data after each render region and preview; otherwise, you might be building up unused memory that slows your renders. You'll find these preferences in File > Preferences > Rendering.

## Hair Segments Versus Geo Approximation

When you are working with longer hair or fur, you'll want each strand to be rendered smoothly, curving along its length from root to tip. Since each hair is composed of segments, one way to improve the shape of the hair is to increase the number of segments per strand. This slows the hair-generation process and adds complexity to the render, so I advise going to higher than 15 segments per strand. To increase the smoothness of the hair further, adding silky glossiness and body to the fur, you can adjust the Geometry Approximation of the hair, just as you may any other object in XSI. If you select a Hair emitter and inspect the properties from the Selection explorer, you will see a shared Geo Approximation PPG. If you click on that icon to open it, you'll be prompted to create a new Geometry Approximation property just for that hair emitter. If you agree, you'll be able to switch to the last tab, the Hair tab, and see the Hair Subdivision parameters. Change the Curve Type drop down to Cubic, and set the Render Level to 2 for best results. Try a test render to see how much plumper and smoother this makes long hair.

## Caching Hair

Initially, the Hair dynamic regenerates the position and shape of the hair all the time, each time you play back the simulation. This is called "Live" mode. But there are several cases where you might want to do the simulation *once* and then reuse it. For instance, perhaps you have a complex simulation with lots of forces and collisions that you have tuned to behave exactly as you want it to. You could then write out that simulation in a series of Hair cache files, to be re-read each time you play back.

Or perhaps you want to render this hair on a render farm where there are many computers. If each computer rendered five frames of the overall animation, but simulated it separately, it would probably come up with slightly different results for each five-frame chunk, and the resulting hair would "pop" constantly. If you cached the hair to a location accessible to all the nodes of the render farm or copied the cache files locally to each node, you would be assured that the results would be consistent on all the rendered frames.

To cache hair, just open the Hair Dynamics operator (if the hair does not have one, it's not dynamic!), and change the Cache mode to Read&Write. Then use the File Name browser button (looks like ...) to set a path to where you want the hair cache files to be written. Using a local directory will be faster than accessing these files over a network. Play back the animation from first frame to last, which will calculate the simulation and write out the cache files. You may even want to begin the playback 20 frames before you need the dynamics to start. This is called Preroll, and it allows the hair dynamics to settle into a stable state before moving. Finally, change the Cache mode to Read Only, so that from here on out XSI will read the cached files and use them to determine the shape of each hair at every frame.

## Lights and Shadows on Hair

The types of lights and shadows you choose to use with your hair can make a great difference in both the look and the speed of rendered hair. In general, you should avoid using Area Lights with hair. Area lights are sampled repeatedly by materials to vary the result color and add softer shadows, but in the case of hair, since the strands tend to be thin and are actually flat ribbons, no great advantage may be gained with area lights.

You may certainly use shadows on lights that are lighting hair, but here also you must take some care. If you use raytraced shadows on the hair (the default type), you may expect to see a doubling or trebling of your hair render time. Some people prefer to use shadow maps with hair instead. If you choose to use shadow maps, you must also use Volumic shadow maps (sometimes called deep shadow maps) to avoid odd chatter and artifacting on moving hair. However, Volumic shadow maps require time and memory to build at each frame. Keep in mind that if you do use Volumic shadow maps, they should be on spotlights that are fairly close to the hair—a distance of no more than five character lengths is a good starting guideline. And in no cases should you use both Area Lights and Shadows, either raytraced or mapped, with hair. Using Area Lights and Shadows on hair results in render time increases of over 10,000% depending on the number of samples in the area light. That's one slow render.

## Motion Blur on Hair

Because hair is so thin and often in motion, a solid plan for motion blurring the hair will generally be required. Because the full 3D motion blur is so slow even in simple scenes, it is rarely appropriate for Hair (see Figure 13.25). Only in cases where the shadows or reflections cast by hair must also be blurred correctly should you use 3D motion blur. In other cases, you'll find some faster solutions. Surprisingly, the 2D output shader motion blur (applied to the Pass output shader stack) may soften the movement of the hair enough to get by on simple projects, and it is lightning fast and simple to use.

For cases where a more sophisticated 2D solution is required, you can download and use the free Material shader named lm2Dmv from La Maison, which generates files that can be blurred with the professional-quality Real Smart Motion Blur from ReVision Effects.

If your budget does not allow for purchasing software or your project does not allow for compositing motion blur, you can also use the mental ray Rasterizer-based 2D motion blur built into XSI. The Rasterizer greatly increases the memory footprint (RAM required to render) of an XSI scene, so it should be used sparingly. To enable the Rasterizer for a hair pass, open the render options for that pass, and in the Optimization tab, change the Scanline Mode Type drop-down to Rasterizer. You might also wish to turn off the Ray Tracing Enable switch to save additional time, since most raytraced effects will be unavailable when using the Rasterizer (transparency will be faked). Next, in the Aliasing

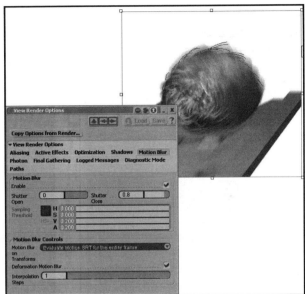

**Figure 13.25**
Motion blurred hair.

tab of the same render options, start with a sampling Min Level of 0 and Max Level of 0, which tells the rasterizer to subdivide all the hairs into micro triangles that fit within a single pixel.

Finally, turn on Motion Blur in the Motion Blur tab, make sure Deformation Motion Blur is checked on, and set the Shutter Close time to something reasonable, like 0.333, which means that the virtual shutter would remain open for one-third the duration of the entire frame. In real life, the actual duration that the shutter remains open depends on the frame rate, but more importantly on the shutter speed chosen by the cinematographer, which depends a lot on light levels, film speeds, and other artistic considerations. Now set your Preview Options to use the Current render Pass Settings, and test render. If you don't see blur, make sure you are on a frame where the hair is moving and avoid the first frame of the sequence. If the blur appears too grainy, you can increase the Collect Rate in the Aliasing tab to 8.

In really extreme cases, such as those where dynamic hair is moving rapidly and needs to be visible through glass, in reflections or in refractions, you can use real 3D motion blur, which is really a form of temporal anti-aliasing. This is computationally slow but very high quality. Just switch the Scanline mode back to Default and adjust the Sampling Min Level to -1, Max Level to 2, and Sampling Threshold to .05 in all RGB and A channels.

# Conclusion

The possibilities that can be realized with SOFTIMAGE's new Hair and Fur module are more than the kinds of hairstyles you can see out there. With this module, you can manipulate exceptionally fine detail for your effects and add that much more realism to your scenes.

# Appendix A
# Getting Started with Rigid Body Dynamics

By Randall Dai

One should approach new experiences with an open mind as well as a childlike desire to play with what you discover.

This is absolutely true when it comes to learning the new and very robust AEGIA Dynamics engine now part of XSI 5.0. AEGIA's PhysX technology is a new approach to real time dynamics that turns any polygonal surface into a Rigid Body Dynamic object.

In this chapter, I will be taking you through building a basic scene that will require very little setup and absolutely no keying. After you learn the work flow of creating a Rigid Body in XSI, you will be able to refine the scene for even more accuracy by keying settings on and off at the appropriate times.

## Building the Better Slingshot

First we will be building a slingshot from a torus (barrel), sphere (projectile) and a spring (plunger). This very simple design will allow us to shoot the sphere at a building constructed of cubes (pillars and floor) and enjoy the ensuing destruction over and over again.

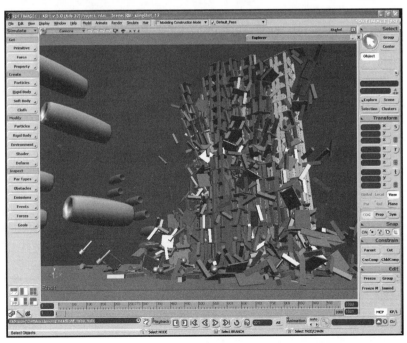

Open a new scene and change the left menu bar to Simulate (or just press hotkey 4 on the keyboard). Change the timeline to 1000 frames. Save the file as RBD_slingshot_001. Remember to save new versions of your scenes as they become more complex.

## Import the Geometry

In previous versions of XSI, using a torus produced mediocre results. Now with the Actual Shape tab, we are able to use a torus for the barrel.

### Create the Barrel

Choose the Get > Primitive > Poly. Mesh > Torus menu command.

Open the torus' PPG and name the torus barrel.

Change the V subdivision to 16.

Manually scale the barrel in Y by 12. Select a polygon loop close to the bottom of the inside portion of the barrel. Duplicate this geometry (Ctrl+D), then scale it into the center (leave a small hole).

Now freeze the geometry. In Object mode, select Create > Rigid Body > Passive Rigid Body.

Under the Rigid Body Properties tab, change collision type to actual shape

Although I have had great fun shooting all manner of shapes at my buildings, we will be using a sphere for this simulation to ensure a straight shot out of the barrel.

## Create the Projectile

Choose the Get > Primitive > Poly. Mesh > Sphere menu command.

Name the sphere projectile. Change the radius to 1.5.

In Object mode, select the Create > Rigid Body > Active Rigid Body command. Under Rigid Body Properties tab, change collision type to actual shape.

The plunger will need to be small enough to fit in the whole at the bottom of the barrel.

## Create the Plunger

Choose the Get > Primitive > Poly. Mesh > Cylinder menu command.

Name the cylinder plunger. Translate the plunger -25 units in Y and change its radius to 2.4.

Select the top-center circle of polygons and duplicate them.

Translate the polygons in Y so that they can pass through the hole left in the bottom of the barrel.

Now freeze the geometry. In Object mode, select the Create > Rigid Body > Active Rigid Body.

Under Rigid Body Properties tab, change collision type to actual shape.

## Create the Gravity

If you play the scene, nothing will happen because there is no force yet.

Choose Get > Force > Gravity. Set the gravity to 20, then hide it.

## Apply the Spring

Many excellent constraints exist for you to choose from while learning how to manipulate the RBDs. We will use a spring to pull the plunger into the center of the barrel. When applying the spring you should first choose your Active Body object (plunger). A spring will appear that will be connected to your object at one end and the other will be at zero X, Y, and Z. You can constrain an Active Body to either another Active body or a Passive one. You will then be prompted to choose a second object (choose the barrel).

Select the plunger, choose the Create > Rigid Body > Rigid Body Constraint > Spring menu command, and then select the barrel.

Open the spring PPG and under the Constraint tab check the Attached Bodies Intercollide tab.

Save the scene as RBD_Slingshot_002.

## Test the New Slingshot

Press play and enjoy the projectile flying through the air. We haven't parented any of the geometry yet due to the Rigid Bodies aversion to hierarchies. Shift-Select the slingshot and translate it in Z until it is out of the way for you to build the building. Once it is out of the way, select the Modify > Rigid Body > Set Initial State command. This will tell AEGIA to re-calculate the collisions from this position.

# Creating the Building

After this tutorial you should attempt using different designs for bridges, buildings, or even cars to blow apart. Before we can do any of that, the building will require a ground to sit on.

## Create the Ground

Select the Get > Primitive > Poly. Mesh > Cube menu command.

Name the new object ground. Scale the ground down .05 in Y and out 25 in X and Z until a good floor has been created for the building to crash down on and slide across.

In Object mode, choose Create > Rigid Body > Passive Rigid Body.

Make the ground unselectable so that you won't mistakenly grab it from now on.

Each floor of the building will have four pillars and one floor. If setup correctly, the floors may be stacked very high. For the sake of this tutorial, we will only be raising the building eight floors.

## Create the Pillars

Again, select the Get > Primitive > Poly. Mesh > Cube menu command.

Name the new object pillar.

Scale the pillar in X and Z until it becomes a tall pillar shape. In Object mode, choose Create > Rigid Body > Active Rigid Body.

Translate up until the pillar sits just above the ground. Select Modify > Rigid Body > Set Initial State. Run the timeline for a few seconds so that the pillar settles down on the ground.

Select Modify > Rigid Body > Set Initial State again. Restart the timeline to test if the pillar has properly settled on to the ground.

Translate the pillar -3 in X and -3 in Z.

Once more, select Modify > Rigid Body > Set Initial State.

Now that we have a dynamic pillar, we will place it and three more into a position that will allow us to stack a floor on top of it.

## Duplicate the Pillar

Duplicate the pillar and translate it to 3 in X, -3 in Z. Duplicate it again and translate it to -3 in X, 3 in z.

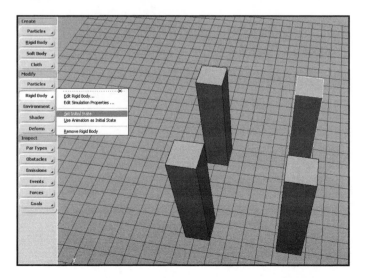

Choose all of the pillars then choose Modify > Rigid Body > Set Initial State.

## Create the Floor

Select the Get > Primitive > Poly. Mesh > Cube menu command.

Name the object Floor and scale it .05 in Y.

Translate it up in Y until just above the pillars. Run the timeline for a few seconds so that the floor settles down on the pillars.

Select the Modify > Rigid Body > Set Initial State menu command.

Re-start timeline to test if the floor has properly settled on to the pillars.

Save the scene as RBD_Slingshot_003.

Now you can duplicate the levels and stack them. Be careful while you place the levels above other ones. If you stack them too high, you will have them bouncing down onto each other. If the geometry is passing through when you begin the simulation, the pieces will take flight in a most undesirable way.

## Raise the Building

Select the pillars and floor then duplicate them. Translate the new floor to just above the first floor,

Select the Modify > Rigid Body > Set Initial State menu command.

Run the timeline for a few seconds so that the second floor settles down on the first.

Select Modify > Rigid Body > Set Initial State again. Re-start timeline to test if the second floor has properly settled on to the first.

Continue the duplicating process until the building is about eight floors high.

Save the scene as RBD_Slingshot_004.

Now you can rotate you weapon into position. If you attempt to rotate the weapon in any other way than described below, you will be disappointed with the results.

# Aim Your Weapon

Shift-select the slingshot and rotate globally (global) in center of gravity (COG) until it is pointed at the building. Translate into a desired position that will allow the projectile to strike the side of the building.

Select the Modify > Rigid Body > Set Initial State menu command.

Run the timeline. Did you knock the building down the first time?

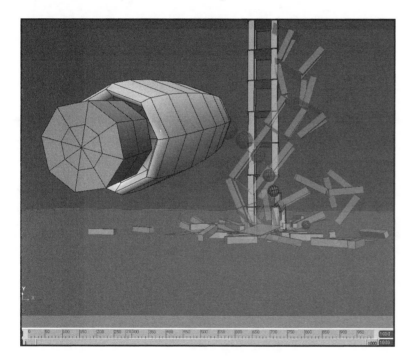

# Cacheing

You can cache the scene for faster playback. This setting will allow you to scrub the scene in real time after it has been cached. Every time that you change something, the scene will need to be re-cached before it can be scrubbed again.

Press the 8 hotkey to open up an Explorer. Change from scene root to environments. Open the Simulation Time Control. Change the Play Mode to Standard.

Check the Caching tab.

In the Explorer, open the Scene_Root_Environment_Cache.

Change the Internal dropdown to External (.xsi binary).

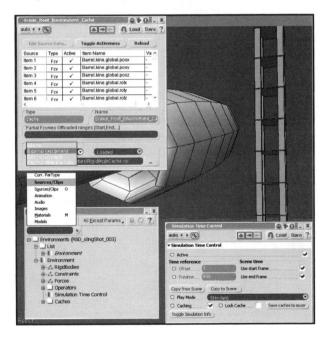

Let the timeline run all of the way through and then scrub the timeline.

# Refine the Scene

There are many ways that you can create a more dynamic scene including increasing the mass of the projectile, duplicating the slingshot, increasing the spring's tension, or erecting the building to an incredible size. I have found that 3,400 rigid bodies was the limit for my computer. Here are several settings that you should check out to change the dynamics of the scene.

**Elasticity** = This setting will allow the object to bounce a lot at 1 and none at 0.

**Static Friction** = How much force is required to get the object moving.

**Dynamic Friction** = How much the object will slide against other objects.

**Mass** = The mass or weight of the object.

**Gravity** = Yep, just like it sounds.

Now go learn, play, and have fun!

# Index

## N

## O

# License Agreement/Notice of Limited Warranty